MW01258496

Sameness in Diversity

CALIFORNIA STUDIES IN FOOD AND CULTURE
Darra Goldstein, Editor

Sameness in Diversity

Food and Globalization in Modern America

———

Laresh Jayasanker

Foreword by Carol Helstosky

UNIVERSITY OF CALIFORNIA PRESS

University of California Press
Oakland, California

Library of Congress Cataloging-in-Publication Data

Names: Jayasanker, Laresh, 1972–2018, author.
Title: Sameness in diversity : food and globalization in modern America /
    Laresh Jayasanker.
Description: Oakland, California : University of California Press, [2020] |
    Series: California studies in food and culture | Includes bibliographical
    references and index.
Identifiers: LCCN 2019041008 (print) | LCCN 2019041009 (ebook) |
    ISBN 9780520343955 (cloth) | ISBN 9780520343962 (paperback) |
    ISBN 9780520975286 (ebook)
Subjects: LCSH: Food habits—United States—History—21st century. | Food
    industry and trade—United States. | Food habits—Social aspects—
    United States. | Food—Social aspects—United States. | Food supply—
    Globalization.
Classification: LCC GT2853.U5 J39 2020 (print) | LCC GT2853.U5 (ebook) |
    DDC 394.1/20973—dc23
LC record available at https://lccn.loc.gov/2019041008
LC ebook record available at https://lccn.loc.gov/2019041009

CONTENTS

TABLES

Laresh Jayasanker's voice rang clear in the crowded and sometimes confusing world of food studies. His book's title, *Sameness in Diversity*, deftly summarizes his argument about contemporary food history: Because of multiple and sometimes competing forces, consumers confront a world of food that seems diverse, but one that is ultimately shared by most Americans, in the same stores and in similar restaurants. It's a complex culinary landscape in which American consumers think they have more food choices than ever, but their options come from only a handful of producers. Few of us have attempted to understand this paradoxical state of affairs, yet Jayasanker explains how our eating habits have come to be with clarity and precision.

In much of his research, Jayasanker sought to explain globalization's impact on the United States by charting changes in immigration, transportation, suburbanization, and commercial practices. His focus here on food—what we eat, how we eat, and how we think about the food we eat—illuminates the "lived experience of globalization in the United States" (p. 2). He connects large, impersonal forces to the everyday choices we make to feed ourselves and our families. Although much has been said and written about the recent culinary and dietary changes in the United States that have negatively impacted our health and the environment, such as the rise of fast food and agribusiness, no one has sufficiently explained the origins and evolutions of these dramatic and sometimes devastating transformations of our eating habits. Taking a broader approach and a longer view, Jayasanker mobilizes the metaphor of sameness in diversity to trace the histories of restaurants, grocery stores, corporations, and cookbooks. With marvelous ease he shifts from discussing massive changes in the corporate structures of grocery chains, to providing a fine-grained analysis of a single menu at a strip-mall Indian restaurant. As a business and cultural history, *Sameness in Diversity* takes seriously the sites of food consumption and excavates a rich and engaging history of food markets where goods are not only bought and sold, but where producers and consumers negotiate daily what is good to eat, how foods are marketed, and how much those foods will cost.

Sameness in Diversity picks up where historian Donna Gabbaccia's influential *We Are What We Eat* left off, in chronicling the impact of immigrants on eating habits in the United States, in this case, after the Vietnam War, an event that exerted a profound influence on American immigration patterns and food habits. Jayasanker's book vividly chronicles the shifts in migration patterns, transportation systems, commercial practices, and labor rhythms that shaped the variety and cost of foods available in stores and restaurants. His analysis moves food history in a new direction, beyond an oversimplified understanding of how immigration influenced food habits. He demonstrates that it was not only the actions of immigrant entrepreneurs who opened doors for so-called ethnic cuisines in the United States, but a host of factors operating in concert that made these foods affordable, desirable, and familiar to the masses. This revolution was most apparent in grocery stores, where Americans shopped for a variety of ethnic foods, fresh produce, and an array of frozen foods, with more aisles and more choices than previous generations could ever imagine. Yet a simple trip to the (now virtual) grocery store reveals the paradoxes we confront as modern eaters: We are offered more food and a range of choices, but we wind up eating the same foods produced and sold by the same companies. This paradox is frequently due to circumstances beyond our control. Although it may seem that changes in our eating habits stem from personal taste or cultural exposure, larger forces weigh heavily, as Jayasanker demonstrates in his analyses of trade, transportation, government policies, and commercial practices. Changes in restaurant culture and cookbook publishing lead the reader to similar conclusions: Though we may be convinced we have more choices than ever in dining out or preparing ethnic foods at home, we inhabit the same culinary world, no matter where we come from, where we live, or where we are going.

Histories of globalization chronicle the vast and impersonal forces of change, oftentimes with little space devoted to individual consumer reactions. *Sameness in Diversity* details how grocers, restauranteurs, corporations, and publishers promoted specific foods and dishes, as well as how consumers understood the food they ate. The unique focus on individual translators, who took the time to explain new foods to wary consumers, suggests how new foods are accepted by American consumers. Jayasanker focuses on translators who made strange foods familiar and, as an unintended consequence, made all foods similar. These translators enabled consumers to navigate a dizzying array of food choices and settle on the familiar. His careful analysis of the cognitive processes by which individuals make connections between familiar and unfamiliar foods suggests that the way we think about food, when reading restaurant menus or examining cookbooks, is also how we grapple with larger issues. The cognitive process by which we decide what to eat is of paramount significance today, when words and phrases like *paleo*, *vegan*, and *gluten-free* define not only what we eat but who we are.

Laresh Jayasanker's thought-provoking work proves how extraordinarily complex and even fragile our eating practices are, derived as they are from an interplay of global, local, and individual forces. Yet the book's passionate conclusion argues that, despite all of the paradox and complexity, food ultimately has the ability to unite us. Warning us against a pseudo-culinary cosmopolitanism, Jayasanker urges us all to eat more thoughtfully, to leave our neighborhoods, to turn off our mobile devices, and to share food with others: "Eat not the other. Eat with the other and we may bridge the many divides" (p. 149). They are words he lived by.

Carol Helstosky
Associate Professor of History
University of Denver

EDITOR'S NOTE

In June 2016, Susanne and Laresh Jayasanker hosted an eclectic mix of guests for a meal to celebrate his earning tenure. He was living up to his suggestion at the end of this book to "share foods with a wider circle of people." Among the guests at their home were colleagues, family, and friends, including a clutch of soccer parents and his daughters' teammates and classmates. When the food was ready, he announced with a wry smile that he was serving tacos. As we filled our tortillas with meat that he had carefully braised, many of us familiar with Laresh's research recognized the reason for his smile. Laresh had talked about tortillas a lot and for a long time. For him, as he demonstrates in this book, a taco wasn't just a taco. Like many commonplace foods that he knew his guests took for granted, the humble taco opened a wide window onto the changes wrought by immigration and globalization in the United States.

Two years later, Laresh was diagnosed with pancreatic cancer. He died soon after at the age of forty-six. Until the end, he was a dedicated scholar and teacher who loved food and friendship. He culminated his teaching career—unaware it was his last term—by treating students in his large class to a tasty and educational lunch. When some of his colleagues in the History Department visited him for the last time in that summer of 2018, he stood at his kitchen counter, weak and unable to drink, sharing flawlessly crafted cocktails from a vintage recipe book that intrigued him.

After his cancer diagnosis, Laresh continued working on this book, which had already been a labor and a passion for more than a decade. In hospice, with what would be only days to live, he was still sending emails and making editorial adjustments. At the same time, he knew that he wouldn't be able to take care of final publication details. When colleagues promised to see the book into print, he asked that they not do so if it was "at all inconvenient."

Far from burdensome, ushering *Sameness in Diversity* through publication has been an honor for members of the Metropolitan State University of Denver's History Department. When Laresh passed, he had finished an intensive round of revisions in response to external referee reports. We were able to resubmit to the press that manuscript as he left it, and, upon its approval, only the production logistics remained. The book, then, is wholly Laresh's work. Thanks to his persistence, we now know far more about how globalization and immigration have affected not just our eating habits, but American culture more broadly.

Granted, not everything turned out as he wished. One of Laresh's final emails explained that he might have to hurry the dedication and acknowledgments. Alas, he faded too quickly to leave us these parts. Given his generosity and selflessness, there is no doubt he would have thanked a long list of individuals and institutions. So, on his behalf, we thank all those he would have mentioned—family members, mentors, friends, colleagues, and others. What little work he left undone we, his colleagues, and the outstanding staff at University of California Press have completed in memory of Laresh, and in honor of his wife, Susanne, and daughters Holly and Ella.

James D. Drake
Professor and Chair of History
Metropolitan State University of Denver

Introduction

Was it the shaking beef? Or the cellophane noodles with Dungeness crab? Perhaps the chicken in a clay pot? Which dish was most transcendent?

Charles Phan created these dishes for the Slanted Door, his signature fine-dining restaurant in San Francisco. Phan's family had escaped Vietnam on a cargo ship in 1975, just after the Fall of Saigon.[1] Today those cargo ships bring Vietnamese and other Asian foodstuffs in containers, but their early voyages across the Pacific in the late 1960s shipped supplies to American troops in Vietnam. Then, it was hard to imagine a war refugee winning awards for his California interpretation of Vietnamese food. When he first opened the Slanted Door in 1995, Phan himself wondered, "Are white people going to eat this? Will they pay me for this?"[2]

They did. Phan made it to the United States in 1977 as a teenager, settling with his family in San Francisco. After working as a busboy, in his family's clothing business, and in the computer industry, he pursued his love of food by opening the Slanted Door. In just a few years, the restaurant garnered a local and then a national following. By the late 1990s, it was among the most celebrated restaurants in San Francisco, serving Vietnamese cuisine in a fine-dining setting. In April of 2000, President Bill Clinton ate there just months before a diplomatic mission to Vietnam, the first sitting president of the United States to do so. While promoting his memoir a few years later, Clinton employed the restaurant to cater a gathering of Democratic Party hobnobbers.[3]

By then the restaurant had moved from the Mission District to the downtown waterfront; it was an anchor in each location, drawing other restaurateurs. At the downtown locale, its reservation staff fielded thousands of phone calls a day. In 2004 Phan won a prestigious James Beard award for "Best California Chef," and a

1

few years later *Gourmet* magazine named Slanted Door the best Vietnamese restaurant in the country.[4]

Phan's story illustrates a major shift in American eating habits over the last fifty years. In the mid-1960s the United States was fighting a war in Vietnam, but few Americans, save those GIs stationed abroad, had tried Vietnamese food. Rarer still would have been a Vietnamese restaurant anchoring a prime waterfront venue, as the Slanted Door now does for the Ferry Building in San Francisco. But in 2005 Charles Phan's spring rolls were photographed on the cover of *Food & Wine* with the headline, "Everyone loves Asian." The Slanted Door's popularity resulted from its exceptionally good food, but it was pathbreaking for a Vietnamese restaurant to charge high prices and win such critical acclaim.[5] It represented a vibrant example of the changes underway for many ethnic restaurants in this era. Ethnic cuisines once unfamiliar to American consumers moved from cheap dives to fancy emporiums as they slowly assimilated into the culture.[6]

Among its many other upheavals the Vietnam War engendered two simultaneous global changes: it ushered in a new way to ship goods more cheaply and efficiently over long distances, and it contributed to mass migration. Phan embodies these two phenomena of the last fifty years in the United States. Millions of immigrants entered the United States over that time, and a disproportionate number of them helped feed Americans, whether by picking strawberries, cooking meals, butchering cattle, or washing dishes. Sometimes those immigrants made "American" fare—hamburgers, hot dogs, and pizza. And sometimes they cooked a version of the recipes from their homeland; menudo, phở, chicken tikka, and pupusas.

SAMENESS IN DIVERSITY

Food shows us the lived experience of globalization in the United States. Food reveals these developments because it is such an integral part of any society. Most Americans eat several times a day, with at least two or three significant "meals." Though we spend less of our budget and time preparing food than we ever have, food rituals are still important to most Americans' lives.[7] And eating is a communal activity, embedded with meaning. Sharing some sort of bread and wine is a ritual for most world cultures. The "bread" can take many forms—tortilla, baguette, rice, cassava, arepa. So too can the "wine"—zinfandel, beer, arrack, grappa, vodka—but the production and sharing of those things is important.[8] Social events usually involve food and drink. When visiting people's homes in almost all parts of the world, the guest is offered food or drink as a sign of hospitality.[9]

Food then can be a lens onto the way we understand culture as it changes over time. The choices we make about our foods, and the manner by which we understand those foods, are both meaningful. Paradoxically, because of immigration and globalization, our food choices have expanded dramatically at the same time that just a few purveyors dominate many food sectors. This tension between sameness and diversity is "integral to globalization."[10]

American food culture has transformed since the 1960s, with Americans eating out much more, getting fatter over time, and partaking of a much wider array of ethnic foods. Fast food became the norm, whether served by McDonald's or Starbucks. And food fads, while always a part of American history, came and went even quicker during this era. Food journalism took off, with newspapers running food sections and magazines devoted just to food—think *Bon Appétit*, *Gourmet*, and *Saveur*. Food television, then blogs and eating Web sites, and then social media all slowly replaced newspapers and magazines, as citizens weighed in on their latest meals, cocktails, or barbecue outings via the internet. In particular, food scholars have in recent years highlighted Americans' expanding waistlines and the latest media fancies over food.

Since the 1960s, the percentage of Americans classified as obese has almost tripled, increasing from about 13 percent of the adult population to about 36 percent.[11] The obesity epidemic has produced dramatically higher rates of type 2 diabetes and is implicated in a variety of other negative health outcomes, including heart disease and cancer. In 2001, the surgeon general estimated that "unhealthy dietary habits and sedentary behavior together account for approximately 300,000 deaths every year."[12] Perhaps most surprising with this new epidemic is that it hits the poor hardest. Whereas for most of human history, the poor were underweight or malnourished, today they are *more* likely to be overweight or obese. How could this happen? The cheapest foods are often the most calorie dense—chips, crackers, soda, and other processed foods derived from tax-subsidized corn or soybeans. The poor binge on these foods because they are uncertain when the next meal may come, thus leading the body to store fat for later. Because racial minorities have higher rates of poverty, obesity and related diseases hit those populations more intensely. In a 2011–2014 survey, 42.5 percent of Hispanic adults and 48.1 percent of black adults were obese.[13]

Food media has a long history, with domestic science advice and recipe roundups in newspapers and magazines in the 1800s and early 1900s. Later, food advice moved to radio, and then television. Betty Crocker, an invention of General Mills, made a mark in all three media with newspaper advice columns, a regular radio show, and then television. Even in the early years of television, food had a place, with cooking demonstrations on news programs and James Beard on a Friday night show after the boxing matches. Julia Child beamed into American homes on public television in the 1960s, and other chefs and celebrities followed.[14] The Food Network made its debut in 1993, harkening a new wave of food television programs.[15] In the internet era, anyone could access recipes and video cooking demonstrations in an instant. Social media introduced a new concept—documenting one's eating habits via photos and video. This new media makes the diversity of the world's foods more accessible. In this study, however, the timeline means I do not delve deeply into the social media age.

As Americans got fatter and social media gained traction, immigrants such as Charles Phan reordered America's ethnic and racial makeup. This shift has had dramatic consequences for American culture, social life, and politics. To some, this change has invoked fear—a new anti-immigrant backlash has slowly emerged since the 1970s. To others, it has provided opportunity, for immigrants form the economic backbone of many industries, including food. It has also presented Americans with a dizzying array of new cultural conveyances, whether in dress, music, language, or food.

American eating habits have changed dramatically since the 1960s because of immigration and globalization and a host of other social and economic upheavals. Globalization is the acceleration of trade and human migration. In times of global integration, such as the present era, people in faraway places are more connected by the goods and the arts they consume, the social relations they forge, and the work they wage. Americans discuss their computer glitches with call center employees in India; they can also eat an approximation of Indian food from restaurants and grocery stores in their hometowns.[16]

Globalization affects all parts of our lives, and it has long been important to the way Americans eat.[17] American supermarkets and restaurants brim with items not available in the 1960s—mangoes, hot sauces, açaí drinks, kale smoothies, and coconut milk. As these choices have exploded in quantity, just a few conglomerates dominate many parts of the food industry, whether in chicken processing, beer manufacturing, or tortilla production. The changes in food reflect other phenomena. These include transportation and communication improvements, car culture and suburbanization, the diversification of the American population, and the increasing power of massive corporations. Using food, this book explains the globalization of American life and culture and the corresponding narrowing of big companies' control over it.

One way that Americans understood this shifting landscape was through food. Indeed, many experienced globalization for the first time and most intimately in grocery stores and restaurants. I examine the sites at which Americans bought food—grocery stores and restaurants—and the vehicles by which they understood their food choices—restaurant menus and cookbooks. This is a business history— one which examines the tortilla manufacturers, food wholesalers/sellers, and chefs to see how they source, prepare, and market foods. This is also a cultural history, or one that makes sense of how and why American consumers seek out and understand new foods and, at the same time, pursue convenience and comfort in their meals. This is the "omnivore's dilemma"—the paradox that we as humans are omnivores and therefore *can* eat anything. However, we don't, whether because we're afraid of poisoning, have been conditioned to eat certain foods by our culture and/or religion, or prefer the familiar. We are, on the one hand, incredibly adventurous in our eating habits, and on the other hand, very mundane. This dilemma has taken on new meaning in the past few decades because globalization presents more choices and yet more familiarity from place to place.[18]

Other scholars have examined some aspects of the introduction of ethnic foods over time and the process by which industrial giants appropriated and sold those foods. Most notably, Donna Gabaccia argued in *We Are What We Eat* that Americans have long welcomed foods from afar and have made hybrids as they appropriated those foods in an American context. Though there was a brief episode of cultural conservatism in the 1800s, she argues that Americans are culinary creoles who take on cuisine from many parts of the world and make it their own. This book updates Gabaccia's study by demonstrating the massive changes in American food over the last several decades, including the rise of suburban ethnic culture. It also uses the new concept of translating diversity to explain how Americans have understood all of the new foods available to them. And it contends that accelerating global trade and immigration since the 1960s has created a fundamental paradox in American food culture, that of sameness in diversity.[19]

The book explains this paradox, resulting from accelerating global trade and immigration since the 1960s, using four themes. First, it reveals how grocers, restaurateurs, and cookbook authors were leaders in marketing ethnic and foreign foods, as they translated diversity for an American audience. Food purveyors sought profit by selling new or "foreign" foods, but consumers frequently needed explanation or instruction to understand them. This is the first study to delve deeply into this process of cultural translation. Second, it demonstrates that cultural homogenization went beyond the McDonaldization variety—one in which American companies dominated abroad. Foreign companies, whether peddling tortillas or chicken tikka, came to dominate certain food sectors in the United States, and they often collaborated with massive American food firms. The process of introducing Americans to foreign foods often resulted in the homogenization of those cuisines in their American context, however. And food choices narrowed in some senses, as just a few firms dominated many food sectors. Third, it highlights globalization's effects on American suburbs, as strip malls and supermarkets became sites to experience foreign foods. Immigrants began to move directly to the suburbs, and these enclaves shifted from bastions of whiteness to hallmarks of diversity. Global exchanges were no longer centered only in big cities; instead, they occurred daily in the ethnic restaurants and grocery stores of the suburbs. Last, the book examines an increasing dialogue about authenticity in the United States, born out of a tension between homogenizing and diversifying culture. Americans sought "authentic" experiences more frequently because of the disorientation associated with globalization, but such experiences were fuzzy and fiercely contested.

IMMIGRATION AND GLOBALIZATION IN THE
LATE TWENTIETH CENTURY

Since the 1960s, immigration has transformed the United States. The numbers are simply astounding. The United States was the largest destination for those immigrants, with some forty-six million foreign-born residents in 2015. In recent decades, over half of the world's migrants left Asia, with India producing the largest number of expatriates.[20]

In the several decades before the 1960s, immigration to the United States had been squelched. In 1924, the US Congress passed a law to severely restrict immigration, targeting those from eastern and southern European countries and Asians. This law, along with stricter border enforcement, came from a surge in racism in the 1910s and 1920s. Anti-immigrant groups gained traction in churches, women's groups, and the halls of Congress. The Ku Klux Klan counted millions of members in the 1920s, its largest total ever, with this wave of anti-immigrant sentiment. The law, and then depression and war in the 1930s and 1940s, dramatically reduced the number of people who immigrated to the United States.[21]

Riding the great wave of the civil rights cause, President Lyndon Johnson engineered passage of a revised immigration law in 1965. It opened the golden door to the United States again. Following the law's enactment, immigration surged, but this time not from Europe. Instead, over the next five decades, immigrants to the United States mostly came from Latin America and Asia.

From 1960 to 2010, the United States admitted over 34 million immigrants, resulting in what one commentator termed a "vast social experiment."[22] In 1970, only 4.7 percent of the American population was foreign-born (the lowest rate in almost two centuries). By 2010, 40 million people, or 12.9 percent of the population, had been born abroad.[23] The racial and ethnic makeup of the country changed dramatically as a result. Whereas in 1970, 1.5 million people identified themselves as Asian on the census, by 2010 that total had surged to 14.7 million. Similarly, in 1970 there were 9.6 million Hispanics in the United States, and by 2010 that number exceeded 50.5 million. The 2010 Hispanic population included 31.8 million Mexican Americans. Table 1 shows this dramatic shift.[24]

In the last half-century then, immigration from Latin America and Asia has replaced that from Europe. From 1820 to 1969, 79.9 percent of immigrants to the United States came from Europe. Between 1981 and 2000, only 12.3 percent were from the European continent.[25]

As immigration surged, so too did global trade. Americans are connected to the world via the goods they possess—the mobile phones, T-shirts, automobiles, or fruit from abroad. As immigrants moved by the millions into the United States, they sought out the foods of their homeland. In any community with a large population of one immigrant group, entrepreneurs figured out that it could

TABLE 1 The Changing US Population, 1970–2010

	1970	2010
% Foreign-born	4.7	12.9
Asian population	1.5 mil.	14.7 mil.
Hispanic population	9.6 mil.	50.5 mil.
Total population	203.2 mil.	308.7 mil.

SOURCES: William H. Frey, *Diversity Explosion: How New Racial Demo-graphics are Remaking America* (Washington, DC: Brookings Institution Press, 2015), 67, 89; US Census Bureau, "A Look at the 1940 Census," https://www.census.gov/newsroom/cspan/1940census/CSPAN _1940slides.pdf (accessed January 22, 2017).

be good business to import foods from afar, knowing it would cure the home-sickness many felt. It wasn't just homesickness that drove immigrant consumption of foods. Habit dictated this too. Certain foods are intimately tied to certain cuisines, making them hard to let go. Think about tortillas for Mexicans, fish sauce for Vietnamese, or olive oil for Italians. Second-generation Americans tell of their immigrant parents clinging to these foods no matter what they eat—pouring fish sauce on fries and burgers or adding tortillas to any meal, no matter the cuisine.[26]

One such Texas entrepreneur was typical of this process. In 1981 he started an Indian grocery store in Houston but soon heard from customers that no such store existed in Dallas. Seeing an opportunity, he moved to Dallas in 1983 and immediately searched the telephone book for areas with Indian surnames. He saw that the Beltline area in the northern suburbs had many Indian immigrants, so he opened his store there. After a tough first year he found success, expanding the store and adding a fast food counter at the back. By the late 1980s his store anchored a shopping center where eight other Indian-owned businesses flourished. He estimated that he had three to four thousand regular customers, including some from Arkansas and Oklahoma. He went to India three times a year to expand his product line and had employees regularly pick up air shipments in Dallas for delivery to local restaurants.[27] While these stores flourished in many places, immigrant customers slowly assimilated and bought fewer of these imported goods from their brethren—in part because managers at major supermarket chains saw that selling immigrant foods could be profitable too.

The success of those immigrant entrepreneurs and large grocers in selling immigrant foods also required communications and trade improvements. Telegraphs, telephones, faxes, computers, mobile phones, and jet planes have all made it possible for merchants to communicate globally. A three-minute telephone call between New York and London fell from $60.42 to $0.40 between 1960 and 2000.[28]

These technological changes make it possible to transact a much wider variety of goods, but they also introduced a sameness over time and space. Workers video conferencing from New York to Shanghai might drink the same Starbucks latte even as their environs differ greatly.

Firms had to move goods more efficiently too. Containerized shipping and air travel made this possible. Falling transportation costs have been key to globalization over the past century. Ocean freight costs fell 70 percent between 1920 and 1990.[29] Since the 1960s, goods have crossed oceans in standardized train boxcars (or truck trailers). Containers can be lifted directly off a train or truck, stacked onto a ship, and ferried across the ocean to a foreign port, there to be crane-lifted again to another train or truck. Today, about 70 percent of all worldwide freight moves by container ship.[30]

As noted by other scholars, globalization can thus create "heterogeneity as well as homogeneity" with local shifts moving national, transnational, and global change.[31] If the United States has had an imperial or hegemonic presence throughout the world since World War II, the cultural dialogue about American power typically centers on the impact of hamburgers, blue jeans, and American movies abroad. Cultural commentators wonder how these American artifacts are adopted, adapted, or rejected around the world. They often focus on the big corporations, which can extend their logistical and marketing budgets widely; McDonald's and Coca Cola loom large in this food imperium. Whether America sought or even created an empire is still heavily debated, but there is no doubt that these snippets of American culture are felt abroad.[32]

Since the 1960s, however, this hasn't just been a one-way street of American beef and soda filling up foreigners. Multinational corporations, such as Gruma and JBS, based in Mexico and Brazil, have had their share in sating the American belly as well. I show how America's daily bread, meat, and fruits are frequently controlled by foreign firms that operate on a massive scale.

Globalization has accelerated in dramatic fashion since the 1960s. The rapid change has been much greater than any previous globalizing era, including from 1870 to 1913. In that earlier period, the United States dove headlong into the global economy and immigration surged dramatically too. Migrants moved far away for work, sharing commodities and culture across national and regional boundaries. Barriers to trade significantly declined, as "international freight rates collapsed" because of new technologies, including steamships, railroads, and canals. This "transport revolution" had an impact worldwide, whether in rich or poor regions. Many governments also opened anew to trade, lifting long-held barriers. Japan is one case in point; it had been relatively closed to trade until 1858, when it suddenly opened to the world's ships.[33] Following World War I, however, global trade declined as governments put up tariffs and worldwide depression and another global war strained international cooperation.

In terms of raw figures, global trade since the 1960s is double that of the 1870–1913 period. Trade comprised 29 percent of world GDP in 1913. It then declined precipitously between the 1910s and the 1940s. In 1972, world trade as a percentage of GDP surpassed 29 percent for the first time in the postwar period, accelerating to 59 percent by 2009.[34] The United States was among the top exporters and importers of goods and services throughout this period. In the past two decades, China and India have trafficked a larger portion of worldwide trade as their economies have surged.[35]

These figures fail to capture the actual lived experience of globalization, however. In both periods, natives and immigrants were astounded by the incredible changes they witnessed. In 1900, the Chicago slaughterhouses teemed with immigrants from all over Europe. They sought lunchtime respite from the abbatoir's hurly burly in the saloons surrounding their workplace and residences. In *The Jungle*, Upton Sinclair describes this milieu of Lithuanians, Poles, Czechs, and others competing for a small wage, a small place to rest after work, and a small bit of dignity.[36] A hundred years later the slaughterhouses had moved from Chicago to rural areas south and west, but Chicago still teems with immigrant workers. They converge on downtown and suburban office parks every day, driving taxis, bussing tables, writing computer code, and brokering international business deals. Many more come from Latin America and Asia, and a large number do not toil at the lowest rung of the labor ladder.

A look at the meatpacking industry in 1900 and 2000 puts the two eras in perspective. In 1900, the large meatpackers in Chicago—Swift, Armour, Morris—got their raw materials (cattle and hogs) from the West, processed most everything in Chicago, and then sent it out to customers in the United States and Europe.[37] In our own era, this is a cross-border enterprise mostly away from Chicago. Piglets born on Canadian farms get shipped to the midwestern United States for fattening and slaughter. The pork cutlets are shipped back to Canada (or to Mexico) for consumption. Similarly, some cattle are weaned in Chihuahua, Mexico, only to grow up in the American Midwest. They're subsequently processed, with much of the beef sold in Mexican Walmarts.[38] The trade is still global, but the routes and connections for that trade are far different today.

Sociologists have examined the many paradoxes of globalization, including that of sameness in diversity in food choices. Their studies identify the growing push for free trade across borders, often at the expense of the poor. In these studies, multinational corporations loom large, pushing governments to enact trade and subsidy policies to benefit their bottom line. One debate among these scholars is the degree to which local foods compete with the multinationals to fill bellies. Some studies, however, portray this as an all-or-nothing proposition. Either local foods must die at the hands of McDonald's or Wal-Mart, or they can only flourish if the "pathologies" of globalized agriculture are eliminated.[39] In reality, consumers in the United States and elsewhere straddle a middle ground, in which "homogenization and heterogenization are both crucial features of modern life."[40] Local foods and imported foods sit side-by-side on store shelves, just as consumers may choose to eat a staid diet or experiment regularly with new, ethnic, or foreign foods.

This debate also turns to the question of "traditional" foods, sometimes conflating them with local foods. Tradition, of course, is invented, and changes are birthed in every era, including the present. However, the fact that recent globalization has compressed time and space causes many to wonder whether it obliterates tradition.[41] It does and it doesn't. Tradition is constantly reshaped, and fast food can be a tradition in many families. To start, *tradition* is a loaded word that can mean very different things. If you just mean what you "normally" do, that need not be loaded up with visions of mom's home cooking. Mom may have hated to cook, and tradition might have meant a quick stop at the drive-thru or TV dinners. Furthermore, "tradition" (or doing things the old way), might happen only on select occasions, such as Sunday dinner or holidays. Many families do whatever they can on the weekdays to just eat but may spend more time on the weekend doing something special because they have the time. This could mean regularly visiting grandma's house for Sunday lunch or special meals with friends on Saturday. So, there is a mix in many families of the standardized fast-food burrito on one night and the home-cooked meal from one's ethnic traditions for another night. Tradition is changing, can (and usually does) involve those multinational corporations, and includes both homogenized and heterogeneous foods.

There is also a question of who benefits from free trade and globalization. The answer is not simple. Consumers see prices decrease slightly. Workers see wages drop in many places. Urbanization accelerates as small farmers are displaced by large agricultural firms. Choices increase in some sense, but that can be an illusion when large firms provide most of those options. The poor may see marginally increased job opportunities in some areas. But some may feel compelled to leave their old way of life for the new—work at a factory or in a city when generations lived in the country. Increased trade has also meant a move away from self-sustaining agriculture. In many poor parts of the world farmers grew crops for their own sustenance and, if they had a good year, to sell the surplus. This was frequently precarious. Nature's whims often bankrupted or starved farmers. With free trade, farmers turn to commodity crops to be sold to the market. This means they also rely on imported goods for sustenance, making them vulnerable to a second master—the market. Those imported goods can change diets, such as when soybean oil or wheat are exported to markets where they were not staples before. Again, this is not entirely new. In the 1800s American farmers, merchants, and bankers were intimately tied to the world cotton market and relied on many imported goods as urbanization took hold.[42]

DIVERSE PEOPLE AND FOODS IN THE SUBURBS

People seeking out the latest food trends and ethnic cuisines used to have dinner out downtown. But as Americans and new immigrants moved in droves to the suburbs, so too did ethnic food. For the best Chinese food, Chinatown was no longer the only option. Indian and Mexican food abounded in the suburbs of D.C., Chicago, and other metropolitan areas where, in some cases, chefs crafted the most innovative cuisine. The suburbs also hosted the homogenized version of ethnic foods, most notably with the Chinese chains of P.F. Chang's and Panda Express, comfortably filling a niche within the mid-range and cheap Chinese food offerings. The changes in ethnic foods reflect the new geography of consumption in the United States, in which the suburbs were at the center of globalization. Immigrants moved directly to the suburbs of major urban areas, no longer having to settle in the segregated ethnic enclaves of old. Food studies has long had an urban/rural bias, in which the focus is on the downtown restaurant or the farm supplying that restaurant.[43] In the last half-century, however, suburbs have exploded in the United States and abroad.

After the 1960s, suburbanization and globalization each increased and intensified. The number of Americans living in suburbs doubled from 1950 to 2000, growing from about a quarter to half the population.[44] At the end of the twentieth century, suburban life was the norm, and the suburban home became the "quintessential mass consumer commodity,"[45] making "suburban culture a consuming culture."[46] It was also a symbol of sameness and mass production. Assembly-line construction techniques widened the province of homeownership beginning in the 1940s. The mass-produced home was cheap to build and cheap to own.[47] Mass production meant the homes from subdivision to subdivision, cul-de sac to cul-de sac, came to "all look the same."[48]

But underneath the superficial sameness hid great diversity. For one, the racial makeup of the suburbs ceased to be predominately white after the 1980s. Hispanics, Asians, and the foreign-born moved into the suburbs in great numbers.[49] People of all races and ethnicities put their individualistic flourishes on the sameness of the suburbs. Even Levittown, New York, the old model for mass-produced suburbia, was no longer a whites-only enclave by the early twenty-first century.[50]

DIVERSITY

Increased global trade brought many more choices to American tables, but it was another matter for consumers to understand and utilize the new fruits (papayas), vegetables (nopales), sauces (tikka masala), and grains (quinoa) on store shelves. Cookbooks, restaurant menus, food advertisements, food television, and social media were among the media in which foreign foods were made comprehensible to an American audience.[51]

That "American" audience should be clarified here. In essence, it means the masses. The population of the United States in the late 1960s and early 1970s was as assimilated into a homogenized "American" culture as it has ever been. The foreign-born population was at an all-time low, and though there had been massive immigration from Europe in the early twentieth century, those immigrants were outnumbered by their second- and third-generation descendants. Together, whites and blacks made up about 95 percent of the US population, with Hispanics and Asians constituting only 5 percent.[52] Therefore, most consumers of Mexican, Indian, or Vietnamese food often needed help in understanding those cuisines. They needed translators or guides to make seemingly strange food understandable.

Cultural translators—grocers, advertisers, cookbook authors, and restaurateurs—played a pivotal role in familiarizing the American public with new foods. Translation changed over time, for the foods Americans were familiar with changed too. For example, a very small percentage of Americans had tried Indian food in the 1960s. Then, the more familiar British Empire was used to translate the "curries" that seemed more slop than sauce to many Americans. Indeed, many Indian restaurants in the United States were run by British ex-pats who had spent time in the old empire. Slowly, as more Indian immigrants moved to the United States, they shed the British legacy and reclaimed an older empire—the Mughal one. The Mughals brought grilled meats and flat breads to India; these were foods Americans could easily interpret, so Indian restaurateurs featured them on their menus next to the curries. But over time, Indian immigrants came from a wider expanse of India, and by the 1990s they re-created the subcontinent's diverse cuisines. Their efforts met with some success because many Americans had become familiar with other spicy cuisines—Mexican and Thai, for example. The translation process was ever changing, adapting to the shifting culture.

That food culture shifted in the 1960s and 1970s when purveyors targeted "gourmet" and counterculture eaters with ethnic foods. This selling of ethnicity was not confined to food, however. Airlines, fashion mavens, music sellers, and others sought out customers who were sophisticated, had traveled abroad, and weren't afraid of the foreign, argued Ernest Dichter, one of the leading marketing experts of the twentieth century.[53] Dichter saw that tastes were changing rapidly in the 1950s and 1960s as more Americans traveled abroad, sought variety in foods, and wanted to try entirely new combinations of foods.[54] These included ethnic or foreign foods.

Dichter and others realized that they could broaden their marketing possibilities by using ethnicity to sell foods.[55] Supermarket and restaurant chains used ethnic foods to capture business from immigrants and their descendants and as a way to entice all customers to try new foods. *Ethnic food* is a term that changes over time, but I define it here as any food that is not considered "American." It is instead associated with another ethnic group—say Chinese or Italian. Although "there is no clear cut universally accepted definition," it is "identified in the public mind with a foreign source or an American minority group."[56]

The term is transient and specific to the American context. The hamburger (named after Hamburg, Germany) was brought by German immigrants to the United States in the 1800s but is now indelibly associated with the United States. Today, one would be hard pressed to find anyone who called a hamburger an "ethnic food" in any part of America.[57] For many years, "Chinese" food in America was really Cantonese food, for it didn't encompass a broad spectrum of foods in China.[58] The term can create controversy because of its malleability. Journalist Gustavo Arellano once said, "Here's what I know. If it's in a tortilla, it's Mexican food. If it's made by a Mexican, it's Mexican food."[59] He's of course ignoring the fact that some Mexican food doesn't contain tortillas (though not much) and non-Mexicans can make Mexican food. A better and simpler test for whether something is an ethnic food in any historical period is to basically ask if most Americans called it that. In times of rapid globalization, the "other" changes over time and ethnic character can migrate. This was the case for the hamburger as it moved from Germany to America, for "each regional and national cuisine is a culinary hybrid."[60] Ethnic foods hybridized because they fit within a major strategy of modern American business—product differentiation, or getting consumers to buy the newest thing.[61]

Food marketing was but one part of the larger trend toward market segmentation in American business. As the supermarket industry discovered that there really was no "typical shopper," it segmented consumers based on various elements, including race, ethnicity, income, and education.[62] Because mass marketing had prevailed from the 1930s to the 1960s, the transition to segmented marketing took time. Grocery stores, food processors, and restaurant chains progressively moved to target smaller subsets of the buying public and used a broader range of products to do so. In the 1970s, grocery chains focused on capturing the "black shopper," even as they realized there might not be a precise formula for targeting her. Over time they developed strategies to sell to Hispanic and Asian shoppers while also attempting to sell the same products to a broader public. By using new technologies, such as computer-aided supply chain management, businesses were later able to target even smaller segments, such as upper-class immigrants from Hong Kong.

SAMENESS

Though the grocery aisles were exploding with choices after the 1960s, another trend flew in the face of all this—the homogenization and consolidation of the food industry. Big food companies got bigger over time by buying up rivals, using their political influence and taking advantage of economies of scale. Although it seemed dozens of companies operated in the bread aisle of the typical supermarket, only a few firms actually controlled that section.

A handful of grocers dominate their industry. In my home state of Colorado, Kroger, Walmart, and Safeway together take 76 percent of grocery sales.[63] One estimate has Walmart selling more than half of all groceries in the United States.[64] We live in an age of oligopoly, as demonstrated by the food industry.

The largest food processors have enormous financial power. The top ten global food companies pull in $1.1 billion in revenue per day. Nestlé, the biggest food firm in the world, had revenues larger than either the nation of Guatemala or Yemen in 2010.[65] Mergers and buyouts produce mega-firms that extend to what we often believe is local or small-scale production. This is true even in the organic industry—a fact that probably surprises many Whole Foods customers. The giant food companies have bought dozens of organic and natural foods brands since the 1990s, including Odwalla (owned by Coca-Cola), Kashi (Kellogg), Cascadian Farms (General Mills), and Applegate Farms (Hormel).[66] Yet another example is the flour industry; most of our bread is milled, baked, distributed, marketed, and sold by just a few companies.[67] Just two companies sell most of the beer in the world.[68] Anheuser-Busch InBev and SABMiller are the giants controlling 71 percent of sales.[69] And just a few processors control the meat industry; four firms produce 65 percent of the nation's pork and 85 percent of the beef. Three firms process almost half of the chicken in the country. Dominance by just a few companies caused meat prices to increase over the past decade.[70]

The food business isn't the only sector dominated by just a few firms. Between 2005 and 2015, the nine major airlines in the United States merged to become just four—United, Delta, American, and Southwest. They control 80 percent of the domestic travel market.[71] One survey found Amazon selling a full 41 percent of books in the United States (print and e-book) and 67 percent of e-books.[72] Three companies—Sony, Universal, and Warner—rule the music industry.[73] Intel held 85 percent of the global market for PC microprocessors.[74]

What should we make of this? Big firms control many of the products we buy. In many cases they drive away or swallow small firms, hold great sway with governments to reduce regulations and taxes, and give an illusion of choice. Most wield massive advertising budgets to persuade us that they have our best interests at heart, even when they don't. And at worst, they are close to monopolies, or at least oligopolies, thereby driving up prices, reducing quality, and peddling foods stripped of nutritional value.[75] There is also a paradox here, however. Even as big firms control sectors, one-stop shops—ethnic grocery stores, mom and pop restaurants, and food trucks still flourish. The big firms get a good portion of our wallets but only so much. Those firms frequently capitalize on the success of the smallholders though.

THE AUTHENTICITY TRAP

The wide availability of foreign foods and the constantly changing food environment raises questions of authenticity when it comes to food. Globalization-disoriented geography and the flattening nature of fast food caused many consumers to search for something real. They often wondered how "Americanized" foods were in their local context, whether at a restaurant or grocery store. This raises all manner of questions about how we perceive culture, especially with respect to race and ethnicity. Must sushi restaurants have Asian-looking hosts and chefs to feel authentic? What decor is expected in an Indian or Mexican restaurant? If food in Japan, Mexico, and India is rapidly changing too, what is really authentic? Consumers—both immigrant and native—sought certain ingredients from afar to make the real taco, bowl of phở, or curry. Paradoxically, however, they also sought local foods. For some, "real" meant a chicken taco from a bird raised behind the restaurant, garnished with radishes and cilantro from a local purveyor. Restaurants simultaneously celebrated the foreign and local origins of their offerings, reflecting the inherent tension for consumers in globalization. Non-food businesses fed this desire too, claiming authenticity for all sorts of other consumer products—travel, furniture, clothing, and music are just a few examples.

Though authenticity was highly contested, it was also something of a shell game. After all, food cultures in Mexico and India are constantly changing, so trying to find the supposedly "authentic" Indian or Mexican food in a strip mall in Seattle might be a lost cause. The authentic or the phony—take your pick—was cultivated by an army of worker-bee immigrants in the fields, slaughterhouses, restaurants, cafés, and grocery stores of American cities and suburbs. When it came to food, the parade of the authentic was evident in the immigrants who picked fruits, butchered meat, cooked, washed dishes, and bused tables. In many cities, no matter the cuisine, it was cooked by recent immigrants.[76]

One study found that in the city of Chicago in 2000, more Mexican men worked as cooks than in any other occupation, including construction and gardening.[77] Many of them were not necessarily making Mexican food, but instead threw pizzas, rolled sushi, and chopped ginger, indicating that the authentic was again a slippery notion. And while it may have been necessary at one time for a sushi bar to have a Japanese-looking person behind the counter, it was slowly becoming acceptable to have Mexican American chefs, or "susheros," crafting tuna rolls at many spots. Roberto Pina was one such chef at Midori, a sushi restaurant in Chicago owned by Korean Americans. Most of Pina's coworkers were Mexican immigrants too. When he began working there in 1990, many Asian customers saw him and immediately walked out of the restaurant. He said those customers "accepted" him over time, however.[78] While Pina basically makes sushi in the standard Japanese American style, he has added some Mexican aspects to his creations, including a roll with arbol chilies plus ten tequilas on his otherwise sake-heavy drink menu. Across Chicago, Mexican cooks were making other foods too—a group of cooks from Zacatecas were found discussing "the finer points of tandoori chicken" as they relaxed after work.[79] And though immigrant workers dominated the underbelly of the restaurant trade, many of the cooks and busboys moved to management positions as well. Pedro Barrera was one such manager. Having come to the United States in 1986 to work at the Lou Malnati's pizza chain in Chicago, he rose through the ranks to become an executive who oversaw kitchens in its two dozen outposts and "jealously" protected "the culinary legacy of the Italian American Malnati clan as if it were his own family's recipes."[80] As he oversees these kitchens, he mostly supervises immigrant Mexican workers like himself.

INGREDIENTS OF THE BOOK

The book investigates four themes about food and globalization since the 1960s. First, it explores how restaurant owners, cookbook authors, grocers, and advertisers marketed ethnic foods, including how they translated the foreign into the familiar. Second, it shows how food became the same across distance and time, as large firms came to dominate certain food sectors, whether based in the United States or elsewhere. Despite the diverse array of choices newly available, they were often peddled by just a few companies. Third, suburbs became a center of the new global food culture, both as immigrants moved there in droves and firms such as Walmart dominated their strip mall landscapes. Last, all of these changes caused many Americans to question what foods were authentic or real, as new choices abounded, but sameness seemed around every corner.

Chapter 1 tells the story of recent globalization's massive impact by examining changes in fruit and vegetable consumption in the United States since the 1960s. Container ships moved fruits thousands of miles to winter markets. Americans developed a taste for grapes and raspberries out of season and could get cilantro or jalapenos anytime. Chapter 2 explains how once foreign fruits and vegetables, and for that matter lots of other foods, were marketed to Americans in grocery stores. Grocers saw ethnic foods as an opportunity to grow and diversify their business, but they debated the best strategies for luring consumers to the latest fad. Of course, the latest fad often became the norm; no American consumer blinks an eye today at the supermarket shelves filled with tortillas or salsa. Even as choices within the stores exploded, the major supermarket chains consolidated. Chapter 3 illustrates how just a few chains came to dominate the grocery landscape by the early twentieth century, with Walmart leading the new food and retail universe. As supermarkets changed, so did restaurants. Americans eat out much more today than ever before. The restaurant industry has expanded and diversified since the 1960s, and one major growth strategy has been via ethnic foods. Chapter 4 surveys the broad changes in the industry and uses restaurant menus as historical artifacts to explain shifting eating habits.

Americans needed help understanding all of these new foods. The book explores the adaptation of three major world cuisines in the United States. Mexican and Chinese food have a long history in the United States and are two of the most popular ethnic cuisines (Italian is the other of the "big three"). Indian food is newer to the American culinary landscape and still has not been adopted or integrated as fully into American life. Chapter 5 makes sense of how Americans understood Indian food as the cuisine diversified and shifted in the United States. By the twenty-first century, diversity was translated anew for American consumers by using examples from Latin American and other Asian cuisines, and indeed, many restaurateurs used those foods to create hybrid menus.

Chapter 6 looks at all three cuisines and more as they were translated in cookbooks. The cookbook is an essential format for translating foreign culture—it allows the readers/cooks to experiment in their own homes. The chapter shows how one major publishing house, Alfred A. Knopf, fashioned its cookbooks to both explain the foreign elements of cuisines and offer familiar signposts for home chefs. Though other scholars have used cookbooks as historical sources, this chapter goes further by examining the private correspondence between editors and authors. Judith Jones of Knopf was among the most important editors of the twentieth century and shepherded dozens of important cookbooks to publication.

Chinese food is both familiar and foreign to American consumers, depending on the context and the dish. It also has a long history in the United States—chop suey restaurants dotted the nation by the mid-twentieth century. Chinese food has undergone a dramatic shift in its American context since the 1960s. The cuisine has diversified beyond its chop suey dullness to include foods from all over China. It has also moved out of the Chinatowns and into the suburbs (which are sometimes new "Chinatowns"). Chinese fast food and casual dining chains have also moved into those suburbs. Chapter 7 shows that, paradoxically, like the other three cuisines, Chinese food has both diversified and homogenized at the same time. Mexican food has done this as well, becoming one of the most widely consumed ethnic foods in the United States. It was not always so. Chapter 8 illuminates how the central food of Mexico, the tortilla, rapidly became a staple in the United States. GRUMA and another Mexican firm, Bimbo, now sell Americans the majority of their daily bread. These and other large firms came to dominate the tortilla and other food businesses through active involvement in politics. They vigorously and effectively lobbied American and other governments to meet their needs, which were not always the same as that of their consumers.

The epilogue concludes with an examination of authenticity and the meaning of race in modern food culture. Food, especially ethnic food, is often wrapped up in our understanding of race, ethnicity, and immigration. Some use food to bridge culture. Others use food to divide. Authenticity is a highly contested notion tied to these collective and divided understandings of racial and ethnic culture. I show how authenticity is a fleeting concept. In some senses everything is authentic, and nothing is authentic—it is all subjective.

All of these chapters illustrate a central paradox in food culture since the 1960s: sameness in diversity.

. . .

Charles Phan's Slanted Door still flourishes in its waterfront downtown location, and some two decades after he founded the restaurant, it still represents something unique about Vietnamese restaurants. Although Vietnamese noodle joints dot the landscape of most major cities, they often have very similar menus and expectations from diners. Most are low-priced affairs, whereas just a few fancy Vietnamese restaurants exist in those cities as well.[81] A selling point for Vietnamese food is still its cheapness—the great attribute of ethnic restaurants for many customers. This has long been the case.[82] The 1961 *New York Times* headline announcing what it claimed was the first Vietnamese restaurant in the city simply said, "Vietnamese Cuisine Is Inexpensive."[83] The transition of ethnic cuisine from simple, cheap grub to a widely variegated set of options works slowly. So, while cheapness and exoticism are still the main selling points for Vietnamese food, now a greater range of places exist serving the cuisine in different form and price. This happened for a number of reasons. The Vietnamese are no longer only newcomers, and second-generation Vietnamese Americans are adept at marketing new versions of the cuisine. Their customers also became familiar with other related cuisines—Thai, Chinese, Indian—so they could translate phở or bánh mì easier. Grocers and food processors got on the bandwagon too, noticing that they could sell fish sauce and rice noodles in the supermarket. Global trade changes made it possible to ship premium products, such as Red Boat fish sauce, from Vietnam to the United States. What remains to be seen is whether Vietnamese food will occupy the same terrain as Japanese after a time; some don't blink at spending a fortune for sushi at Nobu, even as one can pick up a five-dollar set of California rolls at the local supermarket.[84]

1

The Globalization of the Fruit and Vegetable Trade

Follow that mango. Or the fragrant lime, the sprigged cilantro, the shiny apple, the bunched grape. Each has a journey far different from the one it might have taken fifty years ago. Today, fruits and vegetables often travel *long* distances to their consumers on immense ships, supersonic planes, and long-haul trucks and trains. And many are available all the time, no matter the season. An apple a day is only recently possible—after all, in the 1960s, a grocery shopper in Detroit or D.C. was hard pressed to find an apple in the dead of winter. Now she can eat a Braeburn in February, "fresh" off a six-thousand-mile marine journey from Chile.

How is this possible? And what can we make of the fact that we have hundreds more choices in the produce bins of our typical grocery store, but can get the same-looking, tasting, and smelling banana each day for lunch? Or that we have incredible consistency even in a "natural" or "unprocessed" fruit? In sum, in the produce bins, there is sameness in the diversity. Those bins illustrate the explosion of choices resulting from changes in global trade and massive immigration to the United States since the 1960s. They also demonstrate the emphasis on uniformity and consistency, as the same fruits and vegetables have only recently become available at any time of the year. The accelerating diversity of choices was brought on by several factors: millions of immigrants demanding produce and other foods from their homelands; grocers and food processors looking to market new foods; and transportation improvements including container ships and airplanes to bring those foods from afar. As more choices became available, food companies consolidated over time and seasons no longer mattered—one could get the same thing from the same purveyor no matter the time of year or place of purchase. Containerized shipping was key to making these fruits and vegetables available to anyone at any time.

CONTAINERIZATION

The development of containerized shipping was critical to the great expansion in global trade after the 1960s. Whereas the typical merchant vessel carried only around five to ten thousand tons in 1950, the larger container ships hauled over 150,000 tons at the end of the century.[1] For thousands of years, stevedores unloaded goods at the docks by the strength of their backs. Over the course of the last century those docks were outfitted with forklifts, tractors, and trucks, but the unloading process was still cumbersome and time-consuming because individual crates of goods had to be taken off ships in small sets. In the middle of the century, many shippers sought improvements to this "break-bulk" shipping process.[2]

One shipper, Malcolm McLean, proved most important in rethinking that process. McLean came to marine shipping later in life, having built a successful North Carolina trucking business in the 1930s and 1940s. His "obsessive focus on cutting costs" fostered growth in his trucking line, and would do the same when he got interested in shipping.[3] By the 1950s, his trucks were often stuck in traffic along the East Coast and he thought it made better sense to boat goods up and down the Atlantic seaboard. A universal container could make the process move more efficiently; in this manner the whole trailer could be craned from a truck or train and dropped onto a ship. McLean did not "invent" containerization, but he was the first to conceptualize a system to connect all parts of the shipping chain—trucks, rail cars, ships, ports, and storage facilities.[4]

In McLean's new system, the trailer was packed at a factory in Peoria, Illinois, railed to the docks in New York, and loaded on a ship bound for Rotterdam. There, the whole trailer was unloaded by crane at the docks and trucked still further to its ultimate destination, Vienna. Only in Vienna would the trailer need to be unpacked. Major shipping firms such as Matson and American President Lines tested routes between the West Coast and Hawaii in the 1960s, trying various arrangements for shipping containers and cranes.[5]

Containerized shipping did not take hold immediately; only the Vietnam War made McLean a sizeable profit for his innovation. In 1967 he first contracted with the US military to ship supplies to Vietnam via container ships, and by the end of the war in 1973, 80 percent of all cargo shipped to Southeast Asia went by container. During the war, the first circular container ship route was established between Asia and the United States. The route took loaded containers from the US West Coast to Vietnam. There they were emptied, only to be filled again in Hong Kong, Taiwan, and Japan and returned to the largest ports on the West Coast— Seattle/Tacoma, Oakland, and Los Angeles/Long Beach. This Pacific trade dominates imports to the United States today, with China, Japan, Hong Kong, South Korea, and Taiwan heading the list of nations sending goods to the United States via container ship.[6] Until the 1990s, ships typically carried just a few thousand containers. By the 2010s, some ships packed over eighteen thousand containers, making them larger than aircraft carriers. Container ships now carry 70 percent of world freight.[7]

The wars in Southeast Asia also eventually meant a demand for new fruits and vegetables in the United States as millions of refugees brought their food habits to the United States. Prior to the 1970s, Vietnamese food was hard to find in the United States, and ingredients such as lemongrass and fish sauce could not be found on most grocery shelves. Thai and Vietnamese immigrants imported some of these goods from Mexico in the 1970s and 1980s, but mostly to their small ethnic grocery stores in California and elsewhere.[8] New York Chinatown merchants sourced much of their produce from Long Island, and later from Florida and Honduras, creating an alternative network.[9] Over time, new networks emerged on both regional and global scales for produce importers.[10]

The container ships on which these fruits and vegetables traveled is a microcosm for the sameness and diversity in American life since the 1960s. It holds row by row of trailers standardized at 40 × 8 × 8.5 feet so they can be stacked uniformly on the ships.[11] Although the boxes are numbingly uniform, they hide thousands of possible goods—toys and trinkets, persimmons and pears, books and barbecue grills. Paradoxically, the uniformity necessary for containerization of freight has made it possible to ship a much wider array of goods across the oceans, including the Chilean grapes that pass thousands of miles by sea from Santiago to ports in Oakland, Hong Kong, and Rotterdam. For that reason, consumers in each of those locations has a wider choice of goods available to them, but because almost any good can be shipped almost anywhere, those consumers also share their more diverse choices. As they traverse the oceans, these goods huddle together in sameness and diversity.

The changes brought on by McLean and others dramatically transformed the food available in the United States after the 1960s. Apples arrived from Chile in January, raspberries from Guatemala in March, and tomatoes year-round from Mexico. The United States imported four times the variety of goods between 1972 and 2002; foods were just one among the important types of goods arriving to the ports of Los Angeles, Oakland, Houston, and New York on the massive container ships.

This range of choices, when it comes to food, has had a dramatic impact on American eating habits. Whereas cilantro was difficult to find in New York City in the 1970s, one can go to *any* grocery store in the city today to procure it. The mechanisms of shipping foods such long distances are important to this process. Of course, technological changes lubricated the supply chain, including the container ships, but also telephones, faxes, and computerized inventory systems. There was also a change in mindset, in which grocers and restaurant owners capitalized on the availability of new foods, looking to present the next best thing to consumers over and over again. As much as it was nice to be able to import man-goes, it was also important to get customers to understand what to actually do with the mango. While those Asian and Latin American immigrants knew how to use the mango (and used them differently depending on their culinary back-grounds), most Americans did not, and had to have this fruit translated for their own understanding.

Peeling back the story of these fruits reveals the new consumption practices brought on by globalization, changing business practices, and immigration. Pro-duce at the typical grocery store changed dramatically from 1960 to 2010. First, choices expanded over those fifty years, as mangoes, cilantro, jalapeno peppers, bok choy and a host of other items were added to store shelves. Second, more vari-eties of each fruit or vegetable were displayed too. One could buy Pink Lady, Brae-burn, McIntosh, Gala, Fuji, Granny Smith, and Jonathan apples, where there had been only red and green in many grocery stores a few decades before. Third, a shopper could get fresh grapes, tomatoes, and other summer produce in the win-ter. Over time, more and more stores stocked produce shipped from Southern Hemisphere countries like Chile, New Zealand, Australia, and South Africa dur-ing the Northern winter. Together, these changes meant that in 1998 the typical American grocery store carried 345 produce items, whereas in 1987 that store had carried 173, and in 1975 only about 65.[12] A US Department of Agriculture (USDA) report summarized the trends in fruit and vegetable markets during the 1980s and 1990s by noting that changes included an "increasing array of produce varieties," a "greater role" for imported produce, and an expansion of restaurant and takeout foods that used those fruits and vegetables.[13]

Mass immigration from Asia and Latin America also prompted changes in the produce bins. Immigrants demanded fruits and vegetables from their homelands, reordering the way grocers stocked their stores. By 2000, about half of the foreign born had come from Latin America, and about a quarter from Asia; these immi-grants and their descendants requested chilies, mangoes, and other produce that most Americans had little experience with a few decades prior.

Beginning in the 1960s, grocery store managers sought to attract greater busi-ness by marketing different produce items to new immigrants and the native born. Some foreign-grown produce, such as the banana, had been an everyday part of the American diet since the early twentieth century.[14] In the mid-1960s, half of the world's bananas were consumed in the United States, shipped by rail and sea from Central and South America to be held in "ripening rooms" before hitting store shelves.[15] Bananas were long removed from any ethnic connotation—they were simply an easy-to-eat fruit for consumers. Bananas were the exception, not the rule, however. Other than bananas, Americans consumed few fresh tropical fruits and vegetables before the 1960s. At that time, American cuisine was still entrenched in meat-and-potatoes sameness.[16]

Cilantro and limes show immigration's impact on the fruit and vegetable trade after the 1960s. Cilantro is used widely in many Asian and Latin American cuisines, but Americans rarely bought it before the 1960s. Typically referred to in the 1960s and 1970s as Chinese parsley or fresh coriander, cilantro shifted from a difficult-to-find item on supermarket shelves to a must-have for storeowners across the United States. As late as 1979, Elisabeth Ortiz, author of *The Book of Latin American Cooking*, was anxious that she would not have enough cilantro for her book release party in New York City, telling her editor that hot weather made it harder to procure. Cilantro was a seasonal and exotic ingredient at the time.[17] During the 1980s and 1990s, Americans became much more familiar with the ingredient, using it to make the guacamole and curries that they had tasted in restaurants. And whereas cookbooks once had to explain the distinction between cilantro and other herbs, by the 1990s customers demanded cilantro without hesitation. Large restaurant chains even used it in hybrid foods, such as a pollo barabacoa chicken pizza. The El Torito chain sold this at its Italian-Mexican hybrid restaurant chain, Pasta Manana, topping it with barbecued chicken, red onion, and cilantro.[18]

Limes are another case in point. They can be grown in warm areas of the United States, but since the 1960s have largely been imported from Mexico to sate the demand for Mexican and Asian foods in the United States. American consumption of limes grew dramatically in the last couple decades of the twentieth century, from a steady 0.2 pounds per capita annual consumption during the 1970s to about 2.6 pounds by 2004, when they were used to provide acidity and sourness to something other than that occasional cocktail.[19] As an essential ingredient in guacamole and many Asian sauces, the lime slowly became a common item in the American supermarket basket. A full 92 percent of limes eaten in the United States in the 1997–98 growing year were imported, with 99 percent of those imports coming from Mexico.[20]

Although there was greater choice in the produce aisles by 2000, other economic trends heralded a degree of homogenization. Americans had more choices within a typical supermarket, but for the most part they bought their produce at the same places. In 2000, supermarkets captured around 88 percent of retail produce sales because supermarket chains consolidated.[21] Furthermore, the suppliers to those supermarkets had consolidated in the 1980s and 1990s. Although fifty-four bagged-salad companies operated in 1999, the two largest ones accounted for over three-quarters of sales in that food category.[22] The very invention of the bagged salad industry is one example of the desire for consistency and sameness in the consumption experience. Termed a "value-added" product by the industry, a bag of "fresh-cut" spinach presents a uniform package of salad greens. Rumpled, ugly, or discolored spinach leaves have already been taken out of the mix. One estimate found that in the European Union, somewhere between a quarter and third of fruit is rejected by retailers for blemishes that may have nothing to do with the fruit's taste.[23] The buyer of bagged salad wants convenience, but she also wants consistency.[24]

The same is true for the buyer of winter produce. A shopper purchasing a winter peach wants to be able to make peach cobbler in January just as she might in June, when peaches are actually harvested in the United States. During the 1950s and 1960s, newspapers often ran articles dispensing advice to housewives about how to handle surpluses of particular fruits during local growing seasons.[25] At the end of the century, newspapers still ran columns about local fruit harvests, but they could provide recipes at any time of the year with almost any "seasonal" ingredient, knowing that if it was not in season locally, it still could be found on a local store shelf, shipped from afar. The mental disconnect between local growing seasons and availability of produce was so marked that one San Francisco cooking school had to teach its students about the harvest seasons for various fruits and vegetables. In the school's library, a chart illustrated the seasons for which local produce was fresh. It advised that students should try a "new approach" and choose the "best, fresh-picked locally grown ingredients from this list first, *then* [select] the recipes that feature them in the chart below. Red boxes indicated when varieties of fruits and vegetables were harvested in North America."[26] Clearly, the students were used to seeing all produce available in all seasons.

This easy availability was partly responsible for Americans eating more fresh fruits and vegetables over the last few decades of the twentieth century. From 1980 to 2001, per capita consumption of fresh vegetables and melons rose 33 percent. Per capita fresh fruit consumption also rose 11 percent in that period.[27] Consumers rated the produce section the most important priority for a supermarket (alongside cleanliness).[28] Supermarket chains responded naturally by emphasizing produce, making that section the "most exciting part of the store."[29] The trend toward larger stores helped this. In the mid- and late-1980s, Safeway greatly expanded its produce sections as it built more superstores—the larger stores allowed a greater variety of foods. In 1989 the company boasted, "Whereas a few years ago customers could buy approximately 130 different produce items over the course of a year, customers today can buy more than 350 items, including exotic and out-of-season items."[30]

Globalization, rising incomes, and urbanization were all factors in the increased consumption. Higher imports made that consumption possible. Global trade, including that of agricultural products, rose markedly during the last few decades of the twentieth century, as farmers could specialize to better serve an export market. American farmers produced all types of foods, but soybeans, wheat, and beef were high on the list of export commodities.[31] Worldwide trade accelerated dramatically at the end of the century.[32] The global trade in fruits and vegetables also increased both in absolute numbers and as a percentage of overall agricultural trade, growing from $3.4 billion in 1961, or 10.6 percent of agricultural trade, to nearly $70 billion, or 16.9 percent of agricultural trade, in 2001.[33] Even if population increases and inflation for that period are taken into account, global trade of fruits and vegetables doubled from $1 per person in 1961 to about $2 in 2001.[34] One factor in this rise was continuing urbanization and rising incomes. Studies by the Food and Agricultural Organization of the United Nations have shown that when people move to cities, they consume more fruits and vegetables. Farmers worldwide found they had growing export markets not just for the nations that had already urbanized like the United States, but countries for which the middle and upper classes were growing, like China.[35]

In the United States, health concerns have also prompted more Americans to make fruits and vegetables a part of their diets. Media coverage and consumer education campaigns about healthy eating have intensified these concerns. The USDA food guide pyramid, for example, first devised in the 1980s, recommends between five and nine servings of fruits and vegetables per day, and has had some success in educating Americans about the nutritional value of these foods.[36] In sum, rising demand caused the value of imported fruits and vegetables into the United States to roughly double between 1965 and 2000.[37] The United States was also the second largest exporter of fruits among all nations by the end of that period, as consumers in Canada, China, and Japan sought oranges, apples, and grapes from California, Texas, Washington, and Florida.[38]

THE PRODUCE TRADE WITH MEXICO

While the United States exports a good deal of its fruit and vegetable production to its northern neighbor, it also imports a large percentage from its southern neighbor, Mexico. Mexican growers sell around 80 percent of their crops domestically to meet the nation's growing population, but certain crops have been sent in increasing numbers to the United States since the 1960s. These include tomatoes, peppers, asparagus, onions, cucumbers, and mangoes. Mexican growers dominate the US market for items such as green onions and frozen broccoli because they must be processed by hand and growers can pay Mexican laborers less than their American counterparts. Since the 1960s, US firms have also invested heavily in Mexican operations by transferring plant technologies to Mexican growers. During the 1980s and 1990s, as more American consumers demanded a year-round, consistent supply of fruits and vegetables, Mexico stepped up exports of winter vegetables. By the early 1990s, the majority of bell peppers, tomatoes, squash, and cucumbers consumed between January and March each year had come from Mexico. American consumers, like their counterparts in almost any other industrialized or industrializing nation, could enjoy almost any fruit or vegetable at almost any time. Global trade meant more diverse choices for consumers, but a sameness of experience across seasons.[39]

Mangoes are Mexico's most valuable agricultural export and second only to bananas as an export fruit worldwide. Between the 1960s and 1990s, the mango export trade grew dramatically. In the 1990s, 80 percent of Mexican mango exports went to the United States. Mexico stands second in annual world production of mangoes (India is the largest producer, but most of its mangoes are consumed domestically). Mexico exports to the United States from February to September, while Central and South American mangoes fill the void from October to March. An estimated half of all mangoes exported from Mexico to the United States are consumed in Los Angeles, and only about "one-third of all Euro-American homes have ever purchased the fruit." Immigrants in cities and suburbs fuel the demand.[40]

Mangueros, or Mexican mango entrepreneurs, took advantage of US-Mexico trade liberalization in the 1980s and 1990s, including the North American Free Trade Agreement (NAFTA) to make this trade possible. Because "*mangueros* were absolutely subject to USDA requirements for their participation in the export trade," they constructed elaborate hot-water systems to eliminate disease and pests.[41] These certification systems required heavy capital, meaning only a small number could participate.[42] As with the tortilla business (detailed in chapter 8) the US-Mexico produce trade increased after the 1980s but also privileged the largest firms. Shoppers in America had more absolute choices, but those were offered by just a few purveyors. Mexico was not the only country shipping millions of tons of produce to the United States; after the 1970s, Chile was just as important to this business.

CHILEAN FRUIT, CONTAINERIZATION, AND THE GLOBAL TRADE IN FOOD

Chilean growers ship a large proportion of the fruits consumed in the United States during the winter, including grapes, apples, and berries. Beginning in the 1970s, they realized that they could profit from their Southern Hemisphere growing season, refrigerated cargo holds on massive oceangoing container ships, and advances in airline shipping. By the early 1980s, fruit growing was the most profitable agricultural activity in Chile, partly because the Chilean government and trade organizations actively promoted the country's agricultural bounty. The government gave subsidies to large foreign and domestic companies to encourage growth, thereby displacing many peasant farmers. Although other Latin American nations were saddled with debt during the 1980s, Chile's economy grew on the strength of its produce exports, bolstered by private investment in farmland, processing, and export facilities. The Chilean government also introduced new fruit and vegetable varieties, such as the kiwi, to Chilean growers.[43]

The Chilean export promotion agency Pro-Chile was critical to Chile's fruit growing boom. In the 1980s it produced a brochure containing dozens of glossy photos of glistening fruits. It explained how the beauties could be transported across the world by ship or plane. It also advertised the unique geography of Chile, which enabled grape growers in the northern valley of Copiapó to harvest in mid-December, and those in Talca, 1,100 kilometers to the south, to harvest in mid-April.[44] Because of these exports to the United States and elsewhere, fruits grew from 16.7 percent of all Chilean agricultural exports in 1970 to 40.3 percent in 1988.[45] By the beginning of the twenty-first century, Chile was second only to Mexico as a supplier of fruits and vegetables to the United States, and it dominated US fruit imports from December to April.[46]

Grapes have been the most important of these fruits for the Chilean economy since the 1970s, as farmers profited from shipping winter grapes and wine worldwide. The proportion of imported grapes in the US market shifted from only 4 percent in 1972–74 to 53 percent in 2002–04. A great number of those grapes came from Chile between January and April. The concurrent rise in availability of winter fruits and overall produce consumption caused the average American to eat over eight pounds of table grapes in 2006 compared to only two pounds in 1970.[47] Though Chilean vintners had long shipped wine around the world, they also began shipping wine grapes in the 1983/84 growing season to be used by foreign winemakers so they could produce "off-season" wines.[48]

The journey by sea for the Chilean grapes is often quite long—around 6,500 miles in the case of Santiago to Philadelphia—so foods must be handled differently than if trucked to market from a local field. Before airline and container shipping of fresh fruits, vegetables, fish, cheeses, and meats, Americans had basically three options to recreate the ingredients present in other locales. One was to grow those items in a suitable part of the United States. This was possible with a wide variety of foodstuffs and immigrants frequently farmed foods from their homelands. In California, Italian immigrants built large olive oil and wine industries, and Chinese immigrants grew Chinese fruits and vegetables for the San Francisco, Sacramento, and Los Angeles markets.[49] The second option was to ship them by rail or sea, but that often meant risking spoilage, for they had to be kept cold for long periods of time.[50] The third option was to preserve the faraway food and ship it dried, salted, pickled, bottled, or canned.[51] Before the 1960s, fresh ingredients that had to be grown in geographies not found in the United States were expensive for American consumers.

Growers, distributors, and supermarkets enable the shipment of grapes and other produce by stringing together a "cold chain" to ensure that the grapes stay fresh. The very term *fresh* expands when speaking of grapes shipped over oceans, for they take about two weeks to get from the Chilean fields to the American consumer. Just after harvest, grapes must be nestled in boxes alongside sulfur dioxide packs to inhibit fungus growth. They are then trucked to cooling facilities for preservation. Chilean exporters had to create a large infrastructure for cooling and packing in the 1980s; they more than doubled the country's cold storage capacity during that decade.[52] After transfer to these cooling facilities, they are loaded into containers for the ocean voyage. Traveling via the Panama Canal from Santiago to Philadelphia, the containers are trucked to locations around the East or Midwest, where they are finally unloaded. Produce clerks remove the sulfur dioxide packs and pile them "fresh" onto store displays. Philadelphia port authorities and Chilean exporters developed strong connections in the 1980s to enable this process, and by the end of that decade, Chilean fruit represented about one-third of all the dockworker man-hours at the Philadelphia terminal.[53] To capture western US markets, the Philadelphia company that dominated Chilean import traffic established a sister facility in San Diego during the mid-1980s. The grapes, apples, pears, and cherries entering the San Diego terminal traveled as far as Chicago by truck and train.[54] These "fresh" fruits traveling long distances ensured that consumers could truly eat an "apple a day."

Although most Chilean produce is shipped by sea, airfreighted fruit has also made its mark. Before the 1970s, fresh fruits and vegetables rarely traveled by air. Airline and agriculture executives first truly dreamed of air freighting fresh produce by the ton during World War II, when the airline industry dramatically expanded.[55] In 1944, as Henry Ford's Willow Run plant in Detroit cranked out new bombers, the executives organized a conference nearby to discuss the results of their study of the "Air Cargo Potential in Fresh Fruits and Vegetables." To sell conference attendees on air cargo's wonders, they held a luncheon to provide a "dramatic demonstration of how the Age of Flight may affect the dietary habits and gustatory experiences of the American people." The menu was "unique" and "exotic," for it featured "such rarities as tree-ripened bananas, breadfruit, and papayas" flown directly from Guatemala, Mexico, Cuba, and the southern United States. Because airplanes at the time had limited range, the conference focused on shipments from California, Florida, and Texas to the Northeast and Midwest. Several speakers highlighted the advantages of shipping vine-ripened produce, because at the time, tomatoes and bananas were picked green and ripened in special warehouses in destination cities. Another speaker lauded the health benefits of air-shipped produce, citing a Department of Agriculture study that showed a marked decline in vitamin C content for fruits and vegetables as they sat in refrigeration; a bunch of freshly picked strawberries delivered 74 milligrams of vitamin C, but when the strawberries sat refrigerated for five days, their vitamin content slipped to 17 milligrams.[56]

Dreams of air-shipped produce did not come to fruition immediately, for certain technical advances were necessary for large-scale shipments. The development of the long-distance airliner in 1958 and the wide-body jet in 1967 made international passenger and cargo travel easier and cheaper. Air freight dramatically increased in the 1950s and 1960s, particularly in the North Atlantic market, but the airlines did not carry much fresh produce. At the time, airline holds were reserved for high-value items, such as artwork, jewelry, and legal documents, and as late as 1970, the winter peach was still something for the imagination.[57] The leading grocery industry magazine previewed the 1970s by explaining that "lower-cost air freight will make tropical fruits and imported produce available in all markets, and lead to a special section for exotic new lines in some units," adding that guavas would be sold on the East Coast and "vine-ripened tomatoes will be sold in Minnesota in January."[58] The plans hatched in the fervor of World War II only became a reality by the end of the century, when on a bitterly cold January day a Milwaukee supermarket shopper wouldn't blink an eye at an overflowing bin of peaches, nectarines, and grapes.[59] Indeed, by the end of the twentieth century, air freight had made significant inroads; in 1993, 29 percent of US exports and 21 percent of imports by value were transacted by air.[60] The prediction for the 1970s had come true, albeit a couple decades later.

In 2000, LAN Chile, the major Chilean airline, was one of only two passenger airlines in the world to devote most of its tonnage to freight. This freight was mostly fish, fruit, vegetables, and flowers, proving quite profitable for the airline.[61] In particular, LAN Chile air ships fragile and high-value fruits, such as raspberries and cherries during the Northern Hemisphere winter. Predictably, during the weeks that Chilean, American, or Mexican growers could not guarantee fruit shipments to grocers, farmers in other regions filled the void. In the 1990s, Guatemalan growers developed a niche trade in raspberries for short windows of opportunity during the spring and fall.[62]

CONSISTENCY AND VARIETY IN THE SUPERMARKET

The shipment of off-season fruits and vegetables to areas far and wide speaks to a desire for consistency on the part of the consumer. Large food processors and chain restaurants strenuously try to achieve that consistency. In the 1960s, the Stouffer's company operated restaurants in addition to selling frozen foods in supermarkets. On one menu it explained that its creamed chicken entrée was "prepared in small batches," but that "every batch must be exactly the same, so that you may enjoy in your homes the dependability of our quality."[63] Similarly, in 1986, McDonald's explained in its corporate literature that it used shortening for its fries to achieve the "consistency and taste our customers the world over have come to expect."[64] Wanting the same dependability of experience they have in a McDonald's drive-thru or when purchasing a frozen dinner, American consumers want good grapes in their supermarket basket whether they shop in February, when no grape could grow in the United States, or August, when they are shipped from California.[65] Shoppers in Taiwan, Australia, and Malaysia also desire grapes on a year-round basis, and California growers export grapes to those countries in late summer.[66] That this demand is a worldwide phenomenon makes the paradox of diversity and sameness more than just something encountered on American store shelves. Several nations signed trade agreements during the 1990s to enable the consistent shipping of fruits and vegetables year-round. For the 1996–1997 growing season, Taiwan's government responded to consumers' demands for year-round fresh fruits by increasing import quotas of Chilean fruits. In particular, Taiwanese consumers desired apples. American growers shipped $79 million worth of the fruits there that year, and Chilean growers filled additional demand. Overall, exports from the Southern Hemisphere nations of Argentina, Australia, New Zealand, Chile, and South Africa more than tripled between 1974 and 1996.

The commodification and industrialization of fruit production has had one unfortunate consequence—decreasing biodiversity. The varieties of seed stock held by the US National Seed Storage Laboratory in Colorado dramatically decreased for several fruits and vegetables during the course of the twentieth century. Worldwide, the United Nations estimates that about three-quarters of crop biodiversity vanished in the twentieth century. The problem is so acute that one group recently created the Global Seed Vault, a secure bunker in an arctic Norwegian mountain, designed to hold and protect millions of varieties of seeds from extinction. The US government runs similar facilities in Colorado and Georgia. The International Treaty on Plant Genetic Resources was ratified in 2004 to protect thirty-five major world crops. Biodiversity has declined mostly because over the last several decades agricultural corporations have preferred to create "super-breeds" of grains, fruits, and vegetables that they distribute widely. Just nine species of plants supply around three-quarters of human food.[67] One type of banana, the Cavendish, dominates the market.[68] And corn is in an immense array of processed foods, including high-fructose corn syrup, animal feed, cooking oil, and tortillas. Biologists at the University of California, Berkeley, calculated that most parts of a McDonald's meal for three, which included chicken nuggets, a cheeseburger, fries, sodas, a milk shake, and a salad, were in fact composed of corn. Except the fries and the salad components (but not the dressing), most of the meal's carbon content could be traced to corn. The soda was sweetened with corn syrup, the fries and salad dressing were cooked or composed of corn-derived oil, and the chickens and cows turned into nuggets and burgers grew on a corn-heavy diet. Soybeans serve the same purpose as corn, finding their way into thousands of processed foods. As any driver who has passed through Illinois or Iowa in the last few decades knows, the land there is composed of corn and soybeans as far as the eye can see. By one estimate, at the end of the twentieth century one in four Americans visited a fast food chain each day, and the average American ate about three hamburgers and four orders of French fries per week, mostly from those chains. Gazing upon the masses of Miami, Chicago, or Los Angeles, one can imagine millions of people morphing into walking corn and soybean stalks.[69]

Paradoxically, however, despite the ubiquitous nature of corn and soybeans in our lives, another trend of the past several decades has been expanding eating choices. Four times as many types of goods arrived at American ports and airstrips in 2002 as compared to 1972, as the share of imports as a percentage of GDP more than doubled during that period, increasing from 4.8 to 11.5 percent.[70] Some economists studying American trade patterns have concluded that "consumers value variety," thereby encouraging trade flows. They have also found that more product choice meant more real income for Americans during the last few decades of the twentieth century.[71] So even if corn and its homogenizing counterpart, the soybean, were used in thousands of homegrown products, the world's bounty came to the United States over the last three decades of the twentieth century, introducing a new variety of sorts. Growers shipped produce long distances across oceans not just because they could, but also because mass immigration gave them a reason to ship it. Asians and Latin Americans coming to the United States in record numbers after the 1960s sought more of the foods familiar to them in their home countries. And large supermarket chains, in an attempt to widen their business and compete with the superstores that began to dominate the market by the 1990s, actively marketed ethnic foods of all sorts, including fruits and vegetables, to all customers. The demand for fresh produce and new ethnic foods was "transforming the nation's supermarkets" in the late twentieth century as customers were "crazy about new items."[72]

Though large companies such as Dole and Del Monte dominated the produce trade, a variety of local importers, distributors, and sellers worked around those giants. In New York's Chinatown, produce vendors sell inexpensive, high-quality produce by fostering their own trade networks. They sell Chinese and other Asian fruits and vegetables to a wide mix of customers from around the New York area. The vendors and suppliers have created an alternative network for the special mix of produce, sourcing it from Florida, Honduras, and other places.[73] The San Francisco Wholesale Produce Market used to be the nexus for produce distribution in the Bay Area, supplying grocers and restaurants alike. Now that the grocers and many major wholesalers bypass the market, its vendors have turned to high-value and specialized produce, often for the fancy restaurants of the region.[74] Restaurants that demand Satsuma tangerines, organic Adriatic figs, or heirloom tomatoes can get these from the market, for it has reoriented in the last couple of decades to supply the wide range of exotic produce that many eaters have demanded.[75] While the big grocers and wholesalers dominated the market for fresh produce by the twenty-first century, a diverse group of small suppliers also filled niche markets, increasing access to exotic, local, and high-value items.

In American fruit and vegetable consumption, globalization and its subset, mass immigration, created a paradox of diversity and sameness. Americans ate a greater variety of fruits and vegetables even as they ate ever-higher proportions of just two vegetables, corn and soybeans, in the form of fast food or processed food. This sameness in diversity was experienced after the 1960s in the aisles of the biggest supermarket chains that came to dominate their regional markets by the end of the century. One could buy bok choy, cilantro, or seven types of apples in the typical store by 2000, but that store was remarkably similar to others in the area, with its McDonald's franchise within and its Frito-Lay snack displays dominating one aisle just as an array of other processed foods did so in other aisles.[76] Even the produce aisle, abound in choice, was often controlled by a small number of immense firms that packaged and shipped those apples and grapes.[77] Sameness and diversity existed together in the American supermarket, which was but a snapshot of the wider American experience.

2

The Consolidation and Globalization of Grocery Stores

Over the last two decades of the twentieth century, major supermarket chains consolidated and increased their power. The biggest—Kroger, Safeway, Albertsons, and Walmart—obtained a wider share of their regional markets than they had a few decades prior. At the same time, all of these chains operated larger stores with much wider selections. One-stop shopping was the norm by the turn of the century, as American consumers could buy food, toiletries, auto parts, clothing, electronics, and office supplies under one roof.

This meant a certain sameness of experience for the average consumer, particularly when one considers other developments in the food industries. Food processors also consolidated, meaning American consumers ate more products from Nestlé, Kraft, Tyson Foods, and other large companies. The food wholesalers that supplied restaurants, cafeterias, and convenience stores became larger too, with Sysco dominating the market.[1] And to make the eating experience even more homogenized, many food service chains set up shop *inside* the local supermarket or superstore by the early twenty-first century. McDonald's and Starbucks each operated hundreds of stores *within* supermarkets at the turn of the century.[2]

McDonald's has long promoted its connections to large food processors, believing that the brand recognition shoppers develop in their supermarket trips convince them that McDonald's offerings are healthy and safe. A 1986 nutrition pamphlet showed Sara Lee Danishes, Hunt's ketchup, Tyson chicken, Kraft cheese, and Gorton's fish filets on its cover next to the signature fries and hamburgers.[3] In 2006 it still sold the connection, noting in its annual report that "many of the foods McDonald's serves are from the same trusted brands that consumers purchase at the grocery store to enjoy at home—Dannon, Kraft, Nestlé, Tyson, Dasani, Newman's

Own, Heinz, Minute Maid, and many others."[4] Similarly, Southern California's largest grocery chain, Vons, supplied area Jack-In-the-Box and Burger King restaurants with hamburger patties in the 1980s.[5] Even as American shoppers traversing the grocery aisles could get lemongrass, hoisin sauce, or tortillas much easier than they could forty years prior, those foods often came from the same supplier, populated by the same ingredients, no matter which supermarket or restaurant they were purchased from.

What had changed between 1965 and 2015? Quite simply, the global reach of these corporations. By 2015, American brands were available in many places outside the United States. To explain the reach of American corporations, one writer told the story of a Japanese girl who, upon visiting Los Angeles said to her mother, "Look, mom, they have McDonald's here too."[6] Many studies have explored the impact of McDonald's, and more broadly American culture on other parts of the world. This study is concerned more with the impact of globalization on the United States.

In order to see how American consumers have been affected by globalization, one must also see the eating experience across borders. This becomes even more important in an age of migration, when consumers are traversing borders. A consumer in Mexico might well shop at Walmart, H.E.B., or Casa Ley (owned by Safeway), just as consumers in the United States are doing the same. Walmart was the largest supermarket operator in both the United States and Mexico by 2003.[7]

Although Walmart has had an important effect on consumption in Latin America and Asia, European retail giants ventured first to those continents. The hypermarket, a massive supermarket and general store, had been a feature of European life for over a decade before Walmart built them in the United States.[8] The French supermarket chain, Carrefour, opened its first hypermarket in 1963 in France, expanding to Brazil in 1975, and Taiwan in 1989.[9] One-stop shopping slowly took hold in Latin America and Asia as consumers increasingly got their food from superstores and hypermarkets operated by European or American companies. In Chile, supermarkets owned by a small number of operators took hold through the 1990s as they expanded their business beyond the upper-income neighborhoods of Santiago and built stores in the middle- and lower-class sections of smaller cities.[10] Royal Ahold, a Dutch company with many stores in Latin America, also bought the US chains of Giant Food and Stop and Shop during the 1990s to become one of the largest food purveyors in the United States.[11]

So, although supermarkets stocked many more food choices after the 1960s, they also became more and more alike as chains consolidated and stores became larger. The largeness of individual stores ironically made more choices possible, but also made for larger chains. The chapter is mostly concerned with these changes at the end of the twentieth century, but first it is instructive to describe the origin of those chain stores in the early 1900s, for it was during that era that mass consumption habits took hold.[12]

SHOPPING AT THE EARLY CHAIN STORES AND
SUPERMARKETS

In many ways it was remarkable that all groups shopped at the same stores at the end of the twentieth century. Despite the changes of the civil rights era, Americans were still segregated by class, race, ethnicity, and political beliefs.[13] But no matter whether they lived in segregation, Americans of all types shopped at the same chains. Rich and poor San Franciscans both shopped at Safeway. Rich and poor Dallas residents shopped at Albertsons, Kroger, or both. At the beginning of the twenty-first century, some chains found success catering to shoppers wanting primarily organic, gourmet, or specialty foods, such as Whole Foods (nationwide), Central Market (in Texas), and Andronico's (in Northern California), but their sales composed a relatively small portion of the overall grocery trade. Whole Foods, the largest of the stores catering to gourmet and organic shoppers had $1.72 billion in sales in 2001, making it the thirty-fourth-largest grocery chain. In the Houston-Galveston-Brazoria and Dallas-Fort Worth markets, for example, the chain had just over 1 percent of area sales. In the San Francisco-Oakland-San Jose market, it reached 2 percent of sales, small in comparison to Safeway, the largest retailer in the area at a 29 percent market share.[14] By 2012, Whole Foods had surged to become the twelfth-largest grocer, but in many markets it still held only 2–3 percent market share.[15] Just a few companies therefore dominated grocery sales in each region, with Walmart the largest by the early twenty-first century.[16]

This was not the case in the first few decades of the twentieth century. There were two essential differences between grocery shopping during the two bookend eras of mass immigration at the beginning and end of the twentieth century. First, during the early 1900s, "ethnic and racial politics permeated food shopping," whereas this feature of the consumptive experience was absent from the supermarket of the late twentieth century.[17] In the early 1900s, Lithuanian grocers served Lithuanian shoppers in the multicultural environs of Chicago, and Italian or German proprietors who wanted to sell to that market were often shunned. Ethnic and racial tensions frequently exacerbated tensions between shoppers and grocers over the quality of foodstuffs, credit, and prices.[18] As Donna Gabaccia has argued, during the early 1900s, "cultural conflicts associated with nation-building characterized the early years of American consumer society, preventing the free expression and celebration of the multiculturalism that has now become such a familiar part of our own consumer marketplace and sense of national identity."[19] Furthermore, shopping was hard work for women in cities, for they had to navigate multiple stores without automobiles, haggling over prices and food quality with mostly male clerks.[20]

While those grocers often had special products associated with shoppers' ethnic heritages, they typically offered limited selection. Before the invention of grocery chains, however, consumers could one-stop shop using the Sears or Montgomery Ward mail-order catalogs. In the early twentieth century, more Americans lived in rural than urban areas, and small country stores offered limited selection. The mail-order giants were the precursor to Walmart, offering two of its most attractive features—massive selection and rock-bottom prices. Just as consumers of varied backgrounds experience sameness and diversity simultaneously at Walmarts and other supermarket chains, mail order shopping during the height of the last century's immigration had a similar cast. The Sears and Montgomery Ward catalogs listed tens of thousands of items in the 1890s, much as a Walmart superstore carried that number in the 1990s. And tens of millions of Americans shopped "at" each in both eras, sharing a common experience there.[21]

Grocery chains first came into being in the early 1900s and expanded rapidly around World War I as the catalog stores such as Sears and A&P opened hundreds of retail locations in the growing cities.[22] These chains took hold as other forms of mass consumption emerged, such as radio and movies. Significantly too, mass immigration from Europe slowed in the 1920s due to new restrictive immigration laws, making it easier for immigrant communities to share in a national rather than ethnic or local culture.[23] Immigrants slowly turned to the new chain stores, leaving their ethnic grocers to buy mass produced goods. Immigrant groups had once participated in diverse and separate food consumption practices, but after the chains took hold, immigrants ate more and more alike.[24]

Italian food is the most important example of this process. Italians were the largest immigrant group during the 1870–1920 period, when millions of Europeans relocated to the United States.[25] Italian immigrants underwent a homogenization of eating habits on two levels. Before immigrating to the United States, most Italians in fact placed their allegiances with their home village or region. They did not necessarily share an "Italian" identity. In America they became Italian, exchanging cultural traditions with Italians from other regions to create a national Italian cuisine in the United States.[26] Then, as Italian immigration slowed and chain stores took hold, this national Italian food was slowly introduced to non-Italians in the United States. Italian restaurants opened in cities, catering to non-Italians looking for a bohemian experience.[27] At the same time, large food manufacturers created "Italian" canned foods. At first, this was the most common way that Americans experienced Italian food from the grocery store, but restaurants soon opened to serve spaghetti and meatballs, a dish that one would hardly find in Italy itself. By the 1950s, Italian food in America, in both grocery stores and restaurants, was quite common, and could be said to have a stilted sameness to it—spaghetti and meatballs, pizza, and macaroni and cheese were its common denominators.[28]

Some of the early chains, including Safeway, Kroger, and A&P, grew in the 1920s because they capitalized on the tensions between purveyors and customers at the independent stores. (A chain is typically defined as a company that has eleven or more branches, and an independent is an operator of ten or fewer stores. The Census Bureau defined a chain as four or more stores until 1951, when it increased the number to 11.)[29] Before the chains, most grocery operators held goods behind the counter and customers pointed to what they wanted, waiting for a clerk to fetch it. Early grocers also extended credit to cash-poor customers and prices were typically negotiable. Disputes over credit, prices, and the quality of the merchandise often boiled into frustration for customers. The chain stores saw these problems with the independents and responded by standardizing prices and instituting cash-and-carry operations. It must be remembered that early chain stores were not like supermarkets of the post-WWII era. They were still small— most less than a thousand square feet.

The features of the modern supermarket began to take hold only during the 1930s. These included larger size, cash sales, self-service, and a wide range of goods. These supermarkets offered not just dry goods, but also meat, produce, and non-dry goods, which had been sold by separate stores in the past. Another key difference was that supermarkets operated from a central office. Perhaps most importantly, the chain stores, and later, to an even greater extent, the super-markets, sold mass-produced, nationally advertised foods. The earliest supermar-kets shied away from the ethnic brands that grocers had once sold, turning to national-brand goods to serve the mass market. The proprietor of the King Kullen supermarket chain, Michael Cullen, was the "leading figure in the super-market movement in the 1930s." He wanted a "wide variety of goods" for custom-ers, but also wanted them to be "100 percent branded and nationally advertised merchandise," for that "stimulated business." Soon, independent grocers mim-icked the techniques of the supermarkets by centralizing operations and selling mass-marketed goods.[30]

For the most part, then, ethnic and racial tensions faded from the grocery retailing landscape as supermarkets took hold. In looking to capture the masses, those supermarkets also de-emphasized ethnic foods, and as a result, the immi-grants and their children ate a homogenized version of the cuisines from their homelands. There were some exceptions to the relative harmony and sameness in the supermarkets. During the 1960s and 1970s, some black customers rightfully complained that their neighborhood stores had higher prices and worse selection than those in white neighborhoods.[31] And during the Los Angeles riots in 1992, looters targeted Korean-owned grocery stores as tensions overflowed between Korean Americans, blacks, and Hispanics in the city.[32] Overall, however, these conflicts paled in comparison to the general ethnic and racial calm of the grocery shopping experience. By the early twenty-first century, Americans were, in many respects, shopping at similar stores carrying similar products. What had changed, however, was the immense variety of the products available *within* each store. To understand this paradox of diversity and sameness, one must see the overall consolidation of the grocery industry during the last few decades of the twentieth century.

GROCERS EXPAND, CONSOLIDATE, AND DIVERSIFY—THE SAFEWAY STORY

The experience of the Safeway grocery chain after the 1960s is instructive of how the supermarket industry has changed, swaying between the strategy of giving its customers greater product offerings and the need to offer a consistent and familiar shopping environment. Safeway has been one of the largest grocers in the United States since the 1960s. Safeway, like other chains, centralized and streamlined its overall operations while building ever-larger stores during that period. The company shifted from a bottom-up to top-down management strategy in the 1990s and early 2000s. Before the 1990s, the grocery giant operated at the local level, as store managers made many decisions about what to feature at their supermarkets. The company centralized its operations in response to competition from other chains.

As Safeway streamlined its organizational structure, it expanded by adding new locations in booming suburbs, upping the size of individual stores, and increasing the number of products available at each store. The chain built new stores in the expanding western states and bought up rivals in the Midwest and West. But as the company increased its reach into the suburbs, it also consolidated many locations into superstores, eliminating the need for smaller neighborhood supermarkets.[33] Beginning in the 1960s, the industry had articulated a distinction between conventional stores, which in Safeway's case then carried about 7,500 items, and superstores, which held over 40,000 items. Safeway began testing its superstore format in the 1960s, eventually shifting to mostly superstores after the conversion and construction of many stores during the 1980s. By 1992, most of Safeway's outlets were superstores.[34]

The company touted a new superstore format it had tested during the 1980s in Oklahoma, Texas, and California as most representative of the "changing retail food industry."[35] At that time, the conventional Safeway store, typically located in a city neighborhood or old suburb, averaged 25,000 square feet. The typical superstore was much larger at about 41,500 square feet. The superstores included much broader sections for non-food items, stocking toiletries, auto parts, toys, and pantyhose. They also had much more space devoted to food. By expanding meat and bakery displays and building delicatessens, take-out counters, soup and salad bars, and full-service seafood counters, the superstores sought to capture more business. Customers who had purchased items at separate stores moved to one-stop shopping at the supermarket.[36] Between 1980 and 1994, the industry share of conventional supermarkets decreased from 85.0 percent to 49.1 percent, as superstores, combination stores, and warehouse stores filled the void (see table 2). Cor-

TABLE 2 Changing Supermarket Formats in the United States, 1980–1994

Supermarket Format[a]	Share of Supermarkets by Format		Sales Share of Supermarkets by Format	
	1980	1994	1980	1994
	Percent			
Conventional	85.0	49.1	73.1	28.2
Superstore	8.9	26.5	17.7	37.2
Combination	0.9	9.8	4.0	17.9
Warehouse/limited assortment	4.7	11.8	4.2	9.6
Superwarehouse	.5	2.1	1.0	5.6
Hypermarket	NA	0.7	NA	1.5

SOURCE: Gallo, *Food Marketing Review, 1994–95, AER#743*, iv–v, 28.

[a] The US Department of Agriculture provides the following definitions for types of grocery stores:

Conventional supermarket: A store that is primarily self-service in operation, provides a "full range of departments and has at least $2.5 million in annual sales (in 1985 dollars)."

Superstore: "Greater size and variety of products than a conventional supermarket, including specialty and service departments, and a considerable inventory of general merchandise products."

Combination store: Those that feature a "pharmacy, non-prescription drug department," and other health and beauty products.

Warehouse store: Features fewer products than typical supermarkets but sells them in large volume.

Superwarehouse: Has limited product variety, but is larger than warehouse stores and often has "full-service meat, delicatessen, and fresh seafood departments."

Hypermarket: Includes a substantial proportion of non-food items (up to 40 percent of sales), combining a supermarket and department store.

respondingly, as stores got larger, the number of unique items carried in American grocery stores expanded from 14,000 to 25,000 between 1980 and 1994.[37]

Safeway's changes meant that over the last few decades of the twentieth century, Americans could buy a wider and wider variety of items at the typical supermarket. Because this supermarket was designed for one-stop shopping, it became the place where Americans bought the vast majority of their foods. As a result, consumers increasingly shared their food-shopping experience. And because large grocery chains such as Safeway centralized and expanded their operations, customers found the offerings at branches in Baltimore and Phoenix quite similar. The largest chains controlled the grocery business by the end of the century. Furthermore, as supermarkets like Safeway and large food processors such as Kraft, Nabisco, and Campbell Soup expanded overseas operations, immigrants flocking to the United States came to know American brands and consumption practices before they departed from their home countries. So although Americans could find greater choices within a typical store, one-stop shopping and the consolidation of large grocers caused a homogenization of choices for the average American when it came to choosing *where* to shop for food on a regular basis.[38]

TABLE 3 Supermarket Chains Dominate Regional Sales, 2001

Region	Regional Market Share for Top 3 Supermarket Chains (%)			
	Largest Chain	2nd-Largest Chain	3rd-Largest Chain	Total of Top 3 Chains
Chicago–Gary–Kenosha	Albertsons[a]	Safeway	SUPERVALU	**54.1**
	25.3	23.3	5.5	
Dallas–Fort Worth	Albertsons	Kroger	Minyard	**46.4**
	18.7	14.0	13.7	
Los Angeles–Long Beach	Kroger	Safeway	Albertsons	**57.4**
	25.3	18.0	14.1	
Phoenix–Mesa	Kroger	Safeway	Basha's	**56.9**
	28.0	16.7	12.2	
San Francisco–Oakland–San Jose	Safeway	Albertsons	Costco	**61.0**
	29.6	19.8	11.6	
Washington, DC–Baltimore	Ahold USA	Safeway	SUPERVALU	**61.3**
	28.1	21.0	12.2	

SOURCE: Market share data from *Chain Store Guide 2001*, a47–a99, 52–53, 135. Supplementary information from *2005 Marketing Guidebook: The Blue Book of Supermarket Distribution* (Wilton, CT: Trade Dimensions International, 2004).

[a] A number of large national chains kept the brand names of regional chains even after consolidation. In the Chicago area, for example, Albertsons operated Jewel-Osco stores and Safeway ran the Dominick's regional stores. Kroger operated the Ralph's stores in Los Angeles, King Sooper's in Denver, and the Fry's stores in Phoenix. In Washington, DC, Ahold USA ran the Giant Food and Stop & Shop stores.

The largest chains—Kroger, Albertsons, Safeway, Walmart, Publix and Winn-Dixie—held controlling market shares in certain regions. By 2001, Safeway, Albertsons and Costco stores together had a 60 percent market share for grocery sales in the Bay Area. Likewise, in the greater Phoenix area the top three chains together had a 56 percent market share, and in the Washington-Baltimore metropolis the top three shared 61 percent of the market (see table 3).[39] Over a decade later, the biggest firms still dominated. Kroger, Walmart, and Safeway together controlled 76 percent of the grocery market in Denver in 2014. Whole Foods held only a three percent share.[40]

Some chain stores dominated the market by buying competitors. A flurry of consolidation took place between 1998 and 2001. During those three years, Ahold USA, a subsidiary of the Dutch company Royal Ahold, purchased 169 Bruno's supermarkets in the southeast and 176 Giant Food supermarkets in the Washington, D.C., area. The third-largest supermarket chain, Safeway, bought three different competitors in the period, including Randall's of Texas, Dominick's of Chicago, and Genuardi's of the northeast, for a total of 270 stores. And Kroger, the largest chain, took over 74 Winn-Dixie stores in Oklahoma and Texas in 2001. The largest eight chains accounted for 26.6 percent of total US grocery sales in 1994. By 2000, those eight chains accounted for 40.5 percent of sales.[41] Merger mania was a response to the new challenge from Walmart.

WALMART'S RISE

Walmart made rapid inroads in the grocery business in the late 1990s and the first decade of the twenty-first century, as its revenues shot from $33 billion in 1991 to $191 billion in 2002. According to some estimates, by 2002 it was the largest grocery retailer in the United States, largely because it could operate on smaller profit margins for its food items. In the 1990s, Walmart managers found that the addition of grocery products to existing stores raised sales on nonfood goods by 30 percent.[42] Walmart's supercenters lured shoppers with groceries and low prices on everything, hoping customers would buy T-shirts, electronics, or furniture after buying food. Because it priced below cost in its food business, Walmart struck fear in the hearts of other grocers. Walmart's share of US grocery sales leapt from 3.9 percent to 24.7 percent from 1999 to 2005, and the company was just getting started.[43] In 2005, it had planned to open at least forty supercenters in California, and by then it was the largest grocery retailer in the nation.[44] Other large retailers responded to this competition by refocusing efforts on specialty and ethnic foods, including sales to Asian and Hispanic populations, and on high-price gourmet items. H.E.B., a large Texas chain, created its Central Market stores to attract gourmet shoppers. The Kroger chain did the same with "Signature" stores to respond to neighborhood demographics, including ethnic makeup.[45] Walmart and the other chains also developed in-house lines of organic and natural foods to capture that growing business.

Walmart became a giant in the grocery business by using data processing to give it an edge in supply-chain management. In the case of supermarkets, controlling the supply chain meant the ability to reduce both waste and storage space on the shelves and in the backroom. Though Walmart was the mover and shaker in this realm, many other companies had tested data processing in earlier decades.[46] In the 1960s, Safeway moved in the direction of many large corporations—it began using computers to track inventories and sales. In 1966 the company established a central data processing unit at its Oakland headquarters so it could more efficiently manage its operations.[47] Like Safeway, chip-giant Frito Lay realized the advantages of data processing in the 1970s. During that decade the company also first sold its snack foods nationally, and by the early 1980s it was micromarketing, or targeting specific consumer segments by region, age, and other criteria to extend profits. By 1986 it had created a central computing facility to track the delivery of each bag of chips each day. The data processor created new stocking instructions each night and sent them to a network of 161 regional minicomputers and 10,000 hand-held computers. The end-result was the elimination of 500 delivery trucks by the reconfiguration of routes. In this process, Frito-Lay could tell what sold and where, enhancing its marketing strategies in particular regions.[48]

Supermarkets and food processors could also track sales via new barcode scanners at the checkout. In the early 1970s retailers and the federal government together standardized Uniform Product Codes (UPC) (or bar codes) and supermarkets were the first retailers to use them. In 1980, only about 14 percent of grocery stores had scanners, but by 2000, they were in 97 percent of stores.[49] Walmart also pushed many supermarkets to test technological innovations in the 1980s and 1990s as it slowly entered the grocery business. It was the first to use satellites to transfer purchasing data to headquarters, thereby dramatically changing the understanding of inventory and distribution. Rather than having a gut feeling for customer preferences, Frito-Lay, Walmart, and others sought data.[50] As one commentator explained, retailers like Walmart illuminated the fact that supermarket distribution systems were "not so efficient after all."[51] In a 2004 survey, grocery industry members listed Walmart as the second-worst problem for their business, surpassed only by health insurance costs. Walmart had not registered as a concern in the 1990 survey.[52]

The innovations that struck fear in the hearts of other grocery chains owners also caused them to change. They streamlined inventories and responded to the demand for "convenience" from customers. Streamlining was accomplished in its most basic form by adapting elements of just-in-time inventory management. In this system, cookies, crackers, and other products are delivered to retailers just as they are needed, based on information about recent sales derived from checkout scanners. From scanner data a supermarket's central computer system determines that there is only one box of Ritz crackers on the shelf. The system responds by ordering five more boxes to be delivered to the supermarket the next day. The just-in-time process ensures that the item is never out of stock and that the store need not keep extra boxes of crackers in the back, thereby saving on-site storage space. Computer inventory-management systems also had the benefit of giving more accurate data to supermarket owners about sales. This process is ever-changing; Walmart is now testing drones in its warehouses as a new device for cataloging inventory.[53]

Over time, grocers realized that consumers wanted more convenience and greater selection at individual stores.[54] Supermarket chains like Safeway responded by simultaneously turning to one-stop shopping *and* expanding the exotic and specialty items within their stores. Their data told them that customers wanted pineapples and mangoes, but they also wanted them cut and packaged for convenience to add to the "sense of theater and service that modern supermarkets are looking to offer."[55]

That desire for consistency and homogeneity drove the increasing presence of "value-added," products, such as those cut and packaged fruits and vegetables. "Value-added" refers to the process whereby foods have value added to them as they move along the food marketing chain to the consumer. Of course, lettuce can be sold directly from farmer to consumer without even being washed. In that case, no value is added to the original act of growing the lettuce. Alternately, lettuce can be washed, trimmed, sorted, and packaged in plastic as "romaine hearts" to be sold in a supermarket, with the value of each of those activities added along the way. The package of romaine hearts sells for two to three times more than the simple bunch of romaine. Value-added products such as packaged greens have captured a larger share of the food business over the years, especially in high-income nations such as the United States, Japan, and Germany, where processed foods account for around half of all food sales.[56] Some farmers and processors copied the success of these lettuce packs and developed other packaged fresh produce offerings. Brandt Farms, a California fruit grower, sold a "Grab and Bake" cobbler kit containing 1.75 pounds of fresh peaches, nectarines, or plums, and seven ounces of "Whistlestop Caboose Cobbler Mix." Shoppers are instructed to "just add melted butter and bake" for a "delicious 9-inch cobbler."[57] In these products, consumers believed they were eating fresh foods and making something from "scratch," even though the peach farm does most of the work. In the late 1940s and early 1950s, food processors created cake mixes that still required a couple steps—adding eggs and mixing the ingredients. These mixes made the housewife feel as if she still had a role in making the cake from scratch and the added benefit of smelling the cake baking in the oven.[58] Produce companies found a way to give customers the same feeling of making something from scratch. Customers believed they were creating a unique product, even if their peach cobbler came out roughly the same as the next purchaser's.

In addition to value-added goods, both Americans and those in developing nations increasingly spend a large portion of their food budgets on other processed foods made by large corporations. These crackers, cookies, soups and soft drinks are commonplace in American supermarkets. Major processors based in the United States and Europe, such as Nestlé (Switzerland), Unilever (UK), and Altria (US), expanded their operations to China, India, Mexico, and Brazil in the 1980s and 1990s as incomes rose in those nations. In lower- and middle-income nations, the share of processed food sales had historically been low, but that has changed of late.[59] The processors have a tight relationship with Walmart and other large retailers who feature their brands, and in many instances, even shape their products.[60] Processors also looked to open the great China market, one that has long lured American corporations and entrepreneurs. Kraft, Campbell Soup, and other food giants hope Chinese consumers will take to their packaged foods.[61] Completing the trade circle, a large portion of the goods sold at the typical Walmart come from China. By one estimate, Walmart's purchases alone form about 10 percent of the overall goods exported by China to the United States.[62] The company located its global purchasing headquarters in Shenzhen in 2002 to control this supply line. It has also set up shop in China at a rapid pace in recent years, building its first supercenter in Shenzhen in 1996 and growing to 426 total stores by 2016.[63]

The global trade in food by large companies was not confined to Walmart's exploits abroad. In addition to the Chilean and Mexican farms shipping produce,

Brazilian and Chinese meatpackers now have a strong hold on American food consumption. As Walmart expanded abroad and foreign grocers enter the US market, their suppliers are increasingly global in nature as well. Nestlé, a Swiss company, is the largest food manufacturer in the world. JBS, the Brazilian meat-packer, is second.[64]

JBS has grown dramatically in the last decade by buying out other meatpackers and expanding its reach into the United States, Argentina, Europe, Asia, and Austra-lia. Globally, it ranks first in beef, chicken and leather production and second in pork and lamb; it exports to more than 150 countries. It has almost a quarter million employees, with the largest number in the United States. Its major American divi-sions include Swift (beef and pork), Plumrose (pork), and Pilgrim's Pride (poultry). In the United States alone, during 2017, the company processed over 29,000 cattle; 90,000 hogs; and 8.6 million birds, *per day*.[65] It began buying up companies in the early 2000s, taking advantage of the global economic downturn in 2007 and 2008. Brazil's government bank gave robust financing to JBS and other companies looking to expand abroad, including $2.8 billion between 2007 and 2009 for JBS's acquisi-tions of Swift and Pilgrim's Pride.[66] This vigorous investment continued over time; in the first quarter of 2012 alone, JBS spent $1.4 billion on US companies. Though most foreign direct investment in the United States still comes from Europe, the JBS mon-ies are "almost like a reindustrialization of the U.S., with the help of foreign money."[67]

Overall, JBS's revenues grew from $1 billion to $162 billion in just a decade by capitalizing on the expanding global demand for meat.[68] Though it started as a small family business in 1953, over time founder José Batista Sobrinho built an empire processing beef in Brazil. JBS expanded its portfolio to include pork and chicken in part because markets elsewhere demand those meats. Pork is the primary meat in China, and as citizens there and elsewhere become more affluent, they eat more meat. Worldwide, the average person consumed seventy-three pounds of meat in 1991 and eighty-six pounds in 2007, and the United Nation's Food and Agriculture Organization has projected that will rise to ninety-nine pounds by 2030.[69] Some of the meat-eating habits of consumers are shifting too. Argentinians had long been the biggest beef consumers per capita, but they are shifting toward pork and chicken because they are versatile and cheap.[70] Over sixty billion chickens are slaughtered each year, signaling the need for JBS and others to get into this market.[71] When JBS acquired Pilgrim's Pride, it and Tyson (the second largest meatpacker in the United States) each held 22 percent of the US market for chicken.[72] As one JBS executive remarked, it "is betting heavily on chicken to become the top global protein."[73]

Other foreign companies got into the growing meat market too. In 2013, the Chinese company Shuanghui International Holdings (now WH Group) com-pleted a $4.7 billion purchase of Smithfield to become the largest pork manufac-turer in the world. It was the largest Chinese purchase of an American firm at the time.[74] Like other global giants, the company processes and sells millions of hogs in China, the United States, and Europe.[75] And two other Brazilian firms have a major impact on American food consumption—the Marfrig group and 3G Capital. Marfrig has major operations in South America, the United States, and China, supplying restaurant chains such as McDonald's, Subway, and Wendy's.[76] A Brazilian investment firm, 3G Capital, coordinated with American financier Warren Buffet to create Restaurant Brands International, a consolidation of Burger King, Popeye's, and Tim Horton's (the largest Canadian fast food chain). It also engineered a merger to combine Kraft and Heinz, then making it the fifth-largest food company in the world. And the company's head, Jorge Paulo Lemann, helped craft what would become the largest beer company in the world, AB InBev, by combining Brazilian AmBev, Dutch Interbrew, and American Anheuser-Busch.[77]

All of these mergers add up to just a few companies controlling different parts of the food business; the concentration is not just confined to the grocery sector. In meatpacking, JBS, Tyson, Cargill, Smithfield/WH Group, and a select few other corporations have created a tight hold on the nation's meat market. This is not by accident or the supposed whims of the "free market." The largest food firms—whether they are grocers, food processors, restaurants, or meatpackers—lobby governments in the United States and abroad heavily and resist the mostly weak attempts to regulate the industry.[78] For example, the Department of Justice held hearings in 2010 to expose the problems of oligopoly in the poultry industry. Testimony told of enormous pressure put on chicken farmers by the big processors such as Perdue and Tyson. The farmers sign contracts with the firms but typically have little control over the price they receive.[79] In an official comment for the hearings, the National Chicken Council, which represents 95 percent of the chicken firms, argued that "vertical integration is the preferred structure for the broiler industry," and having the whole supply chain for chicken under "one management" was ideal.[80] Although the USDA proposed new antitrust enforcement measures following the hearing, the National Chicken Council and other trade groups lobbied vigorously to scuttle them. Not surprisingly, the enforcement measures received no funding in the USDA's annual appropriations between 2012 and 2015.[81]

Concentration took hold then in both the grocery business and its suppliers. Consumers in many countries ate the same chicken brand purchased from the same store. The increased prevalence of supermarket chains and food manufacturers in Asia and Latin America meant that immigrants from those continents are familiar with the American brands and shopping experience before immigrating to the United States. Walmart, Safeway, and H.E.B. expanded their reach in Mexico during the 1990s.[82] In 1990, supermarkets accounted for around 10–20 percent of food sales in Latin America. By 2000, they accounted for around 50–60 percent.[83] Mexicans were the largest immigrant group to the United States during the 1990s, and Mexican immigrants could be seen shopping in the same stores in Houston and Los Angeles that they patronized in Mexico City.[84] Major American supermarket chains consciously used their experience in foreign countries to market to customers in the United States. One Walmart executive, John Menzer, has acted as both head of the International and US divisions, using experience in each to inform the practices in the other. He said the retail giant used the same "product assortment" in stores in Mexico and Puerto Rico as it did in US stores with large Mexican American and Puerto Rican populations. One tangible crossover was the sale of cakes specially made for the quinceañera, or the celebration when a girl turns fifteen, an important occasion for many families in Mexico and Puerto Rico. The company even considered a gift registry for the event.[85]

As American grocers expanded abroad, more foreign grocers tried to gain a foothold into the US market. Some have succeeded and others have had to retreat in the face of tough competition. Tesco, a major British grocer, tried to introduce its Fresh and Easy concept in the United States, but it didn't work because of the different store layouts and check-out concept. It spent over a billion dollars on the 199 stores it opened.[86] Aldi, however, has had much success in the United States both with its purchase of Trader Joes in 1979 and later by expanding Aldi stores. Based in Germany, Aldi had more than ten thousand locations in eighteen countries by 2013. It hoped to increase its presence in the United States and become the third-largest grocer behind Walmart and Kroger. The chain's strategy is to provide very limited selection with cut-rate prices, few brand names, and cash-only purchases. This allows Aldi to save on overhead and staff. Most stores stock just over a thousand items, compared to the typical Walmart Supercenter with 120,000.[87] Another major German grocer, Lidl, opened its first American stores in 2017.[88]

The homogenizing effect of globalization has been studied rather widely with respect to the increased consumption of American products such as McDonald's and Coca-Cola abroad.[89] Two fundamental impacts of globalization that are important, but less studied, are the cultural and economic effects of globalization on the United States, and the manner in which immigrants become human transporters in consumption habits as they experience the effects of globalization in *more* than one region or nation.[90] Clearly, globalization works in many directions. American companies sought greater influence abroad, whether selling groceries in Mexico or pork in China. And foreign companies invested in American operations, whether processing cattle in the heartland or selling chocolates and candies in the grocery store. The result was concentration and consolidation of food across borders. Consumers increasingly ate the same products from the same purveyors, no matter their residence inside or outside the United States. But there was a paradox wrapped up in all of this. As big food companies got bigger, grocery stores offered a much wider range of choices for consumers. Immigrants came by the millions to the United States after the 1960s, bringing the foods of the world to the American grocery store. Grocers realized that if they marketed all of those new foods well, they would expand their business opportunities.

3

Marketing Ethnic Foods at Supermarkets

In the 1950s, Jeno Paulucci seemed an unlikely promoter of Chinese food in America. In the postwar boom years, Paulucci slowly built Chun King into a canned and frozen food empire from his home turf of northern Minnesota. Paulucci was not Chinese, however, having been born to Italian immigrant parents, née "Luigino Francesco Paulucci."[1] When he was young, Paulucci and his mother ran a grocery store where she made extra cash selling home-canned pasta to town residents. For a time, Jeno attended junior college, but he left to become a produce salesman. He proved adept at hawking food—so good that one boss fired him for hitting higher sales commissions than him. While selling dehydrated garlic in the 1940s he came upon a Japanese community in Minneapolis growing bean sprouts in hydroponic gardens. This piqued his curiosity; he soon discovered that Chinese cooking used the same sprouts. At age twenty-nine he borrowed $2,500, rented a building in Grand Rapids, Minnesota, and began growing the sprouts to meet what he thought was a "tremendous, untapped market for ready-prepared Chinese foods for home use."[2] By 1947 he sold canned chow mein to grocers. Moving on to chop suey, Paulucci thought the type served in many restaurants was bland, so he invented a zestier version with celery, pimentos, and an Italian herb mixture from his mother.[3] By the 1970s, Chun King was the leader in Americanized Chinese food. President Gerald Ford, feting Paulucci at a 1976 bicentennial dinner said, "What could be more American than his business built on a good Italian recipe for chop suey?"[4]

Paulucci's shrewd marketing strategies contributed greatly to his success.[5] He hired the popular comedian Stan Freberg to pen some of his radio and television advertisements in the 1960s. Paulucci appeared on Johnny Carson's *Tonight Show* and packaged a Christmas record attached to frozen dinners. From his improbable start in northern Minnesota, Paulucci sold canned/frozen Chinese food, frozen pizza rolls, and Italian frozen TV-dinners. In the 1950s, newspapers termed his Chun King line "American-Oriental" fare. In 1964, he replaced Freberg with Nancy Lee for a $3 million television advertising campaign. She was a "young Los Angeles homemaker," whom the company called "the first Chinese-American Betty Crocker."[6] Paulucci once noted, "I don't sell chow mein. I sell excitement."[7] Chun King eventually produced $50 million in annual revenues before Paulucci sold it to R.J. Reynolds.[8]

By the 1950s, chop suey joints had blanketed the country, but there wasn't much by way of Chinese ingredients in grocery stores. Chun King and its competitor La Choy saw a market for industrially produced Chinese food. They employed memorable marketing campaigns emphasizing both the foreignness of Chinese food and its familiarity to all of those patrons of chop suey houses. In the mid-1950s, one study found that 65 percent of Americans ate "American-Oriental" dishes either at restaurants or for take-out, and that "85 percent are familiar with some Oriental dishes."[9] Paulucci thought that if Americans ate Chinese food out, they would also eat it at home—they just needed someone to make it easy for them.

Chun King's marketing campaigns emphasized ease of preparation with a hint of exotic Orientalism. At supermarkets in the late 1950s, Chun King created an end-of-aisle display, the "Menu Magic Bazaar," which brought "the ingredients of Chinese menu dishes together under an Oriental-motif bamboo canopy," explained a J. Walter Thompson company newsletter. This advertising firm ran Chun King's marketing efforts, saying the "Bazaar reminds homemakers that they can prepare a variety of Chinese menus with a minimum of trouble."[10] After selling canned Chinese foods for a time, Paulucci entered the rapidly growing frozen dinner market in 1955. That first TV dinner offered chicken almond chop suey, rice, and two egg rolls for 90 cents. A *New York Times* reviewer raved that it was "an outstanding example of what is possible with frozen foods," noting it required heating in the oven for just thirty-five minutes.[11] In the early 1960s, Freberg hosted the "Chun King Chow Mein [Radio] Hour" in honor of Chinese New Year. One New Year Paulucci developed a stunt in which he pulled Freberg through Los Angeles on a rickshaw. By the 1980s, a Chinese American organization in New York wrote an editorial wondering how an Italian American could lay claim to the Chinese holiday.[12]

Chun King was among hundreds of companies to market ethnic foods in grocery stores after the 1960s. Grocers welcomed a new revenue source in ethnic foods, but they struggled with how to best market them. They tried to capture both the rapidly increasing immigrant population and the even larger customer base of non-immigrants. Those consumers experienced both diversity and sameness in the local American supermarket at the end of the twentieth century, for they were able to buy fast food burgers and "fresh" bok choy in a single trip—an unlikely experience forty years prior.

TABLE 4 Number of Items in the Typical Grocery Store, 1920–2004

Year	Average Number Per Store
1920	700
1930	1,000
1940	1,800
1950	3,750
1960	5,900
1970	7,800
1980	14,000
1988	26,430
1998	40,333
2002	35,000
2004	40,000

SOURCES: For the years 1920–1970, Robert W. Mueller, "5 Decades that Revolutionized the Food Industry," *Progressive Grocer*, June 1972, 19–30. For 1980, J. Michael Harris, Phil R. Kaufman, Steve W. Martinez (coordinator), and Charlene Price, *The U.S. Food Marketing System, 2002, AER# 811* (Washington, DC: ERS-USDA, 2002), 22. For 1988, 1998, and 2002, *Food Marketing Industry Speaks 2003* (Washington, DC: Food Marketing Institute, 2003), 18. For 2004, the number listed is for conventional supermarkets. Superstores carried 35,000 items on average, and combination stores carried 42,500, *Food Marketing Industry Speaks, 2004* (Washington, DC: Food Marketing Institute, 2004), 38.

Just as the produce bins diversified in the late twentieth century, so too did the rest of the grocery store. The diversification of food choices was partly a function of the increased global trade described earlier. As shipping methods improved, all sorts of products that had not been available in American stores were there at the end of the twentieth century. In 1960, the average supermarket carried 5,900 items, but by 1998 that number had grown to 40,333 (see table 4).

Supermarkets deliberately offered greater product choice to address three issues. First, supermarket chains, like other businesses, searched for ever-new methods for growth. Because publicly traded companies must always search for ways to grow, the chains theorized that they could increase revenues by selling ethnic foods.[13] Second, grocers operate on very low profit margins as compared to other industries and therefore constantly look for the new thing to offer consumers. Though all industries do this, grocers are especially attuned to the need to shift product lines regularly. Furthermore, after the 1960s, the supermarket business changed from "manufacturer-driven . . . to consumer-driven due to technology such as scanners and computers," which tracked sales.[14] Third, after the 1960s, the chains slowly sought to capture business from the growing population of immigrants and their descendants. But because the chains also wanted to sell ethnic foods to the native-born, grocers often conflated it with two other categories, specialty and gourmet. Of course, some ethnic foods were not typically labeled gourmet, as in the case of the humble tortilla, but even that changed over time, as many "peasant" foods became gourmet so that operators could charge higher prices for them.[15] These chains did not wholly devise the ethnic food strategy. Consumers demanded ethnic foods, and supermarkets and food processors gave them what they wanted. But even as they demanded greater variety, American consumers also sought a shopping experience that felt familiar and comfortable. So, what exactly did consumers and supermarket operators want? Greater product choice? One-stop shopping? Exotic or authentic foods? Americanized, familiar versions of ethnic foods? They wanted all of these things, and they got them.

Paulucci was ahead of the curve for all of these trends. He filled a niche market and then grew it; he also created a vertically integrated company with a global supply chain and pursued new technologies for food processing and packaging. Chun King imported Ecuadoran shrimp and Argentine beef; grew mung beans, sprouts, and other vegetables in Texas, Oklahoma, and Minnesota; and had its own trucking company, the "Orient Express."[16] In 1957, he developed a "Divider Pak" combining two cans for chow mein or chop suey—dividing wet and dry ingredients to keep dry goods crisp.[17] To promote the Divider Pak, Freberg wrote a 1960s television commercial in which a housewife suffering from a headache wonders how she can make a dinner "that's different." Of course, Chun King has a solution. She shows the Divider Pak to her husband who says, "It's what's on top that counts." The wife replies, "On the bottom too. It's the quarter inch tape that makes the difference," showing the cans stuck together.[18]

Recognizing that the Americanized form of Chinese food was already attractive for consumers, Paulucci walked a line between the familiar and foreign. He realized that the average American consumer in the 1960s (mostly white/native-born) was ready to try new foods, but that consumer was rather homogenous. The 1960 and 1970 censuses showed the lowest percentage of foreign-born in the twentieth century—the immigrants of the early century had assimilated in large numbers.[19] But his childhood in northern Minnesota had exposed him to a melting pot where workers from around the world worked the Mesabi Iron Range. They came from over forty countries and produced half the iron mined in the United States during the twentieth century.[20] This environment attuned him to the possibilities of selling ethnic foods. In the 1950s, Chun King capitalized on a fashion trend for "Oriental furniture, beachwear, [and] household accessories," running ads heralding the glamorous, quick, and economical elements of Chun King's foods.[21] Like other food purveyors, he disseminated recipes that featured his foods, both in magazine advertisements and full cookbooks. Chun King's 1962 cookbook, *Quick, Easy and Intriguing Ways with American Oriental Cookery to Add Zest to Your Menus*, published together with Mazola Corn Oil, told readers that Chinese ingredients were not "mysterious and difficult," but instead "flexible and versatile." As might be expected, almost all recipes contained Chun King and Mazola products.

The back of the cookbook listed thirty-five Chun King products. It had "Chinese" recipes, and other recipes for "Mexicali," "South African Bake," and "Italian Tagliarini," all using Chun King sauces or noodles.[22] Chun King emphasized this in a 1966 ad in which Italian, Irish, and Jewish actors talked about their favorite dishes from their homeland. For them, Chinese food provided a nice "change of pace."[23] Often, these advertisements relied on old stereotypes to orient white consumers. In 1969 the company gave away fortune cookies for Chinese New Year. Dick Hanley, a copywriter on the Chun King account at J. Walter Thompson said, "Of course we're going to use old favorites like 'Your laundry is ready' and 'Wink back'" for the fortunes.[24]

Chun King paved a middle way in the marketing of ethnic foods. This proved important in a globalizing era. The proliferation of ethnic foods in supermarkets represented the massive changes going on around the world, as migrants moved from place to place, carrying their food cultures. Many Americans experienced this new era of globalization firsthand by way of the grocery store. That store was about to experience a host of changes beginning in the 1960s.

SAMENESS IN THE MID-CENTURY SUPERMARKET

The story told here is one about ethnic marketing and its role in creating increased choices in the American supermarket after the 1960s. A snapshot of the middle-century grocery store helps one see how dramatically the foods in the average supermarket changed after the 1960s. Grocery store shopping had been rather unadventurous in the 1950s and 1960s. Ethnic food sections were usually confined to a small area for Italian and/or Chinese foods, and one could find some of the same foods in the freezer case. *Progressive Grocer*, the main industry trade magazine, ran a "Store of the Month" article in each issue that included an architectural diagram of the store in question. Diagrams from the early 1970s show a variety of layouts but a tendency toward small ethnic food sections in most stores. A Houston, Texas, store profiled in 1971 was fairly typical. It had a small section of one aisle reserved for Chinese foods, macaroni, and spaghetti. Otherwise, the store did not have any special ethnic sections. To be sure, some foods that had once been labeled ethnic, such as pickles, became mainstream enough to warrant no ethnic designation.[25] Even if this was the case, supermarkets still put little emphasis on ethnic, specialty, or gourmet foods.

Although product variety had grown rather steadily since the inception of chain stores in the 1920s, new products typically did not highlight ethnic elements. In that era, food processing was king, as corporations and scientists unabashedly promoted product differentiation borne by new food technologies. One industry observer called the 1950s the "golden age" of the supermarket, adding that they were ideal venues for food manufacturers and suppliers to expose the public to their innovations. Supermarkets "presented [processors] a direct invitation to develop new products and new sizes in food lines."[26] Appropriately enough, General Foods chose a marketing expert as its new president in 1954.[27] Manufacturers needed new things to market, and they turned to their research and development teams for direction. In response, food chemists worked on additives to enhance "mouth feel" in processed foods, causing one General Foods executive to remark, "we are gradually moving toward a world of designed consumer foods."[28] Food processing journals argued that convenience foods were cheaper than fresh foods and took that argument abroad. The USDA and the Grocery Manufacturer's Association together held a trade show in Germany in 1963 to promote American processors.[29] These companies invented, marketed, and sold many more brands of foods, but a good number simply were not all that different. They may have contained a distinctive size, shape, or color to make them seem different from the other processed goods on the shelves, but they were often basically similar. A trip down the cracker and cookie aisle reveals this today. Though it seems as if the aisle contains dozens of choices, the "products" mostly consist of a few basic ingredients—corn (including corn syrup), wheat, soybeans, and chemically enhanced flavors.[30]

The sameness of store offerings can be seen in the recipes and food tips offered by *Safeway News*, a magazine for the grocery chain's employees, in the late 1960s. One article suggested that a hot dog need not only be served for lunch and dinner—it was a suitable breakfast food too. That same article counseled parents that they could serve hamburgers and peanut butter sandwiches to children who were otherwise unwilling to eat breakfast. That was as "unorthodox" as the publication would be.[31] Another column told readers that it was possible for a housewife to serve ground beef for dinner seven nights a week, because "chances are they won't even realize they're being served the same meat night after night if you follow these suggestions from the American Meat Institute. . . . By the seventh night, the family *may* begin to yearn for steak or pork chops, but they *may* not even have missed them!"[32] While the American Meat Institute had good reason to push everyday ground beef, Safeway liked the idea too. Turkey curry was about as adventurous as many eaters got with everyday food, and only as a way to use leftovers from Thanksgiving and Christmas. Curry powder gave an exotic touch to an otherwise run-of-the-mill dinner. Besides the fact that turkey is rarely eaten in Asian countries, the recipe was a distinctly American concoction of turkey—apples, onion, garlic (one clove only), and but one teaspoon of curry powder, complemented by heavy doses of butter and milk.[33]

Safeway News's editors did not yet know that the country's ethnic makeup was about to transform dramatically. The foods carried in grocery stores were to change starting in the 1960s, for as immigrants entered the United States in increasing numbers from Latin America and Asia, they demanded more of the important fruits and vegetables from their home cuisines, thereby introducing those ingredients to other Americans. Even as Safeway's corporate-sanctioned recipes featured few ingredients that its readers would call exotic, the company was trumpeting its international operations and imported foods in corporate literature. Two locations—an "international store" in downtown Washington, D.C., and the company's flagship store in the Marina district of San Francisco—were favorite places for foreign visitors in the mid-1960s. The Marina location was even on a regular State Department tour of San Francisco. Those stores were a part of Safeway's promotions precisely because they were unique and at the leading edge, despite the firm's "bustling import department."[34] A decade passed before the chain seriously rethought its ethnic food holdings.

ETHNIC MARKETING AFTER THE 1960s

As grocery store managers were just beginning to seek new business by way of new imports and immigrant cuisines in the 1960s and 1970s, a broader development in American business practices contributed to widening product choice—market segmentation strategies.[35] In the middle decades of the twentieth century, companies marketed to the masses by selling the same dish soap or sliced bread to all consumers, whether they were black or white, rich or poor, city or country folk. This strategy continued just after World War II, but in a short time, businesses worried that they would drive each other out of competition if they did not distinguish their customer bases. As historian Lizabeth Cohen has described, business journals first advised companies in the 1950s to tailor their marketing campaigns to specific segments of the consuming public, for they could no longer sell to the masses.[36] One *Harvard Business Review* article explained that a "marketer should break his market down into segments that are smaller and more homogeneous than the market as a whole."[37] The article advised to break down segments by a combination of product dimensions (style, price, or use), or consumer dimensions (income, education, ethnicity, or socioeconomic status).

Rising incomes also allowed marketers to discriminate among various segments, for many products that were "formerly inaccessible" to consumers were then "within reach" of the middle class. Notably, the products included imported wines and spirits, specialty foods, tourism, and air travel.[38] From 1947 to 1997 Americans' real median income grew by 58 percent; this meant more Americans experimented with new cultural forms, including food, whether at the local grocery store or on a trip to Mexico or Italy.[39] To this end, Safeway boasted in 1962 that it was trying to "broaden the appeal of shopping at Safeway" by "the development of a program to offer our customers a much wider variety of imported cheeses," which were more expensive and had gourmet appeal.[40] Just a few years later a Kraft employee explained that foreign and domestic cheeses each saw growing sales because people "move more frequently" and that varieties once sold in delicatessens and "specialty shops" could now be had in supermarkets.[41] In the 1970s, Kraft reordered its line of Casino cheeses by introducing "expensive-looking packaging and [an] advertising campaign glamorizing the exotic, foreign origins of the cheeses." This strategy of "foreign intrigue" only worked so long—by the 1980s Kraft's advertising firm saw that the once exotic cheeses were now "familiar," and the brand needed repackaging.[42]

Marketing specialists writing in the early 1960s knew that they could break down segments by ethnicity, but they had little idea that a whole new group of consumers would form a substantial consumer base by the 1970s—the Asian and Latin American immigrants arriving in the United States. Some major companies such as Pepsi and Esso were already marketing to black customers in the 1940s; this strategy would gain steam with the civil rights movement. Thereafter, businesses slowly paid greater attention to blacks, and later, other racial and ethnic groups, to capture new consumer bases and generate positive corporate images.[43] In the grocery business that meant new campaigns to highlight health and beauty products for blacks and an effort to improve inner-city stores in predominantly black neighborhoods. These campaigns took time; one 1977 report said "ethnic merchandising" of facial and hair products was "spreading slowly" nationwide as "Pathmark, A&P, and Winn-Dixie move to win and hold black customers."[44] Still, at the time, many retailers did not "appreciate" the sales category, partly because it was difficult to operate wholesale facilities to process merchandise that might be sold only in the small number of stores with a large number of black customers.[45] One marketer said a store should "merit special consideration of black shopping needs," only when blacks composed more than 30 percent of the shoppers.[46] That was hardly a low threshold, meaning if a store's makeup included even 10 or 15 percent black shoppers, they would not be targeted. Improved technologies would allow stores to target much smaller groups in the next few decades, making segmentation strategies much more effective for large chains.[47] One trade publication said that the "buzzword of the 1980s was segmentation," for there was no "typical shopper."[48]

INDEPENDENTS AND THE NEW HISPANIC
AND ASIAN CHAINS

Unlike the supermarket chains, independent grocers (defined as having ten or fewer branches) had long marketed to specific ethnic or class segments, adapting to changes in their consumer base.[49] Jeff Brown ran one independent supermarket during the 1980s in South Philadelphia. He redesigned his store with expanded produce and Asian sections to cater to the neighborhood's long-standing Italian American population and a recent Asian and Jewish influx. To target his Italian

American customers, he built large displays of canned tomatoes, pastas, olive oils, and broccoli rabe. He also staged events with food samplers based on customer recommendations. Lastly, he saw the Asian foods market as a "growth opportunity," and planned to emphasize Asian foods more as his store matured.[50]

Just as Brown targeted his customer base in Philadelphia, so too did Victor Najor, an independent grocer in the San Diego area who sought Hispanic and Asian customers. In the mid-1980s, as Safeway and Ralphs opened new supermarkets nearby, Najor decided that an expanded seafood section would capture Asian customers. When the Safeway store opened, he bought 1,500 pounds of ginger and priced it low to lure customers away from the chain. And to attract Mexican American customers, he carried several brands of fresh tortillas and priced eggs, rice, and poultry below cost.[51]

Building on the work of the small ethnic grocers, entrepreneurs created supermarket chains to target specific ethnic groups during the 1970s. One was the Fiesta Mart chain founded in Houston, Texas, in 1972.[52] Its president, Don Bonham, "set out to market to Mexicans" when he opened the first store, and they have formed the chain's primary customer base since.[53] The supermarkets were a neighborhood congregation spot for Mexican immigrants, who could grocery shop, bank, and even catch rides back to Mexico with the shuttle services that picked up passengers in store parking lots.[54] A *Texas Monthly* article in the 1980s said Fiesta Marts "were polyglot universes unto themselves, bumptious souks where you could buy clothing, rent a video, make travel plans, eat a taco, lease a house, or browse through flea market trinkets. . . . Among Fiesta's precarious mountains of chilies and weird tubers and shelves crammed with esoteric foodstuffs even Akeem Olajuwon could find what he needed to cure the homesick blues."[55] The produce sections shone at Fiesta stores, and their "biggest draw" was "ethnic items" such as cactus leaves and chilies, said Bonham.[56] Although he targeted Houston's Mexican immigrants, Bonham was "among the first to realize what a multiethnic stewpot the city was becoming and to capitalize on it."[57] He quickly found that his offerings attracted many other ethnic groups, including Taiwanese, Indians, Cubans, Vietnamese, and Koreans in its Houston, Dallas, and Austin locations. In the 1980s he hired employees from various ethnic backgrounds at one Houston store and charged them with purchasing and display decisions for their areas. Bonham said he was not an "expert on foreign foods" but managed his ethnic food section tightly because it was the "most important" part of the store and his customers expected "variety, variety, variety."[58]

He struggled, however with how to distribute some ethnic items that crossed boundaries within the store, wondering if he should keep all curry spice mixtures together, for example, or sectionalize them according to type—Indian, Chinese, and the like. Unlike the chain stores that pushed ethnic foods with bright displays, recipe cards, and promotional materials from major food processors, Bonham believed that his customers did not need "direction" in their purchasing.[59] When Fiesta expanded to suburban areas populated mostly by whites, however, it changed some of the features of those stores for the "Yuppies who never shopped with us," said Louis Katopodis, general manager for the store, because those customers had not lived in areas of high-immigrant concentrations.[60] In some of the new "upscale" stores, Fiesta installed sushi bars and changed the décor to make it look "high-tech," but continued to emphasize its produce section, including the wide range of ethnic produce, because even in the Anglo stores, "people want to try new things," said Katopodis.[61] Chains in other regions targeted Hispanic customers too, including the Tianguis supermarkets in Southern California.[62]

Executives of the Vons supermarket chain in Los Angeles spun off Tianguis to serve the region's rapidly expanding Hispanic population. The first Tianguis was "strikingly different than other Los Angeles supermarkets," with a bilingual staff and "enormous" produce sections with tomatillos, epazote, and poblano peppers—hardly available in the regular Vons stores.[63] Tianguis also had in-house tortilla makers, meat counters that offered "livers, snouts, feet and jowls," and much less frozen and packaged foods.[64] One newspaper commented, "Tortillas and *platanos* are no longer just mom-and-pop grocery store items. Now they're big business." Vons president Bill Davila, a first-generation Mexican American, appeared in both English and Spanish-language ads. "Soon after the first Tianguis opened, an elderly woman from East L.A. marveled that 'I've seen things here that I haven't seen in years—stuff my grandmother used to make.'"[65]

Asian Americans could shop at supermarket chains targeted to them beginning in the 1980s too. H-Mart on the East Coast and 99 Ranch on the West Coast were among the most successful. Begun by Taiwanese immigrant Roger Chen, 99 Ranch primarily sought Chinese American shoppers, but also appealed to other Asian immigrants.[66] Although small grocery stores had long existed in Chinatowns, Little Saigons, and Mexican barrios to serve immigrant customers, Fiesta and 99 Ranch stood out because they were large supermarkets, and in the case of 99 Ranch, were located in the suburbs. Growing from one store in 1984 in the Little Saigon section of Westminster, California, to over twenty by 2001, the 99 Ranch supermarkets typically served as anchors to Chinese or pan-Asian shopping malls in the suburbs of California, Washington, and Georgia.

The stores combined the big format of American supermarkets with the selection of imported goods theretofore found only in the small grocery stores of ethnic enclaves. One anthropologist argued that 99 Ranch testifies to a pan-Asian ethnic identity because various Asian American groups patronize strip malls anchored by the chain.[67] Chester Wang planned many of these malls in Northern California, locating them in areas with high concentrations of Asians. The malls had a wide variety of Asian restaurants and other ethnic stores, and Wang argued that these centers show that "marketing goods to Asian consumers makes sense."[68] Though they may have identified as just Korean or Chinese before, the malls brought together many Asian groups. And although the centers counted primarily ethnic Asian consumers, one could also find many non-Asians feasting on dishes such as Chinese porridge in the supermarkets.[69] On the opposite coast, the Super 88 chain served a similar panorama of Asian foods, but as one *Boston Globe* article remarked, the store had a "diverse mix of shoppers, strikingly unusual for a city like Boston that's notorious for being segregated and tribal." The slogan on the market's website was "Eat the World."[70]

The 99 Ranch supermarkets also testify to a transculturalism and transnationalism in the globalization of the last several decades.[71] Shenglin Chang examined the experiences of Taiwanese who moved back and forth between Taiwan and Silicon Valley. Most were highly educated, middle/upper class, and lived an existence that was part Taiwanese, part American. Some were called "astronauts" because they spent so much time jetting between Asia and the United States. With high-income careers they supported houses, jobs, and families straddling China, Taiwan, and the United States. The 99 Ranch chain figured prominently in the lives of Taiwanese immigrants in Silicon Valley during the 1990s and 2000s as they sought Chinese foodstuffs from their homeland. The Taiwanese of Silicon Valley shopped at similar stores in Taiwan too. Many of the engineers who walked the aisles of 99 Ranch in Silicon Valley patronized a Carrefour supermarket when they worked or lived in Hsinchu, the center of Taiwan's electronics industry. The Carrefour store in Taiwan had a similar layout to the 99 Ranch stores in Silicon Valley, and for that matter, other American and European supermarkets like Safeway, Target, and Walmart. In 1998, Shenglin Chang attended a Thanksgiving dinner with a Taiwanese family in Cupertino, observing, "There was nothing purely Taiwanese or Californian, Chinese or American, at this Thanksgiving dinner . . . as different cultural practices intertwined with each other randomly."[72] The turkey had been prepared at the 99 Ranch supermarket using Chinese ingredients. While 99 Ranch's stores and the Taiwanese immigrants themselves contributed to the overall diversity of the United States, those immigrants experienced continuity in their consumption habits from Taiwan to the United States and back.[73] Someday, Thanksgiving turkey may appear on the Hsinchu Carrefour's shelves.

This continuity of experience across nations is partly because the large supermarket chains targeted Taiwanese and Chinese immigrants too after the 1970s, hoping to capture some of their business. They also wanted to profit from the burgeoning demand for all ethnic foods after the 1960s.

HOW THE BIG GROCERS MARKETED ETHNICITY

After the 1960s, supermarket chains and their suppliers took a cue from independents and began using market segmentation strategies too. If a storeowner knew a lot of Mexican immigrants lived nearby, he might advertise in Spanish-language circulars, put his tortilla case prominently at the front end of the bread aisle, and have regular sales on beans and tomatoes to attract customers. This is not to say that ethnic or segmented marketing was a completely new strategy for the food businesses in the 1950s and 1960s.[74] Independent or small-chain grocery stores had always tried to target their customer base, and food is one consumption area that is already strongly segmented by ethnicity. Prior to the 1950s, these small, ethnic grocers had imported hard-to-find produce, meats, and canned goods for their particular customer bases. In San Francisco, for example, by the 1870s, there were already 131 Chinese-owned grocery stores. A century later that count stood at over 250.[75]

Some non-ethnic businesses capitalized on differences among ethnic groups, but when it came to market segmentation most companies only divided their customer bases by income. Large food manufacturers and chain stores expected that Americans of all stripes would eat some version of similar foods. And many immigrant foods were homogenized to broaden their appeal—the most important case in point is that of Italian food, which had become the pizza and pasta parade after World War II. In sum, prior to the 1960s, food processors and large supermarket chains sought to attract various immigrant groups regardless of the food habits they carried from their homelands.[76]

Independent operators might have long marketed to specific immigrant and ethnic groups, but only in the 1960s did chains first seek higher revenues through market segmentation analyses.[77] In 1970, *Progressive Grocer* undertook an in-depth study, "How Different Customers Shop the Modern Super Market," focused on the largest supermarket chain at the time, A&P.[78] It commissioned the study to give readers guidance about the major grocery trend at the time—the expansion of superstores. The study's authors argued that the operation of superstores necessitated "greater knowledge and insight" about customers. They saw that grocers "increasingly questioned policies which call for cookie-cutter similarities: the same stores, the same lines, the same brands, the same ratio of employees to sales, regardless of the nature of the community and store clientele." For this reason, the magazine and A&P endeavored to "learn more about its customers" by categorizing them and analyzing their differences. The study also previewed the trend that Walmart later took up with gusto—using data about purchasing to manage inventory efficiently. For their study of Detroit-area A&P stores, the authors ended up with seven categories of shoppers: Negro, Apartment Dweller, Young Family, Upper Income, Blue Collar, Small Town, and Discount.[79]

The upper-income category foreshadowed the direction of eating trends most closely, for those consumers purchased more specialty, exotic, and convenience items. The study said the upper-income customer was on the "vanguard in the revolution of tastes." Understandably, grocery operators sought to capture the market for such shoppers, for they had the most to spend and were a "constantly growing segment of the population."[80] The survey illustrated the fact that leisure spending rose substantially in the 1960s and 1970s.[81] Foods once reserved for the upper classes became available to the common man, even as new niche operators targeted the wealthy. Between 1920 and 1970, food costs for American consumers rose 87 percent, but per capita income grew by 502 percent, meaning money spent on food could extend to far more than staples, even for middle-income shoppers.[82] The A&P survey showed upper-income shoppers searching for "variety," for they had "wide tastes for family eating and entertainment." They also had more "exotic tastes," which pushed them near the top in purchases of Chinese, Mexican, Italian, and other "nationality foods," illustrating the place for ethnic foods among the growing specialty and exotic foods market.[83] The trend toward greater ethnic food purchases accelerated after the 1970s; by 1985, foreign foods were one of the most important attributes for a "perfect supermarket."[84]

So it was around the late 1970s and early 1980s that supermarket chains began to market "ethnic" and specialty foods to both ethnics and non-ethnics. The way these chains identified ethnics typically depended on locale. Some used broad terms—Asians, eastern Europeans, or Hispanics. Others targeted specific groups, such as Mexicans or Chinese. More typically, however, during the 1970s and 1980s, chains picked specific ethnic foods and attempted to sell them to people no matter their ethnicity.

This was a strategy that moved beyond food to other areas of consumption, such as travel. In 1982, Hofstra business school members studied New York City's Italian, Jewish, Polish, Chinese, and Korean markets to see how airlines, banks, and newspapers could target their marketing strategies to these sectors. The case study on airline travel said, "ethnic marketing can be used in conjunction with business establishments to create trends in fashion, food, recreation or whatever," concluding that ethnic marketing does not only pertain to ethnics.[85] It explained that Air India, which had primarily served immigrant Indians before, expanded its marketing strategy to include wealthy New Yorkers who might want to travel to a "fantasy" land. If Air India could market to non-ethnic customers, Alitalia, TWA, or other airlines could too. As airline travel became less expensive and travel businesses marketed their wares more widely and in more targeted pitches, a broader spectrum of American customers could travel to India, Italy, or elsewhere.[86] Those customers need not even travel across the oceans for ethnic experiences, for in food, they could quite literally consume at home. Furthermore, their consumption of ethnic foods could be an everyday experience rather than a once-a-year vacation; after all most people eat a few times a day and shop at a grocery store a couple times a week.[87] The extension of ethnic marketing to the masses was most visible and affecting through food.

By offering many more product choices, supermarket chains widened the consumption experiences of those consumers. This was a major shift after the 1960s, with a trickle-down effect over time. Ethnic foods and the cosmopolitan feel associated with them were first marketed to those with higher incomes. Middle- or upper-income families who liked to entertain could show off their knowledge of authentic Italian or Chinese or Mexican foods. They could also afford more impulse purchases. One study of consumer preferences found ethnic foods had become symbols of sophistication for the middle and upper classes.[88] After a time, many expensive foods became accessible to the lower classes and the upper and middle classes welcomed new products to distinguish themselves.

As many retailers stepped up their efforts to win over the upper-income group, many also looked to mass market ethnic foods. These retailers figured that if the rich could serve guacamole or a stir-fry for a party, why not the average consumer? In particular, they used holidays and special promotions to introduce average consumers to these foods. After running a successful Decemberfest promotion for German foods at one store, a supermarket executive became convinced that he should integrate ethnic foods into all of the store departments rather than put them into a separate gourmet foods section. "I realized we had to stop treating imported items as gourmet foods," he said. "They're really everyday ethnic foods which should be enjoyed by everyone."[89] Analyzing the grocery market in Los Angeles during the 1980s, advertising executive Suzanne Rampton said that availability of ethnic foods would make markets stand out from their competitors.[90]

Grocery chain sales stagnated in the early 1970s, causing many storeowners to theorize about how they could capture more of the market in non-food sales by expanding pharmacy, hardware, and clothing sections.[91] Supermarkets also tried to steal some of the restaurant industry's expanding business by building take-out food counters and expanded delis in their stores. One Northridge, California, store was described as "bucking the discount trend" in 1971 for building a "complete International Foods snack counter/take-out department," carrying Italian, Mexican, Hawaiian, and barbecue foods. The store's bakery also had a "wide assortment of ethnic and special breads" to capture more business.[92] Ethnic and specialty foods, take-out counters, and in-store bakeries and delis together served the purpose of expanding market share for these groceries.

During the 1970s, storeowners disagreed about whether to stock "ethnic" foods in separate sections or integrate them throughout the store, but no matter their placement most proprietors thought of them as impulse purchases. One owner of a suburban supermarket in Rochester, New York, said his customers were more likely to "pick up gourmet or ethnic items on impulse" if stocked with other foods, so he put Spanish, Japanese, Chinese, Jewish, Italian, South American, and Greek foods throughout the store.[93] A San Francisco store instead spurred ethnic food sales by creating an end-of-aisle display with corn, tortillas, taco shells, chili, enchilada flavoring, and Spanish rice on the display. The same display held Italian pastas and cheese as well as horseradish, potato salad, and party dips. As in the Rochester store, ethnic foods were categorized as "impulse" buys, best suited for parties or special occasion rather than a regular dinner.[94] An Alabama storeowner created a whole aisle of gourmet and international foods, stocking them together to win over young families that entertained and traveled a lot. The gourmet and party foods included Italian, Kosher, and Chinese items; purchasers would presumably show off their worldly ways.[95] Another store operator in Long Island used the same strategy, theorizing that his customers had traveled extensively and desired imported, ethnic, and health foods.[96]

Three supermarkets captured the heightened emphasis on ethnic foods. Fazio's Food Emporium, a Cleveland-area store, carried 15,000 items and offered "perishables in depth, featuring ethnic lines and concentrating on specialty products." Walking through the emporium, shoppers saw fresh kielbasa, pasta imported from Italy, bok choy, and sugarcane.[97] Another store in Southern California did the same, pointing toward the coming super stores. *Progressive Grocer* explained that the 46,500 square foot store combined a "deli, bakery, wine, flowers, party items, soft goods, kitchenware, dishes, appliances and pharmacy. It's much more than the chain has ever tried, but it's already coming together at its new Whittier, Calif. store."[98] The "featured" section of the store was the gourmet and ethnic foods department with imported and domestic goods.[99] Although it would seem Los Angeles's ethnic diversity warranted the wide selection of the Whittier store, an Oklahoma City superstore also practiced the same strategy, for owner Fred Wehba Jr.'s mission was to capture impulse purchases on gourmet and ethnic items throughout his store, using the slogan "More Than Just Meat and Potatoes" in his advertising. Godiva chocolates fit the impulse billing; Wehba's was the first American supermarket to carry the expensive truffles. Wehba sought off-the-cuff purchases from upper-income shoppers, but he also realized he needed more than just those customers to sustain the business, advertising "everyday low prices" on common items.[100]

Although many grocers sought to highlight ethnic and specialty foods throughout their stores, others still confined them to special areas, believing that a "sectionalization" strategy was more profitable. One grocery executive put three-foot wide "Israeli" sections in some of his chain's stores in the Northeast because it made it easier for Jewish food suppliers to service the section, causing it to be better stocked, thereby resulting in higher sales.[101] A marketing study commissioned for Rokeach Kosher foods concluded in the 1960s that it was best served by separate sections to highlight its offerings, but that "sprinkling" Kosher foods throughout the store could help push impulse purchases too.[102] Store managers also sectionalized ethnic foods for promotional tie-ins, either to sell a particular product or highlight a holiday that could be used to move those foods. Customers often needed a familiar signpost to guide their purchases of ethnic foods. In the case of Mexican food, the Piñata brand Mexican foods used its namesake to capture customers' attention, quite literally. They distributed small piñatas to stores to be hung above their "Piñata 'Something for Everyone' Line" of foods. Piñata's foods included tortillas, taco shells, sauces, seasoning mixes, frozen burritos, and even frozen corn dogs, which in one advertisement the company claimed were an "American favorite with a taste of Mexico."[103] Similarly, Best Foods created an end-of-aisle display, "Go Chinese with Karo," to sell its Karo corn syrup, Mazola oil, rice, canned pineapple, shrimp, Argo cornstarch, and soy sauce. The display had recipe cards "specially created by a famous Chinese restaurant" and was "one of the best promotions ever run" at a Chicago supermarket.[104] Fittingly, the promotion highlighted the cloying sweetness endemic to Americanized Chinese food.

There was no true "right" method for marketing ethnic foods; grocers, food processors, and marketers employed a buckshot mentality for their schemes, trying anything and everything to make sales. As with other industries, they could quantify higher sales related to those efforts at times. However, at other times they followed the whims of market trends and tried to ride the wave, whether it was the popularity of Mexican food or the increased demand for Asian ingredients. Marketing pushed this process, but consumer demand did too. They tried all sorts of schemes. Sometimes they used exoticism to woo customers. At other times they thought the familiar elements of a new cuisine could attract shoppers to new brands. They stocked foods in separate ethnic food sections at times, but also integrated them into aisles for breads, sauces, or produce. And they used holidays as a way to grab customers who wouldn't otherwise try new foods.

ETHNIC FOODS: HOLIDAYS OR EVERY DAY?

Supermarket operators turned to holiday promotions because customers needed signposts to try ethnic foods. These promotions filled the yearly calendar for grocery managers, beginning in January with Chinese New Year and moving onto Lent, Easter, St. Patrick's Day, Passover, Cinco de Mayo, Fourth of July, Labor Day, Mexican Independence Day, Columbus Day, Halloween, Thanksgiving, and finally, the biggest of them all, Christmas.[105] Those ethnic holidays such as Chinese New Year and Cinco de Mayo became new marketing opportunities for storeowners as they saw more immigrants from countries like China and Mexico enter the United States. They also sought business from non-immigrant customers. A "1970 Merchandising Calendar for the Delicatessen" explained Cinco de Mayo in its May entry with "'Gringos' are buying more and more of the flavorful Mexican foods."[106] The same year, *Progressive Grocer* advised that a Chinese New Year store promotion displaying foods "such as canned chow mein, fried rice, boxes of rice, canned Chinese noodles, soy sauce and hot mustard," could encourage "specialty sales." While Chinese customers would certainly purchase some of these foods, by the inclusion of chow mein and canned noodles, the promotion was more likely targeted at non-Chinese customers.[107] In holiday promotions, grocery store operators sought first to shift the eating habits of the people who rarely ate Mexican or Chinese food. Slowly, they also tried to sell to the new immigrant populations in the United States and, in turn, to the non-immigrants who ate at the restaurants that those immigrants ran. Supermarket operators hoped to capitalize on the new diversity but also create a sameness of sorts, for they would profit most if *all* customers bought Mexican or Chinese food.

As the years passed, the types of foods that the average customer would try became more diverse. After all, more and more immigrants entered the United States in the 1970s and 1980s, and what was once new became old, forcing supermarket operators to look for the new sales edge. If a supermarket chain really wanted to differentiate its offerings, it had to constantly innovate. By the 1980s, ethnic foods became a relatively easy differentiation vehicle because global trade made importing those foods easier.[108] The changes in the grocery store had parallels in other cultural realms. Increasing global trade and migration made music, styles of dress, and television shows more portable. The widening of ethnic foods selection in grocery stores, then, signals an overall trend in the post 1960s period—diversification of choices, especially those that are culturally identified.[109]

In all of these businesses, including supermarkets, widening choice was about profit. "Oriental Vegetables Make Scrutable Money" described well the changes in food marketing. Found in a 1976 issue of *Progressive Grocer*, its headline played on a still-persistent stereotype of the Chinese as inscrutable.[110] Suggesting that the Chinese were in fact no longer mysterious to American consumers, or at least the "sophisticated shoppers," the article argued that supermarket owners could capitalize on this "latest growth category," by selling Chinese vegetables. The author captured most of the key features of diversification on the supermarket aisles. First, the diversification of foods began in "cosmopolitan" cities, where customers were willing to try new foods. Second, it was prompted in part by immigration from Asia and Latin America. Third, the presence of new domestic and foreign suppliers enabled grocers to actually stock the new foods. The article pointed to California supermarkets as the pioneers in Chinese vegetables, saying that some have been "offering bok choy and Napa cabbage as readily as kielbasi or knishes in the appropriate neighborhoods." Until then, Chinese Americans could not find a "full line" of Chinese foods at supermarkets, but slowly options broadened at supermarkets, and as a result, "the white population started buying as well." Lastly, the article contended that low prices and steady supplies made the Chinese vegetables attractive to new buyers.[111]

Passing into the 1980s, supermarket chains slowly added new items to satisfy a growing demand for Asian and Latin American foods. In 1982, the *San Jose Mercury News* ran an article advising readers where to shop for the "truly authentic and exotic meal," providing a list of ten small ethnic stores. The *Mercury News* acknowledged that many readers had "dabbled with ethnic fare," for they were even able to buy some of their ingredients from the big chain supermarkets, which were "catching ethnic-food fever." Those supermarkets already had fresh basil, bok choy, rice vinegar, exotic mushrooms, and chili and curry condiments. Accordingly, many readers had started making food in their newly purchased woks and others had switched from spaghetti and meatballs to linguine with pesto. In the 1980s, supermarket chains slowly realized that they could pick up some of the independents' business by filling the gaps in ethnic foods. And if the Chinese were still viewed as inscrutable in the mid-1970s, that perception was changing by the 1980s, at least when it came to their food. Chinese food constituted a serious "growth category" by the 1980s and 1990s. Grocery chains had to figure out what Chinese goods to sell in order to satisfy both the immigrant consumers and the increasing share of Americans who wanted to make Chinese food year-round.[112]

Safeway upped its ethnic marketing efforts in the 1980s for Chinese and Mexican foods. It built Chinese takeout counters in its supermarkets in the mid-1980s to "capture a greater share of growing consumer expenditures" for takeout food.[113] In this case, Chinese takeout food was just one of many other products that were used to capitalize on changing eating habits—its ethnic connotations were not really important to the corporate strategy. At the same time, an annual report explained that the product selection at its conventional supermarkets had almost doubled in the last five years. Rather than "duplicating similar items," the company put the emphasis on "extending the range of different items" including an "extensive list of ethnic foods and various specialty items."[114] As Safeway sold ethnic foods to a cross-section of its customers, it also targeted its operations to specific segments of its customer base. Five years earlier, Safeway's annual report sold the company's ability to segment its marketing. It trumpeted the company's expanding opportunities with Mexican American shoppers. The report featured a photo of Raj Dogra, who "helped pioneer Safeway's entry into Mexico in 1981," and later as El Paso division head was able to apply knowledge about Mexican consumption habits on a "daily" basis. The company was learning "firsthand what families of Mexican origin expect from their supermarkets," by its experience in Mexico.[115] A full-page photo depicted a Mexican American family just outside a church celebrating a girl's first communion. A table overflowed with tortillas, precut vegetables, a piñata, Safeway cola, and Presidente tequila. The report's cover photo had the family alongside a cross-section of Americans who were "as diverse as America itself." No matter their diversity, they had their Safeway shopping experience in common.[116]

Safeway tried to do both with its ethnic food offerings—capture the growing customer base of Mexican Americans and still please all the rest. The need for the large supermarket chains to address both needs—a specific marketing segment, such as Mexican Americans, and a wider customer base—resulted in those chains expanding the size of their stores in the 1980s and 1990s. After all, if customers demand variety *and* comfort, why not offer massive stores that mostly look the same? Variety was often overwhelming, so familiarity came in the form of a shopping trip at a clean, well-lit, suburban supermarket that overflowed with well-recognized brand name foods.

There was then a steady progression between the 1960s and the 1990s, as supermarkets stocked more and more foods, including many of the "ethnic" sort. Immigrants came to the United States by the millions, asking store managers to stock foods from their homelands. Along the way, some ethnic foods lost their ethnic tags—Americans of all hues ate billions of tortillas annually by the turn of the century. They also ate Chinese foods, employing stir-fry techniques and purchasing soy sauce without hesitation. Chun King and its rival, La Choy, had a significant role in making that possible.

AMERICAN-ORIENTAL

La Choy was the other major food processor to capture a large segment of the "American-Oriental" market in the middle of the twentieth century. La Choy originated in Detroit in the 1920s, and like Chun King made canned noodle dishes and sauces and packaged some of the harder-to-find ingredients used in Chinese cooking. It later moved into the frozen foods business after seeing Chun King's success. La Choy had originally capitalized on the chop suey restaurant craze in the 1920s by supplying bean sprouts to restaurants when they were hard to come by.[117] Ilhan New (a Korean immigrant) and Wally Smith founded the company in Detroit after meeting at the University of Michigan. By the 1920s, La Choy regularly produced marketing cookbooks as a way to explain these new foods.[118] A 1931 version gave "The Chinese Version of Chop Suey," listing four different La Choy ingredients.[119] Later editions assured readers that the recipes were thrifty and nutritious—this was a common theme for those advertising Chinese cooking to Americans.[120] China after all was a poor country—especially compared to the United States in the 1950s and 1960s—and its people had to make do with less. American housewives were long praised for their ability to do the same.[121]

As a result of the combined success of chop suey restaurants and the efforts of these two companies, by the 1960s supermarkets in many parts of the United States stocked Chinese or "Oriental" foods. These sections typically took up a quarter or a fifth of one side of a supermarket aisle, where grocers displayed canned, bottled, and packaged noodles, water chestnuts, soy sauce, and sesame oil. Over time, the frozen foods aisles of the regular supermarket also carried Chinese foods.[122]

By the 1980s, La Choy held 40 percent and Chun King held 20 percent of the market share for canned Asian foods.[123] By that time, Paulucci had sold Chun King. The company passed from one major food conglomerate to another—RJR Nabisco, Beatrice, ConAgra (which bought Beatrice), and a large Singaporean firm.[124] In 1995, Hunt-Wesson merged Chun King and La Choy; together they still captured 45 percent of the canned and frozen Asian food market share in grocery stores.[125] Their market share derived from the fact that the parent companies were behemoths.

Until this point, both companies fully marketed their products to an increasingly familiar audience for Asian or Chinese foods. In the 1980s, as with other ethnic cuisines, Chinese food was coming into its own. By then, Beatrice foods owned both La Choy and Rosarita, a line of Mexican processed foods. The company packaged the two lines together for food-service providers—cafeterias, restaurants, and hotels—as an "East Meets West" proposition. Their marketing material noted the near doubling of Oriental food sales between 1979 and 1984, and Chinese and Mexican foods' higher gross profit margins compared to other ethnic cuisines. Country club and commissary managers could use egg rolls, chips and salsa, chili, and chow mein noodles to spice up their offerings.[126]

By the 1990s almost all Americans ate the three big "ethnic" cuisines—Chinese, Mexican, and Italian—and other less-known cuisines were on their way to familiarity. The "U.S. food industry is going stale . . . finding a supermarket blockbuster has become much harder," explained a 1997 *Wall Street Journal* article, noting that "an entrepreneur such as Jeno Paulucci could hit the jackpot in the 1950s and 1960s with Chun King and Jeno's pizza, simply by packaging still-novel fare." Novelty was harder to achieve, as "Americans are sprinkling on average 3.1 pounds of spices onto food annually, nearly a pound more than a decade ago."[127] This was a far cry from the 1960s, when spice companies sold the exotic nature of their wares, hoping cooks might dash just a bit on their creations.[128] As when he began in the food business, however, Paulucci saw new openings. In the early 1990s, he introduced a line of frozen Italian foods, Michelina's, named after his mother. To follow, he packaged new brands of Mexican and Chinese frozen dishes. He also had to compete with the many in-house brands that grocers latched onto over time.[129] In 2007, Michelina's frozen pasta dishes were first shipped to Shanghai, traveling on rail and container ship from the Jackson, Ohio, manufacturing facility. Instead of selling Chinese food to American consumers, in his old age Paulucci sold Italian food to Chinese customers.[130]

La Choy and Chun King together signified the bridge built by American entrepreneurs for ethnic cuisines. Chun King's "American Oriental" moniker showed the need for someone to make Chinese food less scary for home use—even as many Americans were accustomed to eating it in chop suey joints around the country. While the companies emphasized themes of convenience, thrift, and taste, like other food processors, they added exotic, novel, and unique to the marketing mix. They were careful not to go too far, representing what might be called a "safe exoticism."[131] This may be where they had an advantage over the many Asian-owned manufacturers and distributors in Los Angeles, San Francisco, and

New York. Those firms, typically owned by first- and second-generation immigrants, imported and/or manufactured Chinese ingredients and foods, but mostly for an Asian-immigrant clientele. To put off the fear of the exotic (and the possible taint of those immigrant business owners), La Choy and Chun King emphasized the hygiene, cleanliness, and modernity of their manufacturing facilities. In the 1950s, La Choy published photos of its manufacturing line in Archbold, Ohio, conspicuously not staffed by Chinese Americans. In the 1980s it boasted, "unique to the foodservice industry, all La Choy products undergo voluntary USDA inspection, assuring you of the highest quality products."[132]

La Choy and Chun King bridged the introduction of ethnic foods to the wider public in American supermarkets during the late twentieth century. Those supermarkets were changing rapidly at the same time, becoming larger and larger over time. Along with other food businesses, they consolidated, meaning just a few grocers dominated each region. They needed variety to be all things to all people but provided what customers knew and trusted too. And they did this not just across regions, but across national borders. Paradoxically, sameness lay in the diverse supermarket of the late twentieth century.

4

The Changing American Restaurant

The National Restaurant Association's Best Menu contest in 1983 signaled the newly surging popularity of Mexican food in the United States. The Association commented that the "full-color photo menu" from second-place winner Monterey House "takes all the guesswork out of ordering. This is particularly useful in a Mexican restaurant where many of the guests may not be familiar with the menu items. To be doubly sure there is no confusion, the menu features a glossary of menu items on the back cover."[1] Located in Houston, Monterey House served the combination plates responsible for popularizing Mexican food in the United States. Its menu initiated diners to the ways of the burrito, explaining that it was "an orgy of brazen beans and coy cheese sensuously stuffed into a clingy covering of tempting tortilla. More cheese is draped seductively over the whole daring concoction." Like the Monterey House diners, those eating at the San Diego-based Carlos Murphy's chain needed assistance with their menu choices. The "Mexican Market" section of its menu advised, "The Hot Ones: This means what it says! Gringos should order with caution. We cannot be held responsible for any tears that come to your eyes." A drawing of a fireman drove home the message.[2]

American diners still felt cautious when eating Mexican food in the 1980s, but that would change quickly. While Carlos Murphy's offered Irish, Mexican, and BBQ-style potato skins in the 1980s, by the mid-1990s a review declared that the "Irish-Mexican cafe," had become "virtually all Carlos, no Murphy."[3] By the year 2000, the tortilla had become ubiquitous, and few menus needed to explain the basics of Mexican food. The cuisine had also expanded beyond its historical base in the Southwest.[4] By the end of the twentieth century, even New Yorkers and Chicagoans had integrated Mexican cuisine into their regular diet, no longer regarding the tortilla as "specialty ethnic bread."[5] Celebrity chefs Bobby Flay (New York) and Rick Bayless (Chicago) popularized haute Mexican and Southwestern cuisine with their packed restaurants, glossy cookbooks, and television shows.[6] Variations on Mexican cuisine appeared all over the world. KFC sold "Mexican Twister" chicken wraps in thousands of outlets across China.[7]

Sushi followed a similar trajectory, making inroads in American food culture after the 1970s. One could find Japanese restaurants in the United States in the late 1800s, but only by the 1920s did a number concentrate in some major cities. These were of two types. Those in Japantowns primarily served Japanese immigrants. Those outside of the Japantowns sold a few Japanese dishes to non-Japanese customers as a way to truck in exoticism.[8] One newspaper described the Japanese "colony" in San Francisco in the 1920s, saying that you could find simple "Nipponese" food there, including raw fish, but "patronage of these places . . . is limited to a few of the initiated and they are quite obscure."[9] Only as late as the 1970s did a large number of non-Japanese partake of Japanese food.[10] Los Angeles counted 15 Japanese restaurants in 1965, 43 in 1970, 88 in 1975, and 173 by 1980.[11] The cuisine held new appeal in part because the Japanese economy was surging and the exoticism of eating raw fish appealed to some who sought distinction.[12]

Sushi's appeal to up-and-comers made it part of the "yuppie flotsam" of the 1980s.[13] ("Yuppie" emerged then as an acronym for "young urban professional.")[14] The 1983 film Valley Girl, set in Los Angeles, captured sushi's high status at the time. In the movie, Nicolas Cage, a teenager from the wrong side of the tracks (Hollywood), woos a rich girl from the San Fernando Valley. Cage and his buddy crash a house party in the Valley hosted by aspiring yuppies. They witness par-tygoers gobbling sushi from a large dinner platter, and Cage's friend asks the host, "Wadda ya got going here, a bait shop?" She explains the options, but Cage and his friend recoil in disgust. Clearly, they've entered another world.[15] Just four years later, sushi featured in Bud Fox's rise to riches in Wall Street. Played by Charlie Sheen, Fox comes from a blue-collar family but is entranced by the world of high finance. He's mentored by the devilish Gordon Gekko (actor Michael Douglas in an Oscar-winning role), who encourages him to sell his soul. As part of Fox's initiation, Gekko takes him to the ultimate power lunch spot—the 21 Club—where he eats the signature steak tartare. Once Fox has become fully yup-pified, he's ready for another raw treat. One scene has Fox and his girlfriend (actor Darryl Hannah) making dinner with a sushi machine that cranks out the rolls.[16] Other 1980s films, both good (The Breakfast Club) and bad (Chained Heat and Troop Beverly Hills), had their own sushi moments. Around that time the National Restaurant Association's magazine ran articles on yuppie diners, saying that they ate out more than most and ate Asian food, including sushi, at a higher rate too.[17]

While some restaurants in the 1980s apparently fed diners who were already sushi-wise, many menus described sushi in detail for the uninitiated.[18] Kamon, in San Francisco, offered extensive explanation: "Sushi was first made in the eighth century by the Japanese. They discovered a way to preserve food for travel by mixing their fresh fish catch with the rice, their diet staple, and rolling these ingredients in seaweed. Thus sushi was born. . . . Let's try the marvelous 'SUSHI.'"[19] A Hollywood restaurant menu similarly featured a glossary, calling sushi the "sandwich of Japan," followed by an explanation of sushi preparation.[20]

Just twenty years later, multitudes of Americans ate sushi from plastic takeout cartons without blinking an eye. Sushi had gone from exotic to familiar and highbrow to low brow in the span of two decades. More Americans had toured Japan, sought out other forms of Japanese culture, and eaten other Japanese foods during this period. And the taboo on raw fish—one of the long-standing barriers for American consumers—had slowly receded.

THE AGE OF THE ETHNIC RESTAURANT

After the 1960s, Americans increasingly experimented with ethnic foods at restaurants, whether that meant eating tacos, sushi, or curries. Restaurateurs offering those foods had to make them understandable to their patrons. Mid-century restaurants had offered a rather standard parade of meat and potatoes. Examining menus from the 1940s to the 1960s reveals strikingly similar offerings across the country. There were exceptions of course—chop suey joints could be found nationwide and Mexican restaurants proliferated in the Southwest.[21] Despite some regional exceptions, northern and western European foods dominated the cuisine across the country. Certainly, in most big cities one could find a Chinese, Italian, or Mexican restaurant, but even those restaurants typically served chop suey, spaghetti and meatballs, or enchiladas, rather than the diverse array of foods to be found in each of the countries of origin.

More diverse menus slowly replaced the meat and potatoes sameness of the 1940s and 1950s. Attended by its onslaught of varied goods, the new diversity meant many Americans needed help understanding all their new consumption choices. Incredible choice did not create incredible confusion, for there were plenty of translators to make foreign cultural goods understandable.

The entrepreneurs who write restaurant menus are important translators of cultural norms. Those translators traversed a balancing act between the familiar and the new. In order to sell their foods and their cuisines, they used reference points that Americans of all sorts could understand. At the same time, many of the translators believed they had to make their restaurants distinctive, for they could profit by bringing new or exotic foods to American tables. This business of translating diversity is an important part of understanding how globalization works on an everyday basis, as American consumers experienced the world in their mouths, tasting the foreign and making American hybrids over time.

As the translators made new cuisines understandable, the foods associated with them slowly became old hat for Americans. That meant cuisines that needed translation in the 1960s and 1970s, such as certain aspects of Mexican or Chinese foods, were used to translate *other* cuisines, such as Indian and Vietnamese, by the 1990s. Through the consumption of ethnic cuisines, one can see the process of cultural change over time, for food illuminates how people come to know and understand foreign cultures, making them less foreign over time. This process is an underlying constant in a rapidly globalizing world—because the unfamiliar is so regularly presented to consumers, they seek translation devices.

Menus also became more important after the 1960s because Americans ate out more and more. Between 1929 and 2013, the proportion of meals taken outside the home increased from 17 to 49 percent.[22] Today, 75 percent of Americans eat out at least once a week. Most of that shift has come since the 1960s, as Americans consumed many more meals at restaurants (especially at fast food chains) in the last few decades. As a result, the restaurant industry is the largest private employer in the United States.[23]

Restaurants were a place to experiment with new foods—perhaps more easily than at home. And because food prices have dropped dramatically over time, Americans bought food not just for sustenance, but also for new experiences. In the late 1800s, many urban working-class families spent around half their income on food.[24] Americans spend roughly half as much today on food as compared to the 1920s, shrinking from 22 to 11 percent of disposable income over time.[25] With cheaper food, Americans could get sustenance at the McDonald's or try Thai food for the first time.

Restaurants are a wide and varied lot. Restaurant sales totaled about $294 billion in 2000. Of that amount, sales at fast food chains formed the highest proportion, or about $125 billion.[26] The high total reflects the increasing importance of fast food in America—one study found that fast food calories had increased from about 3 percent of the American diet in 1984 to 12 percent in 2004.[27] While eaten by all groups, the poor and middle class consume fast food more because it is convenient and cheap. Lower- and middle-income teens in California ate a much higher proportion of fast food than affluent teens did. About half of teens living in households at or just above the poverty line ate it once a day.[28] Not surprisingly, poor and/or minority neighborhoods in major cities have a higher proportion of these chains than white/middle class areas do.[29] Those restaurants that did not serve fast food totaled about $114 billion in sales. These included everything from the dive selling cheap barbeque to the parlor charging $50 an entree. In this general restaurant category, chains such as Denny's, Applebee's, and Red Lobster accounted for a large proportion of sales.[30]

The restaurant, at least in its current form, is just a few centuries old. Some scholars argue that it was invented in France during the late 1700s, but restaurants and menus can be found earlier in medieval China. In Hangzhou in the 1200s (then the largest city in the world), food businesses offered waiters/table service, bills of fare, and set prices. Other variations on restaurants existed too, both for lower- and upper-class patrons.[31] Even if such restaurants existed in China much earlier, the restaurant was still new to most Europeans in the 1700s. The modern version of the restaurant developed in France in the 1760s and 1770s and would evolve by the early 1800s to become commonplace in Paris. The French restaurant was copied in other parts of the world, including the United Sates in the mid-1800s.[32] These were mostly fancy—a place where upper-class patrons could distinguish themselves from the rabble. The commoner had long been able to take dinner at taverns and inns, but in the late 1800s middle-class folks began to frequent restaurants in many cities. In some places, even the lower classes did so too. By the 1920s and 1930s, hundreds of restaurants serving varied cuisines dotted the landscape of any major American city.[33] Over time they declined in formality and became a place for all classes, even if there were still many that sought distinction. Restaurants experienced a re-ordering in the 1970s, with even the French spots offering up "nouvelle" cuisine, and others emphasizing local and fresh ingredients—a marked departure from the norm at the time.[34] Meanwhile, ethnic restaurants flourished and expanded in both number and scope. By 2010, one estimate had 579,012 restaurants in the United States. That total included over 40,000 Mexican and 40,000 Chinese restaurants.[35] Chains constituted 45 percent of the total, with independent restaurants at 55 percent.[36]

The ethnic restaurants described here are within the general restaurant category, and for the most part are not chains, though as seen later, ethnic food was eventually sold in large volume by big firms such as Chipotle and Panda Express. There are plenty of cheap ethnic restaurants that cater to specific immigrant groups or to the lunch crowd in business districts. Ethnic restaurants—especially those reviewed in newspapers and magazines, are patronized at a greater rate by the highly educated and wealthy. Young consumers living in major metropolitan areas also frequented them. One survey conducted in 1999 categorized this group as "Internationalists," and they formed a higher proportion of customers at full-service restaurants with meals costing over $15. They tried foods that were of a "somewhat more exotic nature" and loved to "travel and eat in ethnic restaurants where natives of other cultures eat."[37]

This group of internationalists grew over the course of the late twentieth century, and many Americans became so accustomed to ethnic cuisines that they gave little pause.[38] In that time period, Americans not only ate out more, but also tried much more varied cuisines at restaurants. Global trade and immigration were both factors that caused people to eat more foods identified with Asia and Latin

America. Trade brought many more foodstuffs from many more places in much smaller time frames. Getting ingredients from afar meant that making foreign foods was much easier. At the same time, immigrants brought food cultures to the United States that were previously unfamiliar to most Americans, such as those from Vietnam, Thailand, Japan, and El Salvador. They also reinvigorated Mexican, Chinese, and Italian cuisines, taking them from a homogenized version to much more diverse offerings. Restaurant menus were the frontier for ethnic cuisines—a way for Americas to decide how adventurous their eating might be.

RESTAURANT MENUS TRANSLATE DIVERSITY

We take restaurant menus for granted today, but eating out has not always involved a bill of fare. Before restaurants were "invented," travelers had long eaten out at taverns, inns, or a table d'hôte. In these places the proprietors simply told customers what was available. Often, diners had no choice about what to eat. Food was dropped onto a table at a certain time for a fixed price and customers scrambled to get what they could.[39]

The word *menu* is French for "small," to denote the short description of the dishes offered. Though menus were used in medieval China, the origin of the modern Western menu as we know it—a printed bill of fare—seems to have been in France around the same time that restaurants came into shape—during the late 1700s.[40]

Menus changed over time, and as a wider swath of the population frequented restaurants, they became an important way to communicate to customers.[41] By the late twentieth century, cooking schools and restaurant trade organizations advised chefs about the importance of the menu to drive business and signal customers. *The Restaurant Manager's Pocket Handbook* emphasizes that the menu is the "starting point for every new restaurant concept," and is the "one piece of printed advertising that an operator virtually is assured the customer will read."[42] The impact has to be quick, however, as the typical customer reads the menu for just 109 seconds.[43] For ethnic restaurants, where customers may be trying new foods, menu designers emphasize that it is important to "explain as many food items as possible," for diners are "more adventuresome if they know exactly what is being offered, and what the method of preparation is."[44]

Menus are more than just lists of foods, drinks, and their prices. They are a time capsule of public consumption. Examining multiple menus from one time can reveal consumer preferences and adventures. Examining those menus over a long time reveals how and when foods became "standards," what foods are familiar to an audience at any given time, and what foods need explanation and translation. In *The Language of Food*, the linguist Dan Jurafsky explains, "Every time you read a description of a dish on a menu you are looking at all sorts of latent linguistic clues, clues about how we think about wealth and social class, how our society views our food, even clues about all sorts of things that restaurant marketers might not want us to know."[45]

Indeed, they are such powerful snapshots of a culture that they have been used as teaching tools for language instructors and sociologists. One French teacher "exploited" a menu to "introduce many aspects of French culture" to his students.[46] Two sociologists developed an exercise in which their students examined different menus because "using everyday, taken-for-granted institutions and their artifacts, such as restaurant menus, is an excellent way to introduce students to the role of social class in shaping their lives."[47]

One example of the way menus can indicate shifts in eating habits comes from the National Restaurant Association's analyses. The association is among the largest trade groups in the country, counting 500,000 members.[48] In the 1980s and 1990s, the association collected menus from member restaurants for a contest and analyzed their menus at five-year intervals to understand eating trends. Between just 1987 and 1997 those menus changed significantly. In 1993, the association said that the "influence of ethnic cuisines [was] pervasive," and "nearly eight out of 10 menus incorporate dishes from more than one ethnic cuisine."[49] Just a year later it found a large proportion of consumers were looking for new ethnic foods to try, and that a "second wave" of regional Chinese (Szechuan, Hunan, etc.) and other cuisines were making a mark.[50] By 1997, it remarked that "one would be hard pressed to find a menu without any evidence of ethnic influence; all of the menus analyzed had at least one dish of ethnic origin."[51] Later, it acknowledged that many dishes that were once considered ethnic had become so mainstream that they did not qualify as such anymore; these included spaghetti with marinara sauce and tacos.[52]

Here I use menus to make sense of how culinary professionals—restaurant owners and managers—translated important distinctions about the offerings at their businesses. This is a new way of examining how culture changes over time. One can see what is taken for granted and needs no explanation—meat and potatoes on mid-century menus. And one can also see how that changes over time, as Mexican food needed much translation and explanation in the 1970s but is taken for granted as understandable today. Other cuisines, such as Indian, still need translation today, but the process has changed significantly over time. By looking at translation in menus and other vehicles such as cookbooks and advertisements, one can see American culture shifting in a time of rapid globalization.

MEAT AND POTATOES SAMENESS IN MID-CENTURY MENUS

The middle of the twentieth century was a time of relative sameness in American food choices. The period between the beginning of World War II and the 1960s stands in contrast to the early and late twentieth century when globalization and immigration accelerated. The story of meat and potatoes sameness in restaurant fare can be seen in the menus from those establishments. Why were the menus so similar? Immigration slowed dramatically between 1924 and 1965 because of restrictive immigration laws, depression, and war. The proportion of the foreign-born in the US population declined in the 1950s and 1960s, for as immigration slowed, baby boomers also multiplied. The 1970 census showed only 4.7 percent of the population having been born abroad, the lowest proportion for over a hundred years.[53] The march of homogenized eating began in full force in the 1940s, during World War II, and did not abate until the 1960s. The war may have contributed to the dominance of mild foods. Food historian Harvey Levenstein argues that American soldiers ate standardized meals designed for blandness and fullness in their mess halls and rations, causing their ethnic and regional eating habits to become muted during their time in service.[54] That sameness of the mid-century eating experience meant a common departure point for translation efforts of ethnic cuisines afterward.

World War II increased the role of government in most facets of American life, including eating.[55] The Office of Price Administration (OPA) was authorized as a separate federal agency in 1942 to stabilize prices and ration essential goods, including foodstuffs. The agency had regional offices around the country. It monitored a wide swath of businesses, from used car dealerships and landlords to meatpackers, grocery stores, and restaurants. The Food Price Division monitored food growers, processors, and retailers.[56] In 1943, the OPA issued a regulation ordering restaurants to adhere to ceiling prices based on those from the week of April 4 to April 10. Price ceilings applied to a list of basic foods, including coffee, milk, and various cuts of beef. The enforcement component of the regulation required that restaurants file "a copy of each menu, bill of fare, or other price list of meals, food items, and beverages," as well as prices on any other services provided by the restaurant.[57] An OPA enforcement officer stamped these menus with a date, and some found their way into libraries and archives. Because government regulations ordered all restaurants to file their menus, they provide a fairly comprehensive look at the type of foods offered at dining establishments during the war.[58]

The menus of the mid-1940s in the West, as seen under their OPA stamps, reveal a sameness to the restaurant cuisine of that era. Menus at the typical coffee shops, diners, and luncheonettes listed dinners consisting of meat, potatoes, and vegetables. Even the OPA's regulatory letter to restaurants listed a standard list of American food items. It allowed for some variability among entrees, including chop suey or spaghetti, but those were the only ethnic food items mentioned by the agency.[59]

The menu for the Fly Trap Restaurant in downtown San Francisco was fairly representative, containing several sections of what would be considered "American" or French/English derived foods, with a smattering of Italian or Mexican additions. These were soups, salads, fish and oysters, pastas, entrees, omelets, veg-etables, and desserts. The "cooked to order" page added sections for steaks, chops and cutlets, poultry, and sandwiches. The entrees consisted of meats such as a half-broiled squab with carrots, prime roast beef with spinach and French fries, and broiled hamburger steak. The war forced the restaurant to explain that it was "unable at times" to serve all those items listed, but the menu was extensive if not diverse.

The types of foods offered on the menus at restaurants like the Fly Trap were quite similar to those at its counterparts elsewhere. Almost all of the menus con-tained northern or western European foods. The exception was the smattering of Italian, Mexican, or Chinese items, such as spaghetti and risotto, but these amounted to just a few dishes on most menus.[60] Restaurants in Denver and Butte mimicked the Fly Trap's offerings, with pork and beef sandwiches, chops and steaks, simple salads of lettuce or tomato, and breakfast fare of eggs, sausages, and waffles.[61]

Like the Fly Trap, menus from other restaurants in San Francisco and Oakland during this era conformed to this standard of meat, potatoes, and seafood. The Garden Court, Parkwood restaurants, and Bunny's Waffle Shop chain in San Fran-cisco offered similar selections, punctuated by the occasional enchilada plate or pasta dish. Bunny's, with six locations in the city, counted entrees of chicken turn-over, frank and beans, hamburger steak, lamb or pork chops, and fried chicken.[62] Explanations on the menus were typically terse. The listings for "Mexican Enchi-lada with Beans," "Chili with Spaghetti," or "Beans and Frankfurters" needed no explanation, for Americans were typically familiar with these dishes.[63] The Ger-man-origin franks, sausages, and burgers were already long commonplace. Mexi-can food occupied a curious intermediate position, with some explanation and some assumption that diners were familiar. And many menus offered American-ized Chinese fare—chop suey and chow mein.[64] A "special notice for customers" on the Season Café menu explained that "If you wish, we will be glad to offer sug-gestions for your order for Chinese Dishes," adding an advisement to "Take home our Chop Suey and Chow Mein—We furnish containers." But if an explanation about the Chinese items and the possibility of takeout were not enough, the menu also noted that "We not only specialize in 'Chinese Dishes'—Our Steaks, Chops, and other dishes are also our pride."[65]

CHAINS OF THE 1950s AND 1960s: SAMENESS NATIONWIDE

During the 1950s and 1960s chain restaurants proliferated and their menus mostly offered meat and potatoes. The National Restaurant Association ran a contest for the best menus from members in various years. For the 1964 contest, the association also listed the three most popular dishes at the winning restaurants from around the country. With a few exceptions, those entrees were sirloins, prime ribs, hamburgers, or other filets of beef. Some seafood and chicken appeared too, mostly prepared in English or French styles.[66] This fact becomes important in light of the need for translation of Asian and Latin American foods on menus during the 1970s forward, as restaurateurs increasingly looked to differentiate from those chains.

The dishes on menus in the 1950s and 1960s rarely needed translation because they were northern European in cast, were paralleled by processed foods at grocery stores, and had not yet featured the Asian and Latin American foods that would become commonplace after the 1960s. Independent and chain restaurants also regularly shared the same foods.

The chains of the 1950s were designed to have commonalities with the old roadhouse suburban diner, adopting similar marketing strategies and foods (though varying in quality).[67] Howard Johnson's, Sambo's, and the Fred Harvey chains all had quite similar menus at their many branches. Ham steak, tenderloins, creamed or roast turkey, and the obligatory tossed green salad and French fries were standard. With branches all over California, Sambo's provided a map of its locations on its menu cover and advised diners to "Plan your trip from Sambo's to Sambo's." Surely some diners did.[68] The chains had different gimmicks, but similar food. Sambo's, Big Boy, and the Aunt Jemima chains all catered to families, using their cartoon characters to draw families with children.[69] The success of these chains, and eventually the fast-food outlets like McDonald's, had the effect of cutting off business from independently operated diners in many areas. The ethnic food boom of the post-1960s period would invigorate differentiated, rather than correspondent, marketing in the restaurant business.[70]

The white bread image of the 1950s then was no illusion—it could be seen in the menus of the era. Historians have debated the nature of conformity in the immediate postwar era, but whether or not there was an undercurrent of resistance as represented by the Beatniks and others, the period was still more Bobby Darin than Allen Ginsberg.[71] One factor was the constant reach of the Cold War in everyday life, as evidenced in a meeting of Texas state teachers in 1963. They attended the "Cen-Tex Study of America's Heritage" conference, with a mission to "wage deliberate, effective, ideological, classroom warfare against Communism at every grade level."[72] Americanism in this context was fueled by meat and potatoes. Supported by state agencies and the major universities in Texas, the conference participants were served a banquet of "steak, potatoes, beans, tossed salad, bread, drinks, and a good cobbler pie."[73] Based on that menu, they might as well have eaten at Howard Johnson's.

Though the 1970 census showed a low proportion of the foreign born, the nation's ethnic and racial makeup was about to change, and quickly. By 2010, the census showed radically different data, fueled by the mass immigration of the four intervening decades. For this reason, the collective American menu changed, and as a result of the new foods, a new series of translations ensued. The sameness of the 1940s through the 1960s made the diversity of the post-1960s period seem more incredible. Although global trade accelerated rather steadily through the post–World War II period, the combination of that increased trade and the massive immigration surge meant greater diversity after the 1960s. And no matter if ethnic restaurants were to be found in major cities as remnants of previous eras of mass immigration, there was something different about the post-1960s-era food culture, for it included many more people from Asia and Latin America.

Cookbooks were one way to try new cuisines, but increasingly, Americans had more options to try ethnic foods at restaurants in the cities, suburbs, and towns around the country. As they ate away from home more, Americans found themselves interpreting and consuming many more foods from abroad. Indians and their food had been relatively unknown to American diners in the mid-twentieth century. As Indian immigration surged and more restaurateurs opened Indian restaurants, they sought various translation strategies to make Indian cuisine understandable to their customers.

5

Cookbooks Navigate the Globe

In the 1970s, few Americans ate Indian food regularly at restaurants, and even fewer cooked Indian dishes at home. Madhur Jaffrey hoped to change that. She possessed the right skills to make Indian food less intimidating to American consumers. Although she was born and raised in India, she had never cooked until she left her native country. She left Delhi to study at the Royal Academy of Dramatic Arts in London, and at age nineteen found herself homesick, eating terrible cafeteria food, and possessing no cooking skills. She quickly asked her mother to mail recipes from home. She was forced to experiment, substitute, and improvise when fashioning dishes described in her mother's letters. For this reason, she understood the problems of beginning chefs; the cooking process did not come "naturally" to her.

Jaffrey was pretty and articulate, making her attractive to publishers and consumers. She starred in plays and movies, and toured Europe and the United States in the late 1960s and early 1970s. In 1969 she married an American musician as she was slowly establishing a name for herself as a cooking teacher.[1] Between acting gigs she modeled saris for Gimbel's department stores in New York and held "grand parties that were like bits of theater—musicians and conductors and actors oohing and aahing" at the food she prepared until someone suggested she published a cookbook.[2] Her editor at Alfred A. Knopf, Judith Jones, knew these qualities would help sell books, telling an assistant that Jaffrey was "very attractive, an actress . . . which we obviously want to capitalize on."[3]

Like so many of the Knopf authors, she was helped along by Craig Claiborne and James Beard, who together had the eyes, ears, and guts of the New York establishment fixed on their culinary exploits. James Beard regularly hosted events for other chefs and cookbook authors. At one point or another he ran a catering company, cooking schools, and restaurants, and sold cookware. He also sold hundreds of thousands of copies of his own books, including *Beard on Bread*, published by Knopf.[4] Beard, Claiborne, and others had been interested in Jaffrey's cooking skills as early as the mid-1960s, when she toured the United States doing dramatic readings. Craig Claiborne, the *New York Times* food editor, noted that she was as skilled in the kitchen as she was on stage.[5]

Those two qualities helped her understand and appeal to cookbook buyers, but it was the third skill, her ability to translate a foreign cuisine into something appealing, that proved most important. The writing and editing of Madhur Jaffrey's first American cookbook, *An Invitation to Indian Cooking*, illustrates how one relatively unfamiliar and exotic cuisine was translated for an American audience. Although more Indian immigrants came to the United States than ever before in the 1960s and 1970s, Indian food was only a glimmer in the consciousness of most American eaters. Indian cookbooks created an imaginative experience for readers, who had to visualize a cuisine, a culture, or simply the dish they wished to prepare.

In this imaginative sense, Jaffrey's *An Invitation to Indian Cooking* was, in 1973, an exercise in getting Americans to understand India and Indian food. It was likely the most important cookbook about Indian food published during the 1970s, and it came at a time when Indian food was just fomenting renewed interest in the United States and Britain.[6]

In *An Invitation to Indian Cooking* Jaffrey revolted against a sameness inherent in Indian restaurant cuisine in America; the 1970s version in restaurants did not yet reflect the incredible diversity of Indian cooking. She claimed that the food served in Indian restaurants was a "generalized Indian food from no specific area whatsoever," and that the result was the "sauces in such eating places inevitably have the same color, taste, and consistency."[7] She tried to push Americans past the curry house to experience what "authentic Indian food was like."[8]

For that reason, *An Invitation* began with a different title—*Curry: Myth and Reality*—because Jaffrey wanted to educate Americans about Indian cooking at a time when it was just beginning to garner interest. Judith Jones eventually changed the title to *An Invitation to Indian Cooking*.[9] Americans needed information to squelch misconceptions, but as her editor surmised, they also needed an invitation to try the cuisine first. Jones was enthusiastic about the possibilities of the book, telling a counterpart at Penguin press that it "opened up a whole world of cooking experiences to me."[10] Raymond Sokolov, a cook himself, noted in a *New York Times* review of the cookbook that "the recipes come directly from [Jaffrey's] mother but she has translated them with great facility into American terms."[11]

The curry house decried by Jaffrey was, of course, related to the curry powder that had been a mainstay in British and American larders for decades.[12] She explained that curry powder was an adulteration created by the British—an "over-simplified" version of Indian food. Furthermore, unlike the spice mixtures ground on the spot in India, she saw the curry powder, or blend of pre-ground spices, as having the "negative aspects of being standardized and somewhat rancid at the same time."[13] She also claimed, "no Indian ever uses curry powder in his cooking."[14] Though this was hard to believe, the film star/cookbook author was exaggerating for the cameras, so to speak. More to the point, Jaffrey added that her recipes had convinced one friend's children who had been "extremely dubious about all foreign foods," to eat Indian.[15]

This chapter examines how Americans translated diversity on an everyday basis in an era of rapid globalization. With many more consumption choices, Americans had to find a way to understand them. They increasingly ate foods from faraway places, including those from Latin America and Asia that had not previously been a common feature on American tables. One study of food and culture noted that the "complex symbolic, economic, sociological, ecological, or even physiological reasons for how a culture uses food often escape an outsider's recognition."[16] This supposition appeared to be true for many Americans. Many food habits, such as the consumption of dim sum in Hong Kong, the use of the hands as eating utensils in India, or the place of the tortilla in Mexican cuisine had to be explained.

Americans contended with globalization in routine circumstances as they read and experimented with cookbooks. Cookbooks functioned as a safe and controlled way to bring foreign cultures into the home. Americans had done this in another time of globalization, the early 1900s, when they bought trinkets from afar to furnish their parlors and kitchens.[17] In recent years, however, global trade increased even more rapidly, and the immigrants who came to the United States arrived from different places. That meant that Americans could actually cook more of the foods that were described in cookbooks, for ingredients and cookware might actually be available. Cookbook authors played an important role in the translation process, bringing the previously distant cultures of Asia and Latin America home to American kitchens.[18]

Those authors enacted a delicate balancing act, shaping their message with equal dashes of familiarity and exoticism. After all, the readers of ethnic cookbooks had to be able to understand the recipes, so the authors regularly referenced common signposts. But if everything in the cookbook was familiar, the reader would not get anything new, so the authors also had to be skilled at describing the unfamiliar. The authors therefore trucked in exoticism to attract more readers.

The descriptive process in cookbooks changed over time too, as the foreign became familiar. Indian food at first was comprehensible in the United States primarily through references to British colonial rule in India. Later, Americans understood it through the other Asian and Latin American cuisines that had taken hold, such as Mexican and Chinese, for Americans made connections among cuisines that were spicy. Similarly, Latin American cooking was at first understood through Mexican food, for tortillas and beans were the signposts for anything south of the border.[19] But over time, Latin American food in the United States became more than just Mexican cuisine, as American consumers came to know the ceviche, grilled meats, and wines from Latin America.[20] Even British and French food needed translators for cooking techniques, vocabulary, and ingredients.

Through the description and consumption of various ethnic foods, we can see the manner in which Americans understood globalization over the past few decades. As with other areas of consumption, there was an underlying tension between sameness and diversity. Americans needed to understand their new choices, so they made connections to the familiar, creating a certain sameness of experience. But they also increasingly sought out distinction in their consumptive experiences, for globalization made the world available in close quarters. Moreover, they struck a balance between local and regional distinctions and national or continental commonalities as globalization marched on. Trying to understand where American food ended and Indian or British food began was no small task. The definitions of the local, regional, national, and global were rather fluid during this period, making the strategies for translation across cultures fluid too.

COOKBOOKS AS HISTORICAL SOURCES

Cookbooks are the main source used here to examine how foreign cultures and cuisines became known to American consumers. In the case of the cookbook, there is great precedent for its use as a historical artifact. One anthropologist argued, "We need to view cookbooks in the contemporary world as revealing artifacts of culture in the making."[21] Another scholar said that the recipes within cookbooks are a "link to the past" and that the recipes and cookbooks themselves are often invested with much emotional and social meaning.[22] Others have argued that cooking and the texts that describe it "can scarcely be less important to our sense of identity and shared values than food itself."[23] Finally, cookbooks are "like a magician's hat: one can get more out of them than they seem to contain."[24]

Because eating is an everyday activity, cookbooks can provide valuable historical evidence. The everyday motions of life are what are most taken for granted, but they often change. Even the amount we consume can take rather dramatic turns in a short time period. Americans, for example, increased their daily food consumption by about 530 calories from 1970 to 2000, or an astounding 24 percent.[25] The method for measuring this consumption is rather new too. The calorie was neither a widely known nor accepted scientific measure in the United States until about the first decade of the twentieth century, and cookbooks published in the middle

1800s made little mention of calories or other dietary measurements.[26] Indeed, the very writing of cookbooks took on a much more scientific bent in the early 1900s, for the measurement of everything became important.[27] As a reflection of their times, cookbooks can then provide some insight about what people thought about food, hoped to cook, and sometimes, what they actually cooked. In the case of cookbooks about foreign or exotic cuisines, they are "a way to appropriate the other by consuming their cultural products." They might also "aim toward people who generally don't have the wherewithal to go half way around the world to be served a meal," engaging the reader in a sort of "fantasy travel."[28]

This issue of the actual cooking that goes on in kitchens is what makes cookbooks somewhat problematic for some historians. It is hard to know how much people actually cook from any given cookbook. One researcher who studied food in the United States during the 1950s preferred to use food magazines and newspaper articles rather than cookbooks, for readers contributed many of those recipes, indicating that they were invested in both the foods and their associated cultural connotations.[29] Another researcher explained that recipes sometimes do not tell the whole story of consumption, for cookbooks cannot escape the peanut butter and jelly problem. Few cookbooks list a recipe for the peanut butter and jelly sandwich, but Americans eat millions every year.[30] And no matter a recipe, people often make substitutions, omissions, or errors when they turn on the stove or take out the cutting board. Furthermore, some cookbooks that seem interesting on the bookstore shelf may sit unused on the kitchen shelf after a closer look. Well-worn, food-stained pages may provide the best indication of a home cook's favorite recipes, but historians cannot jump into the kitchens of enough homes to scrutinize those recipe pages.

Because it's hard to tell what's actually cooked in homes from any book, the cookbooks examined here meet a standard of influence and sales. All of these cookbooks have been discussed widely in newspapers, magazines, or on television/radio. The cookbooks have also exerted a chain of influence on American food culture. The authors greatly influenced other chefs; were seen as standard-bearers for their cuisine's introduction to an American audience; and were widely regarded as authorities on the cuisines they promote.[31] Some of the authors, though not all, have also sold thousands of copies of their cookbooks, and many have seen those sales continue over the years. The limitation of this approach is that some of the cookbooks examined here were not bestsellers, but instead were bought by only a few thousand readers. Even in those cases, however, the cookbooks still illustrate the larger attempt that many Americans made to explain and understand foreign cultures through food.[32]

My method is to examine the degree and type of explanation necessary in those cookbooks. I examine the text of the cookbooks themselves, but what sets this study apart from others is that I have also examined the cookbook editorial and publishing process.[33] Using the cookbooks published by Alfred A. Knopf from the late 1960s through the early 1980s, I show how those cookbooks evolved from first to final draft during the editing process. This editorial process demonstrates what needed to be translated for an American audience during that time period. It also explains how cultural exchange and cross-cultural translation worked in an era of rapid globalization, for in their cookbooks about various ethnic cuisines, the authors were forced to analyze the elements of the cuisine that were either easily comprehended by Americans or, alternatively, were in need of translation. It answers, in sum, how many Americans dealt with the rapid expansion of cultural choices over the last few decades of the twentieth century in one everyday activity—eating. If diversity meant many more eating choices, Americans had to figure out a way to understand their choices, and this chapter shows how they did that at home with cookbooks. Whether they were trying to understand cuisines that were close to home, such as English or Cajun, or foods that were quite far, such as Indian or Peruvian, they sought markers of common understanding to make sense of the cuisines. Those markers changed over time as globalization and immigration marched on so that what was uncommon language in one decade could be common in the next. By seeing how Americans forged a common language to understand foreign cultures, we can see how globalization affected them in their homes, with cookbooks in hand.

COOKBOOKS IN RECENT AMERICA

Since the 1960s, cookbooks have occupied a contradictory status—as Americans ate out more, they also bought more cookbooks. There are a few possible reasons for this seeming disconnect. One is that cookbooks became an easy way for Americans to translate ethnic cuisines and, in turn, the ethnicities themselves. As Americans traveled abroad more, interacted with more immigrants from Asia and Latin America, and became curious about the cuisines from those regions, they wanted to learn about those cultures. This made the late 1960s and early 1970s a promising time for cookbook authors. In 1973, a publisher purchased rights for *The Joy of Cooking* for $1.5 million, the highest sum for any paperback to date. This signaled a renaissance in the cookbook publishing industry, which was also pumping out more volumes on foreign foods, because "plenty of buyers [were] eager to find out exactly how those foreign dishes could be made with American condiments," including the "footloose" young readers who travel around the world "eating whatever native dish is being sold on the corner pushcart."[34]

Raymond Sokolov, food editor of the *New York Times* and himself a Knopf cookbook author, wrote an article in 1972 praising four cookbooks that interpreted foreign cuisines: "Good cookbooks are rare. The best are more than collections of recipes. They are good anthropology. They set down, in clear language, specific ways in which cultures define themselves, deal with the natural world around them, and survive. Until the last ten years, there were almost no good, authentic cookbooks in this sense. Few people bothered to attempt the very hard work of seriously translating the kitchen of one culture into the kitchen of another."[35] As Sokolov noted, cultural translation was difficult, but the best cookbooks could be a cheap and easy way for Americans to increase their familiarity with a variety of cultures. A year later, Sokolov reviewed *An Invitation to Indian Cooking* alongside Marcella Hazan's *The Classic Italian Cookbook*. Readers may have needed more hand-holding with Jaffrey's cuisine, for with Hazan's book, as he noted, "Everyone can at least cook spaghetti and also knows the proper taste of some dishes."[36] The more exotic the cuisine, the more guidance the American home cook needed. Yet by reading a cookbook and then putting homemade sushi on the table, one might be putting a bit of Japan into a non-Japanese home.

On a very practical level too, cookbooks became necessary. As people ate more take-out and processed food, they possessed fewer cooking skills. These skills were typically passed from generation to generation, from mother to daughter, but over time, women cooked less because they worked more outside of the home. This was one major reason for increased consumption of restaurant and take-out food. In 1950, 25 percent of married women living with their husbands worked outside the home. By the late 1980s that figure had risen to nearly 60 percent. Women with children were working too; about half of all women who had school-age children worked outside the home by the late 1980s.[37] Those numbers continued to rise over the next couple decades. Families in which husband and wife both worked became the norm, rising from 43.6 percent in 1967 to a steady 58 or 59 percent between 1988 and 2004. Women who worked as they supported children also became more common, increasing from 47.4 percent of women in the 1975 workforce to 70.5 percent in 2005.[38] Furthermore, couples divorced at alarming rates in the 1960s and 1970s, meaning many men were suddenly forced to cook for the first time.[39] One divorced woman wrote "Dear Abby" in 1975 complaining that her newly remarried husband called her to request that she teach his new (much younger) wife how to cook.[40] One of the many cookbooks Knopf rejected in 1980 was "The Divorced Man's Emergency Cook Book: How to Avoid Starvation Between Wives."[41]

Whereas children had typically learned cooking techniques "through osmosis" in home kitchens during previous generations, this was not possible with the take-out food generation. As a result, those children became adults and turned to cookbooks "for teaching, for explanation and for hand-holding."[42] By the 1990s the *New York Times* called the "cooking illiterate" the "new lost generation," finding that most *thought* they knew how to cook, but flunked basic tests of cooking skills, such as how to thicken gravy, or how many teaspoons were in a tablespoon.[43] Later in the 2010s, meal-prep companies emerged to make it easier for home cooks afraid of the process.

This need for hand holding was in greater evidence as the years passed, for both the number of individual cookbooks published each year and the total volumes sold have increased since the 1970s. Publishing data is rather hard to pin down, but one estimate shows that there were about 3,168 cookbooks published in the United States in the 1965 to 1975 period, or about 300 a year.[44] By the mid-1990s, the number had increased to just under 1,000 cookbooks each year.[45] Both the variety and total volume of cookbooks increased. In 1991, about 27.5 million cookbooks and wine books were purchased in the United States. By 1995, that number had increased to about 41.8 million. By that time, the Barnes and Noble booksellers chain carried about 4,000 cookbook titles nationally, and many of those were on bestseller lists.[46] So, overall, Americans bought more cookbooks over time, and were able to select from a wider range of those books at the average bookstore. The overall surge in interest about all things food was then a complicated process. People ate out more, tried a wider variety of foods, bought more cookbooks, and cooked for themselves less often, all at the same time. While surging interest in cookbooks included the wealthy and middle class at first, there was a trickle-down effect after a time. Television certainly sped this process, as cookbook authors marketed themselves on this medium—first on the major networks and PBS beginning in the 1950s, and by the 1990s and 2000s on the Food Network and the Cooking Channel.

As many Americans cooked for themselves less frequently, they read cookbooks not just for recipes, but also as literature or entertainment. Some "curl up with them" on the couch to read them as they "would a novel."[47] By looking at what cookbooks were saying, and what the editors and authors of them thought about what they were conveying, we can gain insight about how Americans understood diversity in the late twentieth century.

ALFRED A. KNOPF'S COOKBOOKS TRANSLATE THE WORLD

Alfred A. Knopf was among the most important publishers in twentieth-century America, and Judith Jones was one of its most important editors. Starting in 1957 she marshaled manuscripts to publication for best-selling authors and literary giants. Those writers include John Hersey, Anne Tyler, Langston Hughes, and John Updike.[48] In addition to her significant work as a fiction editor, she and Knopf also made a distinct mark on cookbook publishing, beginning with the release of *Mastering the Art of French Cooking, Volume I*, by Julia Child, Louisette Bertholle, and Simone Beck in 1961. Until this book hit the shelves, cookbooks did not stand out on book publishers' ledger sheets. The exceptions were the *Fannie Farmer Cookbook*, *The Joy of Cooking*, and the Betty Crocker cookbooks. The top cookbooks, however, were mostly published as adjuncts to magazines, with *Better Homes and Gardens* and *Good Housekeeping* putting out top sellers.[49]

As one writer noted, "Knopf not only set the standard for American cookbooks" with *Mastering* and other volumes, "but established its culinary authors as catalysts in what would become a renaissance of cooking in the United States" after the 1960s.⁵⁰ A short list of authors Jones shepherded to publication in the 1970s included Claudia Roden (*A Book of Middle Eastern Food*, 1972), Madhur Jaffrey (*An Invitation to Indian Cooking*, 1973), Marcella Hazan (*The Classic Italian Cookbook*, 1976), Irene Kuo (*The Key to Chinese Cooking*, 1977), and Elisabeth Ortiz (*The Book of Latin American Cooking*, 1979). Invitees to Knopf cookbook release parties included a who's who list of New York literary and media figures.⁵¹ While the Knopf books certainly appealed to upper- and middle-class readers, they listed for a reasonable price. In 1973, the bestseller *Better Homes & Gardens New Cookbook* retailed for $6.95, while *An Invitation to Indian Cooking* cost $7.95.⁵²

Judith Jones saw the task of many cookbooks as one of translation, and she guided her authors to interpret other cultures for their readers beginning in the 1960s and 1970s, a heady time for cookbook publishing. When her authors did not translate enough or translate well, she told them. Her frustration with existing French cookbook authors' inability to translate the nuances of the cuisine had led her to feel confident about Julia Child's first effort, which set the standard for American cookbooks after the 1960s. Other cookbooks, she noted, made no effort in "*translating* the mysteries of French cooking into terms that Americans could understand."⁵³ By Jones's estimate and that of millions of others, Julia Child did just that, and with flair too. *Mastering the Art* was vividly illustrated, had step-by-step directions, explained why certain ingredients might be necessary for a dish, and broke down essential French cooking techniques. For example, in her French onion soup recipe, the quarter teaspoon of sugar is "to help the onions brown," letting the home cook know not to omit it.⁵⁴

Jones had firsthand experience as a translator and had spent significant time in France, where her love of food blossomed. She used this experience to land her first job at Knopf, editing English translations of French authors, including Albert Camus and Jean-Paul Sartre. When she took on Julia Child's first book, she was thrilled with its capacity to render difficult techniques in clear, easy-to-understand language. It was Child's authoritative but comfortable voice that made her a good translator, both of the mysteries of cooking and the mysteries of French cuisine and culture.⁵⁵ Like Jaffrey, she had begun as a poor cook, and through travel, trial, and much work, she learned how to cook well. She remarked once that her intent was to "take French cooking out of cuckoo land and bring it down to where everybody is."⁵⁶ "Cuckoo land" was the province of the grand French restaurants replicated in equally expensive form in major American cities.⁵⁷ In *Mastering* she echoed this theme, explaining that she hoped to make French cooking "available to everybody."⁵⁸

France very well might have been never-never land to many, and Child provided the transition for American cooks so that they could make French food using the ingredients from the American supermarket. As Jones put it, a good cookbook was to be more than a "collection of recipes." Child's role was to "*translate* classic cuisine for the American home cook, explaining to them all the things she had needed to know—what to expect, what the rules were, viable substitutes for ingredients not then available in the States, and, to make life just a little easier, what steps could be done ahead."[59] Her skill at translation and ebullient personality on display in her *French Chef* television show combined to make her books bestsellers from the start, with bookstores scrambling for copies in the first year of publication.[60] By the early 1970s, she consistently sold 30,000–40,000 copies per year of *Mastering, Vol. I.*[61]

The translation skill mastered by Child became more important for other cookbook authors as global trade and immigration intensified. Americans increasingly came into contact with new dishes, cooking styles, ingredients, menu variations, and cooking equipment as cuisines from afar were served in restaurants and described in new cookbooks. And despite America's British heritage, even British food need translation.[62]

TRANSLATING BRITISH FOOD

The differences between the foods and eating habits of Americans and the British were wide enough in the 1960s and 1970s that when Jane Grigson wanted to publish her English cookbook, *Good Things*, in the United States with Knopf, Judith Jones remarked over and over again that elements of the book needed to be "translated" for American readers. Grigson was a successful English author from the 1960s until her death in 1990. She wrote a column for the *Observer Magazine* from 1968 to 1990 and was a cooking authority in her home country. She had published her breakthrough cookbook, *Charcuterie and French Pork Cookery* in England in 1967, which Knopf took on for an American version.[63] *Good Things* had been published in England in 1971, and editor Judith Jones turned to her husband, Evan Jones, himself a cookbook author, to write extensive footnotes to Grigson's text so that Americans would understand it. These footnotes gave advice on where to find English ingredients, translated English preparation methods, and offered American equivalents for English eating styles.

Many of the items requiring explanation were from the seas around England. In the introduction, Grigson mentions laver and sewen, English terms for seaweed and sea trout used on the isle. And the first chapter, "Kippers & Other Fish," describes British techniques for smoking, salting, and cooking herring. In the Knopf version, that chapter required frequent footnotes. Often, those notes explain how American consumers could procure English foods that may have been easier to find in Liverpool than Los Angeles.[64] Judith Jones had decided to use these footnotes rather than change the body text of the English version of *Good Things* so that she would not interfere with Grigson's "style" or "information."[65]

She also had reservations about the ability of the book to hold up with an American audience. She told Grigson that her "book is, of course, very English-oriented for our American audience and it is for that reason we need more than simply translation of measurements to American terms, but in addition notes that would make the book more useful to someone here."[66] Some counseled Jones and Grigson that they should eliminate some of the particularly English parts of the book, but Jones told Grigson that she liked the book's "Englishness" and rather than "disturb" that, she would add the footnotes.[67] She added some other observations about differences between the cuisines, including that leeks are poor man's food in Europe, but were "rich man's asparagus" in the United States. She further counseled that the text must explain English "terms like jugging, double cream, short pastry."[68] In the book itself, the note to a section on leeks said they were rare, and that "some Americans would not even recognize" one, adding that one solution was to simply grow them oneself.[69]

For a later book, *The Mushroom Feast*, the transatlantic confusion compounded itself. There, Grigson had taken some American recipes and adapted them to English means for her first English edition. Then she reconfigured them back to "American" for the Knopf version, but Judith Jones saw that this resulted in "confusion," especially with quantities of ingredients.[70] When discussing the problem of whether to use "broiling" or "grilling" to direct readers on preparation techniques, Jones told her copy editor that "I do wish we could get together with our British cousins on all this culinary terminology, and maybe this effort will be the first step."[71] In a later note, she told her that she felt confident that they had "come closer to standardizing our dual culinary vocabularies."[72] Lastly, Jones told Grigson that she should cut the "European slant" to the book so that she might attract mushroom "freaks" (of which she was surprised to find out there were many), nature lovers, and vegetarians.[73] Even if they were speaking the same language, vocabulary and meaning were not all the same, producing some frustration in the effort to bring English food to America. In this case, uniformity was the desired result, for it made cultural interchange easier. Perhaps because of these issues, Judith Jones's inkling about sales for *Good Things* proved correct. She told one literary agent that "I suspect the resistance" to the book "has been primarily to its Englishness—kippers and such."[74] For a follow-up book project, Jones advised Grigson that she visit the United States so she could better aim it toward an American audience.[75]

Though it was important to have consistent language for cookbook readers, distinction was also important, for a publisher did not want its books to be identical to other publishers'. When Grigson proposed a vegetable cookbook for publication, Judith Jones told her Knopf could not take it on, for she had two of them in the pipeline. She explained that Grigson's book would be perceived as too similar to those books, and that "while you and I know vegetarian books are a far cry from a book on vegetable cookery, our salesmen are not necessarily alert to such fine points."[76] She also argued that the book was too English in nature, adding that they "don't quite reflect a trend here, much influenced by the Chinese, toward simple stir-fried combinations, accenting the freshness."[77] While it was still difficult for bookstore owners to categorize the vegetarian cookbooks that proliferated in the 1960s and 1970s, Jones knew that the better ones would reflect the distinct changes in American cuisine, brought on by the new popularity of Chinese and other Asian cuisines that used vegetables differently than the European cuisines.

If Americans were put off by the Englishness of Grigson's books, what of Frenchness, Indianess, or Mexicaness? How would cookbook buyers respond to the foreign elements of these cuisines? Judith Jones was attuned to the problem of translating foreign foods, and rather than keep the text intact, as in the case of Grigson's book, she made major suggestions to authors such as Julia Child, Madhur Jaffrey, and Elizabeth Ortiz for their works on French, Indian, and Latin American cooking. It is in these cuisines that the effort to translate diversity can best be seen. In the case of Madhur Jaffrey, she, much like Julia Child with French food, was among the first important authors to make Indian food accessible to an American audience.

MADHUR JAFFREY AND INDIAN COOKING IN AMERICA

Jaffrey worked to help Americans understand Indian food, and an important factor, even more than in Jane Grigson's books, was the foreignness of the ingredients used in Indian cooking, such as mangoes. Unfamiliar to many Americans, and unavailable in many grocery stores, ginger, tamarind, cilantro, and other foods had to be explained, partly to lend insight about their uses in Indian cooking, and partly to erase misconceptions. In *An Invitation*, Jaffrey wrote a section on Indian ingredients, complemented by another section with grocery stores and mail-order houses listed. After her first draft of the cookbook, Jaffrey was asked to further explain many of the ingredients so that Americans could make connections to foods they knew. For amchoor, or raw mango, used to "make food tangy and sour," Jones added that it was "used as freely as lemon is in American cooking."[78] Similar advice was needed for cilantro, which could be found in "Chinese, Japanese, and Spanish" markets, and ginger, which was to be used fresh, not as the powder sold in many supermarkets.[79]

Translation also shifted in terms of what connections readers were asked to make when learning a new cuisine. One of the more unique aspects of Indian cuisine is the succession of roasting and frying techniques done in intervals to achieve the correct flavors and ensure that ingredients don't burn. Judith Jones addressed this issue in the first drafts of *An Invitation*. Because it was a "less familiar cookery, the recipes must be as complete unto themselves as possible," Jones told her copy editor, rather than forcing one to "chase" around cross-references on cooking techniques throughout the book.[80] Still, she worried that explaining a technique in each recipe would make the book too long, upping production costs. In the end, Jones erred on the side of explanation, rather than cost, and kept the detail in each recipe. She also thought it important not to refer to the cooking techniques employed by Jaffrey as "stir-fry," for that was "apt to be associated with Chinese cooking and seems to represent an unfamiliar (therefore frightening) technique."[81] Though a copy editor had inserted the term *stir-fry* into many of the recipes, Jones opted to "restore" the text so that readers would not be put off by references to Chinese food.[82] Between the publication of her first American cookbook in 1973 and her memoir thirty-three years later, these cross-references to Chinese or Mexican or other ethnic cuisines slowly became routes to understanding Indian and other cuisines, rather than barriers. Stir-fry became part of the American cooking lexicon, just as spicy foods like Mexican would be easy entrees to other cuisines. Mexican food was grouped with all south of the border foods in Elisabeth Lambert Ortiz's cookbook, published by Knopf not long after Jaffrey's, and it too had characteristic translation issues that marked the march of globalization in American life.

ELISABETH ORTIZ TRANSLATES LATIN AMERICA

Like Madhur Jaffrey, Elisabeth Ortiz had lived in several countries, experiencing the foods of many regions. Born in England in 1915, her family moved to Jamaica, and later, Australia, where she married her first husband. He was killed in military service during World War II. Afterward, she moved to New York, where she married a Mexican diplomat, César Ortiz Tinoco, who was then stationed at the United Nations. His duties would take her to Mexico City and other locales around the world, where she sampled many cuisines. Though she had long worked as a journalist and fiction author, she eventually took up food writing, publishing *The Complete Book of Mexican Cooking* in 1967, with the aid of James Beard and Craig Claiborne. She wrote frequent columns for *Gourmet* and advised *Time-Life* books on the Mexican and Latin American sections of their world cooking series. With Knopf she published *The Book of Latin American Cooking* in 1979, which was also quite successful. As a result, she was termed the "undisputed English-language expert" on Latin American cooking and was rivaled only by Diana Kennedy as a non-native expert on Mexican food.[83]

The Book of Latin American Cooking had to explain a good deal about the continents' foods, even though Mexican food was becoming more popular around the United States in the 1970s and 1980s. Though the terms *Hispanic* and *Latino* were coming into use during those decades, American publishers released few cookbooks surveying and comparing Latin American cooking then.[84] The enormity of describing the cuisine of two continents was a difficult task for Ortiz and her editor, Judith Jones. For this reason, Jones suggested during the editing process that Ortiz revise the cookbook so that it would repeat little-known information for American readers throughout, much like the directions for frying and roasting in Jaffrey's book. For example, if Ortiz described cilantro's uses in the introduction, she should also do so in a separate "ingredients" section and even include a line about it in some of the recipes.[85] Jones also cautioned Ortiz that she was "so deep into refinements" about some descriptions of foods that the overall nature of a particular dish might be lost on American readers.[86] Furthermore, Jones advised Ortiz about her many descriptions of the regional origins for certain foods. She wanted her to generalize more and was put off by Ortiz's hair-splitting about what people ate in various regions. In the final draft, this may have led to a broadening of the cuisine to a bi-continental, rather than nation-specific one, for that was the goal of the book. It was also a way to get a handle on the incredible diversity of the foods consumed all across the lands between the US-Mexico border and Patagonia. Jones told Ortiz that she made "too many fine distinctions about origins and crossing of culture" and that they "get repetitive" in the descriptions for individual dishes. She proposed that discussion of regional variations be subsumed in the introduction.[87] Several months later, Jones asked Ortiz if there was a "way of taking a larger view and encompassing several of the cuisines together?"[88] Diversity was interesting, but at some point, it was overwhelming, as evidenced by Jones's pleas for simplicity.

As with Jaffrey and other cookbook authors on foreign cuisines, Ortiz had to offer substitutions for foreign ingredients not available in the typical American supermarket. Like Jaffrey's, Ortiz's cookbook included a section to explain foreign ingredients and an appendix with lists of suppliers and mail-order houses that could provide ingredients, whether fresh, canned, or packaged.[89] Julia Child had found it easy enough to fashion her first French cookbook around goods found solely within the American supermarket, but this was more difficult for many other cuisines in the 1970s and 1980s.[90] Sometimes substitutions would suffice in the minds of other cookbook authors, but some decided that the original ingredient was required for the proper taste, texture, or balance. In Ortiz's case, she insisted that ancho chilies were necessary for one recipe. She had to assure Judith Jones that they could be readily found in large eastern cities and in the Southwest, though Jones would have wondered if she went to the average suburban supermarket.[91]

Jones had concerns about ingredients such as ancho chilies because she worried that "Mrs. Middle America" might not find such ingredients at her local market and was not willing to search inner-city ethnic grocery stores for them.[92] She hoped lists of specialty importers in her cookbooks might partly solve this problem, but regularly asked authors whether substitution or omission of certain ingredients was possible. One recipe in Simone Beck's French cookbook, *Simca's Cuisine*, had called for a whole chicken to be boiled for several hours in water to make soup. Jones asked if chicken parts could be substituted instead, for they were easier to get in the United States. She explained to Beck, "maybe all this is not the French way of doing things and maybe you don't even get parts as readily in your markets, but it would seem fair for you to translate in this case the French way of doing things for Americans with their different marketing problems," adding that it was necessary to make the cooking process more "attractive" for Americans.[93] Even if the whole chicken was not easily obtainable in American supermarkets, product lists were always changing, sometimes so rapidly that desired ingredients could become available during the two- or three-year process of editing a cookbook. Jones asked Elisabeth Ortiz to submit "more interesting vegetable offerings" from Latin American cuisine in one correspondence. Ortiz responded with a soup recipe for "boniatos sweet potatoes," causing Jones to say she would "keep an eye out for them." Though it was "a long trek up to La Marquetta," a Latin American grocery store in New York City, Jones thought the "wonderful mushrooming of Korean vegetable markets now all over the city" meant she would find some of the sweet potatoes "closer to home."[94]

COOKBOOKS AND TRANSLATION

In creating cookbooks on ethnic cuisines, two major goals—using ingredients readily found in the United States so that the cuisine was accessible for the average American, and maintaining "unusual and varied" recipes from a foreign region— sometimes worked at cross-purposes.[95] If unusual recipes were sometimes desired, they took some effort, especially when it came to getting ingredients. In 1978, Jones hosted a dinner at her house using a recipe from Ortiz's book in advance of its publication. She had to "make an excursion" to a special grocery store to get ancho, pasilla, and mulatto chilies. Making note of this for Ortiz's book, she wanted some aspects of the Mexican cuisine familiar to Americans, but not too many, for the cookbook had to be unique. To distinguish the book, more of the unknown aspects of Latin American cooking were necessary, such as a recipe for feijoada, a common Brazilian stew.[96] The ingredients for such dishes would be readily available in supermarkets a couple of decades later, but they weren't common features at the time. For Knopf, it was a major undertaking to locate grocery stores that carried special ingredients so they could be listed in their cookbooks. In particular, Judith Jones strove to make sure such ingredients were available in small cities—not just New York or Los Angeles.[97] One reader of Claudia Roden's *A Book of Middle Eastern Cooking*, published in 1972, found this problematic. She wrote a letter to Roden saying that although she enjoyed the cookbook and wanted to make some of the recipes, she could not find many of the ingredients in her native Canada, and that the book listed only one Canadian ingredient source. Irritated, she reminded Roden that Canada is a sizeable nation.[98]

Even if Canadian readers were not Knopf's priority, Jones's authors still had to strike a balance between offering something unfamiliar, and thereby exciting to new readers, and giving readers enough familiar markers. Roden and Ortiz listed staples of Mexican and Middle Eastern cooking, such as guacamole and kebabs, in their cookbooks. So too, Madhur Jaffrey included recipes for mulligatawny soup and tandoori chicken in *An Invitation to Indian Cooking*, for those were the most recognizable Indian foods outside India. In her description of those foods, Jaffrey acknowledged their importance in Anglo-Indian cuisine and sought to explain their roots at the same time. She placed tandoori chicken in a "summer cooking and barbecued foods" section, knowing that many Americans barbecued in the backyards of their suburban homes.[99]

Even an American regional cuisine, Cajun and Creole, had to be translated for a broader audience. Rima and Richard Collin, professors at University of New Orleans, wrote *The New Orleans Cookbook* for Knopf in 1975. This was before Cajun and Creole cooking became popular during the 1980s, with Louisiana-influenced restaurants opening in big cities around the country, serving gumbo, blackened redfish, and shrimp Creole.[100] New Orleans cooking boomed because of three trends—the resurgence of interest in local American cooking, the vibrant personalities of Paul Prudhomme and other Louisiana chefs who appeared on television shows, and a new vitality for hot and spicy foods, as evidenced in the popularity of Mexican and Szechuan cooking.[101] Judith Jones pushed the Collins to revise their original draft so that it would be accessible to a wider audience of people. She wanted a "personal and engaging voice" in the book rather than a "pedantic and chauvinistic" one. To this end, she told the Collins that they would have to "seduce" cookbook purchasers by making Creole and Cajun cuisine "*accessible*—not something so special that it can only be appreciated locally."[102] It was also necessary to make the cuisine inviting, even for those who had never tried it, and Jones argued that the Collins need to make an "effort [to] translate recipes so they aren't so dependent on regional specialties."[103] Jones had wondered about the cookbook's accessibility when a friend went fishing on Long Island but could not figure out a recipe to use from the Collins's book, despite the abundance of seafood there.[104] In the end, however, the cookbook was quite successful, selling nearly 100,000 copies.[105]

These problems in translating local methods and peculiarities were reflective of the cultural displacement inherent in globalization. Judith Jones attacked the problem of translation in her cookbooks because she was acting as an intermediary between an author who was familiar with the foreign land and the reader who might not be. As cultural forms were introduced to the reader, however, they often had to be changed so that the cuisine would either be translatable, at the very least, or inviting, at a higher standard. Translatable meant the foreign aspects of that cuisine were explained with sufficient verve and detail. Inviting meant the foods were of the sort that Americans, whether they were New Yorkers or Iowans, might first be willing to try, and second, could acquire the ingredients or cooking utensils to make. Translation and accessibility were always changing, for globalization brought more people into contact and made items such as cooking utensils or ingredients more readily available.

In sum, elements of foreign culture had to be explained, accessed, and marketed. Cookbooks on foreign cuisines did not just explain how to cook food, they told readers what was most important about that cuisine too. In the Knopf cookbooks of the 1970s, we can see how both the more familiar foods of England and France and the less familiar ones from India and Latin America needed explaining. The translation process was one of constant give and take. Authors sought both the most elemental and most tasty components of the cuisines to feature in their cookbooks. In doing so, they made judgments about what was representative of a region or nation and conveyed that to the uninitiated. They also made judgments about one of the fundamental questions inherent in globalization—how do regions change as global trade accelerates? All of the authors had to contend with the manner in which the cuisines they described were changing just as American cuisine was changing too, partly because of their influence. This was all heady and complicated business, and the better cookbooks made sense of it in a small way for American consumers. If globalization brought the world to Americans, cookbooks provided an everyday translation device by using an everyday experience, eating, to explain the incredible variety in the world.

Why were these culinary professionals—the authors and editor good at translating? The main cookbook authors here—Julia Child, Madhur Jaffrey, and Elisabeth Ortiz—were either born abroad or spent considerable time in various countries. Child went to cooking school in France to learn her craft. Jaffrey grew up in India, spent time in London, and then settled in the United States. Ortiz traveled all over the Americas. And Judith Jones spent time in France too, starting as a translator of French texts. The authors were also compelling personalities. Julia Child had a distinctive, humorous style. Jaffrey was a polished actress. Ortiz fit well within New York circles advertising her cookbook. Beyond that, Jones insisted on clear, translatable directions.

Much had changed by 2006, when Jaffrey penned *Climbing the Mango Trees*, a memoir/cookbook describing her childhood in Delhi. By then, mangoes were no longer strange fruits to be found only in Asian or Latino specialty grocery stores; produce distributors imported several varieties to meet demand from both American-born consumers and immigrant customers from Latin America and Asia.[106] Jaffrey illustrated this fact in a *New York Times* article in which she celebrated a US-India pact. The United States had just signed a controversial agreement to sell nuclear technologies to India. President George W. Bush highlighted one small, but tasty, component of the agreement to persuade the American public that this

pact was justified. The United States would, for the first time, allow the importation of Indian mangoes, which had long been banned in the United States due to
concerns about pests. Somewhat fortuitously for Jaffrey, mangoes direct from
India landed in America soon after her memoir hit the shelves. In May 2007 the
first shipment arrived at John F. Kennedy airport in New York, where thousands of
Indian immigrants had debarked in the previous three decades. Indeed, some of
those immigrants had smuggled mangoes as reminders of their homeland. From
Jaffrey's first American book to her most recent, the mango had gone from strange
to desirable—so much so that an American president used their importation to
sell a nuclear trade pact.[107] A reviewer on Amazon.com explained to prospective
buyers that she owned six of Jaffrey's books, that one need be only "moderately
adventurous" to cook from her books, and finally, that she recommended "Indian
CDs and Bollywood for the full experience. Bon Voyage."[108] Americans no longer
needed an introduction to Indian cuisine—they were already well familiar with its
variations.

6

Indian Restaurants in America

A Case Study in Translating Diversity

Indian food was barely a blip on the food radar of most Americans in the 1960s. The changing cuisine served at Indian restaurants in and around San Francisco between the 1960s and 2000s offers insight about the need to translate the complexities of Indian cuisine to an American audience. In 1965, the San Francisco telephone directory listed only three Indian restaurants, and just two, Taj of India and India House, were regularly featured in restaurant or tour guides.[1]

Founded in 1947, India House was the Indian restaurant that San Francisco guidebooks mentioned most until the 1960s. Typical of the time, it featured Indian food by way of Britain. A British couple, David Brown and his "handsome blonde" wife, Patricia, founded the restaurant just a month after India had secured independence from Great Britain.[2] The Browns had learned the "art of curry making" in both India and England, taking some recipes from Veeraswamy—the oldest Indian restaurant in London.[3] One review said David Brown was "as authentically British as Winston Churchill," noting that he paused in his regular rounds about the restaurant "only long enough to commiserate over the loss of India, still a prime conversational topic among his English regulars."[4] That atmosphere made it fit for the "Colorful, Amusing, Exotic" section of the restaurant guide.[5] To give the restaurant its exotic air, the Browns hired local Indian and Pakistani students to wait tables and serve drinks. The restaurant's simple menu echoed India and Britain. Entrees consisted of several curries, distinguished only by a main ingredient, such as chicken, crab, lamb, or prawns. Each curry entrée was accompanied by rice, sambals (pickled fruits or vegetables), and Major Grey's chutney, itself a British invention.[6] Acknowledging that it was a hybrid British/Indian dish, one review testified that the curry at India House was prepared in "true Indian style," rather than British style, for it cooked the "curry flavor" through the meats.[7] Another review explained the nuances of curry for the prospective diner, noting that "authentic curry is, of course, not just one seasoning, but a carefully considered mixture designed to complement the particular food." The menu listed steak and kidney pie for wary diners.[8]

Having such European fare on the menu was common practice in many ethnic restaurants, presumably to please the customer who did not want the sense of adventure that his dining companions craved. One review said dishes such as broiled steak were designed for the "mothers-in-law" who were presumably in tow with an adventurous couple.[9] Many Mexican restaurants of that era served burgers and steaks to please those customers who could not stomach tacos or enchiladas; one even titled that section of its menu "gringo items."[10]

Though in India House's first few years it did not sell cocktails, over time the bar became the selling point of the restaurant, for it contributed to both its exotic feel and its British colonial atmosphere. By 1963, one guidebook proclaimed that the restaurant had a "GREAT bar," next to a drawing of a turbaned Indian barman pouring drinks. Behind him loomed the stuffed head of a Bengal tiger to finish the British colonial scene.[11] A contemporary *Holiday* magazine photo did the same, showing David Brown in front of the bar next to his employee in native Indian garb, both backed by a wall upon which dozens of pewter mugs hung.[12] Consistent with the touristy feel of the restaurant, its menu advised that the British mugs and Indian goblets could be "had through your waiter."[13] To confirm the Britishness of the India House dining experience, Pimm's cocktails were its signature drinks. The restaurant boasted in one press release that it served the greatest number of these libations of any location in the United States, in what was "a cross between English pub and English club," replete with Indians serving the drinks.[14]

Three of the other Indian restaurants in San Francisco during the 1950s and 1960s, Taj of India, Little India, and The Bengal Lancer, also demonstrated how diners might be searching for both the exotic, in the form of Indian culture, and the familiar, in the form of English tradition. One guidebook description of Taj of India used hybrid Indian and British references in which waiters and hostesses wore Indian garments to guarantee authenticity, but the British legacy was still present. The "Hunt Room," one of the "enchanting" parlors in the restaurant, alluded to those British officers and tourists who had hunted tigers and elephants in the Indian subcontinent during the Victorian era.[15] Taj's owner, Sushil Kakar, gave an interview in the *San Francisco Chronicle* in 1965 in which the reporter pressed him about his "missing" turban. Kakar said he normally didn't wear one at home, but in the restaurant it lent "a note of authenticity," adding, "I wear it in the way an actor wears a costume to do a performance. You might say the Taj of India is my stage."[16] Little India played up this aspect as well; it was called "exotic" over and over again in one restaurant guide. Run by the "internationally renowned dance team: producer Bill Carroll and his Indian wife, Cheetah," it was advertised by using drawings of Indian dancers with the tagline, "Gateway to the Exotic East."[17] Similarly, former Imperial Indian Army officer Francis Ingall ran the Bengal Lancer. Although his chef was British, he had grown up in India and brought his British-Indian dishes to their restaurant. Ingall decorated the place with colorful Lancer uniforms, perhaps reminding diners of the popular film, *The Lives of a Bengal Lancer*, which had starred Gary Cooper.[18] The references to old imperial rule showed up in Indian restaurants elsewhere. A 1920s advertisement for a New York restaurant, the Warwick, claimed that an Indian "Rajah" would revel in the restaurant's "translation" of curry, making it "so delicious you'd forego a tiger hunt to taste it."[19]

TRANSLATING INDIAN FOOD

Efforts to explain Indian cuisine to American diners then moved through three distinct phases between the 1950s and the beginning of the twenty-first century. In the 1950s and 1960s, Indian restaurants in America typically referenced Britain and its colonial legacy in India, replete with images of Bengal Lancers, hunt clubs for British officers, and the single word that encapsulated Indian food for American and British diners, "curry." Unlike Mexican or Chinese food, the basic components of Indian food were not familiar to most Americans in 1960. Any American had heard of curry powder, but many had not necessarily tasted Indian food, either in a restaurant or in their homes.[20] By the 1970s and 1980s, Mughal food and tandoor cooking had come of age, both in India and abroad. Restaurants in the United States began alluding to India's Mughal Empire, when Muslim kings had ruled over much of the subcontinent from the sixteenth to the eighteenth centuries. Referencing the Mughal rather than the British Empire was partly a result of Indians asserting their independence, both in India and abroad. No longer having to speak of the British power in India, Indian restaurant owners could celebrate their own great past and civilization—the rule of the Mughals. That wasn't the only reason for the shift, however. Mughal cuisine was especially suited to the American palate. Its grilled meats and puffed breads were no stretch for American consumers.

Over the years, Indian food diversified in the United States. By the 1990s, Indian cuisine in America had jettisoned the British past and combined elements of the Mughal tradition with other properties of the cuisine from the Indian subcontinent. As non-European cuisines became more popular, Indian restaurant owners used examples from widely known ethnic cuisines, such as Mexican and Chinese, to help diners understand what they had in store for them. No longer confined to tandoori chicken and endless variations of meat curries, purveyors could offer vegetarian dishes and foods from the southern regions of India without scaring off some customers. Diversity was translated anew for American consumers by using examples from Latin American and other Asian cuisines, and indeed, many new Indian restaurateurs used those foods to create hybrid menus.

EARLY INDIAN RESTAURANTS IN AMERICA

Associating Indian food with Britain, and later, the Mughal heritage, was in some ways a necessary practice for Indian restaurant owners before the 1960s. India *was* exotic for most Americans, and their perceptions of Indians were often negative. Historian Andrew Rotter has shown how Indians and Americans shared negative perceptions about each other concerning foods, smells, work habits, religion, and masculinity. Around the time of Indian independence, "Americans saw Indians as superstitious, unclean, diseased, treacherous, lazy, and prevaricating."[21] Further- more, because India was a new nation, it was viewed as "immature and therefore bumptious."[22] After independence, India, the predominantly Hindu nation, suf- fered in comparison to Pakistan, a mostly Muslim nation, in both diplomatic and everyday circles. Most Pakistanis ate meat, were monotheistic, and had been pre- ferred by the British as administrators and soldiers during colonial rule because they were thought to be of the "martial race."[23] The journalist Harold Isaacs inter- viewed Americans in the 1950s about their view of Indians, finding that many believed Muslims to be better than Hindus. One observer remarked that Muslims were "good people [and] good fighters, whereas the Hindus are said to be mystics, dreamers, hypocrites," adding that he "was brought up on Kipling, [meaning that] all Muslims fine, all Hindus unattractive."[24]

Americans in the first half of the twentieth century typically viewed India through such a British filter, including via the stories of authors like Rudyard Kipling, who once said that India was "divided equally between jungle, tigers, cobras, cholera, and sepoys."[25] Not surprisingly, a cobra candleholder sat on India House's bar.[26] More generally, Americans held fairly narrow views about Asian and African nations before the end of colonial rule.[27] Popular representations such as, Tarzan, Little Black Sambo, and Bengal Tigers figured heavily.[28]

Americans came to know the Sambo character from a Helen Bannerman book, which conflated dark-skinned stereotypes about India, Africa, and the American South. Before the Civil War, whites used the "Sambo" character to justify slavery by depicting blacks as childlike, irresponsible, lazy, affectionate, and happy. In addition to the book, the Sambo character lived on as the name of a large restau- rant chain doing brisk business during the 1950s and 1960s. The pancake house, Sambo's, had been named such because Little Black Sambo triumphantly eats 169 pancakes in the book. The restaurants featured menus and murals showing Sambo in a bejeweled turban next to a tiger, ready to stuff himself with pancakes.[29] In the late 1970s, Sambo's operated over a thousand restaurants in forty-seven states. Its business dropped precipitously, however, in the early 1980s, because its breakfast-all-day format struggled. By this time, too, the Sambo connotation offended many potential customers. The chain faced civil rights lawsuits in the early 1980s, eventually changing some of its Northeast stores to "Jolly Tiger" and then to "No Place Like Sam's." This was all to no avail; it went bankrupt shortly afterward.[30] Perhaps fittingly, three decades later an Indianapolis strip mall once anchored by a Sambo's outlet instead leased space to an Ethiopian restaurant.[31]

But that was long after the civil rights movement had taken hold. India House and other restaurants had every reason to reference British or Mughal rule before the 1970s, for diners made connections to those elements celebrating the exotic or triumphant past of India rather than the nuances of the food itself. Although many of the early Punjabi restaurateurs in the United States were Sikh or Hindu, they still cooked a heavy dose of Muslim-influenced dishes, which featured meats and breads. This was in good part because even though many Hindus in India eat meat, they were invariably associated with vegetarianism—something not quite attractive during the pre-1960s meat and potatoes era.[32]

In 1968, three Indian immigrants who had started as waiters and barmen at India House bought it from the previous owners, the Browns. They decided to keep some of the spot's British elements while adding distinguishing features to the preparation of the Indian foods. To highlight the change, they issued a press release explaining to reporters that curries were not all the same and that each type was flavored differently. Though they wanted to break a bit from the previous owners, it would have been foolish to get rid of one of the restaurant's main revenue sources, so their release began with a page-long description of the glories of Pimm's Cups, the British drink. A key change, however, was the addition of a tandoor oven, which was slowly becoming a standard feature in many Indian restaurants. One of the new owners, Sarwan Gill, had immigrated from the Punjab region of Northwest India in 1958 and worked as a busboy, bartender, and waiter at India House for ten years before becoming an owner. Like many of the small number of Indian immigrants of his era, he had come as a student to the United States, eventually graduating from the University of California at Berkeley. He and his co-owners opened another restaurant in Berkeley in 1972.[33] An Associated Press series, "American Dream," ran nationwide in small-town newspapers. In 1976 it featured a short biography of Gill, noting that he came to America with only $5 in his pocket and his success demonstrated that "America is still a land of opportunity."[34]

INDIAN IMMIGRANTS AND THEIR RESTAURANTS

The major ethnic cuisines that dominated restaurant fare in the United States for the latter half of the twentieth century were Italian, Mexican, and Chinese. The number of these restaurants was far greater than that of other ethnic cuisines, and when diners were surveyed, they were naturally more familiar with those foods than others. In 1980, one comprehensive analysis of telephone directories throughout the United States found that Chinese, Italian, and Mexican restaurants accounted for 71.1 percent of all ethnic restaurants.[35] A 1983 National Restaurant Association survey had similar findings. It determined that 89 percent of respondents had tried Chinese food, and 88 percent Mexican food.[36] The 1985 survey counted a total of 302,837 restaurants in the United States, with the two largest categories being pizza shops at 10.3 percent of the total, and hamburger joints at 8.8 percent. "Oriental" restaurants (mostly Chinese in this survey) totaled 4.1 percent, and Mexican 3.9 percent. In contrast, the "other ethnic" category totaled only 0.8 percent, folding German, Spanish, Greek, Indian, and Soul food into that group.[37] Certain ethnic cuisines were to be found in higher proportion in some regions, mostly in correspondence to the history of immigration to those areas. About 70 percent of Mexican restaurants were located in the Southwest in the early 1980s, and a similar proportion of Chinese restaurants were concentrated on the East and West Coasts.[38]

The small number of "other ethnic" restaurants grew significantly by the end of the century and also required the greatest degree of explanation for American consumers. Surveys conducted in 1995 and again in 1999 found that Americans as a whole were becoming more familiar with some of the other ethnic cuisines, including Indian, Japanese, and Thai, than they had been just a dozen years prior.[39] In a world in which peoples and goods moved faster and more frequently across regions, Americans were introduced to many cultural forms they had previously only read about at a distance, including food. In the ethnic restaurants in cities, suburbs, and even small towns, Americans negotiated this increasing diversity brought on by globalization. One of the largest sending regions during the post-1965 immigration boom was South Asia, as hundreds of thousands of Indians, Pakistanis, and Bangladeshis came to the United States.

Indian food and Indian culture were relative unknowns in America before the 1960s, partly because immigration from India had been quite low. A few Indian restaurants existed in New York before World War II. Sailors from the Indian subcontinent who had disembarked in the city ran some. Students who had come to the United States for college ran others. And still others served "curry" by way of the Caribbean, which had a long-standing South Asian labor force.[40] Some Indian immigrants sold food from other cultures. In California, they could be found hawking tamales and enchiladas in the early 1900s.[41]

A small number of workers from the Punjab region in Northwest India constituted the first large group of Indians to immigrate to the United States in the first two decades of the twentieth century. They mostly went to California to work on the railroads, in lumber mills, and on farms. A large number of these Punjabis settled in Yuba City and Marysville near Sacramento, and the Imperial Valley at the Mexico border. Anti-Asian laws restricted further immigration from 1917 to 1946, allowing only students, scholars, religious ministers, and merchants. Indians trickled into the country after World War II, often as students.[42] Only 40,796 Indians migrated to the United States between 1820 and 1970. For this reason, Indian restaurants were rare in the United States before the 1970s, limited to a handful in big cities like New York, Chicago, and San Francisco.

The racist and restrictive laws were fully repealed in 1965, opening the door to South Asian migrants. By 2000, about 1.6 million people of Indian origin lived in the United States as well as over 200,000 people hailing from Pakistan, Bangladesh, and Sri Lanka. By 2010 about 2.7 million Indian Americans lived in the United States.[43] Many clustered in the urban centers of New York/New Jersey, Chicago, Los Angeles, Dallas, Houston, and San Francisco/San Jose.[44] A number of these Indian, Pakistani, and Bangladeshi migrants opened restaurants in the United States, serving riffs on their home cuisine after the 1960s. But because this cuisine was new to most Americans, they needed to explain it. This process was one of translation, of making a foreign culture inviting, understandable, and familiar to a new audience.

I examine here the strategies used by restaurant owners and food writers to explain the intricacies of Indian cuisine to Americans in one region of extraordinary diversity, the Bay Area. By contrasting the small number of Indian restaurants found in San Francisco during the 1950s to the wide range of Indian restaurants found in all parts of the Bay Area in the 1990s, one can see the changing nature of Indian cuisine in America and the changing techniques to make that cuisine understandable to the wider public.

ONTO AND INTO THE TANDOOR

During the 1960s, immigrants like Sarwan Gill became more common in some American cities. At the same time, some of the negative images of India softened for many American consumers, for the popularity of everything Eastern in some social circles expanded the broader public's understanding of some aspects of Indian culture. Ironically, British musicians helped change perceptions of Indians from offensive colonial subjects to possessors of a long, glorious culture. British rock groups such as the Rolling Stones and the Beatles introduced "Raga Rock," music tinged with sitars and Indian classical melodies to the American airwaves.[45] Meanwhile, in the United States, aging beatniks and young hippies adopted Zen meditation, yoga, and associated foods such as tofu and brown rice.[46]

Though some Americans newly subscribed to vegetarianism during the 1960s and 1970s, most still craved meat, and the tandoor oven that Sarwan Gill and others employed in their Indian restaurant kitchens suited their urges. The addition of tandoor specialties was a reflection of a bigger change in Indian restaurant cuisine in India and America. Food in India had changed after 1947 as a result of the upheavals of independence. Then, when India was partitioned to create Pakistan, millions fled across new borders to choose sides. The Punjab was particularly affected, as it straddled both countries after partition.

Partition produced terrible violence and discord, but it also gave rise to new food cultures. One Punjabi, Kundan Lal Gujral, moved from Peshawar to Delhi during partition, bringing a tandoor oven with him. Gujral had learned to cook meats in the tandoor, a dugout clay oven, when working at a stall in Peshawar. He opened Moti Mahal restaurant in Delhi in 1947, and it soon became a sensation for its tandoor meats and breads, butter chicken, and dal makhani. He built an elevated tandoor oven for his restaurant, mitigating the back-breaking labor for his cooks. Lal was "portly, florid, somewhat dainty in manner and careful in dress, and possessed of splendid moustaches." He was known to list "the names of ministers and heads of state who regularly arrived in his restaurant's quite unwholesome purlieus."[47]

Gujral may or may not have invented butter chicken, but he certainly helped popularize it.[48] Thought to be the precursor to chicken tikka, Gujral made butter chicken by marinating chicken pieces in yogurt, ground coriander seeds, and black and red peppers.[49] He cooked it in the tandoor, which runs at a very high heat—somewhere between 700 and 900 degrees Fahrenheit.[50] He repurposed leftover tandoori pieces as butter chicken to which he added a creamy sauce of butter, cream, tomatoes, and spices. His dal makhani used the same sauce with black lentils.[51]

Before partition, most of Delhi's residents had not tasted these dishes. The cookbook author Madhur Jaffrey, who lived in the city at the time, called Gujral's creations "food with a new attitude."[52] Gujral's business was helped along by the fact that Prime Ministers Jawarhalal Nehru and Indira Gandhi frequently contracted Moti Mahal for official dinners.[53]

Tandoor foods became the centerpiece of Indian cuisine abroad for many years to come. Though most *Indians* had not tried tandoor foods before the 1940s, the grilled meats and chicken tikka masala were to become *the* dishes most served in Indian restaurants outside India.[54] By 1997 a Gallup poll declared curry the favorite food of Britons, and chicken tikka masala was the most popular "curry" type.[55] The introduction of tandoor dishes and chicken tikka masala was thought responsible for a renaissance in British food beginning in the 1990s. One *New York Times* reporter commented that Indian food had saved Britons from the "bland boiled nursery yuck that generations . . . had little choice but to swill."[56]

After seeing Gujral's success, many fellow Punjabis followed suit and opened restaurants in Delhi and beyond with tandoori specialties and dishes from the Mughal court. This changed the nature of Indian cuisine in America, for it slowly lost its British overtures and instead became associated with Mughal traditions, and later, the vegetarian food movement. This change meant different modes of translation for American audiences. Whereas through the 1960s, Indian restaurants in America used the language of British imperialism to help Americans understand Indian food, that currency was no longer valid by the 1970s, for the British had been long gone by then. Furthermore, the Indians who came to the United States and opened restaurants no longer needed to reference their British past. They instead harkened to a grand Indian empire, the Mughal one, for translatable foods. If the Indo-British version of Indian food had created a certain sameness of cuisine, with curry after curry varied only by the meat within, the Mughal version was simply sameness of another sort. Those menus had to reference the familiar as well, so they kept the curries of the previous restaurants but added grilled meats and bread from the tandoor. Even by the 1990s, when some restaurants began to stray from the tandoori and curry formula, one *San Francisco Chronicle* article asked why the region's Indian restaurants served formula food of little distinction. It concluded that most non-Indian customers desired the "standardized" and familiar form of "tandoor, tandoor, tandoor," making it "risky" to offer other types of Indian cuisine.[57] It did not help that in many restaurants, the uninitiated "got little help from most waiters in deciphering the bill of fare," so introducing new foods would have been a lost cause for those establishments.[58]

Even as many restaurants seemed to "cook from a central kitchen," Indian restaurants became more common all over the United States, partly because of globalization. Indian immigrants came in great numbers to the United States, but they did not present the old image of India as a poverty-addled nation. This was in part because India itself was changing—the Indian middle class began to grow, and the nation was no longer young.[59] In the United States, immigrants from India were much richer and better educated than those from most other nations, and median income for Indian households was 62 percent higher than that of the general population.[60] Many initially went to the United States on special visas to work in the electronics and medical industries or to complete graduate or professional degrees. Those immigrants also created vibrant business connections between the United States and India—ones that went beyond the old First World–Third World construct. Instead, professionals in each nation connected on business prospects.[61]

One of those connections came in the form of restaurants. In the 1980s and 1990s, Indian corporations opened restaurants in the United States, some with several branches in India, Britain, or Canada. Some of these chains, such as Gaylord's, served tandoori fare, and in some branches they toned down the spices resulting in many dishes tasting the same.[62] Gaylord's had begun in India in 1946 and independently owned versions opened in Chicago, New York, and Washington, D.C., during the 1950s and 1960s.[63] In the 1970s the New York iteration even employed a chef who had previously cooked at Delhi's Moti Mahal.[64] Kishore Kripalani opened his first Gaylord India Restaurant in San Francisco in 1976, and by

2007, he had seven locations, including five in California.[65] Chains like Gaylord's were also sustained in part because Indian migration was accelerating after the 1960s.

Immigration from India also slowly included many more immigrants from the southern regions where tandoor foods were not commonplace, causing many Indian restaurants in America to take on a new cast. These immigrants were accustomed to more vegetable and lentil dishes and a profusion of breads made from chickpea and fermented rice flour, as served in the stalls, restaurants, and homes in the southern states of Tamil Nadu, Karnataka, and Kerala.[66] In many restaurants, however, these dishes were still served alongside the standby trifecta of chicken curry, chicken tikka, and tandoori chicken. They served the string of meat curries and tandoor items together with South Indian and vegetarian dishes so that both Indians and non-Indians could find something on the menu. In 1989, the two Indian restaurants listed in one guidebook illuminated this shift. The first, Sabina Indian Cuisine, served precisely the curries and kebobs that had been offered in Indian restaurants ever since India House and Gaylord's installed tandoor ovens.[67] The largest section of the Sabina menu was "Tandoori specialties." Like many Indian restaurants, it made its mark with a lunch buffet, attracting office workers in Oakland's downtown.[68]

A Berkeley restaurant, Sujatha's, instead gave diners both tandoor meats and "Madras" specials, signaling a shift in the cuisine as represented in the United States. The guide said the restaurant's specialties were as "varied as India," with an emphasis on Bombay in the North and Madras in the South.[69] At about the same time that Sujatha's served a combination of Indian regional fare, Vik's Chaat House was founded as a spot to serve "street" food from a wide range of Indian regions. It soon became one of the most popular inexpensive restaurants in Berkeley.[70] The owner's son said they served a variety of non-tandoor specialties because Indians "don't crave naan or tandoori chicken. [They] want to eat the zippy, zesty food."[71] Just over a decade later, Vik's was still thriving, and the number of South Indian restaurants had increased, partly to serve Indian immigrants flocking to work in Silicon Valley.[72] Branches of the successful Woodlands restaurant chain from India had opened in the United States by then, often in areas where large numbers of Indian immigrants lived. So too had iterations of the large South Indian chains, Udupi and Saravana Bhavan, with locations in California, Georgia, New York, New Jersey, Florida, and Texas.[73] More non-Indians had become acquainted with the food, but restaurant reviews still required fairly detailed explanations of the intricacies of the vegetarian cuisine. Utthapams, made of fermented rice flour, were "thick, puffy pancakes topped like pizzas," in one review of Woodlands.[74]

While Indian immigrants craved "zippy" and "zesty" food, so too did the wider American public. In order to explain the new Indian foods for an American audience, many menus and restaurant reviews referenced other cuisines, as in the description of utthapams as hybrid pancake/pizzas. One restaurant in Sausalito, just north of San Francisco, offered "Dungeness crab Punjabi enchiladas" and "curried tender chicken breast Punjabi tostadas." It later started a Punjabi burrito takeout service in a nearby town, capitalizing on the popularity of burritos in the Bay Area, but also seeking to distinguish its offerings from competitors.[75] This hybrid actually had a long legacy. During the first two decades of the twentieth century, when Punjabi men migrated to the United States as laborers, they were unable to marry white women under California state law. Many married Mexican women, introducing a hybrid Mexican-Indian cuisine to the region. Some restaurants in the farming valleys of California during this era served chicken curry and rotis alongside enchiladas.[76]

Though the Punjabi enchilada was not common in American restaurants, the general combination of elements from a number of "spicy" or "hot" cuisines was. Mexican food had been widely available for decades in the United States, but its popularity surged in the 1980s and 1990s. The heat and spice factors in Mexican and other cuisines became attractions rather than put-offs over these decades, as more and more Americans sought these foods. And because Mexican food was so widely eaten, other ethnic cuisines that featured similarly spicy or hot dishes could reference that cuisine as a way to explain their dishes, or better yet, attract those who craved these elements. As early as 1979, the large Mexican fast food chain, Del Taco, created a marketing campaign titled "Hot stuff" to introduce itself to Dallas, Houston, and Atlanta residents, where it was building new stores. The theme was chosen because spicy or hot food was a "positive expectation" that consumers had when they thought about Mexican food, according to the National Restaurant Association.[77] One review of an Indian restaurant in the Bay Area advised readers, "If you like spicy food, but are tired of the same Mexican and Szechuan restaurants, then head for Union City for some Indian heat at a small restaurant called Ganesh."[78] By 2000, the San Francisco telephone directory listed 16 Indian restaurants as opposed to the 3 or 4 it had in the 1960s. The wider Bay Area had many more; 133 Indian restaurants showed up on an online directory in 2007.[79]

The new strategies for translation could be seen even in travel advice for London, the leading site for Indian restaurant cuisine. In 2007, an article in the *New York Times* travel section explained an appetizer of papadum with tamarind, lime, and tomato chutneys at one London establishment as "the Indian restaurant's answer to chips and salsa." A description of another restaurant's concept used two other cuisines to explain it, saying, "all dishes are small, something like Indian tapas—though the gorgeous presentation is more reminiscent of sushi." That three cuisines, Tex-Mex, Spanish, and Japanese, were referenced to explain another, Anglo-Indian, was indicative of the way that translation had changed.[80] Readers of the *Times* were sufficiently familiar with these other cuisines that they could be used to describe variations on Indian fare. Though Indian restaurants had multiplied in the past couple decades, far more Mexican, Chinese, or even sushi restaurants existed in the United States, so Americans' expanding cultural knowledge of those and other Asian and Latin American foods could be used to explain ever-more different cuisines.

Most Americans still required a translation device for Komala Vilas in Silicon Valley. Serving vegetarian food from Kerala, the state on the southwestern coast of India, Komala Vilas offered neither Mughal foods nor the taste of old Britain, and it had no bar or cocktail list. One food blog explained the various nuances of eating at the restaurant, which served food on banana leaves and featured no menu. Instead waiters served courses continuously from stainless steel pots and trays as is customary during some celebrations in Kerala. The article used two references to Chinese cuisine to explain the eating experience at the restaurant. One explained the continuous service by the waiters, noting, "as with dim sum and hotel brunch buffets, it's all about the pacing."[81] Later, it explained how forks were hard to come by in this restaurant, for most everyone was eating with their hands, "At Komala Vilas, you'll learn to get in touch with your food. Just as you would use chopsticks at a Chinese banquet, do follow your fellow diners at a South Indian restaurant," advising that the right hand was proper.[82] Just as some American diners were not comfortable with chopsticks, so too many were not comfortable eating with their hands. A *San Francisco Chronicle* review praised the restaurant's food, but also cautioned, "some may find the practice of eating without utensils unappealing."[83] Diners' familiarity with aspects of Chinese cuisine was used to explain the more exotic fare of South Indian.

As demonstrated by this advice, more things Indian may have slowly become familiar to more Americans, but Indian cuisine was by no means an everyday currency, even by the middle of the 1990s. In one comprehensive 1999 survey about ethnic cuisines in America, the National Restaurant Association found that more than 97 percent of respondents were "aware" of Chinese, Mexican, and Italian cuisines.[84] In contrast, only 74 percent were aware of Indian cuisine, one of the lower groups of cuisines in the survey. The survey also found that only 33 percent had tried Indian cuisine, and 25 percent ate it often or occasionally, with those consumers most likely to eat it having high incomes and education, and most likely to have tried it at a restaurant.[85] This was more than a 1983 survey, which found that only 21 percent had tried Indian food.[86] So in the span of sixteen years, the number trying Indian food had increased by around 57 percent, probably because the number of Indian immigrants coming to the United States had expanded too.

The progression of Indian cuisine in America from the 1960s to the present, then, demonstrates how Americans have found new ways to understand the incredible diversity brought on by globalization. Whereas the very small number of Indian restaurants in the United States in the 1960s had to reference British or Mughal Empires of the past to allay the fears of hesitant American diners, restaurants in the 1990s could instead use elements of the new diversity to explain the still unfamiliar Indian cuisine. To understand the wide range of new food choices, Americans used their developing familiarity with a broad range of non-European cuisines to explore still other cuisines. Spicy Mexican food became a way to understand spicy Indian. Eating styles that had just become familiar to Americans, such as dim sum and tapas, were used to describe the then exotic nature of South India's cuisine. Through food, Americans used their new experiences with globalization to explain the incredible choices brought on by that globalization. But even as Indian cuisine diversified, it still had a homogenized tinge, for curries and tandoor meats still dominated Indian restaurant fare at the beginning of the twenty-first century.

7

Chinese Food from Chinatown
to the Suburbs

Like many immigrants, Grace Zia Chu softened her homesickness by cooking. She first sought ways to replicate foods from her Chinese homeland as a student at Wellesley College in the 1920s. She returned to China after graduating, but by the 1940s called Washington, D.C., home when her husband was stationed at the Chinese Embassy. There she taught diplomats' wives how to cook Chinese dishes, but only as a hobby. It wasn't until 1964 that she embarked on a career teaching Chinese cooking full-time, mostly from her new home base in New York City.[1] By one account she taught over three thousand students over the years. In the process she signed multiple partnerships with American food companies.[2] During the 1960s she promoted Planter's Peanut Oil, American Gas Association stoves, and her own line of teas.[3] She packaged her first cookbook, *The Pleasures of Chinese Cooking* (1962), with a wok sold by a New York company.[4]

Chu taught Chinese cooking with a full appreciation that American students probably had little knowledge about the cuisine. She tried to convey the complexity and nuance of Chinese cooking without scaring off fresh-faced American cooks. Her lessons included an abbreviated history of Chinese cuisine, a description of basic ingredients, and practice of essential techniques. Reviews of both *The Pleasures of Chinese Cooking* and her 1975 volume, *Madame Chu's Chinese Cooking School* noted the progression of techniques from beginner to advanced in the books. One explained, "The result is an almost foolproof book, with complete descriptions of ingredients, utensils, and basic cooking methods, along with menus and eating customs."[5]

She mirrored this process in her cooking demonstrations too. The American Gas Association produced a 1963 film of Chu to promote gas stoves. In the film,

Chu teaches Chinese cooking techniques and a few recipes, regularly plugging the gas stoves. Thousands of people viewed the film at showings organized by the association's local chapters. The Omaha division claimed to have had forty-seven screenings with over 1,500 attendees during 1963. By early 1964, the Brooklyn office had screened it ninety-four times for 8,222 people. The film was even shown at an exhibit hall at the 1964 World's Fair in Queens.[6] Chu began by demonstrating how to serve Chinese meals and how to hold chopsticks. Later she counseled the proper Chinese methods for cooking rice and preparing/serving tea. Then she demonstrated recipes for barbequed spare ribs, fried rice, and lobster Cantonese. Not surprisingly, she advised viewers that Chinese food is best suited to gas stoves.[7]

As she promoted her book, Chu had to navigate the many wants of consumers. Her 1964 Planter's Oil advertisement in women's magazines offered a recipe for sweet and sour pineapple chicken. Her original recipe was for pineapple pork, with sherry listed as an ingredient. But Chu was asked to switch chicken for pork and drop the sherry because the advertising agency for Planter's advised that she could then better cater to the Jewish and teetotaler markets.[8]

Just as Chu taught New Yorkers how to cook Chinese, restaurateur Cecilia Chiang campaigned to have San Franciscans eat something better than egg foo yong or chop suey. Despite the city's long history as a stop for Chinese immigrants, those dishes still dominated its restaurant scene in the 1960s. Regal in her bearing, Chiang introduced many San Franciscans to northern Chinese cuisine at her restaurant, the Mandarin, in 1961.[9] Disappointed at first by slow business, she persuaded another restaurateur to get Herb Caen, the "towering icon" of San Francisco journalism, to visit.[10] He and Chiang hit it off and he wrote about the Mandarin in his *San Francisco Chronicle* column. She fielded over a hundred phone calls the next day. Chiang, ever the smart businesswoman, hired an important San Francisco public relations firm to plug the place.[11] Soon her cramped Polk Street restaurant was always full.

All along, Chiang broke barriers. Chiang was one of few female restaurateurs operating a fancy restaurant serving non-Western cuisine. In 1968 she moved the Mandarin to a prime location in Ghirardelli Square—the tourist-heavy locale on the bay.[12] That was not without a fight. Her initial attempt to lease a space there was refused by the landlord because he argued that Chinese restaurants were filthy rat- and cockroach-infested traps. He relented only after seeing her many influential contacts.[13]

Over the years, the Mandarin attracted socialites, politicians, and food scions, including Alice Waters and Ruth Reichl. Actor Danny Kaye was a regular customer, both of the restaurant and her cooking classes. The Kennedys and the Bushes dined there too. In the 1960s and 1970s, San Francisco newspapers ran rave reviews and featured Chiang regularly in gossip columns. Regulars turned out for the squab wrapped in lettuce, smoked tea duck, beggar's chicken, and Mongolian lamb. The posh surroundings and décor also set it apart from most Chinese restaurants in the city.[14] She expanded to Los Angeles with a second outpost of the Mandarin, in Beverly Hills (opened in 1975), and the "small, unpretentious Mandarette," in West Hollywood (opened in 1985).[15] Chiang sold the San Francisco Mandarin in 1991, but did not fully retire, remaining an advisor to other restaurant ventures.[16]

The Mandarette, run by Chiang's son Philip, eventually inspired his restaurant chain, P.F. Chang's.[17] At the Mandarette he served "simple" food akin to what he ate with employees in the kitchen of the Mandarin, "sort of like home cooking." At first, he used organ meats to flavor a number of dishes, but found quickly that "Americans didn't understand that kind of food" and shifted the menu to make it more "accessible" over time.[18]

P.F. Chang's eventually became the largest full-service Chinese restaurant chain in the United States, with over two hundred locations.[19] Founded by Philip Chiang and Paul Fleming in 1993 (P.F. for Fleming and Chang for Chiang), the restaurant sought "cleaner" and "fresher" Chinese dishes served in a restaurant with great décor and "American-style" service (as desired by Fleming).[20]

Paul Fleming wanted to standardize and franchise Chinese food on a wide scale. He met Philip Chiang at the Mandarette.[21] Impressed by the simple, tasty dishes there, he proposed a partnership based in Scottsdale, Arizona. Fleming had run Ruth's Chris Steakhouses in California and was familiar with what would appeal to a broad American audience. They deliberately located most P.F. Chang's near suburban shopping malls. Fleming cut the oil from some dishes, focused on those that were familiar to Americans, and insisted on an extensive wine list and a full dessert menu. As with many Chinese restaurants in the United States, the meat proportions were upped to suit American tastes. A few dishes from Chiang's past remained, including chicken lettuce wraps, originally created by his mother at the Mandarin.[22]

Less than a year after opening, the first outpost in Scottsdale was the "the talk of the town."[23] Much like his mother, Philip Chiang had hit on a concept that was ready for adoption. Cecilia Chiang had introduced regional Chinese food to many Americans at the chic Mandarin in San Francisco and Beverly Hills, and her son Philip brought a new homogenized Chinese cuisine served alongside swank décor in the suburbs. The Mandarin at Ghirardelli Square was known for its beautiful setting—one walked upstairs to be awed by a grand dining room filled with Chinese decorations. Likewise, P.F. Chang's modern décor was "strikingly beautiful," creating a "glamorous ambience."[24] Massive stone warhorse statues sat outside its restaurants. Inside, the "sleek" adornments "avoided Chinese clichés" (think dragons and pagodas), instead opting for modern flourishes.[25]

It was one of many full-service chains that grew around this time. A review said it had "more in common with Olive Garden or Outback Steakhouse than your local Chinese takeout."[26] While Chinese takeout places had long existed all over the

United States, they offered fairly standard fare. The new standard began to change on the heels of cooking teachers like Chu and restaurateurs like the Chiangs.

Together, the Mandarin and P.F. Chang's embody the changes seen in Chinese food in the United States since the 1960s—diversification of the cuisine at the same time that it was sold by large chains in a homogenized version. Only in the last few decades has Chinese food in America featured the incredible diversity of the cuisine found in China. This has happened for a number of reasons. One is that restaurateurs such as Cecilia Chiang introduced non-Cantonese foods to Americans. A second reason lies in the massive immigration from China, Hong Kong, and Taiwan since 1965. Chinese immigrants have come from all over China instead of the narrow region of Guanghzou. By 2010, about 3.3 million Chinese lived in the United States—the largest group of Asians in the nation.[27] Third, the new Chinese immigrants often had means. They are among the wealthiest immigrant groups in the United States, meaning many could demand the cuisine they were accustomed to in their homelands.[28] Their wealth also meant they could travel back and forth between Asia and the United States. Last, Chinese-Americans increasingly lived in the suburbs. Indeed, the biggest changes in Chinese food came in the suburbs, not in the Chinatowns of old.

The new cosmopolitan suburbs where these immigrants settled were a living, breathing paradox. Over time, more immigrants moved to the suburbs than to the central cities. McDonald's and other fast-food spots expanded in those suburbs, but they were joined by Panda Express, bubble tea shops, and dim sum emporiums. About 62 percent of Asian Americans resided in the suburbs in 2010, the largest of any racial minority group.[29] Americans could find some of the best and most cutting-edge food in these new cosmopolitan suburbs. This was partly a result of mass immigration. The expansion of suburbs was not just an American phenomenon—this happened all over the world. By the start of the new millennium, builders put up office parks and tract homes surrounding not just the suburbs of Atlanta and Dallas, but also the outer rings of Delhi and Shanghai.

THE NEW DIVERSE SUBURBS

We tend to associate the suburbs with sameness—a cookie-cutter mentality that developed in the 1950s. To a degree, that vision holds true. You can travel from the suburbs of Los Angeles to those around Charlotte and imagine that you did not actually cross the country. The mass production techniques that took hold after World War II contribute to this feeling. These techniques were embedded in housing, fast food, hotels and motels, and shopping malls.[30]

Americans have both loved and hated the cast of this suburban life. They moved in droves to the suburbs after World War II, and have continued ever since. The 1970 census was the first in which more Americans lived in suburbs than central cities. By 2000, about 50 percent of Americans lived in those suburbs while only about 30 percent resided in central cities.[31] Though Americans moved to suburbs in great numbers, their pallor-inducing sameness also prompted cultural critiques. As early as the 1920s, Lewis Mumford criticized suburban Brooklyn by saying that it was a "no-man's land which was neither town nor country," but instead a "twilight zone of an essentially suburban civilization."[32] In the early 1960s, Malvina Reynolds penned the song, "Little Boxes" about the houses made of "ticky-tacky," occupied by people who "all look just the same." Her song was inspired by the rows and rows of identical houses on the hills of Daly City, just south of San Francisco.[33] Four decades later, the *Weeds* television series chronicled a suburban housewife who lived in a tract development. Each week, the series' opening credits showed identical figures leaving their identical homes in identical SUV's to purchase identical heat-sleeve-encased coffees on the way to what were presumably identical jobs; fittingly, "Little Boxes" played behind the montage.[34] Although the occupants of American suburbs still had some common consumption habits, their population had diversified to a great degree—something not evident in the trailer for *Weeds*.[35]

Since the 1970s, the suburbs had become more diverse, in part because immigrants moved to them in much larger numbers. Cities still held the majority of the nonwhite population by 2010. However, the nonwhite population of suburbs increased from nineteen to thirty-six million between the 1990 and 2010 census—a much faster rate than the growth of the nonwhite population in cities. Immigration was a major factor in this change. Whereas the majority of immigrants lived in cities at the 1970s census, by 2005, five million more foreign-born resided in suburbs than cities. Many of the largest urban areas featured a number of "melting pot suburbs." In certain parts of the United States—especially Los Angeles and San Francisco—some suburbs had majority Asian populations.[36]

This was a stunning shift from the deliberately lily-white suburbs of the 1940s and 1950s. Save the long-standing Chinese take-out places, Asian foods had been hard to find then in the suburbs partly because Asian Americans were deliberately excluded from a good number of them. Many suburbs (and city neighborhoods, for that matter) used restrictive covenants to bar peoples of Japanese, Filipino, Chinese, and Indian descent. Some blandly referred to foreigners of any sort in their mortgage agreements, while others specified "Malay" or "Chinaman" as groups prohibited from purchasing homes in various suburbs. The Westlake area in Daly City (the suburb of "Little Boxes") mandated that homeowners sign a covenant prohibiting them from selling, renting, or living with anyone "not of the white or Caucasian race." The only exception was for live-in servants. A homeowner who violated this clause had to pay $2,000 to each of his eight closest neighbors for the assumed damage it would do to their property values.[37] Residents and realtors enforced these covenants; the California Real Estate Association actively barred nonwhite peoples from a number of suburbs, whether outside of Los Angeles, San Francisco, Oakland, or San Diego. Though the US Supreme Court officially declared racial covenants illegal in *Shelly v. Kraemer* in 1948, most suburbs enforced them for a couple decades longer. The Fair Housing Act of 1968 finally helped fritter them away.[38]

CHINESE FOOD IN AMERICA, 1849–1960s

Chinese food has been eaten widely in the United States since the early 1900s. Before examining its move to the suburbs, one must see its popularization from the gold mines and Chinatown outward. After several decades in which anti-Chinese sentiment mostly meant Americans shunned Chinese food, Chinese restaurateurs came to sell more food to non-Chinese after the turn of the century.[39] Chinese restaurants had begun sprouting in many cities with sizeable Chinese populations, such as San Francisco, Los Angeles, and New York. San Francisco's Chinatown became a major tourist site only after the 1906 earthquake; the disaster provided an unexpected opportunity for local business leaders to clean up its image. While non-Chinese had come to pre-earthquake Chinatown, a good number were drunken, brawling men who participated in the opium trade, brothels, and gang activity that flourished there. After the earthquake, Chinese American business owners deliberately changed Chinatown's image and attracted the business of respectable tourists who wanted a taste of Chinese culture, including food.[40] By the 1930s anti-Chinese sentiment in the United States slowly began to subside. Pearl S. Buck's 1931 novel *The Good Earth* helped this along, selling over two million copies. When it was turned into a movie in 1937, another 23 million Americans saw her positive depiction of the Chinese people. World War II made China and the United States allies, spurring more positive sentiment for the Chinese.[41]

By the 1940s and 1950s, supermarkets in many parts of the United States stocked Chinese or Oriental food sections and Chinatowns had become flourishing tourist spots. The most famous was San Francisco's.[42] A San Francisco Visitor's Bureau pamphlet was devoted to the "unusual fare that awaits you," including the food. If you wanted to find the unusual fare, however, you had to look hard—the pamphlet's cover featured a crude drawing of a Chinatown street with a marquee listing "CHOP SUEY" in front of one shop.[43] By then, even if Americans mostly ate chop suey and chow mein, both Americanized versions of Chinese food, they were eating a lot of it. Around six thousand Chinese restaurants dotted the country in 1960, with the largest number concentrated in California and New York, but also hundreds from city to town in between.[44]

To be certain, some were interested in something other than chop suey. Buwei Yang Chao replaced chop suey with "stir-fry" in her 1945 cookbook *How to Cook and Eat Chinese*. In later editions of the cookbook she added recipes for more non-Cantonese dishes, including Peking and Szechuan duck. She was both prefiguring and reflecting the change in the way Chinese food was conceived in the United States after the 1960s.[45]

CHINESE FOOD'S SECOND COMING IN AMERICA

If chop suey was the lingua franca of Chinese food in 1960, that began to change by the 1970s—to be replaced by stir-fry, pot-sticker, and kung pao. Joyce Chen, who some called the "Chinese Julia Child," first appeared in a PBS cooking show in 1968, continuing her success at her Cambridge, Massachusetts, restaurant.[46] Chen used authenticity as a selling point in her "highly influential cooking conglomerate" consisting of her cookbooks, television show, mail-order foods, and restaurant.[47] Around the same time, *New York Times* food editor Craig Claiborne published *The Chinese Cookbook* with Virginia Lee, a New York Chinese cooking instructor, with great success.[48] These cookbook authors complemented the efforts of restaurateurs like Cecilia Chiang in San Francisco and television stars such as Martin Yan, whose first show, "Yan Can Cook," ran on PBS in 1978. He could be found on television screens and cookbook dust jackets for thirty years after.[49] By 1980 the number of Chinese restaurants in the United States had grown to 7,796, or 29 percent of all those ethnic and regional restaurants listed in telephone directories. That year, another 412 were listed as "Polynesian Chinese," reflecting the popularity of the Trader Vic's restaurants and associated tiki lounge phenomenon that Victor Bergeron first popularized in the Bay Area.[50] By 1996, one study found around twenty thousand Chinese restaurants in the United States.[51]

Chinese food in grocery stores also changed over time. Although the stores had long carried canned, boxed, and frozen Chinese food, some consumers, including the new immigrants from China, sought ingredients for the diverse range of Chinese foods. One reason was the way food was prepared in China. Without refrigeration in many areas, eating local foods was a necessity. Many Chinese families bought fresh produce, fish, or meat once or twice a day, rather than two or three times a week like Americans. This privileged fresh foods, brought from nearby farms. Changes in global trade brought the two mentalities together, as Chinese produce became available in American supermarkets. Much was grown abroad— in Mexico or even in Asia, and American farms took up the business over time— especially to supply the California market.[52] The *San Jose Mercury News* explained that by the early 1990s in the Bay Area, "even the neighborhood Safeway carries a wide range of vegetables that, sadly, Archie Bunker and the family of Beaver Cleaver would have never found on their plates."[53] This was because the "agricultural, culinary, and business communities have conspired to fill markets with dozens of vegetable varieties once common only to Asian countries."[54] This "metamorphosis" was responsible for "busting the homogeneity of produce in the United States."[55]

REGIONAL CHINESE FOODS IN AMERICA

Chinese food in the United States was diversifying too, reflecting the full range of foods in China. The early immigrants from China mostly came from Canton, so the American version of Chinese food was an improvisation on Cantonese dishes for the American palate.[56] China's foods are much more diverse though—the country can be divided into about four or five major culinary regions, each having their peculiarities of geography and culture. One observer counted four regions, with the northern cuisine centered in Beijing, the eastern centered in Shanghai and the lower Yangtze, the western associated with Sichuan province, and the southern from Canton or Guangdong.[57] Other observers referred to the traditional divisions many Chinese speak of in their cuisines, in which there are at least five principal or "great" ones.[58] They are the Szechwan, Canton, Fukien, Shantung, and Hunan traditions, which "are supposedly characterized by flavors: Szechwan or Hunan-Szechwan food is hot with chilies; Cantonese runs to sweet and sweet-sour dishes; Fukien is most distinctively characterized by its soups; Shantung is the home of sea foods, garlic, and the most venerable skills; Hunan is famous for sweet-sour freshwater fish."[59] Of course, each area has subspecialties and nuances, and one could list additional types—including, for example, the foods of the western region near Kyrgyzstan. Even rice, associated indelibly with Chinese food in America, is the staple only in the South. In the North, wheat and millet are the base grains.[60] All of these foods were called, very simply, "Chinese" by most Americans until about the 1960s. But as one commentator noted, this is akin to calling French, Italian or Hungarian cuisines all "European."[61]

Like Cecilia Chiang in San Francisco during the 1960s, restaurateurs in other cities began offering different regional specialties in the 1960s. Hunan cuisine became known in New York and San Francisco in the 1970s, partly due to the popularity of a signature dish, General Tso's chicken, which was supposed to be derived from a Hunan recipe. Henry Chung in San Francisco and Peng Chang-kuei in New York each operated Hunan restaurants in the 1970s that garnered acclaim nationwide. In a bit, or fit, of hyperbole, the New Yorker called Chung's the "best Chinese restaurant in the world." The menu featured a two-page explanation of the Hunan region's history and food and lengthy descriptions for each dish.[62] One review explained, "Overall, the orchestration of aromas and flavors produced in Hunanese dishes is at first strange, but to me at least, instantly appealing."[63]

Meanwhile, New York magazine restaurant critic Gael Greene regularly surveyed the new Chinese food scene erupting in New York. Going to restaurants that served regional Chinese food, she was wowed by the "smoke of Szechuan pepper curling out of our ears. In the clarity of a cayenne revelation, one might have sensed New York was ripe for the flowering of a Hunan kitchen." Hunam restaurant was "celestial," and Shun Lee Palace experienced a "glorious renaissance" in the early 1970s.[64]

This renaissance was partly due to President Richard Nixon's trip to China in 1972. American audiences were eager for news of the summit, but much of the real negotiations were closed to the public. That meant reporters padded their note-books with stories about the sumptuous banquets, advising the public that chow mein and chop suey indeed were not served there. Enthusiastic Americans, seeing the banquet menu (which was a much-abbreviated version of what was actually served so the hosts didn't appear to be dirty capitalists), began asking for similar banquets at Chinese restaurants, which were all too happy to comply. Restaurants that before could not sell Peking Duck had customers clamoring for it after Nixon's visit.[65] Americans were then becoming familiar with the many Chinese regions in the 1970s and 1980s. A typical article of the time proclaimed the enjoyment to be had by eating at a Chinese restaurant that offered non-Cantonese foods and, even better, could cook the foods of many regions in China. Joseph Izzo Jr. wrote for the *San Jose Mercury News* in the 1980s, and in a number of articles he described the vanguard of Chinese restaurants. In a typical review, he said, "Don't expect typical Chinese food at Foo Loo Soo. The menu draws from not one province but nearly all the provinces representing culinary Mainland China. The styles are unlimited, featuring dishes from Szechwan, Junan, Peking, Mandarin, Taiwan, and Canton. The chef creates gourmet interest by utilizing spices uncommon to the American-ized understanding of Chinese food. Don't be surprised if you taste anise or the sweet lacing of white wine or the pickled tartness of mustard greens."[66] In another article he emphasized that Chinese food was still generally stuck in a homogenized mode at Bay Area restaurants, but that there was an "uncommon gourmet quality to the fare that sets Ging Jee/Yet Wah apart from other Chinese establishments."[67] This local chain of Chinese restaurants had expanded from its origins in 1969 in San Francisco out to the suburbs of the Bay Area over the years, managing loca-tions that served tourists, Bay Area Chinese Americans, and everyone in-between.[68] By the 1980s, many Bay Area guidebooks distinguished the specific type of Chinese cuisine one would get at different Chinese restaurants, listing them under Hunan, Szechuan, Cantonese, and the like.[69] A survey two decades later found non-Cantonese dishes to be among those most frequently featured on Chinese restaurant menus.[70]

CHINESE FOOD IN THE SUBURBS

Many Chinese were able to move to the suburbs because of their relatively high income and education levels. From the 1960s forward, Chinese immigrants came to be seen by the wider American public as part of the "model minority." This ste-reotype was illuminated in a 1966 *New York Times* article about Japanese Ameri-cans, and by the 1980s it had encompassed all Asian Americans. During the 1980s, *Time* and *Newsweek* each ran cover stories about bright, successful Asian Americans in the United States.[71] The high proportion of Asian Americans at the nation's best universities helped sustain the stereotype. The halls of UC Berkeley, Harvard, and Cal Tech were filled with young Asian American students. Many had attended wealthy suburban high schools.[72] Some of the restaurants that sustained these wealthy Chinese Americans were grand, for they had the money to pay for it. This was one major change—high-priced Chinese food served in the suburbs to Chinese immigrants—a phenomenon that did not exist in the pre-1960s era. And whether or not the most expensive food was to be had in the suburbs, many argued that the most authentic was.

The convergence of two seemingly incompatible monikers—homogenized and authentic Chinese food—could be found in the 99 Ranches and strip malls of the suburbs. In the 1940s and 1950s, Chinese Americans had slowly moved in greater numbers to the outer boroughs and suburbs of major American cities.[73] Chinese restaurants followed. By 1973 a directory for the New York region listed more Chinese restaurants for Queens and Long Island than for Manhattan.[74] By the 1980s, more than egg rolls were served in the suburbs of San Francisco, Los Angeles, or New York. In Millbrae, just south of San Francisco, Alice Wong opened a Hong Kong-style restaurant in 1984, spawning two other branches and several copycats that all demonstrated "the growing market for high-quality Chinese cuisine" at the time.[75] Wong's Hong Kong Flower Lounge was a "spinoff of a well-known Hong Kong restaurant" and served "what some consider the best Cantonese food in this country."[76] Adjacent to San Francisco International Airport, Millbrae was convenient for travelers on layovers to and from Asia. The surrounding suburbs were home to many wealthy Chinese families, including those who crossed back and forth from Hong Kong.[77] The menu of another Hong Kong style restaurant in Millbrae prominently showed SFO on its map, advertised its other locations in Singapore and Kowloon, and listed expensive banquet dinners with shark's fin soup for wealthy diners.[78] By the 1980s and 1990s, significant numbers of first- and second-generation Asian Americans lived in the suburbs ringing Chicago, New York, Washington, Houston, Dallas, Los Angeles, San Francisco, and Seattle. Some food writers found great pleasure in searching for culinary delights in the outer reaches of these cities. John T. Edge, director of the Southern Foodways Alliance, found a kaleidoscope of ethnic food served in strip malls around Indianapolis.[79] Calvin Trillin reveled in finding new foods. He marveled at the early food websites such as Chowhound, which were obsessed with finding out-of-reach, out-of-the-ordinary ethnic food.[80] In the early 2000s, the *New York Times* regularly featured the San Gabriel suburbs east of Los Angeles as *the* place for Chinese food. R. W. Apple Jr., the longtime reporter and food savant for the *Times*, enthusiastically wrote about those suburbs in "An Asian Odyssey, Seconds from the Freeway," explaining, "The foods of Korea, Thailand and Vietnam, Shanghai, Taipei and Tokyo, pour from a thousand kitchens in astonishing abundance, from holes in the wall and coffee shops and strip-mall dining rooms in burgs with names like Gardena and Arcadia and Alhambra. Because most of the chefs, like most of the customers, are relatively recent arrivals from Asia, the dishes they serve retain the true tastes and the modest prices of their homelands."[81] The article's title evoked the notion that it was surprising to find the best and most authentic foods next to a suburban free-way. Another *New York Times* article asked why bad Chinese food prevailed around the country, concluding that the remedy lay in tapping into the recent arrivals from China who had settled in Queens and the San Gabriel Valley. Americans just had to be willing to venture to the outer boroughs and suburbs for the authentic foods.[82]

Though there had been initial resistance by longtime residents to the large flow of Asians and Hispanics to these suburbs, by the 1990s both groups composed a large proportion of the population there. San Gabriel's population was about a third ethnic Chinese by 2000, as was Monterey Park nearby.[83] The large San Gabriel Plaza mall fed, clothed, and entertained this population, replete with Asian department stores, restaurants, and supermarkets. One Asian American newspaper remarked "that a transplant from Taiwan or Hong Kong should have no reason to feel homesick" at the plaza.[84] The 99 Ranch supermarket anchoring the mall included a "Tung Lai Shun Islamic Cuisine" restaurant, featuring foods from the largely Islamic western provinces of China. Commenting on Tung Lai Shun and a similarly "authentic" Mexican restaurant in the area, a *Los Angeles Daily News* article noted, "We've gotten so used to versions of ethnic cooking that are in one way or another Americanized, that an encounter with the real thing can be a shock to the system."[85] The shock was the "real" food served in the form of lamb dumplings and sesame bread, all to be had in a strip mall. Of course, one could also order kung pao chicken and other northern or southern Chinese dishes, for the owners could not stray too far, even in a shopping mall that catered to Asian American customers.[86] Kung pao chicken, a dish originating in Szechuan cuisine, had once been novel, but was old hat in Chinese restaurants by the 1980s.[87]

The importance of suburban restaurants was further reflected in the "top" restaurant lists for some publications. *Goldsea*, an online Asian American newspaper, was rife with "top" lists, including those for restaurants in various cities. The Los Angeles and San Francisco suburbs dominated the lists for best dim sum. Seven of the eight San Francisco dim sum houses were suburban and the "most popular," located in Cupertino, "may have something to do with the location next to a Ranch 99 Market," but it was also distinguished by being "upscale."[88]

By this time the idea of nonwhite ethnic congregations in the suburbs were normalized—it was no longer thought unusual that Chinese and other Asian ethnic groups filled the San Gabriel or Silicon valleys. While the cities were still a testament to the white flight of the postwar era, with high black and low white

TABLE 5   2000 Population by Area of Residence, by Percentages

	Urban	Suburban	Rural
Immigrants	47	48	5
Native-born	28	51	21
Non-Hispanic White	22	53	22
Hispanic	48	44	8
Asian	45	51	4
Black	55	31	14

SOURCE: Michael Jones-Correa, "Reshaping the American Dream: Immigrants, Ethnic Minorities, and the Politics of the New Suburbs," in Kevin M. Kruse and Thomas J. Sugrue, eds., *The New Suburban History* (Chicago: University of Chicago Press, 2006), 184.

populations overall, the suburbs—especially in the Sunbelt—were being filled by Hispanics and Asian Americans in increasing numbers (see table 5).[89]

THE GROWTH OF CHINESE FAST-FOOD CHAINS

Set in contrast to these authentic Chinese food experiences were the new Chinese fast-food chains that emerged after the 1980s. Though the suburbs would emerge as a place to get variegated Chinese food, they also spawned a homogenized version. Hamburgers and pizza had been the two cornerstones of the fast food landscape after the 1950s—one a legacy of German immigration and the other of Italian. Both changed as various companies entered and left, but each became available anywhere and everywhere over time. After the 1960s, Mexican and Chinese food purveyors saw they could take some of the growing eat-out and take-out food markets with their own creations. They had to compete with the McDonald's model focusing on efficiency and mass production. McDonald's had also focused on suburban development for many years before opening urban restaurants in the 1960s and 1970s.[90] Many of these start-up chains went by the wayside for the same basic reasons that most other restaurants fail—low profit margins, poor food, or bad marketing. They ranged from the Jo Kwan chain opened first in Honolulu by a Hong Kong entrepreneur, to the Nankin Express chain based out of Minnesota. Jo Kwan modeled itself on McDonald's speed and efficiency, cooking with prepackaged ingredients processed at a central location.[91] Nankin Express automated extensively in its 1985 foray by reducing "the delicate art of Chinese cooking—or part of it, anyway—to four basic steps that can be performed easily in a quick-service setting."[92] This was accomplished by stir-frying meat or vegetables and adding eight to fourteen premeasured seasonings and sauces to the mix.[93] Both chains disappeared quickly.

Others were quick to rise and fall in the mid-1980s including Quik Wok, Charlie Chan's and Leann Chin's. Many of these failed because, as one restaurant industry analyst put it, they served "atrocious" food that was composed of "soggy, over-cooked rice and greasy egg rolls."[94] The Tai Pan chain that had begun in Cupertino, one of the Bay Area's suburban Chinese centers, sought to meet the "challenge" that "Chinese fast food presents," which was to "take the complex and time-consuming art of Chinese cooking and reduce it to a cost-efficient science."[95] The owner's solution was to do the "laborious cutting, slicing, and dicing" at a "central kitchen that will serve all the units."[96] His restaurants were merely responsible for heating and assembling the food, much like McDonald's. The key to getting the restaurants to succeed was taking out the distinctiveness, and hence, the inefficiencies, of food preparation, instead mechanizing and standardizing the process.[97] Over time, the search for authentic Chinese food was as much a reaction to its McDonaldization in America as it was a recognition that it was diversifying in the United States.

Two of the most successful chains were Panda Express and P.F. Chang's. The fast food chain Panda Express first set up shop in 1983 in the Glendale Galleria Mall, just north of Los Angeles. Its owners, Andrew and Peggy Cherng, had operated restaurants for ten years prior in Southern California.[98] By 1993, the chain had one hundred outposts and was looking to expand dramatically, opening new branches all over California, Nevada, Arizona, and Texas, mostly in suburbs. In 2008, it had over one thousand locations nationwide.[99] It was the largest of the Chinese fast food chains, garnering more than double the revenue of Manchu Wok (based in Toronto), Pei Wei Asian Diner (owned by P.F. Chang's), and Pick Up Stix (owned by the same group that runs TGI Friday's) combined.[100]

Ironically, when they first began running their restaurants, the Cherngs were trying to get away from the chop suey sameness of their era. Andrew Cherng's father had been a master chef in China, and the couple wanted to offer "a marvel-ously wide variety of Chinese cuisines to America," including Mandarin and Szechuan.[101] As they served these cuisines however, they homogenized them too. An example lies in one of the chain's most popular entrees, orange chicken, avail-able at a branch in Los Angeles's Dodger Stadium. On one belly-busting visit in 2005, the Los Angeles Times food writer David Shaw spent a game attempting to sample as much of the stadium's new food as possible. After remarking that it was notable to have both Chinese food and sushi at the stadium—surely a sign of the times—he judged the orange chicken to be "starchy and overly sweet," reminding him of "very bad sweet-and-sour chicken."[102]

His opinion was in the minority, apparently, at least judging from the success of the chain. One reader had written to his newspaper over a decade before to find out the recipe for her beloved orange chicken. The Times said that though it was "called orange chicken, the dish does not contain fruit," so one could add orange zest to it instead.[103] The sauce for the chicken did contain five tablespoons of sugar—a common feature of Chinese food served in America (and not so common in China).[104] A skeptical reviewer for the "Picky Eater" column of *Asian Week* went on an expedition to a Panda Express in San Mateo, a suburb south of San Francisco, fully expecting to be disappointed by the inauthentic food there. She was surprised, however, pronouncing the orange flavored chicken a success.[105] Ree Drummond, host of the Food Network show, *The Pioneer Woman*, organized one episode around replicating Panda Express's food. She started the episode by explaining that she and her daughters frequently drive their pickup truck to the local Panda Express drive-thru (in Tulsa, Oklahoma) to get orange chicken, beef and broccoli, and chow mein. She approximates the dishes to the delight of her daughters.[106] Customers got this fast-food or fast-casual Chinese from the drive thru, but could also find it in many supermarkets. At one point, Panda Express had over 10 percent of its locations within Vons supermarkets.[107] Likewise, P.F. Chang's had success in the casual dining market because "above all" its food was "dependable," for it had honed the process of turning out thousands of meals a day that looked and tasted the same.[108]

Even as the chains grew, independently operated Chinese restaurants still flourished. Just as thousands of burger joints competed with McDonald's, kung pao chicken could be found at more than the Panda Expresses. In 1982, when many operators were trying new ventures in Chinese fast food, one study found around ten thousand restaurants owned by Asians serving Asian-style food in California.[109] A couple decades later another estimate found that in Los Angeles, Chinese restaurants were second only to doughnut shops.[110] One trade publication listed 43,000 Chinese restaurants in the United States in 2007, more than the number of McDonald's and Taco Bells combined.[111] In both the independent and chain Chinese restaurants, there was a simultaneous move toward diversity and homogenization.

FROM CHINESE TO ASIAN FUSION

By the 1990s, it was hard to know where Chinese food in America might go. Bruce Cost, a food writer, restaurateur, ginger-beer salesman, and cookbook author, reflected the multivariate directions of Chinese food in the United States. Having trained for several years with Virginia Lee, an important cooking teacher and author, Cost embarked on an exploration of Chinese cooking and culture. He wrote for various newspapers and magazines and penned books about ginger and Asian ingredients. Together with a scholar of Chinese civilization, he translated a fifth-century manuscript of Chinese cooking—"How to Steam a Bear"—thought to be the world's oldest cookbook.

He eventually founded three restaurants in the San Francisco area, all featuring a base of Chinese cooking but offering pan-Asian menus.[112] The first—Monsoon—received great reviews but suffered from a bad location in San Francisco. His head chef was a veteran of an important fusion restaurant, Chinois on Main, run by Wolfgang Puck in Los Angeles.[113] Another, Ginger Island, did better in Berkeley, but reviewers were not sure what to make of it. One said it was "*not* an ethnic restaurant" but was instead emblematic of "'fun ethnic' rather than 'ethnic ethnic' food—that is, chef cuisine that spins off from the food of a particular region but doesn't attempt to recreate it."[114] Others called the restaurant an "Asian potpourri" and "Asian Persuasion with Fusion Confusion." Yet another noted that you can "visit the Pacific Rim without boarding a plane."[115]

When he closed his Bay Area restaurants, Cost moved to Chicago to develop other restaurants and food concepts, including Big Bowl and Wow Bao. Big Bowl was in the Lettuce Entertain You group—a large and successful restaurant portfolio in Chicago.[116] Cost's homemade ginger ale was a hit at all of his restaurants—so much so that he eventually built a production facility in Brooklyn and concentrated on selling it to grocers and restaurants nationwide.[117]

Cost was an early mover into the booming market for cross-ethnic restaurants, dishes, and concepts. Though he loved and appreciated the history and nuances of Chinese cuisine, he was also excited to meld flavors from other cuisines in all of his restaurant iterations. He and other non-Chinese chefs experimented with various flavors. Cost sold Chinese buns (bao) at his Wow Bao outlets in Chicago just a few blocks from a Panda Express, where orange chicken still headlined the menu. One could also travel to Chicago's western suburbs where Asian immigrants lived in large numbers. There you could drive down suburban thoroughfares, just as likely to see a P.F. Chang's as you were a Chinese restaurant patronized only by recent immigrants. Chinese food had integrated into the American paradox—sameness in diversity. So too had Mexican food and its staple, the tortilla.

8

Tortilla Politics

Tortillas were small business in the United States prior to the 1970s. They were usually produced in or around Mexican American neighborhoods in family-run factories. These small tortillerias dotted the landscape of the Southwest, but they typically sold their foods locally.[1]

El Galindo was one such company in Austin, Texas, flourishing regionally for several decades and then expanding on the heels of Mexican food's popularity in the 1970s and 1980s. Like many large and small tortilla producers, El Galindo got caught in the crosshairs of GRUMA, the largest tortilla manufacturer in the world. Despite El Galindo's adoption of modern production and marketing techniques, it was no match for GRUMA's cross-border largesse and political connections. GRUMA, like many large food firms, used its lobbying expertise to gain advantages that only the big players could. The result is a tortilla landscape today dominated by just a few big players. When American and Mexican consumers walk down the tortilla or bread aisle of the typical grocery store, they see dozens of brand names to choose from. That is a mirage. In fact, these brand names and generic offerings mostly start as Maseca, the brand name of GRUMA's flour. In the tortilla business, sameness is masked by what seems to be diversity.

Founded as El Fenix in 1940 by Tomas Galindo Sr. and his wife, Josepha, the small tortilla factory was run by the Galindos with their family in Austin until 1972, when their son Tomas Jr. and daughter-in-law Ernestine bought it, changing the name to El Galindo in 1973.[2] In the early years of the business, the tortilla factory also featured a gift shop with Mexican potteries and housewares. Tomas Galindo Sr. was also active in the central Texas Mexican American community.[3] The factory sold tortillas to a few local grocery stores, restaurants, and sorority houses but did not distribute widely. It prospered over the years by primarily serving the many Mexicans who came to the United States beginning in the 1940s to fill World War II employment shortages, and "as more Mexicans came across the border, [tortilla manufacturing] became good business."[4] From the 1940s to the 1980s, Mexican food manufacturing consisted of many mom-and-pop operations, of which El Galindo was one.[5] As Mexican food's popularity surged between the 1970s and the 1990s, Tomas Galindo Jr. and Ernestine expanded their operations from a six-employee company to over a hundred, selling to many more restaurants and groceries throughout Texas.[6] In the 1980s the factory produced between 15,000 and 20,000 packages of a dozen corn tortillas a day as well as whole-wheat- and white-flour tortillas, chips, and taco shells. Although employees still hand-packaged the products, the factory featured modern conveyor belts, fryers, and metal die-cutters to cut the tortillas into rounds.[7]

In 1996, W. Allen Dark purchased the factory from the Galindo family. By then, its products were shipped to stores and restaurants around the United States, including in Austin, Dallas, Houston, Georgia, and New Jersey. Whereas it once served a mostly Mexican American clientele, El Galindo had shifted to what Dark termed a "niche market" for consumers who wanted "traditional" products. His tortillas fit within the "specialty product" category because, according to Dark, they have "a lot of taste but cost more" than other brands. In addition to corn and flour tortillas, El Galindo manufactured organic and spelt tortillas. In 2004, the organic and spelt versions cost around thirty cents each compared to a few pennies for a common tortilla.[8]

By the 1990s, El Galindo was floundering. Ironically, its troubles resulted from the surging popularity of Mexican food. The family had hired W. Allen Dark as a consultant because he specialized in helping "companies in trouble." Later, he purchased the company. He explained that, although "people in California and Texas have always been familiar with Mexican food," that familiarity had spread recently to the rest of the United States, creating a "snowball effect" for Mexican food in the 1990s. Those who "previously wouldn't recognize a Mexican person started eating Mexican food" in that decade, said Dark. Widening consumption necessitated a change in production, and large manufacturers like GRUMA took hold of the tortilla market. In the mid-1990s, Steve Foster, then a vice president for El Galindo, said that major companies were "expanding into new markets" and that McDonald's and Burger King "increase demand" for tortillas "by advertising products like breakfast tacos. People now know there's more things you can do with a tortilla."[9] He added that as a result, large baking companies entered the tortilla landscape in the United States. W. Allen Dark lamented large producers' ability to pay slotting fees for prime product placement in grocery stores.[10] The retail market became "tough" then for small companies in the 1990s, said Dark, forcing many out of business. Other small food producers survived by selling directly to restaurants rather than in retail stores, signing contracts for bulk production.[11]

Although El Galindo's production techniques were fairly cutting-edge, they differed from those of GRUMA and the other big tortilla manufacturers. Even when GRUMA did not directly press tortillas for supermarkets or restaurants, it often sold them its flour, which they turned into tortillas. H-E-B, the largest supermarket chain in Texas, made tortillas in a 20,000 square-foot production facility in Corpus Christi. The tortilla process began there with GRUMA's dry flours, which were added to water. El Galindo and other small manufacturers, such as Sanitary Tortilla Manufacturing Corporation in San Antonio, Texas, instead used the old wet masa process for their tortillas.[12] But H-E-B made its own tortillas using GRUMA flour and also featured GRUMA brand Mission and Guerrero tortillas alongside its store brands on shelves. Though the brand names were different on various packages, implying a great range of choices, consumers were fooled; they increasingly ate tortillas made just from Maseca flour.

El Galindo had to turn to niche markets; as a result, its new customers were "mostly Anglo-Saxons in the middle- or upper-income groups." Dark thought Mexican Americans did not buy his higher-priced tortillas because they "don't have the money and will buy a lower-priced product" in bulk, probably made by GRUMA. El Galindo could not compete with the grocery store shelves "loaded with 120-count pack tortillas" and, as a result, had long ago left that business. El Galindo "missed the high-volume market." Ironically, Dark's tortilla business manufactured tortillas more like old Mexican *tortillerias*, but he sold most of those tortillas to non-Mexicans.[13] Instead, Mexican Americans, according to Dark, bought from large producers like GRUMA because they used newer production techniques. Indeed, in 1997, the four largest tortilla manufacturers shipped 57.2 percent of the tortillas in the United States for the billion-dollar-plus industry.[14] As with other aspects of the food industry, the largest operators dominated the tortilla market by the end of the 1990s, from Mexico to the United States and beyond, homogenizing the tortilla as they mainstreamed it. By 2010, El Galindo no longer existed, put out of business by GRUMA.[15] Though many small tortilla manufacturers remained in Texas, most had turned to niche markets for their products.

"FREE" TRADE AFTER THE 1980s

There is more to the tortilla story than Americans' growing love of tacos and wraps. Changing eating habits accompanied the changing political economy of the United States and Mexico, linking American and Mexican patterns of consumption, labor relations, and retail to each other. Corn and wheat cultivated on massive corporate farms in both countries were pressed into tortillas in technologically advanced plants, finding their way to American tables with the help of distribution and retail innovations developed and sold by businesses on both sides of the border. The mass-produced tortilla proliferated in the late twentieth-century United States and

Mexico on the infrastructure of low taxes, right-to-work laws, low tariffs, and incentives to attract businesses.

Mexico's leading politicians since the 1980s, the neoliberals, shared the political and economic philosophies of many American politicians and business leaders. Mexican politicians drawn from the Institutional Revolutionary Party (PRI) worked in constant dialogue with the United States to develop reforms in the 1980s and 1990s. Many of these officials, who graduated from American universities and worked for American-based companies, assigned their own vision of the free market for Mexico.[16]

Trade liberalization stood at the center of this reform agenda, and beginning in the 1980s, policy makers on both sides of the US-Mexico border worked progressively to remove restrictions. In the United States, free trade was a bipartisan policy. Meanwhile, neoliberal Mexican leaders privatized state enterprises, deregulated the economy, reprivatized banks, and opened trade and investment to foreign businesses.[17] In contrast to many of its Latin American neighbors, Mexico became much less protectionist over time. Many Mexican business owners vigorously supported free trade too, aiding politicians by means of lobbying and trade associations.[18]

American Sunbelt politicians pushed the North American Free Trade Agreement (NAFTA) as the linchpin of free trade, passing it through Congress in November 1993. Mexico had already opened its market by joining the General Agreement on Tariffs and Trade in 1986, but after NAFTA, cross-border exchanges increased. Direct investment by American firms in Mexico and by Mexican firms in the United States each jumped significantly after NAFTA. The Congressional Research Service estimated that from 1993 to 2013 US foreign direct investment in Mexico rose from $15.2 billion to $101.0 billion, a 664 percent increase. Similarly, Mexico's foreign direct investment in the United States rose from $1.2 billion to $17.6 billion.[19] Mexico's foreign trade, meanwhile, outpaced all of Latin America from the mid-1980s to 2001.[20] The neoliberal, or free market push (depending on which side of the border you stood), meant greater exchanges of all sorts, whether measured by goods or people moving across the border. The number of business visitors and intracompany transferees crossing the border also rose significantly beginning in the 1980s and continued with NAFTA, signaling greater economic exchanges between the two countries.[21] And contrary to popular thought, the story of liberalization goes well beyond southward flows of capital and northward flows of labor. Mexican exports to the United States have increased four-fold since NAFTA, and major Mexican cement, banking, and food companies have pumped capital into American operations too.[22]

Those food companies tell another story of US-Mexico interchange—one in which Mexican firms rule the bread and tortilla industries in the United States. This counters the McDonaldization theory of globalization in which American companies homogenize foreign cultures. That theory argues that McDonald's, Levi's, Hollywood, and other American exports have had outsized influence in the last several decades. That is true, but sameness in global works the opposite way. As with JBS and the big meatpacking firms, or the large grocers based abroad, many foreign companies have a strong foothold in American food. Here, Mexican companies sell Americans their daily bread, and corporate giants get bigger and more powerful over time.

TORTILLA POLITICS

The tortilla, the "daily bread" and most important foodstuff of Mexico, is a lens onto the new transnational Sunbelt political economy of the United States and Mexico since the 1980s. Five companies that make (or made) tortillas were central to this political economy—GRUMA, Bimbo, Walmart, Archer Daniels Midland (ADM), and El Galindo. GRUMA and Bimbo, both Mexican companies, have grown much more powerful because of the new political order. Bimbo is the largest food company in Mexico, and GRUMA is the largest tortilla maker in the world. They are also the largest tortilla and bread sellers in the United States. Walmart is the largest company in the world and the largest grocer in the United States and Mexico. Only a few other companies rival ADM's global reach in food processing.[23] And El Galindo, like many other small tortilla manufacturers, was driven out of business by competition from GRUMA, Bimbo, and Walmart.

Tortillas have spread across the world since the 1980s, and GRUMA was the company most responsible for this change, using an American Sunbelt base for its success in the last part of the twentieth century.[24] GRUMA capitalized on the growing Mexican American population in the United States, the surging popularity of Mexican food in the United States, its ties to the Mexican government, and the liberalization of trade to increase its share of the world tortilla market. GRUMA represented the homogenizing forces that came to dominate the Sunbelt political economy—forces ironically built on the new diversity of increased global trade and migration. Furthermore, the fact that a Mexican company dominated a food business in the United States counters the standard narrative in which American foods such as the hamburger homogenize foreign culture.[25] Mexican food became homogenized not just in Mexico but also across borders in the United States, Europe, and Asia.

Walmart and GRUMA capitalized on the continued Mexicanization of the Southwest and its business-friendly environment to make it a locus point for globalization.[26] These retail and manufacturing colossuses developed practices to ensure that Americans could get both consistency and diversity in their shopping experiences, practices that became engines of globalization. Walmart, based in Arkansas, and GRUMA, based in Monterrey, Mexico, established patterns that would secure the global dominance of large corporations in the food business by creating one-stop shops for sameness and diversity. At the same time, as tortillas became a staple not just for those Americans with Mexican roots but for people of all ethnicities in the United States, GRUMA extended its reach first through the Southwest and later to the rest of the nation. It used brand-name recognition of its Maseca flour, advertising in Spanish-language newspapers, and distribution in small Mexican grocery stores to woo Mexican American customers.[27] By 2007, 45 percent of GRUMA's overall sales came from the United States. American consumers formed the company's largest market, in part because it had expanded sales beyond a Mexican American base.[28]

Walmart established a retail model that companies replicated the world over. The company learned to work with US-Mexican trade and immigration policies, taking advantage of the borderlands to expand within and beyond it. In the 1990s, Walmart expanded to Mexico and opened new distribution centers to smooth retailing in the country.[29] Two decades later it was the largest private employer in the country.[30] Millions of consumers shopped in Walmarts in Mexico and the United States as they crossed back and forth.[31] The "big-box" terrain served familiarized and streamlined consumption patterns for migrants who spent considerable parts of their lives on both sides of the border. Both working-class border families and Mexican professionals from Monterrey hunted for bargains at the retailer, whether they were shopping for just the day or planning their move to gated communities in San Antonio. For a time, the Walmart in Laredo, Texas, was the busiest in the United States, fueled by cross-border purchases.[32] In part, because of this international focus, the company became *the* free-enterprise model after the 1980s. Nelson Lichtenstein described Walmart as a "template business setting the standards for a new stage in the history of world capitalism," having been able to "break trade unions, set the boundaries for popular culture, channel capital through the world, and conduct a kind of international diplomacy with a dozen nations."[33]

Among the most important of those nations was Mexico. Walmart backed NAFTA in 1993 when it was in danger of failing. As Bethany Moreton has observed, "For a brief but decisive moment in US politics, the key to imagining free trade was Walmart in Mexico."[34] The opening of a massive Walmart store in Mexico City convinced American consumers during the NAFTA debate that Mexicans would buy US-made products en masse. At the time, many Americans feared what Ross Perot described as the "giant sucking sound" of jobs moving southward. When NAFTA passed in November 1993, Sunbelt representatives voted for it in greater numbers than their midwestern counterparts, where labor unions argued that American manufacturing firms would suffer. About 55 percent of the overall Congress voted for NAFTA, but 63 percent of Sunbelt representatives supported it. In the days leading up to the vote, a *Washington Post* headline called the vote one of "Sun Belt vs. Rust Belt."[35] In committee hearings, Senator John McCain (R-AZ) pointed to major food lobbying associations' support for the bill, such as the National Corn Growers Association and National Cattlemen's Association, explaining that it was the "American zeal for opportunity and competition in the market place that has fared so well throughout its history" and that both the American economy and agriculture will be "the better for" passing NAFTA.[36]

It was no accident that Walmart experienced its greatest growth during the 1990s when legislators put free trade firmly into law. The decade saw stores open at breakneck speed, with goods sourced mainly from cheap manufacturers abroad.[37] Walmart and other large grocery chains sold GRUMA tortillas in increasing proportion, as both the manufacturers and retailers used economies of scale and "free" trade to freely squelch competition.[38] Walmart paid workers low wages and resisted unions too. The chain paid around 20–25 percent lower wages than Kmart, Target, and Safeway.[39] And, whereas many snowbelters had moved south and west for manufacturing jobs in the mid-twentieth century, Walmart replaced those jobs with lower-paying retail positions. The real value of those job's wages, notes Lichtenstein, had actually declined since 1970.[40] Walmart thus took advantage of and enforced the right-to-work and pro-business environment of the Sunbelt.[41] And in Mexico, the company plainly broke the law. A *New York Times* investigation found that "bribery played a persistent and significant role in Walmart's rapid growth in Mexico," as Walmart executives paid Mexican government officials to get favorable store locations and obtain licenses for stores.[42]

Mexican Americans constituted a sizeable number of Walmart's employees and a strong portion of its customer base, particularly in Texas, the largest Walmart market.[43] Those customers included the farmworkers who provided cheap food for all consumers. Farmworkers had been on the very bottom of the American economic ladder for decades.[44] Many had come from Mexico to work as farm laborers because they had been driven off their own farms. One estimate had just six firms—Cargill, GRUMA, ADM, Minsa, Arancia Corn Products, and Agroinsa—controlling 70 percent of the corn import and export trade to Mexico in 2007. Small farmers could not compete with corporate farms after NAFTA, causing thousands to leave the land for work throughout Mexico and the United States.[45] Today, the majority of the farmworkers working in the United States are from Mexico, earning lower wages than any other class of worker.[46]

Those workers (and consumers) moving north became, in part, the basis of GRUMA's successful tortilla empire in the United States, over time deriving more revenue from sales in America than Mexico. Grocers such as Walmart worked in concert with GRUMA, as supermarket chains slowly sought to capture business from the growing population of immigrants and their descendants, while marketing ethnic foods to a wider audience.[47]

THE TORTILLA AS AMERICA'S DAILY BREAD

The tortilla has long been an essential component for Mexican and Central American food, but its production and consumption has grown in the United States and changed in Mexico over the last several decades.[48] In the Southwest and other areas with well-established Mexican American culinary traditions, inhabitants have long consumed tortillas and other border staples.[49] For several decades, however, most American consumers needed detailed tortilla explanations on menus. At Pepe's, a Mexican restaurant at the tourist-heavy Pier 39 in San Francisco, a 1980 menu explained that tortillas were a "staple" for the Aztecs and that they were served basically "unchanged" there. The menu further advised that diners should enjoy tortillas "in the Mexican fashion; hold the tortilla flat in one hand, butter it, add the hot sauce (sparingly at first), roll and eat," adding, not surprisingly, that they "particularly recommend tortillas with a Frosty Margarita."[50] Across the country in Timonium, Maryland, the Mexican restaurant chain Chi-Chi's offered similar counsel to diners. The back of its menu had a full-page spread titled "Mexican Kitchen Talk." There the basic components of Mexican food were translated—tacos, enchiladas, tostadas, and tamales—along with a pronunciation guide. "TAH-ko—The traditional Mexican 'sandwich,'" appeared with "Tor-TEE-yah—Bread with a Mexican accent—*the* south-of-the-border basic."[51] A cookbook published in 1980 distinguished between Mexican tortillas "made from cornmeal" and the Spanish tortilla, which was an omelet.[52] So, although Americans, particularly in the southwestern states, had been eating Mexican food for decades, many diners still required instruction.[53]

Twenty years later menus rarely explained tacos or tortillas, for they were already established in the wider American food lexicon.[54] The tortilla, in fact, became a means to explain *other* ethnic cuisines, like foods from Asia. One magazine article extolled the virtues of Indian-fusion dishes generally, even as it recoiled at a recipe for "cinnamon-spiced buffalo meat in a shell of tortilla-like Indian bread, matched with mint and mango chutney and served on mixed greens." The "tortilla" here probably referred to a chapati, a flat, round, whole-wheat Indian bread so similar to the tortilla that Indian immigrants in the United States were known to buy hand tortilla presses from specialty stores to recreate chapatis at home. Recently, GRUMA has begun selling packaged chapatis along with other "flatbreads" in various markets.[55]

Americans without vestiges of Mexican heritage slowly increased their tortilla consumption between the 1970s and 1990s. During the 1970s, tortillas had moved out of a small space in most California supermarkets to a prominent end-of-aisle display. And at many stores, tortillas became so common that grocers simply lumped them with the rest of the bread.[56] Tom Caron, a director of marketing for one frozen Mexican entrees manufacturer, remarked in 1980 that "The Mexican food category is experiencing in excess of 30 percent growth per year and this growth is going from the Southwest region of the country, into the Midwest and is moving outward."[57] Another large packaged food company, Del Monte, sought greater opportunities with its Mexican food lines, Patio and Ortega, in the 1980s. Patio was the number one selling Mexican frozen food brand at the time and Del Monte even marketed its A-1 steak sauce as great for "putting a little life into a taco."[58]

By the 1990s, some grocers, including H-E-B, featured large tortilla presses within the retail space. An H-E-B vice president explained that his supermarket chain built a press at a majority "Hispanic" San Antonio branch because "around here, tortillas are like bread." The press was enclosed in glass as an attraction for the "kids."[59] Stores that did not primarily serve Hispanic customers built the mechanical presses for that same sense of theater—a machine pumping out soft, hot tortillas, drew attention.

In the United States, tortilla manufacturing primarily operated as a niche ethnic foods industry through the 1980s, existing mostly to serve Mexican American communities in the Southwest. At first, small tortilla plants could make decent profits within this economy. The industry changed radically, however; as more Mexicans immigrated to the United States, more non-Mexicans in the United States ate tortillas, and Mexican food expanded out of regional consumption beyond the Southwest.[60] In Mexico, tortilla production had already shifted from a domestic, labor-intensive activity to one supplanted and supplemented by modern machinery.[61]

This industrial process came to be dominated by GRUMA.

GRUMA AND TORTILLA POLITICS

At the turn of the twenty-first century, GRUMA became the largest tortilla manufacturer in the world. GRUMA had been founded in 1949 by Roberto M. González and his son, Roberto González Barrera, in Nuevo Leon, but it began its real ascent in the 1960s after developing more efficient tortilla machines. By the 1990s, González Barrera was on Forbes's list of billionaires and the company was rapidly expanding beyond Mexico.[62] According to one estimate, its Texas-based Mission Foods division alone produced a quarter of all tortillas worldwide, amounting to twenty-nine billion tortillas in 2007.[63] In addition to the Mission Foods brand, in the United States GRUMA produced Guerrero tortillas, much of the flour used by major grocers such as H-E-B and Walmart to manufacture their in-house brands, and a large proportion of the tortillas used by major food purveyors such as McDonald's, Taco Bell, and KFC. The company topped tortilla sales in the two largest tortilla markets: Mexico and the United States.[64] The story of GRUMA's ascent is one about how the fates of Mexico and the United States became more closely intertwined in the last half of the century with the help of a new cross-border political order favoring the biggest companies.

After its founding, GRUMA slowly increased its share of the tortilla market in Mexico by developing technologies to grind corn more efficiently and cheaply than existing mills. GRUMA's tortilla technology sought to improve on the centuries-old process whereby millions of Mexican women had boiled and ground corn, which they then rolled into tortillas by hand. Millions still do. In this process, women simmer corn in mineral lime overnight to make nixtamal. This softens the corn and releases important nutrients. The next morning, they grind the corn on a stone to make a dough, or masa, which they press flat and then cook over clay griddles at mealtime for fresh tortillas. The process takes hours.[65] In the last half of the nineteenth century, Mexican inventors developed mechanical corn mills. Then, during the twentieth century, inventors developed three industrial technologies that dramatically reduced the tortilla workload. In the 1900s and 1910s, engineers first created metal rolling presses for the corn dough, and around 1950 new developers designed successful mechanical tortilla presses.[66] GRUMA became the leader in the third innovation: masa harina (dried corn flour), which requires only water for the finished product.[67] To make dry masa, manufacturers boil corn for thirty minutes, blast it with hot air, and package it soon thereafter.[68] Known by GRUMA's trade name, Maseca, the dried flour came to occupy roughly half of tortilla production in Mexico by the early twenty-first century.[69] At the end of the century, the average Mexican consumed around eighteen tortillas per day, or three-quarters of a pound's worth, making its production key to any discussion about food and politics in Mexico.[70]

GRUMA controlled about half of the Mexican tortilla market by 2006, but who controlled the other half? Home producers or, or more likely, the thousands of local tortillerias that dotted the landscape. Some Mexican consumers cooked corn at home and brought it to a neighborhood mill for grinding into masa. Others bought masa from a local mill and took it to a tortilleria to make a morning batch. And still others bought tortillas fresh every morning from local tortillerias that ground, cooked, and pressed the tortillas on a daily basis. In comparison to the United States, fewer Mexican consumers bought packaged tortillas, though GRUMA hoped to change that too.[71] GRUMA commented that the tortilla industry in Mexico was "highly fragmented," which meant opportunities for growth.[72] The company continued to push conversion of tortilla production from wet masa to its Maseca brand corn flour, both by large and small tortilla producers, including tortillerias and supermarkets that made tortillas in-house.[73]

GRUMA came to dominate the Mexican tortilla landscape in part because of its ties to Mexican political leaders. First, it profited from the dismantling of the National Company of Popular Subsistence (CONASUPO), the Mexican state agency that had subsidized food consumption since the 1960s. CONASUPO had operated partly through a massive network of retail tortilla outlets. The neoliberal government leaders reformed this distribution scheme. When Carlos Sali-

nas de Gortari became president in 1988, he reordered CONASUPO. By the early
1990s, the agency had undergone significant changes and was on the way to
privatizing the tortilla trade.[74] His government aided GRUMA by declaring in
1990 that any new growth in the tortilla market must be filled by dehydrated
flour, rather than wet masa. At the time, only GRUMA and a state agency produced the dry version.[75] The next president, Ernesto Zedillo, finally eliminated
CONASUPO in 1999.

The *New York Times* and other newspapers investigated both the Salinas
(1988–1994) and Zedillo (1994–2000) administrations for corrupt ties to GRUMA.
President Salinas's brother Raul was jailed in 1995 for plotting the assassination of
a presidential candidate. As a result of this investigation, his dealings with
CONASUPO also came to light, including speculation that he made significant
profit from the dismantling process. A congressional investigation found only
lesser acts of wrongdoing, but many believed the Zedillo administration had cov-
ered up its involvement.[76] Around the same time, another Salinas administration
member, Commerce Secretary Jaime Serra Puche, had also coordinated the reor-
ganization of CONASUPO and was a leading figure in NAFTA negotiations with
the United States. He enlisted business leaders and organizations to lobby on
behalf of free trade.[77] Some observers of Mexican politics charged that Serra
Puche acted on behalf of GRUMA by discontinuing the Mexican government's
rural corn program, which resulted in a flood of cheap American corn into the
Mexican market. Much of that corn was exported to Mexico by the largest pri-
vately held firm in the world, Cargill, the American agricultural company.[78]
Another congressional investigation examined whether GRUMA had improp-
erly received a $7 million payment from a state agency in the Salinas administra-
tion, which then Senior Budget Official Ernesto Zedillo had "acquiesced" to
accept.[79] The inquiry eventually cleared the company of wrongdoing, but it raised
questions about GRUMA founder Roberto González Barrera's (the "tortilla
king") connection to officials in the Mexican government. Carlos Salinas report-
edly used Barrera's private plane to leave the country when his brother Raul was
jailed.[80] Though it is hard to determine if GRUMA's leadership dealt directly with
the Salinas family on the CONASUPO policy, GRUMA certainly benefited from
the change.[81] Between 1992 and 2006, the proportion of tortillas made with dry
corn flour jumped from about a third to about 48 percent in Mexico, and GRUMA
controlled that market.[82]

GRUMA's designs on dominating Mexico's tortilla market worked hand in
hand with its American operations. Over time, GRUMA saw that the tortilla markets of the United States and Mexico could be connected quite profitably. American consumers did not share the old Mexican aversion to packaged tortillas, and
GRUMA hoped to bring its experience in the United States and the connections
between Mexican Americans in the Southwest and Mexico to help its marketing

strategies. Jorge Hernandez, a GRUMA sales manager in Los Angeles, went so far as to note, "maybe we can teach Mexicans how to sell tortillas back home."[83] He had reason to believe this: at the end of the 1990s, the company controlled around 25 percent of the American tortilla market and 82 percent of the market for corn flour.[84]

GRUMA's American tortilla strategy had moved outward from the Sunbelt. The company first entered the American market in 1976, later buying Mission Foods, the largest tortilla maker in the United States. Mission Foods was headquartered in Los Angeles for many years before moving to the Dallas suburbs in 1998 to be closer to GRUMA headquarters in Monterrey, Mexico. It also moved eastward to capture the growing market east and north of the Southwest.[85] GRUMA located most of its plants in California or Texas, including the world's largest tortilla plant in Rancho Cucamonga, California. The company received a grant of $578,000 from the city's redevelopment agency to build there in exchange for supporting 600 jobs at the plant over the next nine years. California Governor Pete Wilson had developed an initiative while in office to recruit and retain businesses in the state, of which the GRUMA plant was one.[86] That plant ran three different processing lines: one for clients such as Taco Bell, another for retailers, and another for tortilla chips. North Carolina also offered incentives to GRUMA. In 1999, GRUMA sought expansion to the East Coast and bought rival tortilla maker Barnes Foods. To entice GRUMA to locate its new facility in Goldsboro, North Carolina, the city and state offered it $400,000 in initial incentives and an annual $200,000 to offset state income tax. GRUMA was expected to provide a $13 million investment in the area and 100 or more jobs, which it did.[87] On top of GRUMA's headquartering its American operations in Texas, the Texas Panhandle sourced most of the company's food-grade corn and the company built the world's largest corn flour plant in Plainview, Texas.[88]

The company also adapted to American, European, and Asian markets to increase sales by developing different products. Though Mission represented its largest division, GRUMA bought or created other brands, including the Guerrero label, which was marketed to Mexican Americans rather than the general American population. The company also introduced fat-free, flavored, and low-carbohydrate tortillas.[89] Fast food represented one of the largest growth areas for Mexican food in and beyond in the United States, proving a boon for GRUMA, which contracted with, at one time or another, McDonald's, Taco Bell, and 7-Eleven. GRUMA was Taco Bell's exclusive tortilla provider in the western region for a time.[90] In gobbling market share and contracting with large chains, GRUMA gradually bought out competitors in this food-service market. Based in Los Angeles, Candy's Tortilla Factory had derived a quarter of its revenue from sales to Taco Bell but lost its contract. GRUMA then bought Candy's in 1994.[91] GRUMA's rising profits could also be seen in the case of McDonald's, which first offered fajitas and breakfast burritos in 1991 and saw this business grow substantially over time. GRUMA also sought growth in Europe and Asia, typically using its operations in Texas or California as jumping off points for that business.[92] By the late 2000s, GRUMA supplied KFC's China branches by shipping tortillas from its plant in Southern California, until demand became so great that it built a separate factory in Shanghai.[93]

GRUMA dominated the market by leading tortilla-processing technologies, entering agreements with American agricultural firms and buying up small tortilla producers. GRUMA had long led scientific advances in processing corn and wheat flour, something its management regularly boasted about in corporate reports and interviews.[94] Building on this legacy, it signed an agreement with ADM in 1996, whereby ADM purchased almost a quarter of GRUMA's stock—a proportion it held until 2012. ADM is among the leaders in corn-, soy-, and seed-oil processing in the world. It markets its high-fructose corn syrup, soy-derived food fillers, animal feed supplements, and other food products in six continents. The deal allowed ADM to increase corn and wheat flour processing in Mexico for the growing corn syrup, white bread, and pastry markets there. For its part, GRUMA gained greater access to the American markets by taking over ADM's corn-milling plants in California and another in Kentucky to supply the growing eastern market for tortillas.

GRUMA and ADM took advantage of the cross-border business opportunities offered by NAFTA. Eduardo Livas Cantu, GRUMA's chief executive officer, commented that his company ran its corn-flour business "better than [ADM was] running theirs" and would be better suited to operate mills in the United States for tortillas, concluding, "we are dedicated to corn flour, our mills are newer, and we have a better technology."[95] ADM brought industrial food technologies southward in the form of corn syrup, wheat processing, and livestock feed, and GRUMA brought tortilla technology northward. The collaboration allowed GRUMA to "vertically integrate" its US tortilla operations in short order.[96]

ADM committed multiple antitrust violations to secure market share. It was forced to pay court fines or settle civil suits for fixing the price of lysine, citric acid, and high-fructose corn syrup.[97] In 1996, the same year it purchased the stake in GRUMA, the company pled guilty in court and paid a $100 million fine for fixing the price of citric acid, an additive it manufactures for sodas and other foods. In 1999, three ADM executives, including the vice chairman, were convicted for engaging in a "global conspiracy" to fix prices on lysine, an additive for animal feed.[98] Then in 2004, ADM paid $400 million to settle a civil class-action suit for fixing the price of high-fructose corn syrup, a sweetener in thousands of processed foods.[99] The Mexican government formally investigated the firm, and in the middle of the price-fixing scandal, ADM fired the head of its Mexico division.[100]

ADM's questionable tactics extended to the political arena as well. The longtime chief executive of ADM, Dwayne Andreas, gave massive sums to various political campaigns. ADM's political influence reaped dividends; for years taxpayer subsidies for ethanol and corn benefited its bottom line. Perhaps the most stunning revelation about Andreas's political contributions was only recently proved after the National Archives released grand jury testimony from President Richard Nixon in 1975. Under oath, Nixon confirmed that Andreas hand-delivered $100,000 in cash to the White House months before the Watergate burglary. Another $25,000 anonymous contribution by Andreas eventually ended up in the bank account of a Watergate burglar. Nixon and Andreas pushed the limit of election laws in the process.[101] In testimony before the US Senate Andreas said, "When it comes to agriculture, there is no such thing as the free market." Indeed.[102]

As a result of this oligopolistic control of the tortilla market by just a few players, Mexican consumers suffered. After privatization took hold and CONASUPO had been abolished, tortilla prices roughly doubled, for the federal government no longer subsidized tortillas for much of the population. GRUMA controlled increasingly larger shares of the tortilla market just as Walmart did the same with groceries. As NAFTA allowed cheap corn from the United States to flood the Mexican market, small farmers in Mexico found it difficult to compete. The rural poor in Mexico became poorer over time, as Mexican farmers were caught in the double vise grip of NAFTA and their countries' neoliberal domestic reforms. Together, these policies meant cheaper agricultural imports enabled by ADM, GRUMA, and other large firms, whether in the United States, Mexico, or elsewhere.[103] Consequently, NAFTA "triggered the most drastic and profound transformation in the history of agriculture in Mexico."[104]

Many of these farmers left their land for the United States, seeking low-wage work in food industries. Their employers included poultry- and pork-processing plants in Alabama, Mississippi, and North Carolina; tortilla factories in Texas and California; and the fruit and vegetable fields that stretched from Florida to California.[105] As NAFTA pushed farmers away from growing corn, they ate fewer tortillas. Though the overall tortilla market in Mexico decreased, GRUMA executives found comfort in the fact that its dry-flour tortillas might supplant the traditional wet masa ones. And even if Mexicans in Mexico increasingly substituted white bread for tortillas, the American and other foreign markets grew by leaps and bounds.[106]

As the tortilla market boomed in the United States, many small tortilla manufacturers found themselves in dire straits at the precise moment when they should have been profiting. Many blamed GRUMA and other large corporations for their demise. A group of these tortilla manufacturers filed a federal antitrust lawsuit against GRUMA in 2001, charging that it fostered anticompetitive practices in the southern California, northern California, Houston, Arizona, and Michigan tortilla markets. The suit alleged that GRUMA entered into marketing agreements with grocers by which it paid slotting fees to "manage or control the placement, location, availability, visibility and promotional activity of competing retail tortillas."[107] The suit further contended that GRUMA attempted to "monopolize" the retail

TABLE 6 GRUMA's Share of Sales in American Supermarkets, 1999

Market	% of Sales	Rank
Seattle	89	1
Los Angeles	85	1
San Diego	85	1
Dallas	62	1
Phoenix	56	1
Portland	56	1
San Francisco	56	1
Houston	55	1
Denver	51	1
New York	51	1
Washington	45	1
Philadelphia	38	1
Boston	36	1
San Antonio	34	1

SOURCE: GRUMA, *Form 20-F for Fiscal Year Ended 1999*, 13.

tortilla market in violation of the Sherman Antitrust Act.[108] GRUMA countered that it indeed arranged marketing agreements with stores but that it always received payment in excess of its cost on tortillas. Albertsons, one of the largest grocery chains in California and Texas, testified in the case that it received similar payments from other manufacturers for marketing but that it alone controlled product placement in its stores and was not beholden to GRUMA. GRUMA argued that other tortilla brands could be found in grocery stores, so customers had a number of choices.[109] Bimbo had been named as a codefendant alongside GRUMA in the original suit, but it was dropped before the case went to court. The court dismissed the suit in 2004, ruling that GRUMA had not violated the law.[110] A similar suit was entered in Los Angeles Superior Court in 2004, but it too was dismissed the next year. That suit prompted State Senator Liz Figueroa to propose a bill in the California legislature to make retailers inform suppliers of slotting fees and market competition. The bill died, but in its description of GRUMA, it noted that the company controlled "90 percent of the Southern California tortilla market."[111] Her numbers were close. GRUMA indeed dominated many of the biggest urban markets, including southwestern cities with large Mexican American populations. According to the company, its Los Angeles market share increased from 66 to 85 percent from 1996 to 1999.[112] (See Table 6) GRUMA, Walmart, Bimbo, and ADM all achieved dominance in their respective markets by promoting, perfecting, and consolidating the new Sunbelt political and economic order.

Bimbo was yet another example of how big companies cooperated with other big players to control a market. Just as GRUMA signed agreements to produce tortillas for McDonald's, Bimbo contracted to bake buns for its burgers, winning exclusive agreements in Mexico in the 1980s and in Venezuela, Colombia, and Peru in 1999.[113] Bimbo needed to become an "export powerhouse and disciple of globalization" to win contracts from big firms. To supply McDonald's it had to invest $30 million into research and development before the burger giant would sign on, something a small baker could hardly do.[114] Like GRUMA, it first began American operations in the western United States, building both on its acquisitions of American bakeries and name recognition from Mexican American customers. After establishing a presence in the West, it sought greater market share, trying to take a "proactive role in an industry that [was] consolidating," by buying Weston Foods, Inc., a major baker in the East.[115] By doing this, it became the largest baker in the United States, with Oroweat, Entenmann's, Sara Lee, Mrs. Baird's, and Boboli among the many brands under its tent.[116]

As the bread, tortilla, and grocery giants enlarged, many workers and farmers in the United States and Mexico scrambled for decent wages. Delivery drivers for GRUMA in Los Angeles went on strike against the company in August 1996, citing low wages and long workweeks without overtime pay. The drivers, who distributed the Mission and Guerrero brands, had joined the Teamsters Union a few years prior. Their strike garnered local publicity because the Teamsters' national president, Ron Carey, spoke at rallies. After seven weeks of strikes, confrontations, and pledges by some politicians to boycott Mission and Guerrero tortillas, GRUMA signed a pay raise of 22 percent for the drivers.[117] Twelve years later GRUMA settled out of court for similar grievances by Teamsters' drivers from Los Angeles, paying $2.9 million to the plaintiffs.[118] GRUMA dominated the tortilla market in the biggest Sunbelt city by mostly resisting worker demands for higher wages and better working conditions.

To reign over worldwide tortilla consumption, GRUMA capitalized on the Sunbelt political and economic order of free trade, low taxes, business incentives, and anti-unionism. Extending from its headquarters in Mexico to its most lucrative market in the United States, GRUMA also pushed, and benefited, from the changes in the Mexican political order. Mexico's neoliberal leaders—many of whom were educated in the United States and in constant dialogue with American policy makers—opened Mexico's banking, agriculture, and manufacturing industries to private investment and supported NAFTA's passage alongside their Sunbelt compatriots. Concurrently, GRUMA supported the dismantling of CONASUPO, the previous system of subsidized tortilla distribution for Mexico. In concert with Walmart, ADM, and other companies that benefited from the opening of trade with Mexico and other countries, GRUMA was able to increase economies of scale and to market its products to a much larger base. It also built on the great demographic and cultural changes in the United States since the 1960s, capitalizing on the mass migration of Mexicans to the United States and the shift in American eating habits toward more

Latin American foods. Ironically, it pushed out long-established family-run tortilla manufacturers in the Southwest, as it developed highly efficient growing, milling, and processing technologies. As GRUMA, Walmart, Bimbo, and other food producers and retailers became bigger, American and Mexican consumers increasingly ate the same foods in Mexico City or Los Angeles—quite often a piece of fast-food meat wrapped in a GRUMA tortilla.

Conclusion

What Is an Authentic Taco?

When I began writing this book, I had hoped to find that food could transcend racism. My thinking went like this: perhaps when we eat the food of the "other," we are less likely to be prejudiced against that group. That may happen sometimes. *Sharing* food with people from different cultures probably helps bridge the divide.[1] But eating the other—as in the white guy eating a taco—that may not do the trick.

Unfortunately, I found many examples of racism tied to food in contemporary America. One was the case of "Minuteman Salsa," a brand launched on July 4, 2006. The Minutemen were a group of ad hoc border patrol enforcers. Operating without official sanction from federal or state governments, they patrolled the US-Mexico border to keep illegal immigrants out of the United States. Minuteman Salsa donated some of its proceeds to the Minutemen. Ryan Lambert had the notion for this company one day as he watched television with a friend and munched on chips and salsa. He realized that the "salsa we had purchased was at odds with our values," so he created the first "American-made and fully documented condiment."[2] Minuteman Salsa's website said, "Minuteman Salsa is American-made salsa. We are proud of our country and believe it is worth defending." The site further argued that the ingredients and workers came only from the United States, and that you "won't see 'Product of Mexico' on our label, because it's not." In a press release, the company said it was "sick and tired of foreign-grown produce and foreign-made salsa entering our country," and that it supported barring illegal immigration and "illegal salsa." This nativist salsa was manufactured in San Antonio—a city with a majority Hispanic population.[3]

The political climate in recent years has produced other moments in which racists eat food from the very groups they despise. Richard Spencer is one of the new "white nationalist" leaders, and he happens to have an affinity for Asian foods. He coined the term "alt-right," and just after the 2016 election gave a speech in Washington, D.C., in which he said that the United States is a "white country designed for ourselves."[4] The crowd responded with Nazi salutes. "Spencer has managed to seize on an extraordinary presidential election to give overt racism a new veneer of radical chic," said *Mother Jones* magazine.[5] In more than one interview, Spencer ate Asian foods while discussing his white supremacist philosophy. In *Time*, a photo showed him sitting at a Vietnamese restaurant. In *Mother Jones* he ate "togarashi-crusted ahi" and a bowl of Thai noodles at two different restaurants in Whitefish, Montana. He wielded chopsticks at both meals. At the Thai restaurant he deflected questions from a reporter about his past relationship with an Asian woman, despite his proclamations against interracial marriage. Apparently, he is comfortable eating Asian food and dating Asian women, but is uncomfortable with other aspects of race mixing.[6]

This is actually not that unusual—people who harbor racism often eat the foods of the group they most disdain. There was a long history of slave owners relishing food cooked by their house slaves.[7] The British colonists in India, while harboring great disdain for many things Indian, took a fancy for curry and tea.[8] And Americans had a great fascination with things "Oriental" in the late 1800s and early 1900s, even as anti-Asian immigration laws sailed through Congress.[9]

This goes both ways of course. Food is often used as a way to identify and reject the other. Outside a 2016 rally for Donald Trump's presidential campaign in Phoenix, a man was filmed screaming at protestors to "Get the f**k out of here! My country! . . . Go cook my f***ing burrito! Go make my f***ing tortilla mother f***er! They build that f***ing wall for me! I love Trump!" Later, holding a Trump sign, he screams, "This is America!"[10] This sentiment was nothing new, though it was expressed in different forms at times. When the United States Commission on Civil Rights interviewed minority students around the country in 1968 and 1969, many testified about unequal and demeaning treatment by white teachers. One said her teacher called Mexican American students "blanket wrappers and chili beans."[11] "Bean eaters" was a common insult hurled at Mexican Americans at the time.[12] The fake news supermarket checkout magazine *Weekly World News* trucked in these stereotypes by running an "article" in 1995 titled, "Gastronaut: Passing Wind Gets Mexican Spaceman Banned from U.S. Shuttle Flights." The astronaut complains that his daily diet of beans was responsible, but to expect him to give up his usual foods was "clearly discrimination."[13]

This discrimination (not made up, by the way) ignores the facts about the food system in the United States. Without immigrant labor, Americans would pay far more to have their strawberries picked, meat butchered, fish de-scaled, onions chopped, garlic minced, sushi rice cooked, tables set, and dishes washed. The food industry might very well collapse without the low-wage labor of immigrants. This includes thousands of undocumented immigrants who work under the table as busboys, prep cooks, and dishwashers. By one estimate, 40 percent of New York's restaurant workers are undocumented. The fact that they work for cheap wages is not an accident. Seven out of the eleven lowest-paid occupations in the country are in food service.[14] These underpaid food workers are essential to any area's economy—over one in ten Americans works in food service.[15] Over 200,000 people work in restaurants in just the Atlanta area.[16]

Many restaurant workers, whether immigrant or native-born, go on to found their own restaurants. Some cook the foods of their homelands, or some approximation thereof. Others cook entirely different foods because they like to or because that's what their customers want. This results in a kaleidoscope of ethnicities cooking ethnic foods. Chinese, Korean, and Thai restaurateurs front sushi places because they make good money and they know their customers want a Japanese-looking person at the front of the house.[17] Mexican and Ecuadorian chefs cook French.[18] All is not what it seems in the food business. And after a time, many may not care. Ultimately, customers judge the food on their perceived "taste," which is always shape shifting too.

Clearly, race, ethnicity, and food have a strong connection. Even if taste matters most, the supposed authenticity of foods, especially in relation to the racial or ethnic connection of that food is important to many Americans. Webster's defines authenticity as "made or done the same way as the original," providing several food-related examples to explain the definition, including "authentic Mexican fare."[19] Even if we start with that definition, there is clearly a "lack of consensus" surrounding the term, as people construct their own ideas about it.[20]

The wide availability of foreign foods and the constantly changing food environment raises questions of authenticity when it comes to food. Globalization disorients geography and the flattening nature of fast food causes many consumers to search for something real. They often wonder how "Americanized" foods are in their local context, whether at a restaurant or grocery store. This raises all manner of questions about how we perceive culture, especially with respect to race and ethnicity. Must Asian restaurants have Asian-looking hosts and chefs to feel authentic? What decor is expected in an Indian or Mexican restaurant? If food in Japan, Mexico, and India is rapidly changing too, what is really authentic? Consumers—both immigrant and native—sought certain ingredients from afar to make the real taco, bowl of phở, or curry. Paradoxically, however, they also sought local foods. For some, "real" meant a taco cooked with chicken raised behind the restaurant, garnished with radishes and cilantro grown in the garden nearby. Restaurants simultaneously celebrated the foreign and local origins of their offerings, reflecting the inherent tension for consumers in globalization. Non-food businesses fed this desire too, claiming authenticity for all sorts of other consumer products—travel, furniture, clothing, and music are just a few examples. Furthermore, in the United

States we are constantly debating the supposed "true" racial or ethnic nature of our population. As the population's collective heritage shifts, food becomes a way to discuss such issues.[21]

This is not new. During the 1800s, an earlier era of globalization, some debated the authentic nature of Mexican food in the Southwest. As Jeffrey Pilcher has noted, in the late 1800s, "The encroaching homogeneity of industrialization inspired a Bohemian nostalgia for more authentic versions" of foods.[22] Mexican American vendors had long sold tamales and chili in southwestern cities to tourists visiting on new train lines. San Antonio was the center of this tourist trade. Big companies came in and canned these items, removing the authentic feel of the products. Later, in the 1960s, the counterculture movement prompted some to search for the authentic in a fight against corporate power and an identification with the peasants of the world. Today, some middle- and upper-class consumers demonstrate their "*own* authenticity" by finding the real Mexican food of Brooklyn or San Francisco.[23]

Authenticity took on many forms. As a testament to authenticity, the exotic surroundings of a particular restaurant were often as critical as the food. In the 1960s, one can see the carnivalesque masking for authenticity in restaurants. Menus featured pictures of Mexicans in sombreros, Indians in turbans or Jinnah caps, and Chinese in bamboo hats. These pictures were designed to lend an air of authenticity to the burritos, curries, and chow meins on the menus, even if the dishes were rarely served in their exact form in those countries. Guidebooks often claimed these restaurants could genuinely bring the customer south of the border or to the Orient.[24] Today this is not uncommon, if in a different way. Indian restaurants still have Taj Mahal photos on the wall, Chinese restaurants have pagodas and red cloth items. Thai restaurants have gold-painted statues, and Mexican restaurants still have sombreros and colorful blankets.[25]

In the cookware realm, purveyors sought to fill a void for ethnic, real, or authentic cooking items. Williams-Sonoma was one such company, founded by Charles Williams in 1954 as a small cookware store in Sonoma, California. Even as supermarket chains grew larger and offered a greater range of products, Williams-Sonoma grew by offering an unusual variety of cookware to customers. Williams's success began in 1958 when he relocated his store to downtown San Francisco, where wealthy housewives could drop in after hairdressing appointments in Union Square.[26] The company became well known in gourmet circles by the 1970s.[27] In the 1980s and 1990s it expanded much further, going public in 1983 and opening a large distribution center in Memphis to serve its growing national base.[28] Many of the tools offered by Williams-Sonoma were those associated with ethnic cuisines, such as soufflé pans, woks, and tortilla presses. The company made it possible for the white, middle-class, city or suburb dweller to get authentic cooking appliances or ingredients without trucking into "authentic" Chinese or Mexican neighborhoods.[29] If one could buy a wok at Williams-Sonoma in San Francisco's Union

Square or Chicago's Michigan Avenue, or even better, in a suburban strip mall, then one would not have to make a trip to a small store filled with mostly Chinese customers in the local Chinatown. Williams was also concerned with finding tools that made foods the "old-fashioned way." One such device was a pasta roller that he promoted as giving better texture to pastas.[30] His company made a market in the United States for these authentic foods that had not been widely consumed by Americans before, such as crystallized ginger.[31] Williams-Sonoma was one of the many businesses that helped make the authentic available anywhere. Homogenized authenticity took form there and elsewhere too.

As native-born customers of various stripes sought out ethnic foods, immigrants sought the real foods of their homeland as a way to cope with a sense of displacement. In the immigration literature, memory, displacement, and tradition reflect one set of emotions. Excitement, adventure, and change reflect another set. These words speak to migration's effects on the mental, physical, economic, cultural, political, and religious identities of the migrants and the natives. The literature is vast too. Novelists, playwrights, filmmakers, and scholars write about the manner in which migration affects the soul. A good deal of the literature has to do with the sense of becoming rootless—a loss of place in a migratory world. The rootless feeling is attenuated for some by the excitement of new experiences. The internal struggle for many immigrants often becomes one of debating whether the "from whence I came" is more important than the "to where I've gone."[32]

Much of the immigration literature focuses on food. Leaving is also losing, for the sense of place once known becomes lost over time. To mitigate their losses, many immigrants look back to where they came from. Because food is often transferable from place to place, especially with accelerated global trade, immigrants can replicate their home lives in their new land. One Mexican immigrant to the United States explained in the 1920s that her family ate "Mexican style" because they could not "accustom" themselves to "any other kind of food." She and her husband dreamed of going back to "beloved Mexico," but were tied to work in the United States.[33] More recently, another set of immigrants from the Indian state of Bengal negotiated the "siren song of modernity and the nostalgia of tradition" as they adapted the foods they ate in America.[34] And from their first arrival to the United States, Chinese immigrants set to growing the fruits and vegetables they were accustomed to in China. In California and Florida, they created a thriving ethnic economy that supplied other Chinese immigrants and the wider public in San Francisco, Los Angeles, and New York.[35] Immigrants sought an authentic version of their foods from home as they adapted to their new environment.

Immigrant restaurateurs often have mixed feelings about the food they produce for customers; some strive to create the most authentic version from their homelands and others are dismissive of that notion. Jason Wang, the proprietor of Xi'an Famous Foods, a group of New York Chinese restaurants, wants to keep to his father's founding vision. "'We're going to keep it pure, because that's what people are coming to us for. We're even going to keep the cashiers non-English speakers, just because that's more authentic. Except me, of course.'" He noted that like himself, he sees other second-generation immigrants running their family businesses to keep this authenticity in place.[36] Eddie Hernandez, who runs restaurants combining Mexican and Southern cuisine in Tennessee and Georgia had the opposite view. "If the food police don't like it, they can see me." He added, "In Mexico, we eat what we like and don't worry about what is authentic cuisine or that. You make do, and you make it taste good." He uses whatever ingredients he thinks are appropriate.[37] The Mahendro family runs Badmaash, a Los Angeles Indian restaurant where they have a similar attitude. "We want to change the perception of Indian culture in America," said Anu, one of three sons working with father Pawan.[38] Nakul, another son, said, "We're going to serve the most bomb traditional Indian food, we're also going to serve really, really thoughtful American food with Indian flavor, and we're going to play Notorious B.I.G."[39] The restaurant does just that— what they consider real versions of chicken tikka masala and samosas but also Indian hamburgers. Actor Kunal Nayyar, who grew up in New Delhi, said Badmaash "felt very authentic. . . . It actually felt like home," even as the restaurant served a mash-up of Indian and American foods.[40]

Even in universities the authentic is debated. At Oberlin College, students complained about the offerings at the dining hall, arguing they wanted more traditional meals. "The culinary culprits included a soggy, pulled-pork-and-coleslaw sandwich that tried to pass itself off as a traditional Vietnamese banh mi sandwich; a Chinese General Tso's chicken dish made with steamed instead of fried poultry; and some poorly prepared Japanese sushi."[41] Speaking to the student newspaper, The Oberlin Review, Tomoyo Joshi, a student from Japan, said, "When you're cooking a country's dish for other people, including ones who have never tried the original dish before, you're also representing the meaning of the dish as well as its culture. . . . So if people not from that heritage take food, modify it and serve it as 'authentic,' it is appropriative."[42] The Oberlin dining director admitted that the college may have been "culturally insensitive" in trying to provide a more "vibrant menu."[43] Responding on Twitter to the controversy, one person commented, "When you're defending the cultural authenticity of GENERAL TSO'S CHICKEN, you're a living Portlandia sketch."[44]

Scholars Josée Johnston and Shyon Baumann examined this question of authenticity at length in their book Foodies, finding five ways people understand the term: "geographic specificity, [it] is 'simple,' has a personal connection, can be linked to a historical tradition, or has 'ethnic' connections."[45] They acknowledge that globalization can "muddy the waters" when it comes to authenticity, but foodies are still concerned with geographic specificity with foods.[46] Foodies' interest in simplicity harkens to the counterculture, where there is a concern for getting away from corporatism. There is also a class element to this, in which middle- and upper-class eaters celebrate the foods of the poor. The personal connection is individualized, of course, specific to the experience of the eater. Historical tradition validates foods because there is a perceived element of "historical continuity" that can be interpreted as "authoritative."[47] And ethnicity, as we've seen, runs throughout discussions of the authentic. One commenter said, "When I think of authentic, I think of ethnicity."[48]

Even if we can define the broad terms by which authenticity is discussed, for most, the authentic is highly personal, individualistic, and fleeting. *Saveur*, the food magazine with the tagline, "Savor a World of Authentic Cuisine," ran a cover story featuring a photo of an egg roll gleaming in all its fried glory. The author described his childhood as one dominated by these egg rolls, which he ate on a daily basis at a branch of the Empire Szechuan restaurant chain in New York City during the 1980s. He explained that although the "pudgy, cabbage-stuffed snacks didn't actually originate in China," they were "the authentic cuisine of my boyhood."[49] Authenticity was in his mind. Empire's egg rolls were authentically New York, not authentically Chinese. Their significance was still geographically specific, but not of the place one might expect.[50]

The slippery nature of authenticity may be due in part because it can be staged— a fact known by most observers. The Italian scholar Umberto Eco made a trip across the United States, observing that the fake was often more real than the real when seen in wax museums, Elvis impersonators, and Disneyland.[51] Staged realities, such as those found in New York's Times Square, San Francisco's Fisherman's Wharf, or the whole of the Las Vegas Strip, could be more impressive than the real thing they supposedly mimicked.[52] Las Vegas "may be a cliché, but it's a cliché on steroids— phoniness cultivated with a staggering amount of care and money."[53] More recently, speaking to this question, Bruce Springsteen gave a speech in which he said, "We live in a post-authentic world. . . . The elements of what you're using don't matter. Purity of human experience and expression is not confined to guitars, to tubes, to turntables, to microchips. There is no right way, no pure way of doing. There is just doing."[54]

As Rachel Laudan said, we can only really have "our-thentic," not authentic.[55] The search for authenticity is an "exercise in nostalgia"—one that ultimately has us chasing our own tails.[56] But we crave it nonetheless. That craving lies in the disorienting nature of globalization and immigration. If everything is changing and newness is on every corner, in every social media refresh, on every restaurant menu, then what value is there to tradition? If we have sameness in diversity, how do we make a choice? The diversity of foods causes Americans to seek adventure, searching for the authentic taco or dim sum. The sameness of foods, with big corporations and fast food dominating the marketplace also fuels that search. Perhaps we shouldn't search for the authentic, however, because it is not possible to find. Instead, search for the best taste in foods, enjoying each bite for what it is worth. And share foods with a wider circle of people. Eat not the other. Eat with the other and we may bridge the many divides.

ABBREVIATIONS USED IN THE
NOTES AND BIBLIOGRAPHY

BANC   The Bancroft Library, University of California, Berkeley
CHS   California Historical Society, North Baker Research Library, San
            Francisco, CA
CHU   Papers of Grace Zia Chu, 1941–1986, MC 641, MP-42, Vt-91, Arthur and
            Elizabeth Schlesinger Library on the History of Women in America,
            Radcliffe Institute for Advanced Study, Harvard University, Cambridge,
            MA (hereafter CHU)
CCSF   Menu Collection, Alice Statler Library, City College of San Francisco,
            San Francisco, CA
ERS-USDA   Economic Research Service, United States Department of Agriculture
HAG   Hagley Museum and Library, Wilmington, DE
HML   Him Mark Lai Papers, Asian American Studies Archives, Ethnic
            Studies Library, University of California, Berkeley
INS   Immigration and Naturalization Service
JJMC   Judith Jones Manuscript Collection, Series V. Editor Files, Alfred A.
            Knopf, Inc. Records, 1873–1996, Harry Ransom Humanities Research
            Center, University of Texas at Austin
JWT-ACC   Inventory of the J. Walter Thompson Company. Account Files,
            1885–2008 and undated, bulk 1920–1995, John W. Hartman Center for
            Sales, Advertising & Marketing History, David M. Rubenstein Rare
            Book & Manuscript Library, Duke University
JWT-AD   J. Walter Thompson Company. Domestic Advertisements
            Collection, 1875–2001 and undated, John W. Hartman Center for Sales,
            Advertising & Marketing History, David M. Rubenstein Rare Book &
            Manuscript Library, Duke University

JWT-BONA   Nicole Di Bona Peterson Collection of Advertising Cookbooks, John
                W. Hartman Center for Sales, Advertising & Marketing History, David
                M. Rubenstein Rare Book & Manuscript Library, Duke University
JWT-COMP   J. Walter Thompson Competitive Advertisements, John W. Hartman
                Center for Sales, Advertising & Marketing History, David M.
                Rubenstein Rare Book & Manuscript Library, Duke University.
JWT-NEWBUS   J. Walter Thompson Company, New Business Records, 1924–2006,
                John W. Hartman Center for Sales, Advertising & Marketing History,
                David M. Rubenstein Rare Book & Manuscript Library, Duke
                University
JWT-NEWS   J. Walter Thompson Company Newsletter Collection, John W.
                Hartman Center for Sales, Advertising & Marketing History, David M.
                Rubenstein Rare Book & Manuscript Library, Duke University,
                in archive and at http://library.duke.edu/digitalcollections/jwtnews
                letters/
NARA-DEN   National Archives and Records Administration, Denver, Broomfield,
                CO, Record Group 188, Records of the Office of Price Administration
                Records of Regional Land District Field Offices, Region 7, Denver
NARA-PAC   National Archives and Records Administration, Pacific Region (San
                Francisco), San Bruno, CA, Record Group 188, Records of the Office
                of Price Administration
NYPLM   Menu Collection, Rare Books Division, Humanities and Social
                Sciences Library, New York Public Library, Main Branch
OAK   Oakland History Room, Oakland Public Library, Main Branch
OPA   Office of Price Administration
SCH   Arthur and Elizabeth Schlesinger Library on the History of Women in
                America, Radcliffe Institute for Advanced Study, Harvard University,
                Cambridge, MA
SFHC   San Francisco History Center, San Francisco Public Library, Main
                Branch
SFMNHP   San Francisco National Maritime Historical Park, San Francisco, CA
VF   Vertical File

NOTES

INTRODUCTION

1. Alex Witchel, "As a Teenage Refugee, He Was the Family Chef. Now, He's a Lauded Chef," *Washington Post*, September 11, 2017.

2. Ibid.

3. Frederick Z. Brown, "President Clinton's Visit to Vietnam," *Asia Society*, November 2000, http://www.asiasociety.org/publications/clintoninvietnam.html (accessed February 14, 2007); John Wildermuth, "President Spends Sunday in S.F. with Daughter," *San Francisco Chronicle* http://www.sfgate.com/politics/article/President-Spends-Sunday-in-S-F -With-Daughter-3304963.php (accessed February 14, 2007).

4. Michael Bauer, "A Revolving Door: Wildly Popular New Slanted Door Has a Few Kinks to Work Out," *San Francisco Chronicle*, June 20, 2004; Laurie Winer, "Vietnam á la Cart," *Food & Wine*, September 2005; Theresa Di Masi, "Chef Profile: Charles Phan," http:// epicurious.com/features/chefs/phan (accessed February 14, 2007).

5. Winer, "Vietnam á la Cart"; Alan J. Liddle, "Demand up for San Francisco's the Slanted Door," *Nation's Restaurant News*, May 3, 2004, 5–6, 72. Menus, The Slanted Door, March 18, 1997, and September 22, 2010; Vertical File, S.F. Menus, Slanted Door, San Francisco History Center, San Francisco Public Library, Main Branch (hereafter SFHC); Richard Leong, "World Chefs: Phan Shares Food, Journey from Vietnam," *Reuters Africa*, October 9, 2012, http://af.reuters.com/article/commoditiesNews/idAFL3E8L55FE20121009?sp=true (accessed October 10, 2012); Esther Sung, "A Conversation with Charles Phan," http://www .epicurious.com/articlesguides/chefsexperts/interviews/charles-phan-interview-recipes (accessed June 6, 2013).

6. Krishnendu Ray, *The Ethnic Restaurateur* (New York: Bloomsbury, 2016).

7. USDA-ERS, "Food Expenditures by Families and Individuals as a Share of Disposable Personal Income," http://www.ers.usda.gov/data-products/food-expenditures.aspx (accessed January 7, 2016).

8. Sophie Coe, *America's First Cuisines* (Austin: University of Texas Press, 1994), 9–10; Rachel Laudan, *Cuisine and Empire: Cooking in World History* (Berkeley: University of California Press, 2013).

9. General histories of food include Carol Helstosky, ed., *The Routledge History of Food* (New York: Routledge, 2015); Jeffrey M. Pilcher, ed., *The Oxford Handbook of Food History* (New York: Oxford University Press, 2012); Linda Civitello, *Cuisine and Culture: A History of Food and People* (Hoboken, NJ: John Wiley, 2011); Paul Freedman, Joyce E. Chaplin, and Ken Albala, eds., *Food in Time and Place: The American Historical Association Companion to Food History* (Berkeley: University of California Press, 2014); Ken Albala, ed., *Routledge International Handbook of Food Studies* (New York: Routledge, 2012).

10. Frank J. Lechner and John Boli, *The Globalization Reader*, 3rd ed. (Malden, MA: Blackwell, 2008), 3.

11. Centers for Disease Control, "NCHS Data Brief No. 219," November 2015, https://www.cdc.gov/obesity/data/adult.html (accessed April 26, 2019); Cheryl D. Fryar, Margaret D. Carroll, and Cynthia L. Odgen, "Prevalence of Overweight, Obesity, and Extreme Obesity among Adults: United States, 1960–62 through 2011–2012," *Health E-Stat*, September 2014, https://www.cdc.gov/nchs/data/hestat/obesity_adult_11_12/obesity_adult_11_12.htm (accessed April 26, 2019).

12. US Public Health Service, *The Surgeon General's Call to Action to Prevent and Decrease Overweight and Obesity, 2001* (Rockville, MD: GPO, 2001), xiii, 8.

13. Ibid.; Center on Hunger and Poverty and Food Research and Action Center, "The Paradox of Hunger and Obesity in America," http://www.agnt.org/humane/hungerandobesity.pdf (accessed April 29, 2019); Lee M. Scheier, "What Is the Hunger-Obesity Paradox?," *Journal of the Academy of Nutrition and Dietetics* 105, no. 6 (2005): 883–85; "The Shape of Things to Come," *The Economist*, December 11, 2003; Amanda Spake, "A Fat Nation," *US News and World Report*, August 19, 2002; Greg Critser, "Let Them Eat Fat: The Heavy Truths about American Obesity," *Harper's Magazine*, March 2000; Michael Pollan, *The Omnivore's Dilemma: A Natural History of Four Meals* (New York: Penguin Press, 2006).

14. Laura Shapiro, *Something from the Oven: Reinventing Dinner in 1950s America* (New York: Penguin, 2004); Kimberly Wilmot Voss, *The Food Section: Newspaper Women and the Culinary Community* (Lanham, MD: Rowman & Littlefield, 2014).

15. "Exclusive First Read: From Scratch: Inside the Food Network," NPR, https://www.npr.org/2013/09/19/223173797/exclusive-first-read-from-scratch-inside-the-food-network (accessed August 22, 2018).

16. The globalization literature is vast. One place to start is Bryan S. Turner and Robert J. Holton, *The Routledge International Handbook of Globalization Studies*, 2nd ed. (New York: Routledge, 2016). Also see Jurgen Osterhammel and Niels P. Petersson, *Globalization: A Short History*, trans. Dona Geyer (Princeton, NJ: Princeton University Press, 2005); David Held and Anthony McGrew, eds., *The Global Transformations Reader: An Introduction to the Globalization Debate*, 2nd ed. (Malden, MA: Polity, 2003); Timothy Taylor, "The Truth about Globalization," *The Public Interest*, Spring 2002, 24–44.

17. Alexander Nützenadel and Frank Trentmann, "Introduction: Mapping Food and Globalization," in Alexander Nützenadel and Frank Trentmann, eds., *Food and Globalization: Consumption, Markets and Politics in the Modern World* (New York: Berg, 2008), 1–18.

18. Paul Rozin, "Food Is Fundamental, Fun, Frightening, and Far-Reaching," *Social Research* 66, no. 1 (1999): 9–30.

19. Donna Gabaccia, *We Are What We Eat: Ethnic Food and the Making of Americans* (Cambridge, MA: Harvard University Press, 1999). Other fundamental studies include Yong Chen, *Chop Suey, USA: The Story of Chinese Food in America* (New York: Columbia University Press, 2014); Joel Denker, *The World on a Plate: A Tour through the History of America's Ethnic Cuisine* (Lincoln: University of Nebraska Press, 2003); Hasia R. Diner, *Hungering for America: Italian, Irish, and Jewish Foodways in the Age of Immigration* (Cambridge, MA: Harvard University Press, 2001); Marilyn Halter, *Shopping for Identity: The Marketing of Ethnicity* (New York: Schocken Books, 2000); Lucy Long, ed., *Culinary Tourism* (Lexington: University Press of Kentucky, 2004). Jeffrey Pilcher, *Planet Taco: A Global History of Mexican Food* (New York: Oxford University Press, 2012); Ray, *The Ethnic Restaurateur*.

20. "International Migrant Stock 2015: Graphs," Department of Economic and Social Affairs, Population Division, http://www.un.org/en/development/desa/population/migration/data/estimates2/estimatesgraphs.shtml?3g3 (accessed July 1, 2016); "Trends in Total Migrant Stock: The 2005 Revision," Department of Economic and Social Affairs, Population Division, February 2006, http://www.un.org/esa/population/publications/migration/UN_Migrant_Stock_Documentation_2005.pdf (accessed July 1, 2016). Jose Moya and Adam McKeown, "World Migration in the Long Twentieth Century," in Michael Adas, ed., *Essays on Twentieth Century History* (Philadelphia: Temple University Press, 2010), 9–52.

21. Roger Daniels, *Coming to America: A History of Immigration and Ethnicity in American Life* (New York: Harper Perennial, 1990); Mae Ngai, *Impossible Subjects: Illegal Aliens and the Making of Modern America*, updated ed. (Princeton, NJ: Princeton University Press, 2014); Leonard Dinnerstein and David Reimers, *Ethnic Americans: A History of Immigration*, 4th ed. (New York: Columbia University Press, 1999).

22. The exact total was 34,823,784. I count immigrants as people obtaining "lawful permanent resident status," or what is commonly called a "green card." Many thousands more people enter the United States temporarily every year as tourists, students, or on work visas. US Department of Homeland Security, "Table 2: Persons Obtaining Legal Permanent Resident Status by Region and Selected Country of Last Residence," in *2010 Yearbook of Immigration Statistics* (Washington, DC: US Department of Homeland Security, 2011), https://www.dhs.gov/sites/default/files/publications/Yearbook_Immigration_Statistics_2010.pdf (accessed February 28, 2017); US Department of Homeland Security, "Lawful Permanent Residents," Years 2004–2010, https://www.dhs.gov/immigration-statistics/lawful-permanent-residents# (accessed February 27, 2017); US Department of Homeland Security, "Table 2: Persons Obtaining Legal Permanent Resident Status by Region and Selected Country of Last Residence: Fiscal Years 1820–2004," *2004 Yearbook of Immigration Statistics* (Washington, DC: US Department of Homeland Security, 2006), https://www.dhs.gov/sites/default/files/publications/Yearbook_Immigration_Statistics_2004.pdf (accessed February 28, 2017); US Department of Homeland Security, "Table 2: Persons Obtaining Legal Permanent Resident Status by Region and Selected Country of Last Residence Fiscal Years 1820–2000," *2000 Yearbook of Immigration Statistics* (Washington, DC: US Department of Homeland Security, 2002), https://www.dhs.gov/xlibrary/assets/statistics/yearbook/2000/Yearbook2000.pdf

(accessed February 28, 2017). The commentator was Christopher Jencks in "Who Should Get In, Part I," *The New York Review of Books*, December 20, 2001.

23. US Census Bureau, "The Foreign-Born Population in the United States," https://www.census.gov/newsroom/pdf/cspan_fb_slides.pdf (accessed December 1, 2016). In 1970, 9.6 million foreign born lived in the United States. The highest percentage between 1850 and 2010 was in 1890 and 1910 at about 14.8 and 14.7 percent respectively.

24. William H. Frey, *Diversity Explosion: How New Racial Demographics Are Remaking America* (Washington DC: Brookings Institution Press, 2015), 67, 89. The "Hispanic" designation has changed over time, so this number is an approximation for the 1970 period.

25. Jon C. Teaford, *The Metropolitan Revolution: The Rise of Post-Urban America* (New York: Columbia University Press, 2006), 207.

26. Flavor profiles from Elisabeth Rozin, *The Flavor-Principle Cookbook* (New York: Hawthorn Books, 1973). "Beyond Phở," *The Migrant Kitchen*, KCET, https://www.kcet.org/shows/the-migrant-kitchen/episodes/beyond-pho (accessed August 19, 2018).

27. The owner is not named in the account from Caroline R. Brettell, "'Meet Me at the Chat/Chaat Corner': The Embeddedness of Immigrant Entrepreneurs," in Elliot R. Barkan, Hasia Diner, and Alan Kraut, eds., *From Arrival to Incorporation: Migrants to the US in a Global Era* (New York: New York University Press, 2007), 121–42. Other examples abound for this. See Arijit Sen, "Food, Place, and Memory: Bangladeshi Food Stores on Devon Avenue," *Food and Foodways* 24, no. 1 (2016): 67–88; "Ethnic Grocery Store in Houston," in Jennifer Jensen Wallach and Lindsey R. Swindall, eds., *American Appetites: A Documentary Reader* (Fayettville: University of Arkansas Press, 2014); Russell Lee, photo, "Small Mexican Grocery Store, San Antonio, Texas," Library of Congress, at https://www.loc.gov/item/fsa2000013867/PP/ (accessed January 27, 2017); and Valerie Imbruce, "From the Bottom Up: The Global Expansion of Chinese Vegetable Trade for New York City Markets," in Richard Wilk, ed., *Fast Food/Slow Food: The Cultural Economy of the Global Food System* (Berkeley: Altamira, 2006), 163–79.

28. Paul Masson, "Globalization: Facts and Figures," *IMF Policy Discussion Paper*, October 2001, 1–7.

29. Ibid.

30. Danny Hakim, "Aboard a Cargo Colossus: Maersk's New Container Ships," *New York Times*, October 3, 2014.

31. A. G. Hopkins, *American Empire: A Global History* (Princeton, NJ: Princeton University Press, 2018), 11.

32. A. G. Hopkins has the most perceptive analysis of the place of globalization in *American Empire*, esp. 11–41. Also see A. G. Hopkins, *Globalization in World History* (New York: Norton, 2002).

33. Kevin H. O'Rourke and Jeffrey G. Williamson, "When Did Globalization Begin?" National Bureau of Economic Research Working Paper 7632, http://www.nber.org/papers/w7632 (accessed August 28, 2007), 15–19, quotes on 15.

34. Esteban Ortiz-Ospina and Max Roser, "International Trade," *OurWorldinData.org*, https://ourworldindata.org/international-trade (accessed March 1, 2018). This surveys several studies and data sets. Perhaps the most comprehensive historical data is in Angus Maddison, *The World Economy: A Millenial Perspective* (Paris: Development Centre of the

Organisation for Economic Co-operation and Development, 2001); and Angus Maddison, *Contours of the World Economy, 1–2030 AD* (New York: Oxford University Press, 2007).

35. Charles Van Marrewijk, *International Trade* (New York: Oxford University Press, 2017), 3–51. Marrewijk's analysis summarizes the broader trends in the other studies mentioned here. One study shows globalization increasing in more than just economic terms since the 1970s. It measured economic, social, and political interchanges, with twenty-three variables used to create a globalization index. This index showed an overall 56 percent increase in globalization from 1970 to 2010. The economic indices included measures of trade and investment; the social indices factored communication improvements, international tourism, and the presence of McDonald's and Ikea stores worldwide; and the political indices counted international treaties and participation in international organizations. Niklas Potrafke, "The Evidence on Globalisation," *The World Economy* 38, no. 3 (March 2015): 509–52. This article makes sense of the KOF Swiss Economic Institute's Globalisation Index. The "Components of the 2013 Index of Globalisation" included twenty-three variables, of which only some are mentioned above. KOF Swiss Economic Institute, "KOF Globalisation Index," https://www.kof.ethz.ch/en/forecasts-and-indicators/indicators/kof-globalisation-index.html (accessed February 25, 2018).

36. Upton Sinclair, *The Jungle*, ed. Christopher Phelps (Boston: Bedford/St. Martin's, 2005), esp. 66–68, 115–19; James R. Barrett, *Work and Community in the Jungle: Chicago's Packinghouse Workers, 1894–1922* (Champaign: University of Illinois, 1987).

37. William Cronon, *Nature's Metropolis: Chicago and the Great West* (New York: W.W. Norton, 1991).

38. "Why Farmers Are Anxious about NAFTA," *The Economist*, June 29, 2017.

39. Harriet Friedmann, "Feeding the Empire: Pathologies of Globalized Agriculture," in Leo Panitch and Colin Leys, eds., *Socialist Register 2005: The Empire Reloaded* (London: Merlin, 2004). Friedman also refers to the "food regime" (a term used by many sociologists) and the "crisis of the world economy" after 1973 in Harriet Friedmann and Philip McMichael, "Agriculture and the State System: The Rise and Decline of National Agricultures, 1870 to the Present," *Sociologia Ruralis* 29, no. 2 (1989): 93–117, quote from 108.

40. Reidår Almas and Geoffrey Lawrence, "Introduction: The Global/Local Problematic," in Reidår Almas and Geoffrey Lawrence, eds., *Globalization, Localization and Sustainable Livelihoods* (Burlington, VT: Ashgate, 2003), 10.

41. Ibid., 3.

42. Philip McMichael, "Rethinking Globalization: The Agrarian Question Revisited," *Review of International Political Economy* 4, no. 4 (Winter 1997): 630–62; Evelyn Hu-Dehart, "Globalization and Its Discontents: Exposing the Underside," *Frontiers: A Journal of Women Studies* 24, nos. 2–3 (2003): 244–60; Paul Krugman, Richard Cooper, and T.N. Srinivasan, "Growing World Trade: Causes and Consequences," 25th Anniversary Issue, *Brookings Papers on Economic Activity* 1 (1995): 327–77; Christian Broda and David Weinstein, "Globalization and the Gains from Variety," (Working Paper 10314, Cambridge, MA: National Bureau of Economic Research, 2004); Nicholas Crafts, "Globalisation and Economic Growth: A Historical Perspective," *The World Economy* 27, no. 1 (January 2004): 45–58; Felipe Fernández-Armesto, "Global Histories of Food," *Journal of Global History* 3 (2008): 459–62; Jacinto F. Fabiosa, "Globalization and Trends in World Food Consumption," in

Jayson L. Lusk, Jutta Roosen, and Jason F. Shogren, eds., *The Oxford Handbook of the Economics of Food Consumption and Policy*, (New York: Oxford University Press, 2011), 591–611.

43. Most studies about food either discuss farming, a typically rural activity (though some focus on urban farming) or major cities, such as New York or San Francisco. A few recent studies have begun looking at the diverse suburbs of recent years, whether in Los Angeles or Toronto. Examples include Haiming Liu, *From Canton Restaurant to Panda Express* (New Brunswick: Rutgers University Press, 2015) and Camille Bégin and Jayeeta Sharma, "A Culinary Hub in the Global City: Diasporic Foodscapes across Scarborough, Canada," *Food, Culture and Society* 21, no. 1 (2018): 55–74.

44. "Population: Urban/Suburban/Rural," in *The First Measured Century*, PBS, http://www.pbs.org/fmc/book/1population6.htm (accessed August 18, 2007).

45. Lizabeth Cohen, *A Consumer's Republic: The Politics of Mass Consumption in Postwar America* (New York: Alfred A. Knopf, 2003).

46. Roger Silverstone, "Introduction," Roger Silverstone, ed., *Visions of Suburbia* (New York: Routledge, 1997), 8.

47. Kenneth Jackson, *Crabgrass Frontier: The Suburbanization of the United States* (New York: Oxford University Press, 1985), 239–41; David Halberstam, *The Fifties* (New York: Fawcett Columbine, 1993), 131–43.

48. The line is from the 1962 Malvina Reynolds song, "Little Boxes." Malvina Reynolds, *Malvina Reynolds Sings the Truth* (New York: Columbia, 1967).

49. Michael Jones-Correa, "Reshaping the American Dream: Immigrants, Ethnic Minorities, and the Politics of the New Suburbs," in Kevin M. Kruse and Thomas J. Sugrue, eds., *The New Suburban History* (Chicago: University of Chicago Press, 2006), 183–84.

50. Silverstone, "Introduction," in Silverstone, ed., *Visions of Suburbia*, 6; "Quick Facts, Levittown CDP, NY," *US Census Bureau*, https://www.census.gov/quickfacts/fact/table/levittowncdpnewyork/PST045217 (accessed August 20, 2018).

51. Food globalization has received much attention recently, including by Richard Wilk, *Home Cooking in the Global Village: Caribbean Food from Buccaneers to Ecotourists* (New York: Berg, 2006); Richard Wilk, ed., *Fast Food/Slow Food: The Cultural Economy of the Global Food System* (Berkeley: Altamira, 2006); David Inglis and Debra Gimlin, *The Globalization of Food* (New York: Berg, 2009); Susanne Freidberg, *Fresh: A Perishable History* (Cambridge, MA: Harvard University Press, 2009); Kenneth F. Kiple, *A Moveable Feast: Ten Millenia of Food Globalization* (New York: Cambridge University Press, 2007); James L. Watson, ed., *Golden Arches East: McDonald's in East Asia* (Stanford, CA: Stanford University Press, 1997).

52. Approximately 5.8 percent of the population was Asian or of Spanish heritage, and 74.5 percent of the foreign-born were from Europe. *1970 Census of Population* (Washington, DC: US Department of Commerce, 1973), 591–98. Hispanics often identify as black or white on the census, so the numbers are inexact for any era.

53. On Dichter's influence, see Daniel Horowitz, *The Anxieties of Affluence: Critiques of American Consumer Culture, 1939–1979* (Amherst: University of Massachusetts Press, 2004), 48–78. Ernest Dichter, President, Institute for Motivational Research, Inc., "A Creative Memorandum on the Introduction of Beedi in the US," submitted to the Consulate General of India, New York, NY, February 1965, in Hagley Museum and Library, Wilming-

ton, DE (Hereafter HAG), Box 82, Ernest Dichter Papers, Research Reports, Accession 2407, Folder 1841E-1842A—Report 1841E.

54. Ernest Dichter, "Proposal for a Motivational Research Study for Unsatisfied Needs in the Food World," submitted to General Foods Corporation, White Plains, NY, December 1959, in HAG, Ernest Dichter Papers, Research Reports, Accession 2407, Box 9, Folder 214.2A.

55. Marilyn Halter, *Shopping for Identity: The Marketing of Ethnicity* (New York: Schocken Books, 2000).

56. William G. Lockwook, "Ethnic Cuisines," *Encyclopedia of Food and Culture*, ed. Solomon H. Katz, vol. 3 (New York: Scribner, 2003), 442–46.

57. Ground beef had been used in many cultures for hundreds of years, but in Germany there was a "Hamburg steak" that some believe was the origin of the American hamburger. This claim is disputed by others who argue for different origins of the name and the food. Linda Stradley, "History of Hamburgers," *What's Cooking America*, http://whatscookin gamerica.net/History/HamburgerHistory.htm. (accessed March 13, 2008); "Hamburger," in David A. Bender, *A Dictionary of Food and Nutrition, Oxford Reference Online* (New York: Oxford University Press, 2005), http://www.oxfordreference.com/views/ENTRY.html?entry =t39.e2593 (accessed March 13, 2008). When discussing the basic category of American food, the anthropologist and food historian Sidney Mintz said it included, "certainly hamburgers, and probably Southern fried chicken, and clam chowders and baked beans, steak, ribs, and perhaps chili, and hot dogs, and, now pizza, and baked potatoes with 'the works.'" Sidney Mintz, "Eating American," in Carole M. Counihan, ed., *Food in the USA: A Reader* (New York: Routledge, 2002), 23–40, quote on 27. Also see Donna Gabaccia, "What Do We Eat," 35–40 in the same reader. Fittingly, the reader's cover photo shows a double-decker hamburger accompanied by fries. Not everyone agrees that hamburgers or hot dogs are American foods. Some argue that true American foods are those present before the arrival of Europeans, such as the turkey and certain chili peppers. See Raymond Sokolov, *Why We Eat What We Eat* (New York: Summit Books, 1991), 148–49.

58. Lucy M. Long, "Introduction," *Ethnic American Food Today: A Cultural Encyclopedia*, ed. Lucy M. Long (Lanham, MD: Rowman & Littlefield, 2015), 1–5. Also see Yong Chen, "Food, Race, and Ethnicity," in Pilcher, ed., *The Oxford Handbook of Food History*, 428–43.

59. Julia Moskin, "How the Taco Gained in Translation," *New York Times*, April 30, 2012.

60. Don Yoder quoted in Linda Keller Brown and Kay Mussell, eds., *Ethnic and Regional Foodways in the United States: The Performance of Group Identity*, (Knoxville: University of Tennessee Press, 1984), 4.

61. One study estimated that about half of all new packaged consumer goods each year were foods or beverages. See John M. O'Connor, "Food Product Proliferation: A Market Structure Analysis," *American Journal of Agricultural Economics* 63, no. 4 (1981): 607–17.

62. *Progressive Grocer* said that the "buzzword of the 1980s was segmentation," for there was no "typical shopper." "The History of the Supermarket Industry," in *Progressive Grocer's 1992 Marketing Guidebook* (Stamford, CT: Progressive Grocer Trade Dimensions, 1991).

63. Steve Raabe, "Losing Shelf-Doubt," *Denver Post*, February 12, 2014.

64. Jordan Weissmann, "Our Monopoly Economy," *The Atlantic*, April 2013.

65. Oxfam International, "Behind the Brands: Food Justice and the 'Big 10' Food and Beverage Companies," Oxfam Briefing Paper, February 2013, https://www-cdn.oxfam.org

/s3fs-public/file_attachments/bp166-behind-the-brands-260213-en_2.pdf (accessed January 14, 2016).

66. Philip H. Howard, "Organic Processing Industry Structure," at https://msu.edu /~howardp/organicindustry.html (accessed January 14, 2016), and "Consolidation in the North American Organic Food Processing Sector, 1997 to 2007," *International Journal of Sociology of Agriculture and Food* 16, no. 1 (2009): 13–30.

67. Philip H. Howard, *Concentration and Power in the Food System* (New York: Bloomsbury, 2016).

68. Philip H. Howard website, https://msu.edu/~howardp/beer.html (accessed September 15, 2016).

69. AB InBev purchased SABMiller in 2016. See "Combination with SABMiller," AB InBev press release, http://www.ab-inbev.com/investors/sabmiller/pressrelease.html (accessed June 30, 2017). "AB InBev and SAB Miller Merger Focuses on Markets Outside the US," *Forbes*, November 16, 2015, http://www.forbes.com/sites/greatspeculations/2015/11/16/ab-inbev-and -sabmiller-merger-focuses-on-markets-outside-the-u-s/#3db4876612cd (accessed July 1, 2015).

70. Christopher Leonard, "How the Meat Industry Keeps Chicken Prices High," *Slate*, March 3, 2014.

71. Ben Mutzbaugh, "Era of Airline Merger Mania Comes to a Close with Last US Airways Flight," *USA Today*, October 16, 2015, http://www.usatoday.com/story/travel /flights/todayinthesky/2015/10/15/airline-mergers-american-delta-united-southwest /73972928/ (accessed January 7, 2015).

72. Jim Milliot, "BEA 2014: Can Anyone Compete with Amazon?," *Publisher's Weekly*, May 28, 2014, at http://www.publishersweekly.com/pw/by-topic/industry-news/bea/article /62520-bea-2014-can-anyone-compete-with-amazon.html (accessed January 14, 2016).

73. Ben Sisario, "EMI is Sold for $4.1 Billion in Combined Deals, Consolidating the Music Industry," *New York Times*, November 11, 2011.

74. Weissmann, "Our Monopoly Economy."

75. Philip H. Howard offers the most compelling overview about this in various food industries in *Concentration and Power in the Food System* (New York: Bloomsbury, 2016). Michael Pollan discusses the nutritional consequences of this in many publications, including *The Omnivore's Dilemma: A Natural History of Four Meals* (New York: Penguin Press, 2006).

76. There is a massive literature on labor in agriculture and food industries. See Daniel Rothenberg, *With These Hands: The Hidden World of Migrant Farmworkers Today* (Berkeley: University of California Press, 1998). The more recent work by Latin American immigrants in poultry, pork and other food processing plants in the South and Midwest is told in Raymond A. Mohl, "Globalization, Latinization, and the Nuevo New South," *Journal of American Ethnic History* 22, no. 4 (2003): 31–66; Lionel Cantú, "The Peripheralization of Rural America: A Case Study of Latino Migrants in America's Heartland," *Sociological Perspectives* 38, no. 3 (1995): 399–414; William Kandel and Emilio A. Parrado, "Restructuring of the US Meat Processing Industry and New Hispanic Migrant Destinations," *Population and Development Review* 31, no. 3 (2005): 447–71; Saru Jayaraman, *Behind the Kitchen Door* (Ithaca, NY: Cornell University Press, 2013); On the changing groups of immigrants who labored in the restaurant industry from the 1800s to the present in New York City, see Ray,

"Ethnic Succession and the New American Restaurant Cuisine," in David Beriss and David Sutton, eds., *The Restaurants Book: Ethnographies of Where We Eat* (New York: Berg, 2007), 97–114.

77. Oscar Avila and Antonio Olivo, "A Foot in the Kitchen Door," *Chicago Tribune*, November 26, 2006. On the Mexican impact on the food service labor force, see Rob Paral, "No Way In: US Immigration Policy Leaves Few Legal Options for Mexican Workers," *Immigration Policy in Focus* 4, no. 5 (2005) http://robparal.com/downloads/nowayin.htm (accessed February 8, 2008).

78. Oscar Avila and Antonio Olivo, "Blending Cultures, Blending Flavors," *Chicago Tribune*, November 26, 2006.

79. Ibid. A Salvadoran immigrant won a major sushi-preparing contest in Los Angeles in 2005, and Mexican sushi chefs are numerous in Chicago, giving rise to the term *sushero*. Claire Levinson, "How Do You Say 'Sushi' in Spanish?," *NY Resident Magazine*, April 10, 2007, http://74.54.115.114/node/606 (accessed February 13, 2008).

80. Quoted in Avila and Olivo, "A Foot in the Kitchen Door." Many of the "back-of-house" staff in restaurants work for low wages and in conditions in which they have little chance for promotion because of their poor education and/or poor English-language skills. As with previous immigrant groups, there are more examples of Mexicans rising to become owners or managers of non-Mexican restaurants too, such as Carlos Nieto, who owns Carlos' a French restaurant just north of Chicago that is often named among the best in the area.

81. The high-priced restaurants include Cassia in Santa Monica and Le Colonial in Chicago.

82. "Beyond Phở," *The Migrant Kitchen*.

83. Craig Claiborne, "Vietnamese Cuisine Is Inexpensive," *New York Times*, August 15, 1961.

84. Krishnendu Ray discusses the transition for some (but not other) cuisines from cheap to haute in *The Ethnic Restaurateur*.

1. THE GLOBALIZATION OF THE FRUIT AND VEGETABLE TRADE

1. Paul Krugman, Richard Cooper, and T. N. Srinivasan, "Growing World Trade: Causes and Consequences," 25th Anniversary Issue, *Brookings Papers on Economic Activity* 1 (1995): 363.

2. Marc Levinson, *The Box: How the Shipping Container Made the World Smaller and the World Economy Bigger* (Princeton, NJ: Princeton University Press, 2006); Brian Cudahy, *Box Boats: How Container Ships Changed the World* (New York: Fordham University Press, 2006).

3. Levinson, *The Box*, 52.

4. Levinson, *The Box*, 46–71.

5. American President Lines News Releases, July 1, 1966 and October 21, 1966; Letter, Tom Wheeler, American President Lines to Mike Harris (Reporter for *Time Magazine*), February 16, 1966; and clipping of *Traffic Management*, February 1966, all in HDC 279, American President Lines, Box 336, Series 6.3, Subgroup IV, Folder 3, Parts 1 and 2, Public

Relations Files Kept by Tom Wheeler Re: Containerization, 1965–66, San Francisco National Maritime Historical Park, San Francisco, CA.

6. Malcolm McLean initiated the first container ship voyage on April 26, 1956, sending a vessel from Port Newark, New Jersey, to Houston. He signed his first contract to work in Vietnam in 1966, but it was not until 1967 that he was able to sign a further deal to containerize shipping through Cam Ranh Bay. Pacific trade import values for 2004 in Cudahy, *Box Boats*, ix–41, 106–11, 238–41; Levinson, *The Box*, 3–7, 171–88; Marc Salvatore R. Mercogliano, "The Container Revolution," *Sea History* 114 (2006), http://www.sname.org/newsletter /SeaHistoryContnrShps.pdf (accessed July 9, 2007), 8–11.

7. Danny Hakim, "Aboard a Cargo Colossus: Maersk's New Container Ships," *New York Times*, October 3, 2014; Carl Nolte, "Huge Container Ship Sails into S.F. Bay Records," *San Francisco Chronicle*, March 22, 2012.

8. Tanachai Mark Padoongpatt, "Too Hot to Handle," *Radical History Review* 110 (Spring 2011): 83–108.

9. Valerie Imbruce, *From Farm to Canal Street: Chinatown's Alternative Food Network in the Global Marketplace* (Ithaca, NY: Cornell University Press, 2015).

10. Tim Zagat said he could not remember a Vietnamese or Thai restaurant when he started his first "Zagat Survey" restaurant guide with his wife, Nina, in 1979. Megan Barnett, "Grabbing a Bite: A Zagat Fave," *U.S. News and World Report, Executive Edition*, March 15, 2004, http://www.usnews.com/usnews/biztech/articles/040315/15eesuite.lunch.htm (accessed January 27, 2007). Thanh Long claimed it was the "first authentic Vietnamese restaurant on the West Coast" when it opened in 1971 in San Francisco. Opening Night menu and announcement of Thanh Long Vietnam Restaurant, 1971, San Francisco, CA in CCSF, Folder—Calif, San Francisco, S-T. In a 1961 review, *New York Times* critic Craig Claiborne wrote that Viet Nam restaurant in New York City was "reputedly the only Vietnamese restaurant in America," in "Vietnamese Cuisine Is Inexpensive," *New York Times*, August 15, 1961. One article reported that "several restaurants that feature Vietnamese, Thai, and Laotian food," had newly sprung up in the vicinity of Ft. Bragg in North Carolina because many servicemen had married women they met in those countries during the Vietnam War, Kenneth Reich, "Chop Suey n' Grits, Anyone?" *Los Angeles Times*, April 2, 1971.

11. The International Standards Committee set the size in 1961. Ships also carry half-length trailers at 20 × 8 × 8.5 feet, Mercogliano, "The Container Revolution," 9.

12. For the 1998 and 1987 numbers, Linda Calvin and Roberta Cook, *U.S. Fresh Fruit and Vegetable Marketing: Emerging Trade Practices, Trends, and Issues* (Washington, DC: ERS-USDA, 2001) http://www.ers.usda.gov/publications/aer795/aer795.pdf (accessed June 28, 2007), 3. For the 1975 estimate, Roberta Cook, "Challenges and Opportunities in the U.S. Fresh Produce Industry," *Journal of Food Distribution Research* 21.1 (1990): 67.

13. Phil R. Kaufman et al., *Understanding the Dynamics of Produce Markets: Consumption and Consolidation Grow*, AIB #758 (Washington, DC: ERS-USDA, 1999), 10.

14. Steve Striffler and Mark Moberg, eds., *Banana Wars: Power, Production, and History in the Americas* (Durham, NC: Duke University Press, 2003), 9–15; "Exotic" fruits such as the banana were eaten by American consumers because they were cheaper and better shipped by the banana "trust," despite their distance from consumers. "Apples and Bananas," *New York Times*, April 26, 1913.

15. Abel F. Lemes, "The Banana . . . It's Incredible but Edible!," *Safeway News*, December 1965, 8.

16. On the homogenizing effect of American cuisine during that era, see Kenneth F. Kiple, *A Moveable Feast: Ten Millenia of Food Globalization* (New York: Cambridge University Press, 2007), 226–37; Harvey Levenstein, *Paradox of Plenty: A Social History of Eating in Modern America*, rev. ed. (Berkeley: University of California Press, 2003), 91. Americans did eat canned tropical fruits, especially pineapples, in significant amounts, but the fresh version was rare.

17. Elisabeth Ortiz to Judith Jones, June 3, 1979, Judith Jones Manuscript Collection, Series V. Editor Files, Box 854.2, Folder—Ortiz, Elizabeth, in Alfred A. Knopf, Inc. Records, 1873–1996, Harry Ransom Humanities Research Center, University of Texas at Austin (Jones manuscript collection hereafter shortened to JJMC). The cookbook was Elisabeth Ortiz, *The Book of Latin American Cooking* (New York: Knopf, 1979). In 1972, Madhur Jaffrey explained to readers that cilantro could be found at specialty stores, suggesting that it was not widely available at supermarkets. Copy Editing Comments, July 6, 1972, JJMC, Box 851.11. Cilantro is explained and given a pronunciation guide on the menu for the chain of El Torito Restaurants, Inc., Irvine, CA, reprinted in *Great Menus: 1985* (Washington, DC: National Restaurant Association, 1986).

18. Richard Martin, "El Torito Founder Creates Mexican, Italian Hybrid," *Nation's Restaurant News*, October 26, 1992, 16. See also "Familiar Mexican Fare Awaits at Carlos Murphy's, *The Virginian-Pilot* (Norfolk), August 7, 1994.

19. Judith Jones Putnam and Jane E. Allshouse, *Food Consumption, Prices, and Expenditures, 1970–97, Statistical Bulletin No. 965* (Washington, DC: ERS-USDA, 1999), http://www.ers.usda.gov/publications/sb965/sb965.pdf (accessed June 21, 2007), Table 17; Gary Lucier et al., *Fruit and Vegetable Backgrounder, VGS-313-01* (Washington, DC: ERS-USDA, 2006), 13.

20. Maria Margarita Calleja Pinedo, "Distribution Channels in the U.S.A. for Mexican Fresh Fruits and Vegetables" (PhD diss., University of Texas at Austin, 2001), 95.

21. Kaufman et al., *Understanding the Dynamics of Produce Markets*, 9–16; Calleja Pinedo, *Distribution Channels in the U.S.A.*, 184.

22. Calvin and Cook, *U.S. Fresh Fruit and Vegetable Marketing*, v.

23. Raphael Minder, "Tempting Europe with Ugly Fruit," *New York Times*, May 25, 2014.

24. Roberta Cook, *The Evolving Global Marketplace for Fruits and Vegetables*, (Davis, CA: Agricultural Issues Center, 2003), http://www.agmrc.org/NR/rdonlyres/DCE3CA96-A372-4522-BD18-1FFD84A0CFF1/0/globalmarketplace.pdf (accessed June 26, 2007), 1.

25. In her column, Marian Manners, Home Economics writer for the *Los Angeles Times*, often gave advice about canning fruits for off-season consumption, "Fruit Needed in Each Day's Menu," January 21, 1947; "Its Time Now for Putting Up Berries," June 28, 1948; "Fine for Nutrition: Winter Fruits Add Zest to Menu Plans," November 3, 1950.

26. Wall Chart, "Seasonal Produce," posted in the computer laboratory at the Alice Statler Library, City College of San Francisco, San Francisco, CA, observed by the author on July 26, 2007. William Cronon best documents the separation of farm and table in *Nature's Metropolis: Chicago and the Great West* (New York: Norton, 1991).

27. Sophia Wu Huang, *Global Trade Patterns in Fruits and Vegetables* (Washington, DC: ERS-USDA, 2004) http://www.ers.usda.gov/publications/WRS0406/WRS0406.pdf (accessed June 28, 2007), 20.

28. Walter Heller and Jenny McTaggart, "The Search for Growth," *Progressive Grocer*, April 15, 2004, 31–41; Richard Turcsik and Walter Heller, "Produce Persona" *Progressive Grocer*, October 2000, 59–63.

29. Thomas R. Pierson, agricultural economist, quoted in Bruce Keppel, "Number of Items Displayed Triples in Decade," *Los Angeles Times*, February 19, 1985.

30. Safeway Stores, *Annual Report* (Oakland, CA: Safeway Stores, 1989), 3. Safeway had long emphasized produce as among the most important sections of its stores.

31. USDA, *Agriculture Fact Book 2000* (Washington, DC: USDA, 2000), 97–101; Pollan describes the drive for farmers to specialize in commodity crops in *The Omnivore's Dilemma*, 32–64.

32. Timothy Taylor, "The Truth about Globalization," *Public Interest*, 147 (Spring 2002): 25.

33. Huang, *Global Trade Patterns*, 1. These numbers are not adjusted for inflation.

34. In 1961, the world population was about 3.1 billion, making the global trade in fruits and vegetables about $1 per person that year. In 2001, the world population was about 6.2 billion, meaning global trade in fruits and vegetables had increased to about $11 per person by then. For population figures, United Nations Population Division, "World Population Prospects: The 2006 Revision," http://esa.un.org/unpp/ (accessed July 19, 2007). When adjusted for inflation, the 2001 amount converts to about $1.90 in 1961 dollars, using Robert C. Sahr, "Consumer Price Index (CPI) Conversion Factors 1800 to Estimated 2015 to Convert to Dollars of 2001," http://oregonstate.edu/cla/polisci/faculty-research/sahr/cv2001.pdf (accessed March 26, 2008).

35. FAO studies referenced in Huang, *Global Trade Patterns*, i–26, 44–45, 77–78. Huang also discusses the China import and export market. For a selection of comments about consumption by the growing middle classes in developing countries, including China, see Betsy Taylor and Dave Tilford, "Why Consumption Matters," in Juliet B. Schor and Douglas B. Holt, eds., *The Consumer Society Reader* (New York: The New Press, 2000), 469–70. The worldwide percentage of people residing in urban areas increased from 32.8 percent in 1960 to 46.7 percent in 2000, causing fruits and vegetables to be traded over longer distances to urban areas. United Nations Population Division, "World Population Prospects: The 2006 Revision."

36. The food guide pyramid was the latest of various food guides the US government had issued as part of nutrition education campaigns. The first food guide was published in 1916. See Susan O. Welsh, Carole Davis, and Anne Shaw, *USDA's Food Guide: Background and Development* (Hyattsville, MD: USDA, 1993).

37. I calculated the value of fruits and vegetables imported to the United States as a percentage of GDP by combining agricultural import data in "Table B-102: U.S. Exports and Imports of Agricultural Commodities, 1945–2001" and GDP data from "Table B-1: Gross Domestic Product, 1959–2001," *Economic Report of the President, 2002 Report Spreadsheet Tables* http://www.gpoaccess.gov/eop/tables02.html#erp8 (accessed June 28, 2007). USDA data show that imports have doubled as a share of total US fruit and vegetable consumption between 1977 and 1999, in Judy Putnam and Jane Allshouse, "Imports' Share of U.S. Diet Rises in Late 1990s," *Food Review* 24, no. 3 (2001), http://www.ers.usda.gov/publications/FoodReview/septdec01/FRv24i3.pdf (accessed September 11, 2007), 21.

38. Huang, *Global Trade Patterns*, 44–45, 77–78.

39. Huang, *Global Trade Patterns*, 21–22, 41, 45; Susan L. Pollack and Linda Calvin, *U.S.-Mexico Fruit and Vegetable Trade, 1970–92, Agricultural Economic Report 704* (Washington, DC: ERS-USDA, 1995), 5–7.

40. Robert B. Alvarez Jr., *Mangos, Chiles and Truckers: The Business of Transnationalism* (Minneapolis: University of Minnesota Press, 2005), 4–8, quote on p. 5; Robert Alvarez, "Neoliberalism and the Transnational Activity of the State: Offshore Control in the U.S.-Mexico Mango and Persian Lime Industry," in Thomas Weaver et al., eds., *Neoliberalism and Commodity Production in Mexico* (Boulder: University Press of Colorado, 2012), 51–66.

41. Alvarez, *Mangos, Chiles and Truckers*, 10–11.

42. Alvarez, "Neoliberalism," 60.

43. University of Chile graduate students who studied horticulture at the University of California at Davis introduced a number of these varieties. Claudio Barriga et al., *The Fruit and Vegetable Export Sector of Chile: A Case Study of Institutional Cooperation* (US Agency for International Development, 1990), v–12, which also details government and private sector initiatives to promote growth in the agricultural sector. Gabriel Casaburi, "Dynamic Production Systems in Newly Liberalizing Developing Countries: Agroindustrial Sectors in Argentina and Chile" (PhD diss., Yale University, 1994), 47–68; and Casaburi, *Dynamic Agroindustrial Clusters: The Political Economy of Competitive Sectors in Argentina and Chile* (New York: St. Martin's Press, 1999), 27–156.

44. International Fruit World, in cooperation with ProChile, eds., *Chile: An Exporting Country for Fruit and Vegetables* (Basel, Switzerland: International Fruit World, 1987); and Agricultural Marketing Service, Fruit and Vegetable Division, Market News Branch, USDA, *Marketing Chile Fruits and Melons: 1981 Season*, (Bronx, NY: USDA, 1981).

45. Barriga et al., *The Fruit and Vegetable Export Sector of Chile*, vii, 15. Chile also had a large export trade in livestock and lumber. Throughout the 1970s and 1980s, copper remained the most important Chilean export and source of foreign exchange for the Chilean economy, but the fruit trade was a new avenue for growth in the Chilean economy.

46. Foreign Agricultural Service, Horticultural and Tropical Products Division, USDA, *United States Horticultural Import Situation, 2002,* http://www.fas.usda.gov/htp/News /News02/03-02/Freelance%20Graphics%20-%20IMSUMARY.pdf (accessed June 26, 2007), 5, 9, 18–19, 33. Other major fruit and vegetable suppliers were Costa Rica, Ecuador, and Guatemala, with bananas dominating much of the trade from those countries.

47. Lucier et al., *Fruit and Vegetable Backgrounder*, 8–9; Putnam and Allshouse, *Food Consumption, Prices, and Expenditures*, 88. Grape consumption was also abnormally low in the late 1960s and early 1970s due to boycotts organized by Cesar Chavez and the United Farm Workers. Sonora, Mexico, also exported grapes in large volume to the United States after 1980. See Rebecca Helen Carter Duvall, "Tracing the Trail of Table Grapes: The Globalization of the Sonoran Table Grape Industry" (PhD diss., University of Arizona, 2002).

48. International Fruit World et al., *Chile: An Exporting Country for Fruit and Vegetables*, 33.

49. On the Chinese in California agriculture, see Peter C. Y. Leung and Tony Waters, "Chinese Vegetable Farming: A Case Study of the Mok Farm in Woodland, California" *Origins and Destinations: 41 Essays on Chinese America* (Los Angeles: Chinese Historical Society of Southern California and UCLA Asian American Studies Center, 1994), 437–52; Him

Mark Lai, "Chinese Regional Solidarity: Case Study of the Hua Xian (Fah Yuen) Community in California," in *Chinese America: History and Perspectives 1994* (San Francisco: Chinese Historical Society, 1994), 19–60; Sucheng Chan, *This Bittersweet Soil: The Chinese in California Agriculture, 1860–1910* (Berkeley: University of California Press, 1986). On the Italians in California agriculture, see the oral histories on food and wine from BANC, such as Robert Di Giorgio and Joseph A. Di Giorgio, "The Di Giorgios: From Fruit Merchants to Corporate Innovators," Oral History Interview conducted in 1983 by Ruth Teiser, Regional Oral History Office, BANC, 1986; Hans Christian Palmer, "Italian Immigration and the Development of California Agriculture" (PhD diss., UC Berkeley, 1965).

50. On advances in refrigeration, James Comer, "North America from 1492 to Present," in Kiple and Coneè Ornelas, eds., *The Cambridge World History of Food*, vol. 2, 1315. An early article on the changes that refrigeration was making on the fruit industry is William A. Taylor, "The Influence of Refrigeration on the Fruit Industry," in *Yearbook of the Department of Agriculture, 1900* (Washington, DC: USDA, 1901), 561–80. The yearbook said, "Since 1897 several shipments each year of grapes, peaches, plums, summer apples, and pears from Canada to British markets have been made on the subsidized refrigerated steamers controlled by the Dominion government. These have usually reached their destination in sound condition and sold at encouraging prices," 580. It also highlighted those apple varieties that "endure refrigeration well," 571.

51. On the preservation of foods and industrialized methods for packing and shipping, see Jack Goody, "Industrial Food: Towards the Development of a World Cuisine," in Carole Counihan and Penny Van Esterik, eds., *Food and Culture: A Reader* (New York: Routledge, 1997), 338–56; Sue Shephard, *Pickled, Potted, and Canned: How the Art and Science of Food Preserving Changed the World* (New York: Simon & Schuster, 2000).

52. Barriga et al., *The Fruit and Vegetable Export Sector of Chile*, 19–20; Casaburi, *Dynamic Production Systems*, 47–68.

53. Rich Pirog, "Grape Expectations: A Food System Perspective on Redeveloping the Iowa Grape Industry." Ames, Iowa: Leopold Center for Sustainable Agriculture, 2002. http://www.leopold.iastate.edu/pubs/staff/grapes/Grape.pdf (accessed June 28, 2007); Walter L. Goldfrank, "Fresh Demand: The Consumption of Chilean Produce in the United States," in Gary Gereffi and Miguel Korzeniewicz, eds., *Commodity Chains and Global Capitalism* (Westport, CT: Greenwood Press, 1994), 267–79.

54. Greg Johnson, "Plan to Ship Fruit to S.D. Port Would Add 40 Jobs," *Los Angeles Times*, December 4, 1985.

55. The United States produced a fantastic sum of 299,293 aircraft during the war, whereas only a small fraction had been produced before. David M. Kennedy, *Freedom from Fear: The American People in Depression and War, 1929–1945* (New York: Oxford University Press, 1999), 653–55.

56. Wayne State University researchers published their study in December 1943. The conference was convened in March 1944 with the various industry, government, and academic representatives. The study is Spencer A. Larsen, *Air Cargo Potential in Fresh Fruits and Vegetables* (Detroit: Wayne University Press, 1944). Conference speeches are collected in N. Stanley Oates, ed., *Outlook for Air Cargo in Fresh Produce* (Detroit: Wayne University Press, 1944), vi–vii, 78–82, 88–89.

57. On the general technological advances in air transportation, see Rigas Doganis, *Flying off Course: The Economics of International Airlines*, 3rd ed. (New York: Routledge, 2002), 9–14; John E. Richards, "Toward a Positive Theory of International Organizations: Regulating International Aviation Markets," *International Organization* 53, no. 1 (1999): 25–27. Air freight in the North Atlantic market increased from 10,938 tons in 1955 to 331,049 tons in 1968.

58. "37th Annual Report: What Super Markets Will Sell in the 1970s," *Progressive Grocer*, April 1970, 148–49.

59. On shipments of fresh peaches and nectarines to the US market, see Pollack and Calvin, *U.S.-Mexico Fruit and Vegetable Trade, 1970–92*, 119.

60. Krugman et al., "Growing World Trade: Causes and Consequences," 364.

61. This figure excludes freight-only airlines, such as FedEx and UPS. Korean Airlines was the other airline that trafficked mostly freight, but significantly, other Asian carriers such as Cathay Pacific, China Eastern, and JAL had large freight percentages. So too did major transatlantic carriers such as Lufthansa and Air France. Freight accounted for about 30 percent of total traffic worldwide among International Air Transport Association Members. Doganis, *Flying off Course*, 23, 149; Boeing company, "LanChile Adds Three Boeing 767-300 Freighters to Its Fleet," press release, at http://www.boeing.com/news/releases/2000/news_release_001218a.html (accessed June 21, 2007); LAN Airlines, S.A., *Annual Report 2006*, http://plane.lan.com/files/about-us/lanchile/memoria2006.pdf (accessed June 21, 2007), 4–5, 40–41.

62. Huang, *Global Trade Patterns*, 17–21.

63. Luncheon Menu, The Stouffer Corporation, circa 1960, CCSF, Folder—Chains, General Menu, USA; Stouffer's, "About Us," http://www.stouffers.com/Index/AboutUs.aspx (accessed August 28, 2007).

64. *McDonald's Food: The Facts* (Oak Brook, IL: McDonald's Corporation, 1986), 7, in CCSF, Folder—Chains, General Menu, USA; Eric Schlosser, *Fast Food Nation: The Dark Side of the All-American Meal* (New York: Perennial, 2002), 6.

65. On grape growing seasons, see California Table Grape Commission, "Commodity Fact Sheet: Table Grapes," http://www.cfaitc.org/Commodity/pdf/TableGrapes.pdf (accessed June 22, 2007); Pablo M. Vial, Carlos H. Crisosto, and Gayle M. Crisosto, "Early Harvest Delays Berry Skin Browning of 'Princess' Table Grapes," *California Agriculture* 59, no. 2 (2005), http://calag.ucop.edu/0502AMJ/pdfs/GrapeBrowning.pdf (accessed June 22, 2007), 104.

66. Australia opened its market for US table grape exporters in 2002 after many years of negotiations. Agnes Perez, "Grape Expectations: Abundant Quantity, High Quality," *Agricultural Outlook* (December 2002), 10–12.

67. Paul Harrison and Fred Pearce, *AAAS Atlas of Population and the Environment* (Berkeley: University of California Press, 2000), 58, 160–66. The number of pea seed varieties held at the National Seed Storage Lab in 1903 was 408. In 1983, the laboratory held only 25, or a 93.9 percent decrease. This study bases its analysis partly on data from the Food and Agriculture Organization of the United Nations. Another study disputes FAO data that list a low number of species dominating consumption worldwide. Those authors argue that the FAO uses globally aggregated statistics rather than looking at national supply statistics.

Instead, they count at least 100 species that contribute to the diets of most nations, and assert that there are other significant crops, such as turmeric and lemongrass, that are low in relative weight, but important to the food cultures of certain nations because they impart a unique taste. See Robert and Christine Prescott-Allen, "How Many Plants Feed the World?," *Conservation Biology* 4, no. 4 (1990): 365–74. The estimate of three-quarters of species having disappeared and information on the Global Seed Vault can be found in Elisabeth Rosenthal, "Near Arctic, Seed Vault Is a Fort Knox of Food," *New York Times*, February 29, 2008. On the treaty ratification, see Legal Office, Food and Agriculture Organization, United Nations, "International Treaty on Plant Genetic Resources for Food and Agriculture," at http://www.fao.org/legal/TREATIES/033s-e.htm (accessed March 1, 2008). The treaty itself is at ftp://ftp.fao.org/ag/cgrfa/it/ITPGRe.pdf (accessed March 1, 2008). On the United States involvement in the treaty, Kelly Day-Rubenstein and Paul Helsey, "Plant Genetic Resources: New Rules for International Exchange," *Amber Waves*, June 2003, http://www.ers.usda.gov/AmberWaves/June03/Features/PlantGeneticResources.htm (accessed March 1, 2008). Chelsea Harvey, "The Tangled Roots of Global Food Supply," *Toronto Star*, June 25, 2016. The US government facilities to protect seeds are the National Center for Genetic Resources Preservation in Fort Collins, Colorado, and the National Seed Laboratory in Dry Branch, Georgia.

68. Ron Harpell, review of *Banana Wars: Power, Production and History in the Americas* (Durham, NC: Duke University Press, 2003) by Steve Striffler and Mark Moberg, eds., *Business History Review* 79, no. 3 (2005): 661–64.

69. On corn, see Pollan, *The Omnivore's Dilemma*, 1–119. Pollan asked scientists at UC Berkeley to "run a McDonald's meal through [a] mass spectrometer and calculate how much of the carbon in it came originally from a corn plant." The topic of biodiversity and globalization is among the most controversial in the globalization debates of the 1990s and beyond, generating intense debate about the function of large corporations in the global marketplace. See lectures by Vandana Shiva, Tom Lovejoy, and John Browne, delivered for BBC Radio in 2000, "Reith Lectures 2000, Respect for the Earth," http://news.bbc.co.uk/hi/english/static/events/reith_2000/default.stm (accessed August 13, 2007). On the sameness of commodified corn and other crops, see Cronon, *Nature's Metropolis*, 98–147. Fast food consumption estimates cited by Schlosser, *Fast Food Nation*, 3, 6. See also Mark D. Jekanowski, "Causes and Consequences of Fast Food Sales Growth," *Food Review* 22, no. 1 (1999): 11–16, http://www.ers.usda.gov/publications/foodreview/jan1999/frjan99b.pdf (accessed January 4, 2007).

70. Levinson, *The Box*, 3.

71. Christian Broda and David Weinstein, "Globalization and the Gains from Variety," (Working Paper 10314, Cambridge, MA: National Bureau of Economic Research, 2004), quote on p. 1.

72. Keppel, "Number of Items," *Los Angeles Times*, February 19, 1985.

73. Imbruce, *From Farm to Canal Street*.

74. The market only does wholesale trade and does not sell directly to the public. There were thirty merchants at the market as of August 8, 2007, San Francisco Wholesale Produce Market, "Merchants: Complete Alphabetical Listing," http://www.sfproduce.org/merchants/merchname.html (accessed August 8, 2007). During the middle to late 1990s, about 55 percent of fruits and vegetables were sold for home consumption in the United States. The other

45 percent was sold to foodservice establishments. Out of the amount sold for home consumption in the United States, only $1.1 billion out of $42.2 billion, or 2.6 percent, was sold in direct markets such as farmer's markets, in which farmers sell directly to consumers. The other 97.4 percent was sold to consumers at food stores, including everything from convenience stores to supermarkets. One study calculated that at the end of the twentieth century, supermarkets sold about 88 percent of all produce sold for home consumption (with direct markets selling the other 12 percent). The other large seller of produce for home consumption was supercenters, which captured greater and greater sales between the late 1990s and 2007. The San Francisco Wholesale Produce Market sold mostly to independent restaurants or small chains, so the consumer who ate at chains such as McDonald's or Chili's, would not eat produce from this market. See "U.S. Fresh Fruit and Vegetable Marketing Channels, Mid/Late-1990s," Produce Marketing Association, at "U.S. Supply Chain Flow Chart," http://new .pma.com/cig/intl/usMarketAndTrends.cfm (accessed August 8, 2007); Calleja Pinedo, *Distribution Channels in the U.S.A.*, 184.

75. Newsletters, Greenleaf Produce, week of June 25, 2007, http://www.greenleafsf.com /newsletters/GLN062507.pdf, July 9, 2007, http://www.greenleafsf.com/newsletters/GLN0709 07.pdf, and Spring Seasonal Guide, http://www.greenleafsf.com/Seasonal%20Guide/Spring SeasonalGuide07.pdf (all accessed July 13, 2007), and Cooseman's Worldwide, http://www .coosemans.com (accessed July 13, 2007). Produce order forms from O. Lippi & Company, and Universe Co., LLP, July 20, 2006 (in possession of author). Not all grocery chains eschew the market. In 2006, Whole Foods Market and Mollie Stone's used the market to supply area stores, but their sales were much smaller than Safeway's.

76. There were over 900 McDonald's franchises in just Walmart's and gas stations in the late 1990s. Jekanowski, "Causes and Consequences of Fast Food Sales Growth," 11. Frito-Lay was one of the largest food processors in the world, and the "fastest-growing" segment of the larger PepsiCo. It sold goods in around 120 countries in 2005. Benjamin Senauer and Luciano Venturini, "The Globalization of Food Systems: A Conceptual Framework and Empirical Patterns" (St. Paul: The Food Industry Center, University of Minnesota, 2005), http://agecon.lib .umn.edu/cgi-bin/pdf_view.pl?paperid=15899&ftype=.pdf (accessed August 16, 2007), 18.

77. This was true in the case of Chilean fruit exports, Casaburi, *Dynamic Agroindustrial Clusters*, 64, 119.

2. THE CONSOLIDATION AND GLOBALIZATION OF GROCERY STORES

1. Steve W. Martinez, *The U.S. Food Marketing System: Recent Developments, 1997–2006, ERR #42* (Washington, DC: ERS-USDA, 2007), 46.

2. Starbucks licensed 530 stores in supermarkets in October 2000. Starbucks also sold its ground coffee and bottled drinks in supermarkets and to a variety of other food service establishments, from airlines to wholesale clubs. Starbucks Corp., *10-K Filing with the United States Securities and Exchange Commission for 10/1/2000*, http://www.secinfo.com /dr643.524k.htm (accessed August 17, 2007). McDonald's had about 700 franchises within Walmart retail locations in early 2003, *Meat Retailer*, January 1, 2003.

3. *McDonald's Food: The Facts* (Oak Brook, IL: McDonald's Corporation, 1986), 7, CCSF, Folder—Chains, General Menu, USA.

4. McDonald's, "McDonald's Facts Summary," 2006, found at http://www.mcdonalds .com/corp/about/factsheets.html (accessed August 17, 2007).

5. "Vons Grocery Company Fact Sheet," c. 1987, JWT-NEWBUS, Box 86, Folder: Vons Supermarket Industry Presentation 1986–1987.

6. The story is told by McDonald's officials. See Thomas L. Friedman, editorial, "Big Mac II," *New York Times*, December 11, 1996. Rob Kroes discusses the local and global effects of McDonald's and Friedman's column in "Advertising: The Commodification of American Icons of Freedom," in Reinhold Wagnleitner and Elaine Tyler May, eds., *"Here, There and Everywhere": The Foreign Politics of American Popular Culture* (Hanover, NH: University Press of New England, 2000), 273–87.

7. Walmart became the largest grocer in the United States in 2003, according to Tom Weir, "Walmart's the 1," *Progressive Grocer*, May 1, 2003, 35. Other estimates place it as the largest grocer by 2002. Walmart was the largest supermarket chain in Mexico by 2001. Rita Schwentesius and Manuel Ángel Gómez, "Supermarkets in Mexico: Impacts on Horticulture Systems," *Development Policy Review* 20, no. 4 (2002): 492. Albertsons took over Safeway in 2015 and sold its share of Casa Ley in 2018. Albertsons press release, "Albertsons Announces Closing of Sale of 49% Interest in Casa Ley," January 30, 2018, http://investor.safeway.com/phoenix .zhtml?c=64607&p=irol-irhome (accessed October 1, 2018). Christine Wilcox, "Albertsons and Safeway Complete Merger Transaction," January 30, 2015, https://www.albertsons.com /albertsons-and-safeway-complete-merger-transaction/ (accessed October 1, 2018).

8. A hypermarket is defined by the USDA as "the largest of supermarket formats, typically 150,000 square feet or more of selling area. General merchandise accounts for 40 percent of sales, while food and nonfood grocery products represent 60 percent of sales," in Michael J. Harris, Phil R. Kaufman, Steve W. Martinez (coordinator), and Charlene Price. *The U.S. Food Marketing System, 2002, AER# 811* (Washington, DC: ERS-USDA, 2002), 23.

9. Carrefour Group, "History," at http://www.carrefour.com/cdc/group/history/ (accessed September 1, 2007). Walmart, Carrefour, and Royal Ahold (based in the Netherlands), were the three largest grocery retailers in the world. Thomas Reardon and Julio A. Berdegué, "The Rapid Rise of Supermarkets in Latin America: Challenges and Opportunities for Development," *Development Policy Review* 20, no. 4 (2002): 7. On the place of the large retailers, see also Benjamin Senauer and Luciano Venturini, "The Globalization of Food Systems: A Conceptual Framework and Empirical Patterns" (St. Paul: The Food Industry Center, University of Minnesota, 2005), http://agecon.lib.umn.edu/cgi-bin/pdf_view.pl?paperid=15899&ftype= .pdf (accessed August 16, 2007), 21–27. Royal Ahold and Carrefour laid the "groundwork" for Walmart in Asia, according to one Walmart executive, quoted in Misha Petrovic and Gary G. Hamilton, "Making Global Markets: Walmart and Its Suppliers," in Nelson Lichtenstein, ed., *Walmart: The Face of Twenty-First Century Capitalism* (New York: The New Press, 2006), 128.

10. Sergio Faiguenbaum, Julio A. Berdegué, and Thomas Reardon, "The Rapid Rise of Supermarkets in Chile: Effects on Dairy, Vegetable, and Beef Chains," *Development Policy Review* 20, no. 4 (2002): 459–71. The large supermarket chains were both Chilean and non-Chilean.

11. Royal Ahold, "About Us—History," at http://www.ahold.com/page/14.aspx (accessed August 18, 2007). In addition to its operations in the Netherlands, Royal Ahold had supermarket ventures in the Czech and Slovak Republics in 2006.

12. See Richard S. Tedlow, *New and Improved: The Story of Mass Marketing in America* (Boston: Harvard Business School Press, 1996); Susan Strasser, *Never Done: A History of American Housework* (New York: Pantheon Books, 1982); Lizabeth Cohen, *Making a New Deal: Industrial Workers in Chicago, 1919–1939* (New York: Cambridge University Press, 1990).

13. James T. Patterson, *Restless Giant: The United States from Watergate to "Bush v. Gore"* (New York: Oxford University Press, 2005), 307–10; Segregation in schools decreased for some time after the *Brown v. Board of Education* (1954) decision but returned to high levels by the early twenty-first century. See Gary Orfield and Chungmei Lee, *Brown at 50: King's Dream or Plessy's Nightmare?* (Cambridge, MA: Civil Rights Project, Harvard University, 2004), www.civilrightsproject.harvard.edu, (accessed May 23, 2004), 1–35. On politics, Robert Putnam has shown that social networks in modern America are weaker in areas of greater racial and ethnic diversity. He argues that "immigration and ethnic diversity challenge social solidarity and inhibit social capital," in "*E Pluribus Unum*: Diversity and Community in the Twenty-First Century, The 2006 Johan Skytte Prize Lecture," *Scandinavian Political Studies* 30, no. 2 (2007): 137–74.

14. *Chain Store Guide 2001 Directory of Supermarket, Grocery and Convenience Store Chains* (Tampa, FL: Business Guides, Inc., 2001), a59, a67, a91.

15. "The Super 50," *Progressive Grocer*, May 2012; Steve Raabe, "Colorado's First Three: Trader Joe's Unlikely to Threaten Big Grocers," *Denver Post*, February 12, 2014. It remains to be seen what Amazon's purchase of Whole Foods means.

16. The top 10 grocers controlled 70 percent of grocery sales in 2012. "The Super 50," *Progressive Grocer*, May 2012.

17. Tracey Deutsch, "Untangling Alliances: Social Tensions Surrounding Independent Grocery Stores and the Rise of Mass Retailing," in Warren Belasco and Philip Scranton, eds., *Food Nations: Selling Taste in Consumer Societies* (New York: Routledge, 2002), 160.

18. Deutsch, "Untangling Alliances," 160.

19. Donna Gabaccia, "As American as Budweiser and Pickles? Nation-Building in American Food Industries," in Belasco and Scranton, *Food Nations*, 177. Gabaccia also makes this argument in *We Are What We Eat: Ethnic Food and the Making of Americans* (Cambridge, MA: Harvard University Press, 1999).

20. Tracey Deutsch, *Building a Housewife's Paradise: Gender, Politics, and American Grocery Stores in the Twentieth Century* (Chapel Hill: University of North Carolina Press, 2010), 1–112.

21. Susan Strasser, "Woolworth to Walmart: Mass Merchandising and the Changing Culture of Consumption," in Lichtenstein, *Walmart*, 31–56.

22. Tedlow, *New and Improved*, 188–99.

23. Cohen, *Making a New Deal*, 324–27.

24. Deutsch, "Untangling Alliances," 156–74.

25. INS, *2001 Statistical Yearbook of the Immigration and Naturalization Service: Tables Only* (Washington, DC: INS, 2001), 6–7.

26. Hasia R. Diner, *Hungering for America: Italian, Irish, and Jewish Foodways in the Age of Immigration* (Cambridge, MA: Harvard University Press, 2001), 19–25, 224–28.

27. Audrey Russek, "Appetites without Prejudice: U.S. Foreign Restaurants and the Globalization of American Food between the Wars," *Food and Foodways: Explorations in the History and Culture of Human Nourishment* 19 (2011): 34–55.

28. Simone Cinotto, "'Now That's Italian!' Representations of Italian Cuisine in American Popular Magazines, 1950–2000," The Italian Academy for Advanced Studies in America (2004), 6–9, http://www.italianacademy.columbia.edu/pdfs/cinotto.pdf (accessed March 19, 2007). Harvey Levenstein calls the eating of Italian food in America the "pasta-and-spicy-tomato-sauce syndrome," in *Paradox of Plenty: A Social History of Eating in Modern America*. Berkeley: University of California Press, 2003, 51–52, 216, 223, quote on 51. On the popularity of spaghetti and meatballs, also see Christopher Lee, "Bay Area Restaurateur," conducted by Kirstin Jackson in 2004 (Regional Oral History Office, BANC, 2006), 8, 13. Elizabeth Paulucci's cookbook explains a recipe for "Liz's Spaghetti Sauce with Meatballs" by saying that it was a "revelation on her first trip to Italy, [where] Lois kept asking for spaghetti and meatballs and not one restaurant offered it on the menu!" *Cookbook from a Melting Pot* (New York: Grosset & Dunlap, 1981), 168.

29. Tedlow, *New and Improved*, 198; "Definitions," *Progressive Grocer*, April 1971, 61.

30. Quotes from Tedlow, *New and Improved*, 226, 228. Tedlow's is the clearest summary of the shift from independents to chains to supermarkets, 182–258. On the nature of local ethnic versus national mass merchandise, see, Deutsch, "Untangling Alliances," 156–74. Deutsch gives estimates for the size of the stores. On the rise of chain stores in relation to mass consumption and ethnicity, see also Cohen, *Making a New Deal*, 99–120. Cohen qualifies that some of the features of the chain store, such as self-service, did not take fully take hold until the 1930s even if chain stores captured a great deal of business in the 1920s. One history of the supermarket industry claims that the term "supermarket" came into being when eastern grocers traveled to the West Coast to look at combination stores there that sold both dry groceries and the meat, produce, and non-dry groceries that grocery stores had not purveyed before. "The History of the Supermarket Industry," in *Progressive Grocer's 1992 Marketing Guidebook* (Stamford, CT: Progressive Grocer Trade Dimensions, 1991).

31. "GMA Concentrates on 70s, Ghettos, Consumerism," *Progressive Grocer*, January 1970, 9; Abel F. Lemes, "Safeway Lends Hand to Failing Co-op," *Safeway News*, June 1968, 2–5.

32. Patterson, *Restless Giant*, 245; Kyeyoung Park, "Use and Abuse of Race and Culture: Black-Korean Tension in America," *American Anthropologist* 98, New Series, no. 3, (1996): 492–99.

33. Safeway had 2,451 stores in 1975 and 1,689 stores in 2001. In 1977 it was the largest grocery chain. In 2001 it was the third-largest. *1977 Progressive Grocer's Marketing Guidebook* (New York: American Can Company, 1976), 19; *Chain Store Guide 2001*, 221. Industry publications such as *Progressive Grocer* abound with tales of consolidation and mergers in the 1990s.

34. Safeway, Inc., *Annual Report, 1964* (Oakland, CA: Safeway, Inc., 1965), 11. The first year for which superstores, defined by the company as 35,000 square feet or larger, formed the majority of Safeway's stores was 1992. That year there were 407 conventional supermarkets at an average of 26,200 square feet and there were 461 superstores, averaging 44,800 square feet each, Safeway, Inc., *Annual Report, 1992* (Oakland, CA: Safeway, Inc., 1993), 14. At the end of 1991, 49 percent of Safeway's stores were superstores. Safeway, Inc., *Annual Report, 1991* (Oakland, CA: Safeway, Inc., 1992), 8.

35. Safeway, Inc., *Annual Report, 1982* (Oakland, CA: Safeway, Inc., 1983), 32.

36. The company said it operated 523 conventional supermarkets and 372 superstores at the end of 1988. Safeway, Inc., *Annual Report, 1988* (Oakland, CA: Safeway Stores, Inc., 1989), 2–3. Though it is commonly said that Walmart and other one-stop shopping establishments put butchers and bakers out of business, the number of "specialized foodstores" as measured by the Census of Retail Trade continued to rise from 1980 to 2000. These are defined by the USDA as foodstores "primarily engaged in the retail sale of a single food category such as meat and seafood markets, dairy stores, candy and nut stores, and retail bakeries." From 1992 to 1997, the number of specialized foodstores decreased slightly, but their sales increased. One type of specialized store, the butcher and fishmonger, declined, but other stores, such as bakeries, increased overall. See Harris et al., *The U.S. Food Marketing System*, 22–23, 58.

37. Anthony E. Gallo, *Food Marketing Review, 1994–95, AER#743* (Washington, DC: ERS-USDA, 1995), 28.

38. On the growth and desirability of one-stop shopping, Paul R. Messinger and Chakravarthi Narasimhan, "A Model of Retail Formats Based on Consumers' Economizing of Shopping Time," *Marketing Science* 16, no. 1 (1997): 1–23. On overseas expansion, see Terry Bivens, Ken Goldman, and Charles Z. Yan, *Packaged Food, China: This Time It's for Real!* (New York: Bear Stearns Equity Research, May 2007). This report was generated to "better understand the market from the perspective of food processors" like Kraft, Heinz, and General Mills to see if they could run "a Chinese business that meaningfully moves the corporate needle" like the "KFC restaurant chain." On consolidation and overseas operations, also see Harris et al., *The U.S. Food Marketing System, 2002*.

39. The San-Francisco-Oakland-San Jose, CA area market share had 735 total stores, including Safeway, Inc., with 156 stores and a 29.6 percent share, Albertsons, Inc., with 134 stores and a 19.8 percent share, and Costco Wholesale Group with 22 stores and a 11.6 percent share. The Phoenix-Mesa area had 382 total stores with The Kroger Co. operating 85 stores at a 28.0 percent share, Safeway with 42 stores and a 16.7 percent share, and Basha's, Inc., with 60 stores and a 12.2 percent share. The Washington, D.C.–Baltimore area included several counties in Maryland, D.C., and Virginia and 795 total stores. Ahold USA had 168 stores and a 28.1 percent market share (Giant Food Store and Stop & Shop are its largest store names), Safeway 119 stores and a 21.0 percent market share, and SUPERVALU with 63 stores and a 12.2 percent market share. All market share figures from *Chain Store Guide 2001*, a47–a99, 452–53

40. Raabe, "Colorado's First Three," *Denver Post*, February 12, 2014.

41. Data for 1994 from Gallo, *Food Marketing Review*, 27. Data for 2000 from Harris et al., *The U.S. Food Marketing System*, 21–29.

42. "Making Global Markets," in Lichtenstein, *Walmart*, 107, 123. For 2002 sales figures, see Jack Plunkett, *Plunkett's Food Industry Almanac* (Houston: Plunkett Research, Ltd., 2003), 9–10.

43. Walmart's retail share figure cited at "Food Industry Consolidation," *Produce Marketer's Association*, http://new.pma.com/cig/intl/usMarketAndTrends.cfm (accessed August 8, 2007).

44. Lichtenstein, *Walmart*, x. Walmart took over the top grocery retail spot, as measured by sales, in 2002. It was also the "greatest gainer" in terms of the number of stores

during 2003. *2005 Marketing Guidebook: The Blue Book of Supermarket Distribution* (Wilton, CT: Trade Dimensions International, 2004), 30, 44.

45. Plunkett, *Plunkett's Food Industry Almanac*, 9–10. On the overall impact of Walmart on the American economy, see the articles in Lichtenstein, *Walmart*; Walter Heller and Jenny McTaggart, "The Search for Growth," *Progressive Grocer*, April 15, 2004, 31–41.

46. Jean Kinsey, "A Faster, Leaner, Supply Chain: New Uses of Information Technology." Proceedings Issue, *American Journal of Agricultural Economics* 82, no. 5 (2000): 1123–29.

47. Safeway, Inc., *Annual Report* (Pleasanton, CA: Safeway, Inc., 2000), 6.

48. This description of Frito Lay's operations is borrowed from Barbara E. Kahn and Leigh McAlister, *Grocery Revolution: The New Focus on the Consumer* (Reading, MA: Addison-Wesley, 1997), 8–10. Frito-Lay distributed its products to over 440,000 retail outlets by 2006. It merged with PepsiCo in 1965. By 2015, PepsiCo owned many of the most recognized consumer brands in world, including Pepsi Cola, Doritos, Frito-Lay, Tropicana, and Quaker Cereals, http://www.pepsico.com/Company/Global-Brands (accessed June 5, 2015).

49. Kahn and McAlister, *Grocery Revolution*, 38; Jay Coggins and Ben Senauer, "Grocery Retailing," in *U.S. Industry in 2000: Studies in Competitive Performance* (Washington, DC: The National Academy Press, 1999), 159. By the first decade of the twenty-first century, supermarkets were testing grocery carts with scanners attached to them. See Terry Hennessy, "The Front-End Frontier," *Progressive Grocer*, April 2000, 93–96; Robert F. King and Paul F. Phumpiu, "Reengineering the Food Supply Chain: The ECR Initiative in the Grocery Industry," Proceedings Issue, *American Journal of Agricultural Economics* 78, no. 5 (1996): 1181–86.

50. Nelson Lichtenstein, *The Retail Revolution: How Walmart Created a Brave New World of Business* (New York: Metropolitan Books, 2009), 36–44

51. Coggins and Senauer, "Grocery Retailing," 156.

52. For the 2004 survey, "Problem Severity Index," in Heller and McTaggart, "The Search for Growth," 31–41. For the 1990 survey, *Progressive Grocer's 1992 Marketing Guidebook*, 18–19. Walmart not only competed well in terms of supply chain innovation, but also had much lower labor costs than most grocery chains, many of which were unionized. See the preface and various essays in Lichtenstein, *Walmart*, ix– xii, 213–83.

53. Rachel Abrams, "Drones Fly about Walmart Warehouses to Take Stock," *New York Times*, June 3, 2016.

54. Coggins and Senauer, "Grocery Retailing," 156–75.

55. Richard Turcsik and Walter Heller, "Produce Persona," *Progressive Grocer*, October 2000, 59–63.

56. Mark Gehlhar and Anita Regmi, "Shopping the Global Market for High-Value Foods," *Agricultural Outlook*, December 2002, 38–42; Susanne Freidberg, *Fresh: A Perishable History* (Cambridge, MA: Harvard University Press, 2009), 190–93.

57. "Turn Your Tree Fruit Sales Up a Notch," Brandt Farms Treeripe Home, http://www.treeripe.com/index.htm (accessed June 22, 2007).

58. Laura Shapiro describes how the companies theorized that women wanted to add something to the cake mix. This was not the only factor—dehydrated egg was not a suitable substitute for the real thing, and the cake mix left more time for women to decorate cakes, meaning a boost in sales of frosting and cake decorations. Eventually, many women came

to see making cakes from a cake mix as "homemade" (as opposed to making it entirely from separate ingredients). See *Something from the Oven: Reinventing Dinner in 1950s America* (New York: Penguin, 2004), 68–84; "Box Score," *Gourmet*, August 2002, at http://www .epicurious.com/gourmet/kitchen_notebook/cake (accessed September 3, 2007).

59. Gehlhar and Regmi, "Shopping the Global Market," 38–42.

60. On Walmart's connections to the food processors, see "Making Global Markets," in Lichtenstein, *Walmart*, 107–41; Jonathan P. Feeney, John Baumgartner, and John P. San Marco, "800 Lb. Gorilla Goes on a Diet," Equity Research Report (New York: Wachovia Capital Markets, LLC, 2007).

61. On the search for the China market by food processors, see Bivens et al., "Packaged Food, China"; Fred Ruppel, "Globalization of the Processed Foods Market: Part One: U.S. Trade in Processed Foods," *Agricultural Outlook*, January–February 1997. On the long allure of the China market for US goods, see William Appleman Williams, *The Tragedy of American Diplomacy* (New York: W.W. Norton & Company, 1972), 34–57; Walter LaFeber, *The New Empire: An Interpretation of American Expansion, 1860–1898* (Ithaca, NY: Cornell University Press, 1963), 408–17; Thomas J. McCormick, "Insular Possessions for the China Market," in Thomas G. Paterson, ed., *American Imperialism and Anti-Imperialism* (New York: Thomas Y. Crowell, 1973), 64–73.

62. "Making Global Markets," in Lichtenstein, *Walmart*, 140.

63. Walmart Stores, Inc., "Our Locations: China," http://corporate.walmart.com/our -story/locations/china#/china (accessed December 10, 2016).

64. JBS, "JBS Day Presentation," December 7, 2017, São Paulo, http://jbss.infoinvest .com.br/?idioma=enu (accessed March 4, 2018).

65. JBS, "JBS Day Presentation"; Juan Forero, "An Industry Giant, from Farm to Fork," *Washington Post*, April 15, 2011.

66. Paulo Prada, "The Easy Credit that Fueled Brazil's Boom Now Imperils It," *Wall Street Journal*, June 13, 2011.

67. Joseph Carson, an economist at Alliance Bernstein, quoted in Neil Shah, "Foreign Investment Surges—U.S. Attracts Billions of Dollars as Investors Seek Relief from Global Turmoil," *Wall Street Journal*, June 15, 2012.

68. JBS, "JBS Day Presentation"; Forero, "An Industry Giant, from Farm to Fork."

69. Jacob Bunge, "What's for Dinner? Pass the Protein, Please," *Wall Street Journal*, June 11, 2014.

70. Jacob Bunge, "Demographic Destiny: 2050: Chicken Feeds the World," *Wall Street Journal*, December 5, 2015; Shane Romig, "In Grains, Argentina Doesn't Keep Distance," *Wall Street Journal*, December 26, 2007.

71. Bunge, "Demographic Destiny."

72. Jeffrey McCracken and Lauren Etter, "Brazilians Bid for U.S. Meat Titan," *Wall Street Journal*, September 3, 2009.

73. Wesley Batista, son of José Batista Sobrinho, quoted in Bunge, "Demographic Destiny."

74. Bunge, "What's for Dinner?"

75. WH Group, Annual Reports and Corporate Presentations, 2015–2017, http://www .wh-group.com/en/global/home.php (accessed April 20, 2018).

76. Marfrig Global Foods, "Sustainability Report 2016," http://www.marfrig.com.br /Uploads/Arquivos/Marfrig_RA16_eng.pdf (accessed September 26, 2018).

77. 3G Capital, "Restaurant Brands International" http://www.3g-capital.com/rbi.html.

78. Christopher Leonard, "How the Meat Industry Keeps Chicken Prices High," *Slate*, March 3, 2014.

79. Michael Pollan, "Why Did the Obamas Fail to Take on Corporate Agriculture?" *New York Times*, October 5, 2016.

80. Quotes from Letter, William Roenigk, senior vice president and economist, National Chicken Council, to Legal Policy Section/Antitrust Division, US Department of Justice, December 21, 2009. The full hearings and comments are at Antitrust Division, United States Justice Department, "Public Workshops: Agriculture and Antitrust Enforcement Issues in our 21st Century Economy," https://www.justice.gov/atr/events/public-workshops-agriculture-and-antitrust-enforcement-issues-our-21st-century-economy-10#dates (accessed October 7, 2016).

81. Pollan, "Why Did the Obamas."

82. H.E.B., and Casa Ley, for which Safeway, Inc., has a 49 percent share, are both American companies that have expanded operations in Mexico in the 1990s and early part of the twenty-first century. Walmart is now the largest supermarket operator in Mexico. Schwentesius and Gómez, "Supermarkets in Mexico," 492.

83. Reardon and Berdegué, "Rapid Rise of Supermarkets," 371–84.

84. *2001 Statistical Yearbook of the INS*, 5–9.

85. Don Longo, "Walmart, Still at Large," *Progressive Grocer*, January 1, 2006, 38–39. On labor and competition issues concerning Walmart in Mexico, see Chris Tilly, "Walmart in Mexico: The Limits of Growth," in Lichtenstein, *Walmart*, 189–209.

86. Paul Sonne and Peter Evans, "Five Years, $1.6 Billion Later, Tesco Decides to Quit U.S.," *Wall Street Journal*, December 6, 2012.

87. Zeke Turner, "Aldi Bets Limited Choice Will Lure U.S. Shoppers," *Wall Street Journal*, September 22, 2017; Stephanie Clifford, "Wal-Mart No, Aldi Yes?: A Giant Grocer, from Germany, Arrives in Queens," *New York Times*, March 30, 2011. Andrew Martin, "The Allure of Plain Vanilla," *New York Times*, September 7, 2008.

88. Lidl, "About Us," https://www.lidl.com/about-us (accessed September 28, 2018).

89. Claude Fischler, "The 'McDonaldization' of Culture"; Jean-Louis Flandrin and Massimo Montanari, "Today and Tomorrow," in Flandrin and Montanari, eds., *Food: A Culinary History*, trans. Albert Sonnenfeld (New York: Columbia University Press, 1999), 530–53; Watson, *Golden Arches East*.

90. Schwentesius and Gómez, "Supermarkets in Mexico," 487–502.

3. MARKETING ETHNIC FOODS AT SUPERMARKETS

1. Mike Pehanich, "Make Way for the New Jeno's," *Prepared Foods*, February 1984, JWT-NEWBUS, Box 22, Chun King Corporation, General Files 1956 Sep.–1965 Feb. (Milton Moskowitz Files).

2. June Owen, "News of Food: Chinese Dishes," *New York Times*, June 15, 1955; "Sweet Success, Chinese Style," *Time*, February 16, 1962; Joel Denker, *The World on a Plate: A Tour*

Through the History of America's Ethnic Cuisine (Lincoln: University of Nebraska Press, 2003), 100–105.

3. T. Rees Shapiro, "Jeno Paulucci, Pioneer of Frozen-Food Business, Dies at 93," *Washington Post*, November 30, 2012.

4. Gerald Ford, "Remarks at the Bicentennial Dinner of the Italian-American Foundation," September 16, 1976, Gerhard Peters and John T. Woolley, *The American Presidency Project.* https://www.presidency.ucsb.edu/documents/remarks-the-bicentennial-dinner-the-italian -american-foundation (accessed May 2, 2019).

5. "Now 1 out of 5 Persons Eats Asian-American Foods," *Sales Management*, September 21, 1956, and various financial statements in JWT-NEWBUS, Box 22, Chun King Corporation.

6. "Chun King Gives $3,000,000 Drive American Twist," *Advertising Age*, September 21, 1964; "Oriental Foods Take All-American Slant," *Sponsor*, September 21, 1964; "Preview: The Oriental All-American," *Broadcast*, September 21, 1964, all in JWT-NEWBUS, Box 22, Chun King Corporation.

7. William Swanson, "The Paulucci Imposition," *Corporate Report*, January 1977, JWT-NEWBUS, Box 22, Chun King Corporation.

8. Paulucci sold Chun King to R.J. Reynolds for $63 mil. in 1966. Khai Sheang Lee, Guan Hua Lim and Soo Jiuan Tan, "Limitations of Conventional Strategy Frameworks when Applied to SMEs: Lessons from a Case Study," at Small Business Advancement Center, University of Central Arkansas, http://sbaer.uca.edu/research/icsb/1999/28.pdf (accessed October 2, 2014); Stephen Miller, "Earned His Chops on Canned Entrees," *Wall Street Journal*, November 26, 2011.

9. "Oriental Recipe Magic . . . Occidental Sales Magic," *J. Walter Thompson Company News*, September 27, 1954, JWT-NEWS.

10. JWT-NEWS, September 8, 1958.

11. Owen, "News of Food," *New York Times*, June 15, 1955.

12. Shapiro, "Jeno Paulucci, Pioneer of Frozen-Food."

13. On the growth imperative in the American economy, see R. Glenn Hubbard, "An Agenda for Global Growth," December 6, 2002, http://www.whitehouse.gov/cea/agenda _for_global_growth_dec6_2002.pdf (accessed September 6, 2007). On the imperative of growth in the food industry see "Grocery Stores," *Encyclopedia of American Industries.* Online Edition (Farmington Hills, MI: Gale Group, 2006), http://galenet.galegroup.com .content.lib.utexas.edu:2048/servlet/BCRC (accessed April 25, 2006); Walter Heller and Jenny McTaggart, "The Search for Growth," *Progressive Grocer*, April 15, 2004, 31–41.

14. Memo and attached presentation, Michelle Silverstein to Bert Metter, September 25, 1986, "Supermarket Industry," JWT-NEWBUS, Box 86, Folder: Vons Supermarket Industry Presentation 1986–87. Grocer profit margins averaged just 1.8 percent in 1985.

15. One example of the changing use of tortillas in the United States is Karen Howarth, *Gourmet Tortillas: Exotic and Traditional Tortilla Dishes* (Santa Fe, NM: Clear Light Publishers, 2000), 2–9. Howarth's cookbook includes orange tortillas with Montmorency cherries, lavender tortillas with garlic chives, and sunny-side up fried rice over tortillas.

16. James J. Nagle, "The Twain Meet in Middle West," *New York Times*, March 17, 1957; "Sweet Success, Chinese Style"; "Oriental Recipe Magic . . . Occidental Sales Magic,"

JWT-NEWS, September 27, 1954. The trucks brought packaged goods from plants and returned with vegetables from company farms.

17. "Chow Mein Package Patented," *New York Times*, September 5, 1957; Robert Alden, "Advertising: Chow Mein to Be Reoriented," *New York Times*, March 13, 1960.

18. "Chun King Chow Mein," Television Commercial, 1960, Historic Films Archive, http://www.historicfilms.com/search/?type=all&q=%22chun+king%22#p1t7096i20 4802109 (accessed September 24, 2014).

19. US Census Bureau, *Historical Census Statistics on the Foreign-Born Population of the United States: 1850–1990*, Working Paper No. 29, February 1999, at http://www.census.gov /topics/population/foreign-born.html (accessed July 24, 2007).

20. His sister, Elizabeth Paulucci, wrote about the region in *Cookbook from a Melting Pot* (New York: Grosset & Dunlap, 1981). Statistics from David LaVigne, "The 'Black Fellows' of the Mesabi Iron Range: European Immigrants and Racial Differentiation during the Early Twentieth Century," *Journal of American Ethnic History* 36, no. 2 (Winter 2017), 14–18. There were a small number of Chinese residents in the major towns of this region in the early 1900s. Paulucci's father was a miner from Italy.

21. JWT-NEWS, September 10, 1956.

22. Chun King and Mazola Home Service Department, *Quick, Easy and Intriguing Ways with American Oriental Cookery to Add Zest to Your Menus* (Chicago: Consolidated Book Publishers, 1962), 1–35, JWT-BONA, 1960s-6, Item#1960s-0204.

23. JWT-NEWS, May 13, 1966.

24. JWT-NEWS, February 14, 1969.

25. Leonard Daykin, "Randall's Super Is Houston's Newest 'Tranquility' Base," *Progressive Grocer*, February 1970, 122–32. The store measured 22,400 square feet. Other stores that fit this mold included a 22,000-square-foot Food Fair Quality/Discount store in Williamsburg, Virginia, that had an ethnic foods section comprising a fifth of an aisle, the same size as the pickles section. The store also had a macaroni products section taking half of an aisle. Stephen Ackley, "Colonial Williamsburg Sets Mood for New Food Fair," *Progressive Grocer*, March 1970, 145–52. Another was the Martin's Super Market in Elkhart, Indiana, at 25,600 square feet. It had a gourmet section that was 15 feet long, a Chinese section of about 12 feet between the diet and convenience sections, and a Mexican and Jewish section of about 15 feet. See Gerry Beatty, "Tight Scheduling Makes Martin's More Productive," *Progressive Grocer*, February 1975.

26. Robert W. Mueller, "5 Decades that Revolutionized the Food Industry," *Progressive Grocer*, June 1972, 29.

27. Mueller, "5 Decades," 19–38. Harvey Levenstein called his chapter about food in 1950s America "The Golden Age of Food Processing," in *Paradox of Plenty: A Social History of Eating in Modern America* (Berkeley: University of California Press, 2003), 101–18.

28. The executive was V. D. Ludington, vice president of General Foods Corporation, in Henry Schact, "Food Industry's Vast Change," *Safeway News*, September 1968, 4.

29. The trade show, held in Munich, had a booth jointly sponsored by the USDA and the Grocery Manufacturer's Association, "Food Industry in Focus," and "Convenience Foods," *Food Field Reporter*, August 12, 1963. Another journal, *Management's Food Processing and Marketing*, extols the virtues of industrial processing for food. During 1966, the

magazine ran monthly "spotlight" issues for the industry. The spotlights for January through April were on computers, sanitary design, cryogenic freezing, and packaging.

30. Levenstein makes this point in *Paradox of Plenty*, quoting from David Riesman's *Abundance for What? And Other Essays*, to note that even the upper classes practiced a policy of "'conspicuous underconsumption,' which meant serving more or less the same food as everyone else," 117. He argues also that this partly came from a belief on the part of Americans that they were at the top of the world in all respects, and that their food needed few changes as a result. Also see Pollan, *Omnivore's Dilemma*.

31. "Home Hints," *Safeway News*, March 1965, 17.

32. "Home Hints," *Safeway News*, May 1968, 17, emphasis in the original.

33. "Home Hints," *Safeway News*, December 1965, 8. Curry powder had long been a common item in American pantries, Kristin Hoganson, *Consumer's Imperium: The Global Production of American Domesticity, 1865–1920* (Chapel Hill: University of North Carolina Press, 2007), 110, 114.

34. Safeway Stores, Inc., *Annual Report,1965* (Oakland, CA: Safeway Stores, Inc., 1966).

35. There is much debate about the history of marketing and its periodization. Hartmut Berghoff, Philip Scranton, and Uwe Spiekermann, "The Origins of Marketing and Market Research: Information, Institutions and Markets," in Berghoff, Scranton, and Spiekermann, eds., *The Rise of Marketing and Market Research* (New York: Palgrave Macmillan, 2012), 1–26.

36. Lizabeth Cohen, *A Consumer's Republic: The Politics of Mass Consumption in Postwar America* (New York: Alfred A. Knopf, 2003), 292–344. Cohen cites two articles as critical early elaborations of market segmentation. Wendell Smith, "Product Differentiation and Market Segmentation as Alternative Marketing Strategies," *Journal of Marketing* 21, no. 1 (1956): 3–8; and Pierre Martineau, "Social Classes and Spending Behavior," *Journal of Marketing* 23, no. 2 (1958): 121–30. See also, Harper W. Boyd Jr. and Sidney J. Levy, "New Dimension in Consumer Analysis," *Harvard Business Review* 41, no. 6, (1963): 129–40; Daniel Yankelovich, "New Criteria for Market Segmentation," *Harvard Business Review* 42, no. 2 (1964): 83–90; Steven C. Brandt, "Dissecting the Segmentation Syndrome," *Journal of Marketing* 30, no .4 (1966): 22–27. For a historical overview by Daniel Yankelovich, one of the early theorists of market segmentation strategies, see Daniel Yankelovich and David Meer, "Rediscovering Market Segmentation," *Harvard Business Review* 84, no. 2 (2006): 122–31.

37. Robert Mainer and Charles C. Slater, "Markets in Motion," *Harvard Business Review* 42, no. 2 (1964): 82.

38. Ibid., 77.

39. Median income for families rose dramatically between 1947 and 1977 but slowed between 1977 and 1997. This slowdown was mitigated in part by the declining size of families in the latter period, which meant breadwinners needed to support fewer family members. Major income disparities continued throughout the last half of the twentieth century when comparing men to women, whites to blacks and/or Hispanics, and the richest quintile of Americans to the poorest. U.S. Bureau of the Census, *Measuring 50 Years of Economic Change Using the March Current Population Survey, Current Population Reports, P60-203* (Washington, DC: GPO, 1998).

40. Safeway Stores, Inc., *Annual Report, 1962* (Oakland, CA: Safeway, Inc., 1963).

41. Tom Carrato, national product sales manager for processed cheese at Kraftco's Kraft Division, quoted in "Dairy Products Display New Vitality," *Progressive Grocer*, September 1970, 144–46.

42. "Kraft RFG Casino Cheese Case Study," June 15, 1982, JWT-NEWBUS, Box 50, Kraft, Case Histories, 1982–1986.

43. Karol Stronger, "New Ethnic Group Marketing Specialists Woo Negro Buyer," *North-west Arkansas Times*, June 8, 1967. In its advertising campaign for the 1964–65 World's Fair, the J. Walter Thompson Agency analyzed the "Negro Market" as part of its strategy. JWT-ACC, World's Fair (New York, 1964–1965), 1939–1965 and undated; Marilyn Halter, *Shopping for Identity: The Marketing of Ethnicity* (New York: Schocken Books, 2000), 42–44. Halter covers many of the same themes concerning ethnic marketing extensively in her book. She explains that "My idea in this book has been to look at the appropriation of ethnicity by businesses, whether ethnic-based or not, as a strategy to sell to wider markets in the United States" (193).

44. Quotes from "Ethnic: Moving to a Faster Beat," in "Health and Beauty Aids Report, 1977," *Progressive Grocer*, August 1977, 73–74

45. Ibid. On the general expansion of marketing campaigns to black consumers in the late 1960s, see Cohen, *A Consumer's Republic*, 324–28; From June to December of 1968, *Safeway News*, a corporate publication for employees ran a series of articles about race and Safeway stores in response to tense race relations around the nation. One article portrayed Safeway as a responsible corporation, for it was helping a co-op grocery store in Hunter's Point, a mostly black ghetto of San Francisco, Abel F. Lemes, "Safeway Lends Hand to Failing Co-op," *Safeway News*, June 1968, 2–5. Another article profiled Adam Peters, a black Safeway baker from San Anselmo, CA, by obliquely referring to recent race riots, "Peters will never be mistaken for one of the passionate, angry, young blacks whose resentment of ancient and modern wrongs sometimes overflows with hatred and violence." *Safeway News*, December 1968, 6. Susannah Walker details the commodification of the Afro by hair-care companies in the late 1960s and early 1970s in "Black is Profitable: The Commodification of the Afro, 1960–75," in Philip Scranton, ed., *Beauty and Business: Commerce, Gender, and Culture in Modern America* (New York: Routledge, 2001), 254–77.

46. Robert F. Dietrich, "Know Your Black Shopper: Race May Be One of Your Least Important Clues," *Progressive Grocer*, June 1975, 45–46, 52, 56. The next month, the magazine ran its first study of how black shoppers rated various sections of the supermarket.

47. Jean Kinsey, "A Faster, Leaner, Supply Chain: New Uses of Information Technology," Proceedings Issue, *American Journal of Agricultural Economics* 82, no. 5 (2000): 1123–29.

48. "The History of the Supermarket Industry," in *Progressive Grocer's 1992 Marketing Guidebook*.

49. A chain was defined as eleven or more branches, and an independent as ten or fewer. This definition is used by *Progressive Grocer* and the US government bureaus in their analyses. "Definitions," *Progressive Grocer*, April 1971, 61.

50. Mary Ann Linsen, "Taking Upscale Downtown," *Progressive Grocer*, November 1989, 30–36.

51. Najor's store was located in National City, CA. "Outstanding Example of Independent Style: Beating California Chains with 50,000 Pounds of Fish," *Progressive Grocer*, March 1984, 56.

52. "Your International Store," Fiesta Corporate website, http://www.fiestamart.com/ (accessed August 16, 2007).

53. Erin Sullivan, "A View from the Top," *Progressive Grocer*, February 1988, 47–51.

54. "On Weekends and Holidays, Vans Travel to the Border," *New York Times*, October 28, 1984. The vans were collectively called the "Monterey Express" because most shuttled passengers to that northern Mexican city.

55. Alison Cook, "Exotic Goods at Bargain Basement Prices Have Strapped Suburbanites Shopping to a Third World Beat," *Texas Monthly*, December 1986.

56. Sullivan, "A View from the Top."

57. Cook, "Exotic Goods."

58. Sullivan, "A View from the Top."

59. Ibid.

60. Steve Weinstein, "Fiesta for Everyone," *Progressive Grocer*, September 1989, 48–50.

61. Ibid.

62. Marian Burros, "Supermarkets Reach Out to Hispanic Customers," *New York Times*, July 18, 1990. The Tianguis division opened in 1987 but failed in the early 1990s, when most stores were reconverted to regular supermarkets.

63. John Nielsen, "California Store Woos Hispanic Community," *New York Times*, February 11, 1987.

64. Ibid.; Marian Burros, "Supermarkets Reach Out to Hispanic Customers."

65. Jack Feuer, "Make Way for the Superbodegas," *Santa Fe New Mexican*, September 24, 1989.

66. The chain is often referred to as Ranch 99 in American media reports, but is called 99 Ranch by its parent Tawa corporation, http://www.99ranch.com/AboutUs.asp (accessed August 17, 2007); Alfred Yee, *Shopping at Giant Foods: Chinese American Supermarkets in Northern California* (Seattle: University of Washington Press, 2003), 164–65; "Roger's Ranch," *Transpacific*, August 1, 1994; "H-Mart Timeline," http://company.hmart.com/eng /company_timeline.asp (accessed June 16, 2014). H-Mart began in New York but eventually added western locations too.

67. Bernard P. Wong, *The Chinese in Silicon Valley: Globalization, Social Networks, and Ethnic Identity* (Lanham, MD: Rowan & Littlefield, 2006), 202–3.

68. Ibid.

69. Ibid., 146.

70. Chris Berdik, "Super Power," *Boston Globe Magazine*, August 14, 2005. Peter Luu, a Vietnamese refugee of Chinese descent, came to the United States in 1979 and began the Super 88 chain in the 1990s. Slogan at http://www.super88market.com/index.htm# (accessed August 17, 2007). On Asian grocery chains, see Dan Turner, "Market Forces," *Transpacific*, October 1, 1994.

71. This phenomenon is not entirely new, but it is made different by rapid travel between Asia and the United States. On the transnational connections between China and the United States in an earlier era, see Madeline Y. Hsu, *Dreaming of Gold, Dreaming of Home: Transnationalism and Migration between the United States and South China, 1882–1943* (Stanford, CA: Stanford University Press, 2000); and Yong Chen, *Chinese San Francisco, 1850–1943: A Trans-Pacific Community* (Stanford, CA: Stanford University Press, 2000).

72. Shenglin Chang, *The Global Silicon Valley Home: Lives and Landscapes within Taiwanese American Trans-Pacific Culture* (Stanford, CA: Stanford University Press, 2006), 88.

73. Chang, *The Global Silicon Valley Home*, esp. 86–122; On globalization's effects on the Chinese in Asia and the Bay Area, see also Wong, *The Chinese in Silicon Valley*; AnnaLee Saxenian, *Local and Global Networks of Immigrant Professionals in Silicon Valley* (San Francisco: Public Policy Institute of California, 2002) and *Silicon Valley's New Immigrant Entrepreneurs* (San Francisco: Public Policy Institute of California, 1999); Jeff Goodell, "The Venture Capitalist in my Bedroom," *New York Times*, May 28, 2000.

74. George Sanchez has argued that ethnic marketing, "usually considered a recent phenomena, has long-standing roots" in the 1920s by showing that entrepreneurs in Los Angeles sold a wide range of goods targeted specifically to the city's Mexican American consumer market in *Becoming Mexican American: Ethnicity, Culture and Identity in Chicano Los Angeles, 1900–1945* (New York: Oxford University Press, 1993), 171–87 (quote on 174). Halter, *Shopping for Identity*, 25–47.

75. Chen, *Chinese San Francisco*, 64; Byron Huey, "Chinese Grocers and the Golden Gate Neighborhood Grocers Association," in Him Mark Lai, Papers, 1778–2002 (bulk 1970–1995), AAS ARC 2000/80 at UC Berkeley Ethnic Studies Library, Asian American Studies Archives, Carton 7:16.

76. On the homogenizing and nationalizing of the American diet, see Levenstein, *Paradox of Plenty*, 27–39, 90–100; Halter, *Shopping for Identity*, 42.

77. Marilyn Halter addresses these themes in a chapter from *Shopping for Identity*, using Kosher and other foods as case studies, 104–16. She does not, however, fully extend her analysis to the paradox of diversity and sameness inherent in the changes in eating habits over the course of the last few decades.

78. "How Different Customers Shop the Modern Super Market," *Progressive Grocer*, October 1970, 35–70. As measured by sales, A&P was the largest, followed by Safeway and Kroger. "75 Leading Grocery Chains and Stores Operated for the Years 1969, 1968 and 1967," *Progressive Grocer*, April 1970, 66–67.

79. "How Different Customers," 35–70.

80. Ibid., 36–39.

81. See table, "Expenditure Share for Non-Necessities," in US Department of Labor, *100 Years of Consumer Spending: Data for the Nation, New York City, and Boston, Report 991*, (Washington, DC: U.S. Department of Labor, 2006), 57.

82. Mueller, "5 Decades," 60.

83. "How Different Customers," 41.

84. John F. Hayes and Kimball Nedved, "Perfect Supermarket U.S.A.," 1985 survey in JWT-NEWBUS, Box 86, Folder: Vons Supermarket Industry Presentation 1986–1987.

85. Jeff Resner, "Italian Ethnic Market and the Airlines," in Maria Starczewska-Lambasa, ed., "The Ethnic Markets in New York City: A Study of Italian, Jewish, Polish, Chinese and Korean Markets and their Profit Potential for the Airlines, Banking and the Dailies," *Hofstra University Yearbook of Business* (Hempstead, NY: Hofstra University, 1982), 94.

86. Ibid.

87. One survey conducted in 1990 found 100 percent of consumers visiting a supermarket each week, at an average of 2.3 trips per week. That is about 119 trips per year. *Progressive Grocer's 1992 Marketing Guidebook*, 30.

88. "A Motivational Research Study of the Major Problem Areas for Rokeach within the Kosher Food Market," March 1961, Accession 2407, Ernest Dichter Reports, Research Reports, Box 62, HAG, 103–4.

89. Len Schechter, executive vice president of Kings Super Markets, in "Should Imported Foods be Treated as Gourmet?" *Progressive Grocer*, March 1978, 130.

90. Suzanne Rampton to Peter Kim, "Re: Vons," March 19, 1987, JWT-NEWBUS, Box 86, Folder: Vons Supermarket Industry Presentation 1986–87.

91. Mueller, "5 Decades," 36; Glenn H. Snyder, "The 'Combination Store': Growing New Approach for Super Markets," *Progressive Grocer*, January 1972, 41–45; "'Combination Store' Roundup," *Progressive Grocer*, January 1972, 46, 70–72, 78.

92. "Bucking the Discount Trend with Selection and Service," *Progressive Grocer*, March 1971, 78–84; "Food Retailers See Big Potential in Fast Foods," *Progressive Grocer*, April 1970, 72–73; and "America's Favorite Restaurant Soon May Be the Supermarket," *The Valley Independent* (Monessen, PA), July 13, 1967.

93. David Kitchel, "Produce and Lighting Build Storewide Sales," *Progressive Grocer*, January 1973, 28–36. Hyman Benatovich owned this store in Irondequoit, NY.

94. "QFI Helps Sales with an Ethnic Case," *Progressive Grocer*, January 1973, 94.

95. Joseph S. Coyle, "A Discount Super that Costs Less to Run," *Progressive Grocer*, March 1973, 58–66. The store was Food World East in Birmingham, Alabama.

96. "Old-Line Chain Is 'Reborn' in Suburbia," *Progressive Grocer*, September 1973, 50–58, about the King Cullen Grocery Store in Port Jefferson Station, NY.

97. "Inside Fazio's First Food Emporium," *Progressive Grocer*, March 1975, 94–100. The store was in Mayfield Heights, Ohio.

98. "Ralph's Raises the Ante for Super Stores," *Progressive Grocer*, June 1975, 67.

99. Ibid.

100. Joseph S. Coyle, "Superest Store of Them All?" *Progressive Grocer*, August 1976, 42–47.

101. Herb Brody, Vice Chairman, Pathmark, quoted in "Jewish Foods . . . A Growing Success Story at Pathmark," *Progressive Grocer*, February 1973, 100.

102. "A Motivational Research Study of the Major Problem Areas for Rokeach within the Kosher Food Market," March 1961, Accession 2407, Ernest Dichter Reports, Research Reports, Box 62, HAG, 93–97.

103. Advertisement in *Progressive Grocer*, November 1978, 71; "Hanging Piñata Spotlights Mexican Foods Section," *Progressive Grocer*, June 1979, 96F. It's not clear from the advertisement what was Mexican about the corn dog, except perhaps the long history of corn consumption in Mexico.

104. "Retailing Roundup," *Progressive Grocer*, March 1973, 100. Best Foods later ran a "Go Chinese" recipe contest and published a cookbook, *Award Winning Chinese Recipes* (Englewood Cliffs, NJ: CPC International, 1983).

105. One example is the "Frozen Food Planning Calendar," *Progressive Grocer*, August 1972, 146–47.

106. The California Delicatessen Council produced the calendar. *Progressive Grocer*, January 1970, 131.

107. Most of these promotions were run in areas of the country with small Chinese American populations. Furthermore, around 1970 the overall ethnic Chinese population in the United States was small—about 436,062. The number, from Census estimates, is an approximation because ethnic Chinese have migrated from a variety of places in large numbers besides mainland China to the United States, including Taiwan, Hong Kong, and Vietnam. Roger Daniels, *Coming to America: A History of Immigration and Ethnicity in American Life* (New York: Harper Perennial, 1990), 351–53.

108. A typical example of this is "Set Your Store Apart with Specialty Foods," *Progressive Grocer*, July 1988, which began, "Today's Specialty Is Tomorrow's Staple."

109. On the general consumption of ethnically identified goods in the post 1960s period, Halter, *Shopping for Identity*; Bandana Purkayastha, *Negotiating Ethnicity: Second-Generation South Asian Americans Traverse a Transnational World* (New Brunswick, NJ: Rutgers University Press, 2005); Matthew Frye Jacobson, *Roots Too: White Ethnic Revival in Post-Civil Rights America* (Cambridge, MA: Harvard University Press, 2006).

110. On the persistence of American views of the Chinese as inscrutable, Harold R. Isaacs conducted a study in the 1950s in which 41 percent of respondents described the Chinese as "inscrutable, difficult to communicate with," *Images of Asia: American Views of China and India* (New York: Harper and Row, 1972), 72–89. Rey Chow, "How (the) Inscrutable Chinese Led to Globalized Theory," *PMLA* 116, no. 1 (2001): 69–74.

111. "Oriental Vegetables Make Scrutable Money," *Progressive Grocer*, July 1976, 22.

112. Joseph Izzo Jr., "Ethnic Fare: A Guide to Exotic Cuisine at Your Neighborhood Market," *San Jose Mercury News*, October 6, 1982.

113. Safeway, Inc., *Annual Report, 1989* (Oakland, CA: Safeway, Inc., 1990), 4.

114. Ibid., 3.

115. Safeway Stores, Inc., *1984 Annual Report* (Oakland, CA: Safeway Stores, Inc., 1985), 5.

116. Ibid., 1–4.

117. Samantha Barbas, "'I'll Take Chop Suey': Restaurants as Agents of Culinary and Cultural Change," *The Journal of Popular Culture* 36, no. 4 (2003): 677–81; J. A. G. Roberts, *China to Chinatown: Chinese Food in the West* (London: Reaktion Books, 2002), 199; Madeline Y. Hsu, "From Chop Suey to Mandarin Cuisine: Fine Dining and the Refashioning of Chinese Ethnicity during the Cold War Era," http://www.instrcc.ubc.ca/History485_2008/Hsu.pdf (accessed February 18, 2008), 15.

118. Jacqueline M. Newman, "La Choy: Going on Seventy-Five," *Flavor and Fortune* 11, no. 2 (Summer 2004): 5, 32–33.

119. La Choy Food Products, *The Arts and Secrets of Chinese Cookery* (Detroit: La Choy Food Products, 1931), HathiTrust Digital Library, http://babel.hathitrust.org/cgi/pt?id=uc1.31822035093574;view=1up;seq=10 (accessed May 22, 2014).

120. La Choy, *The Arts and Secrets of Chinese Cookery* (Archbold, OH: Beatrice, 1949), 1–2, JWT-BONA, Box 1940s-11, Folder 1940s-0318.

121. Many cookbooks emphasized this including the 1953 *Better Homes and Gardens New Cook Book*, which begins by noting that the purchaser will make "economical meals" and purchase in "thrifty quantities." *Better Homes and Gardens New Cook Book* (Meredith Publishing, 1953).

122. *Progressive Grocer* ran a "store of the month" feature for many years that showed an architectural diagram of a store's layout. The layouts from the 1960s and 1970s show many stores with a Chinese or Oriental section. Chinese frozen foods were a standard by this time. A report in 1970 said that Spanish, Italian, Jewish, and Chinese foods were "now standard" at the time and that a new "international foods" frozen section might be needed in the future. "37th Annual Report: What Super Markets Will Sell in the 1970s," *Progressive Grocer*, April 1970, 149. For architectural layouts, see Daykin, "Randall's Super," 122–32; "Ralph's Newest Scores Success in Los Angeles," *Progressive Grocer*, August 1970, 92–104. Another showed Martin's Super Market in Elkhart, Indiana, with a Chinese section of about twelve feet between the diet and convenience sections, Beatty, "Tight Scheduling." On a store in Dallas, TX, Joseph Coyle, "A Big Bright Bid for the Young Consumer," *Progressive Grocer*, June 1971, 70–78.

123. Janet Key, "RJR Sending Chun King to Orient," *Chicago Tribune*, June 22, 1989.

124. Ibid.; "ConAgra Finishes Deal for Beatrice," *New York Times*, August 16, 1990.

125. Russell Redman, "Hunt-Wesson Acquires Chun King," *Supermarket News*, May 8, 1995.

126. Various Beatrice Foods advertisements, dated 1984–1987, JWT-AD, Box BF1 (Beatrice Foods 1984–1987). Beatrice used the East meets West tagline in its marketing materials.

127. Michael J. McCarthy, "Slim Pickings," *Wall Street Journal*, May 6, 1997.

128. Advertisement for McCormick spices in *Woman's Day* clipping, November 1965, JWT-COMP, 1965 Box 11, Folder 1965 F114, Flavoring Extracts and Spices, 11:14.

129. Richard Gibson, "Marketscan: Michelina's Frozen Entrees Trip Up Giants," *Wall Street Journal*, September 21, 1993.

130. Kathy Sexton, "Michelina's Ships Pasta to China," *The Jackson County Times Journal*, June 14, 2007.

131. Sherrie A. Inness, *Dinner Roles: American Women and Culinary Culture* (Iowa City: University of Iowa Press, 2001), 107.

132. Photograph from Ohio Development and Publicity Comm., "A view of the line for filling, labeling and packaging La Choy Brown Gravy Sauce, La Choy Plant, Archbold, Ohio," c. 1950s, Reproduction #LC-USZ62-53160, Library of Congress, http://www.loc.gov/pictures/item/2005696138/ (accessed June 17, 2014); Advertisement, 1984, JWT-AD, Box BF1 (Beatrice Foods 1984–1987). When owned by Beatrice in the 1950s, La Choy requested regular government factory inspections even though this was not mandated by law. Newman, "La Choy"; Inness, *Dinner Roles*, 106–7.

4. THE CHANGING AMERICAN RESTAURANT

1. *Great Menus: 1983* (Washington, DC: National Restaurant Association, 1983).

2. Ibid.

3. "Familiar Mexican Fare Awaits at Carlos Murphy's," *Virginian-Pilot* (Norfolk), August 7, 1994.

4. Jeffrey M. Pilcher, "Tex-Mex, Cal-Mex, New-Mex, or whose Mex? Notes on the Historical Geography of Southwestern Cuisine," *Journal of the Southwest* 43, no. 4 (2001): 659–80.

5. Tortilla Industry Association, *1991 Tortilla Industry National Research Survey* (Encino, CA: Tortilla Industry Association, 1992), 13.

6. In 1991, Flay opened Mesa Grill restaurant in New York. "Bio" at http://www.bobbyflay .com (accessed April 2, 2009). Bayless opened Frontera Grill in 1987 and Topolobampo in 1989 in Chicago. "About Rick Bayless," www.rickbayless.com (accessed February 26, 2010). Both chefs sold packaged foods and cooking utensils.

7. KFC had more than 1,500 locations in China when the Shanghai plant opened, which was to distribute outside of China also. "Wrapping the Globe in Tortillas," *Business Week*, February 26, 2007, 54; Lu Haoting, "Mexican Mission," *China Business Weekly*, July 10, 2006.

8. Audrey Russek, "Appetites without Prejudice: U.S. Foreign Restaurants and the Globalization of American Food between Wars," *Food and Foodways: Explorations in the History and Culture of Human Nourishment* 19 (2011): 34–55

9. Robert H. Willson, "The Japanese," December 23, 1923, *San Francisco Examiner*, in Robert H. Willson and George and Emilia Hodel, *Foreign Nationalities in San Francisco* (San Francisco, CA: 1951), SFHC.

10. Although Craig Claiborne remarked that Japanese food became popular in New York in the 1960s, that did not happen in the rest of the country. Craig Claiborne, "1960's: Haute Cuisine in America," *New York Times*, January 1, 1970.

11. Katarzyna J. Cwiertka, *Modern Japanese Cuisine: Food, Power and National Identity* (London: Reaktion, 2006), 182.

12. Theodore C. Bestor, "Supply-Side Sushi: Commodity, Market, and the Global City," *American Anthropologist* 103, no. 1 (March 2001): 76–95; Sasha Issenberg, *The Sushi Economy: Globalization and the Making of a Modern Delicacy* (New York: Gotham, 2007), 92–105.

13. Rita Kempley, "Wall Street," *Washington Post*, December 11, 1987.

14. "Yuppie," *New Oxford American Dictionary*, third edition edited by Angus Stevenson and Christine A. Lindberg, 2010.

15. *Valley Girl*, directed by Martha Coolidge (1983; MGM, 2003), DVD.

16. *Wall Street*, directed by Oliver Stone (1987; 20th Century Fox, 2010), DVD.

17. Issenberg, *Sushi Economy*, 98–99; "Yuppies," *NRA News*, October 1985.

18. Some menus from the era simply list types of sushi on menus without explanation. See Menu, Genroku Sushi, 1985, New York, NY, New York Public Library, Call #1985-0032 _wotm, http://menus.nypl.org/menu_pages/53188 (accessed January 18, 2016); Catering menu from Creative Gourmets, Boston, MA, in *Great Menus: 1983*.

19. Menu, Kamon, 1985, San Francisco, CA, CCSF, Folder, San Francisco, H–L.

20. Menu, Amagi, 1980, Hollywood, CA, Los Angeles Public Library Menu Collection, http://dbase1.lapl.org/images/menus/fullsize/a/13346-inside.jpg (accessed January 18, 2016).

21. Jeffrey M. Pilcher, *Planet Taco: A Global History of Mexican Food* (New York: Oxford University Press, 2012), 202–9; Andrew Coe, *Chop Suey* (New York: Oxford University Press, 2009), 198–216.

22. USDA-ERS, "Food away from Home as a Share of Food Expenditures," at http:// www.ers.usda.gov/data-products/food-expenditures.aspx (accessed January 7, 2016).

23. Paul Freedman, "Restaurants," in Freedman, Joyce E. Chaplin, and Ken Albala, eds., *Food in Time and Place: The American Historical Association Companion to Food History* (Berkeley: University of California Press, 2014), 253.

24. Katharine Leonard Turner, *How the Other Half Ate: A History of Working-Class Meals at the Turn of the Century* (Berkeley: University of California Press, 2014), 1–3.

25. USDA-ERS, "Food Expenditures by Families and Individuals as a Share of Disposable Personal Income," at http://www.ers.usda.gov/data-products/food-expenditures.aspx (accessed January 7, 2016).

26. Michael J. Harris, Phil R. Kaufman, Steve W. Martinez (coordinator), and Charlene Price, *The U.S. Food Marketing System, 2002* (Washington, DC: ERS-USDA, 2002), 35–40. The percentage of fast-food sales as a proportion of all restaurant sales was relatively steady from 1993 to 2000. According to the USDA, there were about 844,000 food service eating establishments in 2000, with total sales of $358 billion. Commercial sales totaled $294 billion and noncommercial sales totaled $64 billion. Noncommercial sales included food service at schools, hospitals, day cares, prisons, and other establishments, as well as vending machines. In billions of dollars, commercial sales were composed of fast food stores (125), restaurants (114), lodging places (13), retail hosts (20), recreation (10), social caterers (7), cafeterias (3), and drinking places (2).

27. This total included not just burgers and fries, but a large increase in soda consumption. Jason Block, Richard A. Scribner, and Karen B. DeSalvo, "Fast Food, Race/Ethnicity, and Income: A Geographic Analysis," *American Journal of Preventive Medicine* 27, no. 3 (2004): 211.

28. Theresa A. Hastert, Susan H. Babey, Allison L. Diamant, and E. Richard Brown, "More California Teens Consume Fast Food and Soda Each Day Than Five Servings of Fruits and Vegetables," *UCLA Health Policy Research Brief*, September 2005, 4–5, http://www.healthpolicy.ucla.edu/pubs/files/teen_fastfood_PB.pdf (accessed March 25, 2008).

29. Block et al., "Fast Food," 211–17. This study mapped fast food restaurants in New Orleans, finding that there were 2.4 per square mile in black neighborhoods as compared to 1.5 in white neighborhoods. See also Marla Reicks, "Fast Food Consumption among Minority Adults and Adolescents," *Nutrinet*, January 2005, http://www.fsci.umn.edu/outreach/faculty_outreach/nutrinet/archives/january_2005/fast_food.html (accessed March 25, 2005).

30. Harris et al., *U.S. Food Marketing System, 2002*, 35–40.

31. Nicholas Kiefer, "Economics and the Origins of the Restaurant," *Cornell Hotel and Restaurant Administration Quarterly* (August 2002): 58–64; Jacqueline Newman, *Food Culture in China* (Westport, CT: Greenwood Press, 2004), 129–31; Andrew P. Haley, "Restaurant Culture," in Michael D. Wise and Jennifer Jensen Wallach, eds., *The Routledge History of American Foodways* (New York: Routledge, 2016). 214–32.

32. Rebecca Spang, *The Invention of the Restaurant* (Cambridge, MA: Harvard University Press, 2000).

33. Andrew Haley, *Turning the Tables: Restaurants and the Rise of the American Middle Class: 1880–1920* (Chapel Hill: University of North Carolina, 2011).

34. Freedman, "Restaurants," in *Food in Time and Place*, 253–75; Harvey Levenstein, *Paradox of Plenty: A Social History of Eating in Modern America* (Berkeley: University of California Press, 2003)), 213–36.

35. Krishnendu Ray, "Migration, Transnational Cuisines, and Invisible Ethnics," in Freedman et al., *Food in Time and Place*, 222.

36. NPD Group, "U.S. Total Restaurant Count Increases by 4,442 Units over Last Year, Reports NPD," January 23, 2013, at https://www.npd.com/wps/portal/npd/us/news/press -releases/us-total-restaurant-count-increases-by-4442-units-over-last-year-reports-npd/ (accessed January 11, 2016). This report estimated a total of 611,566 restaurants in 2011.

37. *Ethnic Cuisines II* (Washington, DC: National Restaurant Association, 2000), 1–73, quote from 53.

38. Ibid., 5.

39. Elliot Shore, "Dining Out: The Development of the Restaurant," in Paul Freedman, ed., *Food: The History of Taste* (Berkeley: University of California Press, 2007), 301–4.

40. Spang, *Invention of the Restaurant,* 76–79.

41. Haley, *Turning the Tables,* 118–44.

42. David V. Pavesic, *Restaurant Manager's Pocket Handbook* (New York: Lebhar-Friedman, 1999), 3

43. Ibid., 18.

44. Judi Radice, *Menu Design* (Locust Valley, NY: PBC International, 1985), 86.

45. Dan Jurafsky, *The Language of Food: A Linguist Reads the Menu* (New York: Norton, 2014), 9.

46. Michael G. Hydak, "The Menu as Culture Capsule," *Modern Language Journal* 62, no. 3 (2002): 58–64.

47. Wynne Wright and Elizabeth Ransom, "Stratification on the Menu: Using Restaurant Menus to Examine Social Class," *Teaching Sociology* 33, no. 3 (July 2005): 310–16, quote on 316.

48. National Restaurant Association, "About Us," http://www.restaurant.org/About-Us (Accessed May 6, 2019).

49. *Menu Analysis 1993* (Washington, DC: National Restaurant Association, 1993), 8.

50. *Restaurants USA,* December 1994, 26–27.

51. *Menu Analysis 1997* (Washington, DC: National Restaurant Association, 1998), 1.

52. Ibid., 41.

53. Campbell Gibson and Kay Jung. *Historical Census Statistics on the Foreign-Born Population of the United States: 1850 to 2000* (Washington, DC: US Census Bureau, 2006). http://www.census.gov/population/www/documentation/twps0081/twps0081.pdf (accessed March 18, 2007).

54. Levenstein, *Paradox of Plenty,* 90–92.

55. Federal expenditures exploded during World War II. The federal government's budget increased from 10.3 percent of GDP in 1939, when the war effort was just ramping up, to its highest level of the twentieth century in 1945, at 43.7 percent. From 1950 to 2000, it hovered between 15 and 23 percent. See *Historical Tables: Budget of the United States Government, Fiscal Year 2004* (Washington, DC: GPO, 2003) at http://www.gpoaccess.gov/usbudget/fy04 /pdf/hist.pdf (accessed December 14, 2007), 7, 23–24.

56. Administrative History, NARA-PAC; Meyer H. Fishbein and Elaine E. Bennett, *Preliminary Inventory Number 32: Records of the Accounting Department of the Office of Price Administration* (Washington, DC: National Archives, 1951), 1–6; Meg Jacobs, "'How about Some Meat?': The Office of Price Administration, Consumption Politics, and State Building from the Bottom Up, 1941–1946," *Journal of American History* 84, no. 3 (1997): 910–41.

57. Quote from Office of Price Administration, "Part 1448—Eating and Drinking Establishments, Restaurant Maximum Price Regulation 2—Food and Drink Sold for Immediate Consumption," June 29, 1944, 3, NARA-PAC, Accounting Records Field Offices, Region 8, San Francisco District Office Case Files, Ch-Co, Box 151, Folder—Gene Compton's Corporation, D-229-SF San Francisco, CA; War and Price Rationing Board, "It's Amazing!" (Washington, DC: OPA, 1945).

58. My claim that they are representative is based on a review of hundreds of these menus. Though it seems rather arbitrary which menus got collected in archives, I found OPA-stamped menus at CHS, CCSF, and BANC. I found just a few menus at the NARA-PAC, but many more at NARA-DEN. I also surveyed menus from the 1940s and 1950s posted online by the New York Public Library and the Los Angeles Public Library.

59. Letter, Office of Price Administration, Denver Office, to Proprietors of Restaurants and other Eating and Drinking Places (1943), PI 120, NARA-DEN, Enforcement Records, Entry 278, Records of Enforcement Activities, 1943–46, ARC 1105004, Box #105, (E278), Folder: Restaurant Drive (Dist. Office).

60. Menu, Fly Trap Restaurant, San Francisco, CA, April 5, 1944, Richard Brautigan Papers, 1958–1984, BANC MSS 87/173c, Box 3:25A, San Francisco Restaurant Menus.

61. Memo, Innes W. Lundsen to Max L. Keenan, August 8, 1944, about Carl's St. Paul Café, Exhibit B, PI 32, NARA-DEN; Accounting Dept. Records, Denver, CO, Entry 495, Case Files 1943–46, ARC 1104453, Box No. 8, Entry 495, Company Files: Beckett–Colo. Springs, Folder: Carl's St. Paul Café, Denver, Colorado, NARA-DEN; Menus of Butte, Montana, restaurants Green's Café, Raymond's Cube Steak House, Norma's Dog House, Creamery Café, all in Box 193, PI 95, NARA-DEN, Entry 1281, Records Concerning Price Regulations, 1942–46, ARC 1116789.

62. Menus, Carte du Jour, San Francisco, CA, July 15, 1945, and Parkwood, San Francisco, CA, November 7, 1945, CCSF, Folder, Calif.-San Francisco, P-R; Menu, Bunny's Waffle Shops, April 6, 1944, San Francisco, CA, CHS, Menu, A–O, Folder-C.

63. Menu, Bunny's Waffle Shops.

64. These were just the menus I found in the collections. There were surely more. See Menu, Skyline Café, San Francisco, CA, April 6, 1944, CHS, Menu, San Francisco-S; Menu, The Eddy Café, San Francisco, CA, September 8, 1944, CHS, Menu, E; Menu, Season Café, April 12, 1944, CHS, Menu, San Francisco-S; Menu, Casino Café, San Francisco, CA, (No date—circa 1930s or 1940s), CHS, Menu, A–O, Folder-C; Menu, Dong's Café, San Francisco, CA, April 12, 1944, CHS, Menu, San Francisco, Folder—D; Menu, Peacock Café, Oakland, CA, November 26, 1943, CHS, Menu, A–O-Oakland; Memo, Charles D. Pooley, District Accounting Executive, San Francisco District Office, OPA, to Charles Aikin, District Price Executive, San Francisco District Office, OPA, October 24, 1944, NARA-PAC, RG 188, OPA, Accounting Records, Field Offices, Region 8, San Francisco District Office, Case Files, Co-Di, Box 152, Folder-Dixie Coffee Shop, Richmond, CA, D-304-SF. This restaurant was opened in June 1944, and in September of that year began listing Chinese foods on its menu. The restaurant seated 120 and served 452 meals on average during the weekends in 1944. It was owned by a group of five men with Chinese surnames but employed mostly non-Chinese front-of-the-house personnel. Also see Menu, Kent's Chicken Shop, San Francisco and Oakland, CA, November 16, 1940, CCSF, Folder, Calif-San Francisco, P-R. Menu,

Aladdin Studio Tiffin Room, San Francisco, CA, CHS, Menu, Folder—Menu Collection, A—San Francisco. Menu, Casino Café, CHS. Menus, Beresford Dining Room and Casino Café, CHS. Menu, Skyline Café, CHS.

65. Menu, Season Café, April 12, 1944, CHS.

66. *Great American Menus* (Chicago: National Restaurant Association, 1964). One study of families in Medford, Massachusetts, during 1952 and 1953, showed that meat was served as the main dish in 80 percent of the main meals in any given day. Beefsteaks and hamburgers were the most common dishes. Harry E. Allison, Charles J. Zwick, and Ayres Brinser, "Menu Data and Their Contribution to Food Consumption Studies," *Journal of Farm Economics* 40, no. 1 (1958): 5, 9.

67. Andrew Hurley, "From Hash House to Family Restaurant: The Transformation of the Diner and Post–World War II Consumer Culture," *Journal of American History* 83, no. 4 (1997): 1302–6.

68. Menu, Sambo's, No Date (circa 1950s or 1960s), and second menu, 1966 (Locations throughout the West and Midwest). See also Menu, The Alvarado Fred Harvey, Albuquerque, NM, 1953; Menu, Fred Harvey Union Terminal Restaurant, Los Angeles, 1965; Menu, Howard Johnson's (Location—notation for "Route 2, Mass.," on menu) no date (circa 1950s); Menu, Stouffer's, Location Unknown, 1960, and second menu, Stouffers's (circa 1959 or 1960). All in CCSF, Folder—Chains, General Menus, USA. Also see Menu, International House of Pancakes, (Various locations), 1963, Oakland History Room, Oakland Public Library, Main Branch (hereafter OAK), VF–Restaurants, A-K; Menu, Sambo's Pancakes, (California locations), 1961, OAK, VF-Restaurants, Q-Z.

69. Menu, Uncle John's Pancake House (lists fifty locations nationwide), 1964; Menu, Aunt Jemima's Kitchen (Location Unknown), (date circa 1950s); Menu, Frisch's Big Boy (shows 195 locations in Florida, Indiana, Ohio, and Kentucky), 1965. All in CCSF, Folder—Chains, General Menus, USA.

70. On ethnic marketing, see Purkayastha, *Negotiating Ethnicity*, 118–26; Halter, *Shopping for Identity*.

71. David Halberstam noted that social ferment was "beginning just beneath this placid surface" of the 1950s, but that in general it was an era of "good will and expanding affluence," and "few Americans doubted the essential goodness of their society." He also writes that many were beginning to question the focus on material goods in America, but that this was again, something fermenting below the surface. See *The Fifties* (New York: Fawcett Columbine, 1993), ix–xi.

72. "Americanism in the Schools," *The Texas Observer*, October 18, 1963, 6.

73. Ibid.

5. COOKBOOKS NAVIGATE THE GLOBE

1. Madhur Jaffrey, *Climbing the Mango Trees* (New York: Knopf, 1973), 240–43.

2. Marilyn Bender, "The Sari Becomes Western Fashion," *New York Times*, May 13, 1966. Gimbel's held a "Salute to India" promotion to sell Indian products at the store. Jaffrey quoted in Eric Pooley, "Tops in Toques," *New York*, December 25–30, 1991, 80.

3. Judith Jones to Millie, July 7, 1972, JJMC, Box 851.1.

4. "James Beard's Books," *James Beard Foundation*, https://www.jamesbeard.org/about /james-beard-books (accessed March 2, 2017).

5. Craig Claiborne, "Indian Actress Is a Star in the Kitchen Too," *New York Times*, July 7, 1966. Jaffrey was also in a New York play at the time, *The Guide*. Clive Barnes, "Theater: Reluctant Guru," *New York Times*, March 7, 1968.

6. The curry houses of England began to flourish in the 1960s and 1970s, partly because of a reappraisal of English food by the English, and partly because of large-scale immigration from South Asia to Britain. Laresh Jayasanker, "Food and Migration in the Twentieth Century," in Carol Helstosky, ed., *The Routledge History of Food* (New York: Routledge, 2015), 313–30; Lizzie Collingham, *Curry: A Tale of Cooks and Conquerors* (New York: Oxford University Press, 2006), 224–43.

7. Madhur Jaffrey, *An Invitation to Indian Cooking* (New York: Knopf, 1973), 3.

8. Ibid., 4.

9. Elaine Markson to Judith Jones, November 10, 1971, JJMC, Box 851.11.

10. Judith Jones to Jill Norman, Penguin Books, Harmondsworth, England, November 16, 1973, JJMC, Box 851.1.

11. Raymond A. Sokolov, "Current Stars: Books on Indian, Italian, and Inexpensive Food," *New York Times*, April 19. 1973.

12. For the British example, see an early cookbook by Eliza Acton, which has a chapter on "curries" and "potted meats." Acton also gives recipes for curry powders. Acton, *Modern Cookery, in All Its Branches* (Philadelphia: Lea and Blanchard, 1858), 221–26. Curry powder had long been a common item in American pantries. See Kristin Hoganson, *Consumer's Imperium: The Global Production of American Domesticity, 1865–1920* (Chapel Hill: University of North Carolina Press, 2007), 110, 114.

13. Jaffrey, *An Invitation*, 6–7.

14. Ibid., 6.

15. Ibid., 4.

16. Pamela Goyan Kittler and Kathryn P. Sucher, *Food and Culture*, 3rd ed. (Belmont, CA: Wadsworth/Thomson Learning, 2001), 11.

17. Hoganson, *Consumers' Imperium*.

18. Janet Theophano also uses this idea of cooking as translation in "Home Cooking: Boston Baked Beans and Sizzling Rice Soup as Recipes for Pride and Prejudice," in Sherrie A. Inness, ed., *Kitchen Culture in America: Popular Representations of Food, Gender, and Race* (Philadelphia: University of Pennsylvania Press, 2001), 139–56.

19. Jane Benet, "From North America to the Antarctic," *San Francisco Chronicle* (undated, circa 1972 or 1973) in JJMC, Box 854.2. This was a review of Elisabeth Lambert Ortiz's cookbook, *The Book of Latin American Cooking*, which is detailed below. The author starts her article with, "Latin American cooking is not all tortillas and beans, by any means," adding that the food of the region is as "varied as the climate."

20. See for example Himilce Novas and Rosemary Silva, *Latin American Cooking across the U.S.A.* (New York: Alfred A. Knopf, 1997); Norman Van Aken, *Norman's New World Cuisine* (New York: Random House, 1997); Joan Nathan, *The New American Cooking* (New York: Alfred A. Knopf, 2005).

21. Arjun Appadurai, "How to Make a National Cuisine: Cookbooks in Contemporary India," *Comparative Studies in Society and History* 30, no.1 (1988): 22.

22. Barbara Haber, *From Hardtack to Home Fries: An Uncommon History of American Cooks and Meals* (New York: The Free Press, 2002), 208–21, quote on 210.

23. Quote from Janet Floyd and Laurel Forster, "The Recipe in Its Cultural Contexts," in Janet Floyd and Laurel Forster, eds., *The Recipe Reader* (Burlington, VT: Ashgate, 2003), 1. Two other examples of the importance of cookbooks link their writing to national identity. See Igor Cusack, "African Cuisines: Recipes for Nation Building?" *Journal of African Cultural Studies* 13, no. 2 (2000): 207–25; and Jeffrey Pilcher, *¡Que Vivan los Tamales! Food and the Making of Mexican Identity* (Albuquerque: University of New Mexico Press, 1998).

24. Barbara Wheaton, "Finding Real Life in Cookbooks: The Adventures of a Culinary Historian," in Leslie Howsam, ed., *Food, Cookery and Culture* (Windsor, ON: Humanities Research Group, University of Windsor, 1998), 3.

25. This estimate is truly rough. The USDA calculates this number by dividing the total food supply in calories by the number of people in the United States, minus an estimate of the amount of food wasted by each person. The USDA added that wastage estimate in 1970, so the 1970 to 2000 comparison is a bit more accurate than comparisons from before 1970. The USDA estimates that the 1970 to 2000 increase was due mostly to a rise in added fats, sugars, and grains to the American diet. Sugary soda was one of the chief culprits. See *Agriculture Fact Book, 2001-2002* (Washington, DC: USDA, 2003), 14–15.

26. Nick Cullather, "The Foreign Policy of the Calorie," *American Historical Review* 112, no. 2 (2007), 337–63.

27. Ibid.; Laura Shapiro, *Perfection Salad: Women and Cooking at the Turn of the Century* (New York: Farrar Strauss & Giroux, 1986), 3–10, 163–68.

28. Ken Albala, "Cookbooks as Historical Documents," in Jeffrey Pilcher, ed., *The Oxford Handbook of Food History* (New York: Oxford University Press, 2012), 234.

29. Shapiro, *Something from the Oven*, xviii–xxiii. Shapiro did analyze some of the major cookbooks from the era but was careful to point out their limitations.

30. Sandra Oliver, "Ruminations on the State of American Food History," *Gastronomica: The Journal of Food and Culture* 6, no. 4 (2006): 91–98. Oliver did find a peanut butter and jelly recipe in the 1965 *Fannie Farmer Cookbook* under "Simple Sandwich Fillings."

31. The authors of the cookbooks analyzed below meet all these requirements. They include Julia Child, Claudia Roden, Jane Grigson, Madhur Jaffrey, and Elisabeth Ortiz. On the influence of Alfred A. Knopf's cookbooks, see "2006 James Beard Foundation Award Nominees Announced," at http://www.jamesbeard.org/about/press/pr/jbfawd06NOMI NATIONS%20for%20jbf.org%203.16.06%2010AM.pdf (accessed December 12, 2007); Lisa Jones, "Alfred A. Knopf" in Alice Arndt, ed., *Culinary Biographies* (Houston: Yes Press, 2006), 223–24. The Knopf archives at the Ransom Center include some information about sales figures, but it is often incomplete.

32. Cookbooks are not perfect sources, but when read with an eye to the author's intent, perspective, and historical setting, they are valuable tools for food historians. One methodological treatise on food research called cookbooks "both essential and potentially profoundly misleading" when not read in historical and anthropological context. See Jeremy MacClancy, "Food, Identity, Identification," in Helen Macbeth and Jeremy MacClancy, eds., *Research Food Habits: Methods and Problems* (New York: Berghahn Books, 2004), 63–73, quote on 65.

33. Many studies about food and food history make use of cookbooks. Some even use the files of certain authors, such as Julia Child, which are deposited at the Schlesinger

Library at Radcliffe College, Cambridge, Massachusetts. But few detail the publishing process and the interchange between editor and author. One issue of *Gastronomica* was devoted to Julia Child, and some articles made use of those files, including Joan Reardon, "Mastering the Art of French Cooking," *Gastronomica* 5, no. 3 (2005): 62–72.

34. "Culinary Arts Find a New Market," *Berkshire Eagle*, April 11, 1973.

35. Raymond A. Sokolov, "Cultures of the World Depicted in Ounces, Cups and Spoonfuls," *New York Times*, October 5, 1972. Knopf published two of the cookbooks praised by Sokolov. They were Claudia Roden's *A Book of Middle Eastern Food* and Simone Beck's *Simca's Cuisine* (New York: Knopf, 1972). With Knopf, Sokolov published *The Saucier's Apprentice: A Modern Guide to Classic French Sauces for the Home* (New York: Knopf, 1976). For that book, he wished to describe French sauces in "language accessible to the American amateur cook," Raymond Sokolov to Lynn Nesbit, International Famous Agency, February 5, 1973, JJMC, Box 856.4.

36. Raymond A. Sokolov, "Current Stars: Books on Indian, Italian, and Inexpensive Food," *New York Times*, April 19, 1973

37. Steven Mintz and Susan Kellogg, *Domestic Revolutions: A Social History of American Family Life* (New York: The Free Press, 1988), 204.

38. Bureau of Labor Statistics, "Women in the Labor Force: A Databook" (Washington, DC: Bureau of Labor Statistics, 2006) at http://www.bls.gov/cps/wlf-databook-2006.pdf (accessed December 5, 2007), 19–20, 63–64.

39. National Center for Health Statistics, *Monthly Vital Statistics Report*, Vol. 41, No. 33, September 28, 1993, www.cdc.gov (accessed November 29, 2016), 3–5.

40. Abigail Van Buren, "Navy Man Asks Ex to Teach Wife to Cook," *Northwest Arkansas Times*, December 18, 1975.

41. JJMC, Box 853.1, Folder, Manuscript Rejections, July–December, 1980.

42. On the rise of takeout food, see Hayden Stewart, Noel Blisard, Sanjib Bhuyan, and Rodolfo M. Nayga Jr., *The Demand for Food away from Home: Full Service or Fast Food? AER-829* (Washington, DC: ERS-USDA, 2004), 1–11. Quotes from Judith Jones, senior editor, Alfred A. Knopf, Inc., in David Belma, "200 Years of Cooking by the Book," *Restaurants USA*, November 1996, 35.

43. Trish Hall, "New 'Lost Generation': The Cooking Illiterate," *New York Times*, January 15, 1992. The National Pork Producers Council conducted one test of 735 adults. The test had twenty questions and nearly three-quarters of the takers failed, which meant they missed 30 percent or more of the questions.

44. This figure is cited in both L. Patrick Coyle Jr., *Cook's Books: An Affectionate Guide to the Literature of Food and Cooking* (New York: Facts on File Publications, 1985), 25; and Alice Payne Hackett and James Henry Burke, *80 Years of Best Sellers: 1895–1975* (New York: R.R. Bowker Company, 1977), 47. Cookbook publishing data usually includes just those put out by formal publishing houses. There are a wide range of cookbooks published by church groups, clubs, community organizations, and the like for fundraising purposes. These cookbooks are not typically included in the counts by either *Publisher's Weekly* or the American Bookseller's Association.

45. Eben Shapiro, "Publishing: Thousands of Cookbooks in Search of Some Cooks," *Wall Street Journal*, March 2, 1994.

46. These data were cited as coming from the American Booksellers Association in David Belma, "200 Years of Cooking by the Book," *Restaurants USA*, November 1996, 34. The number was skewed by a jump in sales from the publication of *In the Kitchen with Rosie*, a cookbook by Oprah Winfrey's personal chef that sold over eight million copies. See Suzanne Hamlin, "Too Many Cooks, Yes, But Never Too Many Cookbooks," *New York Times*, January 22, 1997. The jump in sales seemed to occur most dramatically in the late 1980s and early 1990s. Another figure cited from *Publishers Weekly* said that 400 cookbooks and food-related books were sold in 1987, and that by August 1988, 436 had already been published, Trish Hall, "A New Spectator Sport: Looking Not Cooking," *New York Times*, January 4, 1989; The Barnes and Noble sales figure is from Martin Arnold, "Making Books: A Culinary Fantasy Life," *New York Times*, October 29, 1998.

47. Caryn James, "Recipes for Success in Cookbooks," *New York Times*, March 27, 1985; Hall, "A New Spectator Sport," *New York Times*, January 4, 1989.

48. "Judith Jones to Receive James Beard Foundation Lifetime Achievement Award," Press Release, The Knopf Publishing Group, at http://www.randomhouse.biz/media/pdfs /Judith_Jones.pdf (accessed September 24, 2007).

49. Cookbooks published under the *Better Homes and Gardens, Betty Crocker*, and *Good Housekeeping* imprints dominated the list of books that sold over 750,000 copies in the period between 1895 and 1975. See Hackett and Burke, *80 Years of Best Sellers*, 10–20. *Mastering* did not appear on that list, though it was said to have sold over a million copies by its fortieth anniversary in 2001. For that figure, see Judith Weinraub, "40 Years by the Book," *Washington Post*, October 3, 2001. Julia Child and Simone Beck's *Mastering the Art of French Cooking, Volume II* (New York: Knopf, 1970), which extended the information in volume I, and Julia Child's *The French Chef Cookbook* (New York: Knopf, 1968), which was based on her television programs, also sold many thousands of copies.

50. "Alfred A. Knopf," in Arndt, ed., *Culinary Biographies*, 223–24.

51. One example is the "Invitation List for James Beard's Party Honoring Claudia Roden," 1972, in JJMC, Box 854.8. Booksellers as well as editors, publishers, and writers from most major newspapers and magazines were on the guest list, including Cecily Brownstone, Daniel Okrent, Nora Ephron, and Christopher Lehmann-Haupt.

52. Raymond A. Sokolov, "Current Stars: Books on Indian, Italian, and Inexpensive Food," *New York Times*, April 19. 1973; Advertisement for Boscov's bookstore, *Lebanon Daily News*, Lebanon, PA, December 21, 1973.

53. Quote from Judith Jones, Alfred A. Knopf, Inc., "The Borzoi Reader Looks Back with Editor Judith Jones," created August 1998, http://www.randomhouse.com/knopf /about/juliachild.html (accessed September 24, 2007). Emphasis in the original.

54. Julia Child, Louisette Bertholle, and Simone Beck, *Mastering the Art of French Cooking, Volume I* (New York, Knopf, 2001, 2008), 43.

55. Judith Jones, *The Tenth Muse: My Life in Food* (New York: Knopf, 2007), 17–64

56. "Everyone's in the Kitchen," *Time*, November 25, 1966.

57. Some claimed to be purely French, and some used American cooking elements. One ballyhooed restaurant was the Four Seasons in the Seagram's building in New York City. See Leslie Brenner, *American Appetite: The Coming of Age of a Cuisine* (New York: Bard, 1999), 39, 51–52; Tom Wolfe, *From Bauhaus to Our House* (New York: Bantam Books, 1999), 58.

58. Child et al., *Mastering, Volume I*, vii.

59. Jones, *The Tenth Muse*, 63.

60. Paul Child to Avis DeVoto, November 22, 1961, in Avis DeVoto Papers, 1952–1968, A-167, Box 1, Folder 13, SCH.

61. Robert H. Johnson, Hill & Barlow, Boston, MA (Julia Child's attorney) to Judith Jones, April 11, 1975, JJMC, Box 851.17.

62. On the British influence on American cuisine, see Harvey Levenstein, "Immigration, Travel, and Internationalization of the American Diet," in *Food Selection: From Genes to Culture* (Paris: The Danones Institute, 2000), http://www.danoneinstitute.org/publications /book/pdf/food_selection_10_levenstein.pdf (accessed April 16, 2007), 158–59.

63. Wayland Kennet, "Grigson (Heather Mabel) Jane (1928–1990)," in H. C. G. Matthew and Brian Harrison, eds., *Oxford Dictionary of National Biography* (Oxford: Oxford University Press, 2004), http://www.oxforddnb.com.ezproxy.lib.utexas.edu/view/article/39832 (accessed May 7, 2007). The American version was *The Art of Charcuterie* (New York: Knopf, 1968). Knopf published the paperback in 1976.

64. Many of these footnotes went beyond the issue of translation to include additional preparation techniques for foods or different versions of the dishes in question, Jane Grigson, *Good Things* (New York: Knopf, 1971) xi, 3–15.

65. Judith Jones to Jane Grigson, August 21, 1970, JJMC, Box 850.7.

66. Ibid.

67. Judith Jones to Jane Grigson (undated, circa 1970) and Judith Jones to Mrs. Michael Joseph, Michael Joseph Ltd., (undated, circa 1970), JJMC, Box 850.7.

68. Judith Jones to Jane Grigson, August 21, 1970, JJMC, Box 850.7.

69. Grigson, *Good Things*, 186.

70. Judith Jones to Jill Norman, Penguin Books, Harmondsworth, Middlesex division, November 16, 1973, JJMC, Box 851.1.

71. Judith Jones to Millie, October 22, 1973, JJMC, Box 851.1.

72. Judith Jones to Millie, December 2, 1973, JJMC, Box 851.1.

73. Judith Jones to Jane Grigson, December 13, 1973, JJMC, Box 851.1. Jones and Grigson courted the mushroom "freaks" when Knopf published *The Mushroom Feast*. They wrote letters to chapters of the North American Mycological Association, alerting them about the book. See Judith Jones to Jane Grigson, October 6, 1975; and Harry S. Knighton, President, North American Mycological Association, to Judith Jones, October 28, 1975, in JJMC, Box 851.1.

74. Judith Jones to Claire Smith, Harold Ober Associates, October 24, 1972, JJMC, Box 850.7.

75. Judith Jones to Jane Grigson, August 23, 1974. Jones and Knopf did publish Grigson's book, *The Mushroom Feast*, in 1975, so Jones's advice to Grigson about *English Food* (published in Britain in 1974), a book she rejected, was not necessarily about the author's writing or cooking capacities.

76. Judith Jones to Jane Grigson, November 9, 1977, JJMC, Box 851.1. The books were Anna Thomas's *Vegetarian Epicure, Book Two* (New York: Knopf, 1978) (a first book was published in 1972), and Madhur Jaffrey's *Madhur Jaffrey's World of the East Vegetarian Cooking* (New York: Knopf, 1981).

77. Judith Jones to Jane Grigson, November 9, 1977, JJMC, Box 851.1.

78. Copy Editing Comments, July 6, 1972, JJMC, Box 851.1; Jaffrey, *An Invitation*, 25.

79. Copy Editing Comments, July 6, 1972, JJMC, Box 851.1.

80. Judith Jones to Millie, July 7, 1972, JJMC, Box 851.1.

81. Ibid.

82. Ibid.

83. Quote from Paul Levy, "Ortiz, Elisabeth Lambert (1915–2003)," *Oxford Dictionary of National Biography*, online edition, Oxford University Press, Jan 2007, http://www.Oxford dnb.com/view/article/92492/ (accessed November 28, 2007). See also Paul Levy, "Obituary: Elisabeth Lambert Ortiz," *The Independent* (London), November 25, 2003; Tom Jaine, "Obituary: Elisabeth Lambert Ortiz," *The Guardian* (London), November 27, 2003.

84. *Hispanic* came into usage in the 1970s and was used widely from that time forward. On the term *Latino* coming into usage during the 1980s and 1990s, see Tom W. Smith, "Changing Racial Labels: From 'Colored' to 'Negro' to 'Black' to 'African American,'" *Public Opinion Quarterly* 56, no. 4 (1992): 510. See also Laura E. Gómez, "The Birth of the 'Hispanic' Generation: Attitudes of Mexican-American Political Elites toward the Hispanic Label" *Latin American Perspectives* 19, no. 4 (1992): 45–58. On the scarcity of pan-Latin America cookbooks, see Judith Jones to Jane Grigson, May 15, 1979, JJMC, Box 851.1.

85. Judith Jones to Elisabeth Ortiz, August 1, 1977, JJMC, Box 854.2.

86. Memo, "Notes and Queries on Meats & Poultry Chapter," Judith Jones to Elisabeth Ortiz, August 8, 1977, 3, JJMC, Box 854.2.

87. Judith Jones to Elisabeth Ortiz, November 11, 1977, JJMC, Box 854.2.

88. Judith Jones to Elisabeth Ortiz, July 26, 1978, JJMC, Box 854.2.

89. Three of the major ethnic cookbook surveys by Knopf of the 1970s included such lists. See Jaffrey, *An Invitation*; Ortiz, *The Book of Latin American Cooking* (New York: Knopf, 1979); Roden, *Book of Middle Eastern Food*.

90. Child et al., *Mastering Volume I*, vii.

91. Elisabeth Ortiz to Judith Jones, November 27, 1977, JJMC, Box 854.2.

92. Jones asked other authors to adjust recipes for those outside of big cities, but she used the term "Mrs. Middle America" with Simone Beck, who created a raspberry dessert with a special bottled syrup that would not be available outside of France, so Jones substituted frozen raspberries. See Judith Jones to Simone Beck, May 20, 1971, and Judith Jones to Simone Beck, February 2, 1972, JJMC, Box 847.7.

93. Judith Jones to Simone Beck, November 8, 1971, JJMC, Box 847.7, Folder, Beck, Simone—Simca book, 1971–77.

94. Judith Jones to Elisabeth Ortiz, December 13, 1977, JJMC, Box 854.2, Folder, Ortiz, Elisabeth.

95. Judith Jones to Elisabeth Ortiz, March 17, 1978, JJMC, Box 854.2.

96. Ibid.

97. Judith Jones to Claudia Roden, May 4, 1972; and the series of letters to such stores including Judith Jones to "Manager," Model Food Importers, Portland Maine, in JJMC, Box 854.2. There were indeed shops listed in Memphis, Louisville, Cleveland, Richmond, Indianapolis, and other smaller cities around the United States that carried these ingredients.

98. Pat McManus to Claudia Roden, May 20, 1973, JJMC, Box 854.8.

99. Jaffrey, *An Invitation*, 38–39, 151–64.

100. On the rise of Cajun and Creole cooking and Paul Prudhomme's role, see Barbara Hansen, "Let's Eat Out ... Answering Seductive Call of the Bayou," *Los Angeles Times*, November 15, 1984; Ruth Reichl, "Cajun Cooking—Going Home to the Source," *Los Angeles Times*, April 21, 1985; "Totally Hot," *Los Angeles Times*, September 14, 1986; Phyllis C. Richman, "Mardi Gras Memories," *Washington Post*, February 29, 1984.

101. Jones told the Collins that for their cookbook, "the history and lore (such as the derivation of the dish) is important because this makes good reading—and recently Americans, I think, have been taking a pride in their own culinary heritage." Quote in Judith Jones to Richard and Rima Collin, May 22, 1973. See also Judith Jones to Bob, Tony, March 5, 1973, both in JJMC, Box 848.12. On the popularity of spicy foods, see Menu, Ha's Restaurant, San Francisco, CA, 1985, CCSF, Folder, San Francisco, H-L, which has many "hot" Hunan and Szechuan entrees, and Menu, Postrio, San Francisco, 1989, a Wolfgang Puck-owned restaurant which had several Asian influenced dishes that were spicy too, in CCSF, Folder, San Francisco, P-R. This trend would continue from the 1980s forward. See Florence Fabricant, "Riding Salsa's Coast-to-Coast Wave of Popularity," *New York Times*, June 2, 1993.

102. Judith Jones to Richard and Rima Collin, May 22, 1973, JJMC, Box 848.12 (emphasis in the original).

103. Judith Jones to Bob, Tony, March 5, 1973, JJMC, Box 848.12.

104. Judith Jones to Rima and Richard Collin, July 20, 1973, in JJMC, Box 848.12.

105. Judy Walker, "Restaurant Critic's Legacy Includes Book: 'New Orleans Cookbook' Remains a Staple," *The Times-Picayune* (New Orleans), January 28, 2010.

106. Jaffrey, *Climbing the Mango Trees*.

107. Madhur Jaffrey, "The Fruits of Diplomacy," *New York Times*, March 12, 2006; Press Release, U.S. Embassy in India, "Indian Mangoes Head to the United States," April 26, 2007; David Karp, "A Luscious Taste and Aroma Arrives from India at Last," *New York Times*, May 2, 2007. Jhumpa Lahiri reminisced about how her family used to smuggle Indian foods back to the United States after every trip to Calcutta but, after decades, no longer needed to, for most of the desired goods were available in the United States. "Indian Takeout," *Food and Wine*, April 2000.

108. Marianne O. Schmidt, "Wonderful Evocative Journey through India's Past," comment on Madhur Jaffrey's *Climbing the Mango Trees*, posted January 3, 2007, http://www.amazon.com/Climbing-Mango-Trees-Memoir-Childhood/dp/140004295X (accessed May 16, 2007).

6. INDIAN RESTAURANTS IN AMERICA: A CASE STUDY IN TRANSLATING DIVERSITY

1. *Yellow Pages* (San Francisco: Pacific Telephone, 1965), 759–76. I counted those restaurants that had identifiably Indian names or referenced Indian landmarks or foods in their titles. India House was often the lone Indian restaurant listed in San Francisco guidebooks. See Raymond Ewell, *Dining Out in San Francisco and the Bay Area*, 2nd ed. (Berkeley, CA: Epicurean Press, 1948), 33. Doris Muscatine profiled India House and Taj of India in *A Cook's Tour of San Francisco* (New York: Charles Scribner's Sons, 1963), 306–16. She counted

four Indian restaurants in 1963, including a Curry Bowl restaurant not listed in the 1965 directory. See also *San Francisco Restaurants* (San Francisco: San Francisco Convention and Visitor's Bureau, 1969), CCSF, Folder-Calif-SF-S-T.

2. Quote from press release, "India House Restaurant on Historic Jackson Square," undated, circa 1975, VF, Restaurants, S.F. Restaurants (Misc.), SFHC. On the restaurant's origins, see Ewell, *Dining Out in San Francisco*, 33.

3. Ewell, *Dining Out in San Francisco*, 33; Jean Fay, "Off-Shore Is a Neighborhood," *San Francisco Chronicle*, November 29, 1953.

4. *Holiday*, April 1961, 167.

5. Ibid.

6. Menu (no date, circa 1950s), India House, San Francisco, CA, Folder, Calif—San Francisco, H-L, CCSF. Major Grey's Chutney is thought to have been developed by a British officer who had traveled in India. The formula was eventually sold to Crosse and Blackwell, a major British food manufacturer, probably in the early 1800s. See Mimi Sheraton, "De Gustibus; Tea and Chutney: 2 Different Greys," *New York Times*, July 10, 1982; "Chutney," in John Ayto, ed., *An A–Z of Food and Drink, Oxford Reference Online* (New York: Oxford University Press, 2002), http://www.oxfordreference.com/views/ENTRY.html?subview=Main&entry=t134.e285 (accessed February 27, 2007). On the adoption, changes to, and popularity of Indian chutneys in Britain, see Lizzie Collingham, *Curry: A Tale of Cooks and Conquerors* (New York: Oxford University Press, 2006), 147.

7. Ewell, *Dining Out*, 33.

8. Muscatine, *A Cook's Tour of San Francisco*, 308.

9. Ibid., 312. Taj of India in San Francisco served chicken baked en casserole and broiled steak.

10. The Acapulco y Los Arcos chain, mostly in California, had one section of the menu with "Gringo Items and Egg Dishes," that listed a hamburger, cheeseburger, New York steak, and several omelets. Menu, Acapulco y Los Arcos, (multiple locations), 1984, CCSF, Folder—Ethnic/Mexican. The Santa Fe restaurant in Kansas City, Missouri, had an "American Selections" section on the menu with a K.C. strip sirloin steak, hamburger, steak and enchilada, and Santa Fe burger. These offered guacamole on the burger, a rather uncommon topping at the time and a nod to the Mexican cuisine in the restaurant. A Mission, Kansas, restaurant did the same, with hamburgers, fried chicken, and hot dogs in its "American food section." This was also common in many Chinese restaurants, such as August Moon in Kansas City, Missouri, which devoted half its menu to Chinese food and half to American food. See Menus, Santa Fe, Kansas City, MO, Don Chilito's Mexican Food, Mission, KS, and August Moon, Kansas City, KS, in Robert C. Mortimer, Charles C. Mortimer, and Eleanor Nelson, *The Menu Guide of Kansas City* (Pacific Palisades, CA: Corm Enterprises, 1976), 8–9, 12–13, 23.

11. Leonce Picot, ed., *Gourmet International's Recommended Restaurants of San Francisco* (Ft. Lauderdale, FL: Gourmet International, 1963), 8, emphasis in the original.

12. *Holiday*, April 1961, 167.

13. Menu, India House, (no date—circa 1950s), Folder, Calif-San Francisco, H-L, CCSF. The date on this menu is derived from comparison to a partial menu listed in *Menu Magazine*, Fall 1961, SFHC. That menu lists slightly higher prices for some menu items.

14. Press Release, "India House Restaurant on Historic Jackson Square," undated, circa 1975, VF, Restaurants, S.F. Restaurants (Misc.), SFHC. Quote from Muscatine, *A Cook's Tour of San Francisco*, 307. Pimm's Cups were mentioned in many restaurant reviews, including, Claire Chamberlain, "Dine Amongst Bengal Tigers at India House," *The Stanford Daily*, July 28, 1978.

15. The Gray Line Tours, *San Francisco Bay Area Welcome Map* (San Francisco: The Gray Line, 1962), VF, SF Guides, 1962, SFHC; Pamphlet, *Citibook: San Francisco*, published by the American Automobile Association, 1968, OAK, VF, San Francisco County—1951-(I), OAK. Another contemporary review of Taj tried to give credence to the merits of Indian cuisine. It quoted the owners, who founded the restaurant in 1956, as saying that the cuisine of Indian was much more than curries. The reporter did refer often to the presumably exotic décor of the restaurant, including the "sensuous Eastern music." J. L. Pimsleur, "Taj of India: Currey and Ghee and the Beat of the Tablas," *San Francisco Chronicle*, June 21, 1959.

16. Monique Benoit, "A New Life in America," *San Francisco Chronicle*, March 8, 1965.

17. *San Francisco Hotel Greeter's Guide*, August 1963 (New York: Guide Group Magazines, 1963), 51–52; VF—SF Guides, 1963, SFHC.

18. "The Lancers' Glamour: Gone with the War," *San Francisco Examiner*, November 6, 1968.

19. Advertisement, "The Warwick," *New York Times*, April 30, 1927.

20. "Home Hints," *Safeway News*, December 1965, 8; Eliza Acton, *Modern Cookery, in All Its Branches: Reduced to a System of Easy Practice, for the Use of Private Families* (Philadelphia: Lea and Blanchard, 1858), 221–25; Kristin Hoganson, *Consumer's Imperium: The Global Production of American Domesticity, 1865–1920* (Chapel Hill: University of North Carolina Press, 2007), 110, 114.

21. Andrew J. Rotter, *Comrades at Odds: The United States and India, 1947–1964* (Ithaca, NY: Cornell University Press, 2000), xvi-xvii.

22. Rotter, *Comrades at Odds*, xvi-xvii. Also see Andrew J. Rotter, "In Retrospect: Harold R. Isaacs's *Scratches on our Minds*," *Reviews in American History* 24, no. 1 (1996): 177–88.

23. Rotter, *Comrades at Odds*, 196. Most Hindus eat meat too, but many Americans did not know that, and Hinduism and Buddhism are indeed the two most widely followed religions with large numbers of vegetarians. In *A Historical Dictionary of Indian Food* (New Delhi: Oxford University Press, 1998), K. T. Achaya estimates that a quarter of the Indian population is vegetarian. Meat is not consumed in as high a proportion in India as in America, even by non-vegetarians, because of India's relative poverty. Most importantly, Achaya notes, "being a vegetarian occasions little surprise in India," 262–63.

24. Harold R. Isaacs, *Images of Asia: American Views of China and India* (New York: Harper and Row, 1972), 277.

25. Rotter, *Comrades at Odds*, 8.

26. Photo of Indian House restaurant from April 1961 issue of *Holiday*, https://webbie1 .sfpl.org/multimedia/sfphotos/AAB-2688.jpg (accessed May 26, 2017).

27. Before the 1950s many Americans viewed Vietnam through British and French filters. See Mark Philip Bradley, *Imagining Vietnam and America: The Making of Postcolonial Vietnam, 1919–1950* (Chapel Hill: University of North Carolina Press, 2000).

28. Rotter, *Comrades at Odds*, 8, 150–61.

29. Rotter, *Comrades at Odds*, 150–51. Menu, Sambo's, no date (circa 1950s or 1960s), and second menu, 1966 (Locations throughout the West and Midwest), CCSF, Folder-Chains, General Menus, USA; Menu, Sambo's Pancakes, (California locations), 1961, OAK, VF-Restaurants, Q–Z.

30. Robert Metz, "Why Sambo's Is in Trouble," *New York Times*, November 27, 1981; Tom Goldstein, "Fight to Keep Sambo's Name," *New York Times*, May 4, 1979; "Job Bias Laid to Sambo's," *New York Times*, May 21, 1980; "Sambo's Profit Outlook," *New York Times*, May 4, 1983. The Jim Crow Museum of Racist Imagery at Ferris State University, Big Rapids, Michigan, catalogs well the racist images of the past, including Sambo, http://www.ferris.edu /jimcrow/. Joseph Boskin, *Sambo: The Rise and Demise of an American Jester* (New York: Oxford University Press, 1986); Charles Bernstein, *Sambo's: Only a Fraction of the Action* (Burbank, CA: National Literary Guild, 1984).

31. John T. Edge, "Around a Midwest City, the World Comes to Eat," *New York Times*, February 23, 2011.

32. The "sacred cow" was one of the problems associated with Indians in this era. Americans wondered how cows, monkeys, and other animals could be so revered, especially when India was so often struck by famine. Rotter, *Comrades at Odds*, 17.

33. Notes, Sarwan S. Gill, accompanying press release (undated, circa 1970s), "India House Restaurant on Historic Jackson Square," SFHC, VF, Restaurants, Folder "Misc." Gill's co-owners were Abdul Rhman and Shanti Patel. Much of the press release was quite similar to Doris Muscatine's section on India House in *A Cook's Tour of San Francisco*, published in 1963, but the handwritten notes added new information about Gill. Indian immigrants between 1952 and 1965 were mostly professionals or students. David M. Reimers, *Still the Golden Door: The Third World Comes to America*, 2nd ed. (New York: Columbia University Press, 1992), 31; Karen Isaksen Leonard, *The South Asian Americans* (Westport, CT: Greenwood Press, 1997), 67–71.

34. "American Dream," *Gazette-Telegraph*, Colorado Springs, CO, June 17, 1976.

35. Wilbur Zelinsky, "The Roving Palate: North America's Ethnic Restaurant Cuisines," *GeoForum* 16, no. 1 (1985): 63.

36. "A Glowing Year Ahead," *NRA News*, December 1983, 16. Although the survey only included eight hundred telephone respondents, its findings corresponded to the data found by Zelinsky and others.

37. "What You Eat May Depend on Where You Are," *NRA News*, February 1985, 40. In this count, 94,456 restaurants, or 31.2 percent, were unclassified, so there could have been many additional restaurants in any category. The classifications included ethnic types, such as Italian or French, and food types, such as café, barbecue, or donut.

38. "New Study Shows Restaurant Distribution across U.S.," *NRA News*, September 1983, 35–36.

39. I compared results from three National Restaurant Association surveys in 1983, 1995, and 1999. The 1983 telephone survey found that 50 percent of respondents had tried Japanese, 21 percent had tried Indian, and 21 percent had tried "other Oriental." A 1995 survey, by contrast, found that 53 percent of respondents had tried Japanese, 30 percent had tried Indian, 22 percent had tried Thai, 19 percent had tried Vietnamese, and 17 percent had tried Korean. So, between 1994 and 1999, the number having tried Japanese and Vietnamese

remained the same, Indian increased 3 percent, Thai increased 4 percent, and Korean dropped 2 percent. In contrast to the 1983 survey, the 1994 and 1999 surveys separated the last three Asian cuisines, which likely would have been those mentioned in "other Oriental" in the previous survey. The separation indicated greater familiarity with those cuisines and greater diversity in food consumption. See "A Glowing Year Ahead," *NRA News*, December 1983, 16; *Ethnic Cuisines: A Profile* (Washington, DC: National Restaurant Association, 1995), 11–13. The 1999 survey said that ethnic cuisines were "more common, more available, and more often offered by non-authentic providers," *Ethnic Cuisines II* (Washington, DC: National Restaurant Association, 2000), 5, 17.

40. Krishnendu Ray, *The Ethnic Restaurateur* (New York: Bloomsbury, 2016), 39–45.

41. *San Francisco Chronicle*, January 18, 1909 and March 19, 1911; *San Francisco Call*, January 14, 1909.

42. Leonard, *The South Asian Americans*, 40–105. Congress passed a bill in 1946 to open immigration to nationals from India and the Philippines—the quota remained low, at 100, but more importantly, the bill opened the door to naturalization for these groups. Reimers, *Still the Golden Door*, 15.

43. Pew Research Center, *The Rise of Asian Americans* (Washington, DC: Pew Research Center, 2013), 59.

44. Immigration and Naturalization Service, *2001 Statistical Yearbook of the Immigration and Naturalization Service: Tables Only*, http://www.ins.gov/graphics/aboutins/statistics/immigs.htm, (accessed December 10, 2002), 6–9. There were 41,428 Bangladeshis, 155,509 Pakistanis, and 19,708 Sri Lankans in the United States. *The Asian Databook* (Millerton, NY: Grey House Publishing, 2005), 1.

45. Jonathan Bellman, "Indian Resonances in the British Invasion, 1965–1968," *Journal of Musicology* 15, no. 1 (1997): 116–36; David R. Peck, "Beatles Orientalis: Influences from Asia in a Popular Song Tradition," *Asian Music* 16, no. 1 (1985): 83–149.

46. Warren Belasco, *Appetite for Change: How the Counterculture Took on the Food Industry*, 2nd ed. (Ithaca, NY: Cornell University Press, 2007). Richard Alpert, who conducted studies on Harvard University students to determine the effects of psilocybin mushrooms, turned to Hinduism after leaving academia. Allen Ginsberg read Zen texts extensively. Maurice Isserman and Michael Kazin, *America Divided: The Civil War of the 1960s*, 2nd ed. (New York: Oxford University Press, 2004), 151, 161; Bruce Schulman describes hippies' predilection for brown rice, tofu, and Zen bakeries in *The Seventies: The Great Shift in American Culture, Society, and Politics* (Cambridge, MA: Da Capo Press, 2001), 14, 88–90; In *Slouching Towards Bethlehem*, Joan Didion's essay about life in San Francisco's Haight-Ashbury neighborhood during the 1960s, she observes one woman cooking seaweed in a makeshift living space called the "Warehouse" and shares tempura with one hippie-turned-businessman in Japantown. Joan Didion, *Slouching Towards Bethlehem* (New York: Farrar Straus & Giroux, 1968), 95, 103.

47. Quotes from James Traub, "Fare of the Country: Tandoori Artistry in Delhi," *New York Times*, January 8, 1984. Also see Collen Taylor Sen, *Food Culture in India* (Westport CT: Greenwood Press, 2004), 133–36.

48. The origin of chicken tikka masala is disputed, but some argue that it is really a derivation of the butter chicken created by Kundan Lal Gujral. Colleen Taylor Sen, "Kundan

Lal Gujral," in Alice Arndt, ed., *Culinary Biographies* (Houston: Yes Press, 2006), 193–94. Sen agrees that Gujral basically invented butter chicken and popularized tandoori cooking. The BBC calls the provenance of chicken tikka masala "hazy" but suggests it may have been introduced by Bangladeshi chefs in Glasgow in the 1950s. No matter if this happened, Gujral had popularized butter chicken by that time. "Chicken Tikka Masala: Spice and Easy Does it," *BBC News*, April 20, 2001, http://news.bbc.co.uk/1/hi/special_report/1999/02/99/e -cyclopedia/1285804.stm (accessed November 2, 2007).

49. Sen, *Food Culture in India*, 133–36.

50. As described by Madhur Jaffrey in "Taking High-Heat Tandoor Techniques to the Backyard Grill," *National Public Radio*, July 1, 2013, http://www.npr.org/blogs/thesalt/2013/07 /01/197652733/taking-high-heat-tandoor-techniques-to-the-backyard-grill (accessed July 5, 2013).

51. "Moti Mahal: Delhi's Gastronomic Pearl," *Wall Street Journal*, December 22, 2011.

52. Madhur Jaffrey, *Climbing the Mango Trees* (New York: Knopf, 2006), 191–92.

53. Monish Gujral, *Moti Mahal's Tandoori Trail* (New Delhi: Thomson Press, 2004), 8, 14–15.

54. Madhur Jaffrey said tandoori items are "what everyone associates with India," in Debbie Elliott, "In the Kitchen with Madhur Jaffrey," *All Things Considered*, National Public Radio, November 25, 2006, http://www.npr.org/templates/story/story.php?storyId=6525257 (accessed October 26, 2007); Also see Sen, "Kundan Lal Gujral," 193–94.

55. Shrabani Basu, *Curry in the Crown: The Story of Britain's Favourite Dish* (Delhi: HarperCollins, 1999), xv–xvii, 185.

56. Henry Shukman, "Where Indian Cuisine Reaches for the Stars," *New York Times*, March 4, 2007.

57. First two quotes from unidentified local Indian immigrants, and "risky" from Julie Sahni, New York-based cookbook author, in Maria Cianci, "Why So Many Menus Look So Much Alike," *San Francisco Chronicle*, April 12, 1995. The food served to New Yorkers was also quite similar among Indian restaurants. The four restaurants listed in one Manhattan guidebook in 1983 had the standard tandoori and curry items. One, Raga, featured a few more regional specialties, including dishes from Goa and Hyderabad, but it still had a tandoori mixed grill on the bill of fare. The restaurants were Akbar, Bombay Palace, Gaylord, and Raga, all in Manhattan. *Manhattan Menus: The Great Restaurant Guide* (New York: Author, 1983), 103–4, 127–28, 177–78, 237–38. See also Menu, Bengal Tiger, Los Angeles, reprinted in Robert C. Mortimer and Charles C. Mortimer, eds., *The Menu Guide of Los Angeles* (Pacific Palisades, CA: Corm Enterprises, 1976), 14–15.

58. Susan Spedalle, "Once Exotic Indian Cuisine Gaining Momentum in the U.S.," *Nation's Restaurant News*, August 27, 1984, 29.

59. On the Indian middle class and its role in globalization, see Tulasi Srinivas, "'A Tryst with Destiny': The Indian Case of Cultural Globalization," in Peter L. Berger and Samuel P. Huntington, eds., *Many Globalizations: Cultural Diversity in the Contemporary World* (New York: Oxford University Press, 2002), 89–116.

60. This figure is from Mike Swift, "Illegal Immigration from India Growing," *Contra Costa Times*, February 20, 2008. Household income for Asian Indians in 1999 was $70,708, second only to Japanese Americans among Asians (at $70,849). Indians had the highest

education levels among Asian Americans, with 63.9 percent of adults twenty-five and older having a bachelor's degree or higher, compared to 24.4 percent of the overall population and 44.1 percent of the Asian population. The high education levels of Asians in general likely contributed to the overall impression that Indian immigrants were not from the teeming immigrant masses. See Terrance J. Reeves and Claudette E. Bennett, *We the People: Asians in the United States* (Washington, DC: Census Bureau, 2004), 12, 16, 20.

61. On the professional nature of the new immigrants and the vibrant business connections, see David W. Lyon, *Global California: The Connection to Asia* (San Francisco: Public Policy Institute of California, 2003), 1–4; AnnaLee Saxenian, *Local and Global Networks of Immigrant Professionals in Silicon Valley* (San Francisco: Public Policy Institute of California, 2002), viii. Saxenian estimated that in 1990, around 15 percent of the engineers in Silicon Valley were Indian or Chinese.

62. John Canaday, "Dining: Off to India by the Short Route," *New York Times*, April 26, 1974; Menu, Gaylord (India) Restaurant, in *Manhattan Menus*, 176–77.

63. "About Gaylord India Restaurants," Gaylord India Restaurants corporate website, http://www.gaylords.com/history.html (accessed November 9, 2007).

64. Craig Claiborne, "A Rare Thing: Indian Restaurant with Food to Get Excited About," *New York Times*, September 26, 1974.

65. Jing Zhou, "Gaylord India Restaurant Keeps Standards High as it Expands," *Nation's Restaurant News*, August 6, 2007; Myra MacPherson, "Embassy Chefs Transfer their Allegiance," *New York Times*, August 21, 1968.

66. Sen, *Food Culture in India*, 81–138.

67. India House installed its tandoor oven in the 1970s, and one reviewer said its menu had "evolved very little" over time. It closed in 1995. See also Menu, Gaylord India Restaurant, San Francisco, CA, in Mara Theresa Caen, *San Francisco Epicure: A Menu Guide to the San Francisco Area's Finest Restaurants* (Seattle: Peanut Butter Publishing, 1986), 58–59.

68. Menu and review of Sabina Indian Cuisine, Oakland, CA, in *Cityguide 1989/90: Alameda and Contra Costa Counties* (Danville, CA: Shandra Publications, 1989), 138.

69. Ibid.

70. Amanda Berne, "Master of Spices," *San Francisco Chronicle*, April 19, 2006. Vik's opened in 1989 but expanded after that to a different, warehouse location to serve a larger customer base. See also Joan Zoloth, "Breads of India, Viks Chaat Corner Cover Dining Spectrum," *Oakland Tribune*, October 10, 1997.

71. Ibid. Quote from Amod Chopra.

72. Lyon, *Global California*, 1–4; Saxenian, *Silicon Valley's New Immigrant Entrepreneurs*. Arijit Sen, "Curry Mahals to Chaat Cafés: Spatialities of the South Asian Culinary Landscape," in Krishnendu Ray and Tulasi Srinivas, eds., *Curried Cultures: Globalization, Food, and South Asia* (Berkeley: University of California Press, 2012), 196–218.

73. Jane Tunks, "Bargain Bite: Udupi Palace," *SFGate*, August 28, 2008, http://www.sfgate.com/cgi-bin/article.cgi?f=/c/a/2008/08/28/NS1J12GPPS.DTL&type=printable (accessed August 28, 2008); "Saravana Bhavan—Passion—Milestones," at Saravana Bhavan corporate website, http://www.saravanabhavan.com/milestones.php (accessed May 1, 2016).

74. Aleta Watson, "Fresh Vegetarian Eating: Popular Chain in India Comes to Newark," *San Jose Mercury News*, October 18, 2002.

75. The restaurant also featured Jamaican-Indian and Cajun-Indian combinations, owing to the similar spices and ingredients used in those cuisines. David Sason, "Avatar's," *North Bay Bohemian*, August 16–22, 2006, http://www.metroactive.com/bohemian/08.16.06/bite -0633.htm (accessed October 29, 2007); Keith Power, "Sausalito Spot offers Indian with Something Extra," *San Francisco Chronicle*, August 7, 1998.

76. Collingham, *Curry*, 218–21.

77. "Promotions Are Your Lifeblood," *NRA News*, March 1983, 18–19; Florence Fabricant, "Indian Spices Go Mainstream as Cumin, Cardamom, and Fenugreek Curry Favor with Chefs," *Nation's Restaurant News*, January 22, 2007.

78. Stephen Wright, "Ganesh Will Warm You Through and Through," *San Jose Mercury News*, February 1, 1984. For the national view, see Ann Levin, "Indian Food Curries Favor with Americans," *South Florida Sun-Sentinel*, sun-sentinel.com/entertainment/restaurants /us-fea--food-indian_food_rising-20100105,0,383810.story (accessed January 8, 2010).

79. *Pacific Bell Smart Yellow Pages* (San Francisco: Pacific Bell, 2000), 1372–405. This directory had two restaurant listings. One was simply an alphabetical listing of restaurants. In that listing, I counted sixteen Indian restaurants. There could have been more that did not possess either Indian names or landmarks. The second section listed restaurants by cuisine. That section had thirteen Indian restaurants for San Francisco; "South Asian Restaurants in San Francisco Bay Area," at http://www.thimmakka.org/Activities/Restaurants /restaurants.html (accessed April 6, 2007).

80. Shukman, "Where Indian Cuisine Reaches for the Stars," *New York Times*, March 4, 2007.

81. Thy Tran, "South Indian Rice Courses," *KQED Food Blog: Bay Area Bites*, March 4, 2007, at http://www.kqed.org/weblog/food/labels/india.jsp (accessed October 29, 2007); Komala Vilas Restaurant, Sunnyvale, CA, at http://www.komalavilas.com/ (accessed November 3, 2007).

82. Tran, "South Indian Rice Courses."

83. Ben Marks, "Dazzling Flavors Shine in Komala Vilas' Humble Setting," *San Francisco Chronicle*, July 2, 1999.

84. The 1999 survey showed a slight increase over the 1995 results, where 95 percent were "aware of" those cuisines. For the 1999 results, see *Ethnic Cuisines II*, 15. For 1995, *Ethnic Cuisines: A Profile*, 9.

85. *Ethnic Cuisines II*, 19, 117–21. Those who had tried Indian cuisine also tended to live in higher proportion in the West and in large metropolitan areas. This meant people in the Bay Area were more likely to be familiar with Indian cuisine than those in other cities in the Midwest or South, and much more familiar than rural dwellers in those regions.

86. "A Glowing Year Ahead," *NRA News*, December 1983, 16. Although the survey only included eight hundred telephone respondents, the data fit with the overall number of restaurants of each type.

7. CHINESE FOOD FROM CHINATOWN TO THE SUBURBS

1. A Finding Aid, June 2010, Papers of Grace Zia Chu, 1941–1986, MC 641, MP-42, Vt-91, CHU.

2. Award speech, "Dynamic Years, Margaret Stader/Lorena Fletcher Farrell," Folder 1.1 Awards, 1969–1986, CHU.

3. Advertisement clipped from *McCall's*, circa fall 1964, attached to Florence Baldwin to Madame Grace Chu, June 5, 1964, Box 1, Folder 1.2—Biographical and Correspondence, 1941–1979, CHU. Teas in pamphlet version of her cookbook in Folder 2.15, Publications: The Pleasure of Chinese Cooking, 1962, 1 of 2, CHU.

4. Folder 2.15, Publications: The Pleasure of Chinese Cooking, 1962, 1 of 2, CHU.

5. Quote from Mimi Sheraton, "The Best New Cookbooks of 1975," *New York Magazine*, November 24, 1975, in Folder 2.16, Publications: Madame Chu's Chinese Cooking School (1975), 2 of 2, CHU. Other reviews in *Kirkus Reviews* and the *Denver Post* in this folder.

6. Periodical clippings in Folder 2.13, Film, 1963–1965, CHU.

7. "The Pleasures of Chinese Cooking," 16 mm film, Bob Bailey Productions, ca. 1963, Archival Record: MP-42, CHU.

8. Florence Baldwin to Madame Chu, January 9, 1964, Folder 1.2—Biographical and Correspondence, 1941–1979, CHU.

9. Martin Halstuk, "Mistress of the Mandarin," *San Francisco Chronicle*, August 30, 1989.

10. Michael J. Ybarra, "Herb Caen, 80, San Francisco Voice, Dies," *New York Times*, February 2, 1997.

11. Cecilia Sun Yun Chiang, *The Mandarin Way*, rev. and expanded edition (as told to Allan Carr) (San Francisco: California Living Books, 1980), 266–67; Cecilia Chiang, *Cecilia Chiang: An Oral History*, conducted by Victor Geraci, 2005–2006, Regional Oral History Office, BANC, 72–73; Gerald D. Adams, "Mia D. Conrad," *San Francisco Chronicle*, April 29, 2001.

12. Andrew Coe, *Chop Suey* (New York: Oxford University Press, 2009), 220–21.

13. Chiang, *Cecilia Chiang: An Oral History*, 75–77.

14. Menus, The Mandarin, San Francisco (c. 1973 and 1989), in *San Francisco Menus: The 1989 Restaurant Guide*, in Folder, VF Restaurants, S.F. Menus, and S.F. Menus, The Mandarin, SFHC; Menu, The Mandarin, Beverly Hills, (1980), Los Angeles Public Library Online Menu Collection, https://www.lapl.org/collections-resources/visual-collections/menu-collection (accessed September 2, 2016); Herb Caen and Pat Steger each wrote about Chiang in the *San Francisco Chronicle*. Pat Steger, "Social Scene," April 22, 1975; May 1, 1975; November 12, 1975; Herb Caen, October 8, 1973; Madeline Y. Hsu, "From Chop Suey to Mandarin Cuisine: Fine Dining and the Refashioning of Chinese Ethnicity during the Cold War Era," in Sucheng Chan and Madeline Y. Hsu, eds., *Chinese Americans and the Politics of Race and Culture*, (Philadelphia: Temple University Press, 2008), 173–93.

15. Steger, "Social Scene," *San Francisco Chronicle*, April 22, 1975; Michael Bauer, "The Tables of Two Cities," *San Francisco Chronicle*, March 30, 1988.

16. Herb Caen, "Pocketful of Phlug," *San Francisco Chronicle*, February 21, 1991; Michael Bauer, "At the Mandarin, Cecilia Chiang Changed Chinese Food," *San Francisco Chronicle*, May 25, 2011, http://insidescoopsf.sfgate.com/blog/2011/05/25/at-the-mandarin-cecilia-chiang-changed-chinese-food/ (accessed May 15, 2014).

17. Michael Bauer, "These Eight Trendsetters Made Bay Area Dining What It Is," *San Francisco Chronicle*, July 17, 2011.

18. Judith Cummings, "Out West, Restaurants Divide to Conquer," *New York Times*, June 18, 1986; Menu, Mandarette (1985), Los Angeles Public Library Online Menu Collection, https://www.lapl.org/collections-resources/visual-collections/menu-collection (accessed September 2, 2016).

19. P.F. Chang's China Bistro, Inc., "Corporate Overview," http://www.pfcb.com/Investor CorporateOverview.html (accessed August 30, 2016).

20. Summer Whitford, "Facts about P.F. Chang's That Would surprise You," *The Daily Meal*, July 12, 2016; John Heckathorn, "An Interview with Philip Chiang, Founder of P.F. Chang's," *Honolulu Magazine*, October 10, 2011.

21. Heckathorn, "Interview with Philip Chiang."

22. Joel Kotkin, "Will Chinese Food go the Way of Pizza?" *New York Times*, March 26, 2000; Penny Parker, "Chang's Opens Upscale Doors at Park Meadows Location," *Denver Post*, December 20, 1996; "Q&A with Cecilia Chiang of the Mandarin Restaurant," PBS, April 9, 2015, at http://www.pbs.org/food/features/qa-cecilia-chiang-mandarin-restaurant (accessed December 30, 2015); Menu, P.F. Chang's (2004), Los Angeles Public Library Online Menu Collection, https://www.lapl.org/collections-resources/visual-collections/menu-collection (accessed September 2, 2016). Cathy Thomas, "Changing Chinese," *Orange County Register*, September 4, 1996.

23. *Mesa Tribune* (AZ), March 25, 1994.

24. Richard Jay Scholem, "Chinese with American Heartland Slant," *New York Times*, June 27, 1999; Mary D. Scourtes, "Chain Bistro Revs Up Chinese," *Tampa Tribune*, June 13, 2003.

25. Kotkin, "Will Chinese Food go the Way of Pizza?"

26. P.F. Chang's Expands, Succeeds Where Others Have Failed," *The Lima News* (OH), May 16, 2004.

27. Elizabeth M. Hoeffel, Sonya Rastogi, Myoung Ouk Kim, and Hasan Shahid, U.S. Census Bureau, *The Asian Population 2010*, March 2012, https://www.census.gov/prod /cen2010/briefs/c2010br-11.pdf (accessed October 23, 2016), 14. This included 3,137,061 Chinese and 196,691 Taiwanese.

28. The median household income for Chinese Americans was $65,050 in 2010 as compared to the overall median of $49,800. "Asian Americans Lead All Others in Household Income," *Pew Research Center*, April 16, 2013, http://www.pewresearch.org/daily-number /asian-americans-lead-all-others-in-household-income/ (accessed February 8, 2017). The American Community Survey of the U.S. Census Bureau for 2010 gave the median income as 64,965.

29. Willow Lung-Amam, "The Vibrant Life of Asian Malls in Silicon Valley," in John Archer, Paul J. P. Sandul, and Katherine Solomonson, eds., *Making Suburbia: New Histories of Everyday America* (Minneapolis: University of Minnesota Press, 2015).

30. Kenneth Jackson, *Crabgrass Frontier: The Suburbanization of the United States* (New York: Oxford University Press, 1985), 239–41; David Halberstam, *The Fifties* (New York: Fawcett Columbine, 1993), 131–43.

31. Frank Hobbs and Nicole Stoops, *Demographic Trends of the 20th Century* (Washington DC: U.S. Census Bureau, 2002), 33.

32. Quoted in Becky Nicolaides, "How Hell Moved from the City to the Suburbs: Urban Scholars and Changing Perceptions of Authentic Community," in Kevin M. Kruse and

Thomas J. Sugrue, eds., *The New Suburban History* (Chicago: University of Chicago Press, 2006), 87. Nicolaides describes how the suburbs replaced cities as the objects of criticism by major writers, including Mumford, Jane Jacobs, and William Whyte.

33. Smith and Schimmel, "Little Boxes." "Little Boxes" has a 1962 copyright. Reynolds was on her way from her home in Berkeley to a meeting south of San Francisco when she passed through Daly City and was inspired to write the song.

34. *Weeds*, Season 1, DVD (Santa Monica, CA: Lion's Gate Home Entertainment, 2006).

35. On Hispanics, Asians, and blacks moving to the suburbs, see William H. Frey, "Melting Pot Suburbs: A Census 2000 Study of Suburban Diversity," *The Brookings Institution: Census 2000 Series*, June 2001, at http://www.frey-demographer.org/reports/billf.pdf (accessed February 8, 2008), 1–17.

36. Alan Berube, "The State of Metropolitan America: Suburbs and the 2010 Census," Presentation and Remarks, July 14, 2011, Brookings Institution, at https://www.brookings .edu/on-the-record/the-state-of-metropolitan-america-suburbs-and-the-2010-census/ (accessed September 17, 2016); William H. Frey, "Melting Pot Cities and Suburbs: Racial and Ethnic Change in Metro America in the 2000s," *Metropolitan Policy Program at Brookings*, Brookings Institution, May 2011, at https://www.brookings.edu/wp-content/uploads/2016 /06/0504_census_ethnicity_frey.pdf (accessed September 17, 2016).

37. Carol Lloyd, "Westlake Wars: Residents in Daly City Subdivision Fight their Homeowner's Association," *SFGate*, December 10, 2002, http://articles.sfgate.com/2002-12-10 /entertainment/17573320_1_hoa-homeowners-association-westlake-homeowner-improve ment-association (accessed October 5, 2010).

38. On the history of these covenants more generally, see Jackson, *Crabgrass Frontier*, 190–218. For the role of the California Real Estate Association and California's housing segregation see Daniel Martinez HoSang, *Racial Propositions: Ballot Initiatives and the Making of Postwar California* (Berkeley: University of California Press, 2010); Cindy I-Fen Cheng, "Out of Chinatown and into the Suburbs: Chinese Americans and the Politics of Cultural Citizenship in Early Cold War America," *American Quarterly* 58, no. 4 (December 2006): 1067–90; Grace Tzeng, "Chinese Real Estate Association Guarantees Fair Housing for All," *Asian Week* http://www.asianweek.com/2008/02/28/chinese-real-estate-association -of-america-guarantees-fair-housing-for-all/ (accessed October 5, 2010).

39. Two recent volumes survey the broad history of Chinese food in the United States quite well, with different emphases/interpretations. Coe's *Chop Suey* and Yong Chen, *Chop Suey, USA: The Story of Chinese Food in America* (New York: Columbia University Press, 2014). On the early history of Chinese food in the United States, see Netta Davis, "To Serve the 'Other': Chinese American Immigrants in the Restaurant Business," *Journal for the Study of Food and Society* 6, no. 1 (2002): 71; Jacqueline M. Newman, "Chinese American Food," in Andrew Smith, ed., *The Oxford Encyclopedia of Food and Drink in America*, vol. 1 (New York: Oxford, 2004), 235; Chi Kien Lao, "The Chinese Restaurant Industry in the United States: Its History, Development and Future," (master's thesis, Cornell University, 1975). The prejudice against the Chinese in the late 1800s was accompanied by a prejudice against their food too. See Alexander Young, "Chinese Food and Cookery" (Unknown magazine, dated 1872), in HML, Carton 54:17, Food and Cooking, Chinese Food in the U.S., 1870–1987, 2001; "Report of the Joint Special Committee to Investigate Chinese

Immigration," *S. Rept.* 689, 44 Cong., 2 sess. (1877); Luther W. Spoehr, "Sambo and the Heathen Chinee: Californians' Racial Stereotypes in the Late 1870s," *Pacific Historical Review* 42, no. 2 (1973): 190–91; J. A. G. Roberts, *China to Chinatown: Chinese Food in the West* (London: Reaktion Books, 2002), 144–45.

40. Chen, *Chinese San Francisco*, 64–69, 90–92, 186–87, 196–99; Ivan Light, "From Vice District to Tourist Attraction: The Moral Career of American Chinatowns, 1880–1940," *Pacific Historical Review* 43, no. 3 (1974): 367–94; Roberts, *China to Chinatown*, 144–55; Samantha Barbas, "'I'll Take Chop Suey: Restaurants as Agents of Culinary and Cultural Change," *Journal of Popular Culture* 36, no. 4 (2003): 669–79.

41. Harold R. Isaacs, *Images of Asia: American Views of China and India* (New York: Harper and Row, 1972), 155–58.

42. Some of the old images of the dangerous Chinese remained through the 1950s—one pamphlet produced by the city's Visitor's Bureau advised that Chinatown was not dangerous, despite the "narrow streets and dark alleys," and that the residents are "peaceful, law-abiding American Chinese," San Francisco Convention and Visitor's Bureau, "Chinatown," Pamphlet, 1959, OAK, VF-San Francisco County—1951 (I). A typical walk through San Francisco's Chinatown could be found in Vincent McHugh, "San Francisco: Little China," *Holiday*, April 1961.

43. San Francisco Convention and Visitor's Bureau, "Chinatown," 1959.

44. Roberts, *China to Chinatown*, 164.

45. Chen, *Chop Suey, USA*, 163–65.

46. Gerry Schremp, *Celebration of American Food: Four Centuries in the Melting Pot* (Golden: Colorado: Fulcrum Publishing, 1996), 101; "Joyce Chen Foods," at http://www .joycechenfoods.com/ (accessed February 20, 2008).

47. Malinda Lo, "'Authentic' Chinese Food: Chinese American Cookbooks and the Regulation of Ethnic Identity," paper presented at the Association for Asian American Studies, March 2001, http://www.malindalo.com/chinesefood.htm (accessed March 23, 2007), 8.

48. Craig Claiborne and Virginia Lee, *The Chinese Cookbook* (Philadelphia: J.B. Lippincott, 1972).

49. Amanda Gold, "Martin Yan's Can-Do Attitude," *San Francisco Chronicle*, February 20, 2008.

50. Roberts, *China to Chinatown*, 165–66. Victor Bergeron founded Trader Vics in 1934 in Oakland, establishing the Polynesian/Chinese connection. He opened a San Francisco location in 1951, later operating dozens around the world. He used a Chinese oven to cook many foods, and employed Chinese chefs at most of his restaurants, serving a mélange of Asian and Polynesian foods and drinks. Many restaurants followed suit. Other popular culture influences, such as the musical *South Pacific*, made these places popular. See "South Sea Isle Trading Post Becomes Popular," *Oakland Tribune*, 1940 (date unknown), and "New Home, New Ear for Trader Vic's," *Oakland Tribune*, November 23, 1972, OAK, Folder, Oakland, Restaurants, M-Z; Pat Steger, "Raising a Glass to the Last Mai Tai," *San Francisco Chronicle*, February 25, 1994.

51. Charles F. Tang, with Robert Goldberg, "Chinese Restaurants Abroad," *Flavor and Fortune* 3, no. 4 (1996) at http://www.flavorandfortune.com/dataaccess/article.php?ID=87 (accessed January 27, 2007).

52. Peter C. Y. Leung and Tony Waters, "Chinese Vegetable Farming," in *Origins and Destinations: 41 Essays on Chinese America* (Los Angeles: Chinese Historical Society of Southern California and UCLA Asian American Studies Center, 1994), 437–52.

53. Joyce Gemperlein, "Asian Vegetables Hit Markets," *San Jose Mercury News*, February 5, 1992.

54. Ibid.

55. Ibid.

56. Immigration continues from the southern areas in large numbers, but there are more immigrants to the United States in recent years from other parts of China. See Bernard Wong, *Ethnicity and Entrepreneurship: The New Chinese Immigrants in the San Francisco Bay Area* (Boston: Allyn and Bacon, 1998), 9–15. Before 1965, the largest numbers of Chinese immigrants were from the Taishan area of Guangdong Province. The commercial connections between the United States and China were strongest there, leading to significant migration from that area. See Chen, *Chinese San Francisco*, 11–48. Madeline Y. Hsu found that the majority of Chinese immigrants in the United States before 1960 came from Taishan province. See *Dreaming of Gold, Dreaming of Home: Transnationalism and Migration between the United States and China, 1882–1943* (Stanford, CA: Stanford University Press, 2000), 3.

57. Roberts, *China to Chinatown*, 23

58. E. N. Anderson Jr., and Marja L. Anderson, "Modern China: South," in K. C. Chang, *Food in Chinese Culture: Anthropological and Historical Perspectives* (New Haven, CT: Yale University Press, 1977), 353–55. Also see Lao, "The Chinese Restaurant Industry in the United States," 25–30.

59. Anderson and Anderson, "Modern China," 354.

60. Ibid., 321–26; Jack Goody, *Cooking Cuisine and Class: A Study in Comparative Sociology* (New York: Cambridge University Press, 1982), 106.

61. Kian Lam Kho, quoted in "Think 'Chinese Food' Means Lo Mein?" *All Things Considered*, NPR, October 6, 2016, http://www.npr.org/sections/thesalt/2016/10/06/496560317/think-chinese-food-means-lo-mein-home-cooking-brings-more-to-the-table   (accessed October 8, 2016).

62. The *New Yorker* line is repeated in a proclamation by San Francisco Mayor George R. Moscone on January 26, 1977, to "salute the proprietors of the Hunan Restaurant" on that day. The proclamation made note of the food's "unique combination of seasonings." See Office of the Mayor, George R. Moscone, San Francisco, "Proclamation," January 26, 1977, in SFHC, VF-Restaurants, Folder, Hunan Restaurant. In that same folder, see also Henry W. S. Chung and Diana Chung, "My Country and My People: Introducing Hunan, China"; Menu, Hunan Restaurant (undated); "Hot Hunan," *Sunset*, October 1976. See also Harvey Steinman, "Hunan Food Is More Than Hot and Spicy," *San Francisco Examiner*, August 16, 1978. On General Tso's chicken, Fuchsia Dunlop, "Hunan Resources," *New York Times*, February 4, 2007.

63. Robert Finigan, Jack Juhasz, and Jack Shelton, *Jack Shelton's Private Guide to Restaurants*, vol. 7, no. 8, April 1974, in SFHC.

64. Quotes from Gael Greene, "Star Struck at Hunam," *New York*, October 1, 1973. She also surveyed these restaurants in "High-Rent Chinese," *New York*, September 27, 1971.

65. Coe analyzes this best in *Chop Suey*, 221–46; Nancy Ross, "China's Cuisine," *Washington Post*, February 17, 1972; John Burns, "Peking Drafting Best Chefs to Prepare Delicacies for U.S. Visitors," *The Globe and Mail* (Toronto), February 19, 1972; Raymond Sokolov, "Menus at Peking Banquets Didn't Do Justice to the Foods," *New York Times*, February 26, 1972; Raymond Sokolov, "When It Comes to Food at Least, Chinese Still Cling to the Past," *New York Times*, February 17, 1972; Margaret MacMillan, *Nixon and Mao: The Week That Changed the World* (New York: Random House, 2008), 149–50; Chiang, *Cecilia Chiang: An Oral History*, 119–20; Hsu, "From Chop Suey to Mandarin Cuisine," 188.

66. Joseph Izzo Jr., "Good Fortune Foretold at the New Foo Loo Soo," *San Jose Mercury News*, April 25, 1982.

67. Joseph Izzo Jr., "Rare Gourmet Quality Pops up at Ging Jee," *San Jose Mercury News*, June 19, 1983.

68. Bill Chan and Stephen Rich, *The Yet Wah Story* (Burlingame, CA: Advanced Pub., 1989), 39–51, in SFHC.

69. One typical guide listed eight Chinese restaurants in San Francisco, variously under Cantonese, Hunan, Peking, and dim sum. *Where San Francisco*, May 7–20, 1983, OAK, VF, San Francisco County—1951—(V); Another had twenty-four Chinese restaurants, the most of any category after American, with thirty-three listed. There were another twenty-three for Continental and twenty-three for French. The restaurants that qualified as Chinese were described as "Chinese—all regions," "Cantonese," "Cantonese and Hunan," "Cantonese/Mandarin," "Cantonese/Mandarin/Dim Sum," "North Chinese," "Peking, Szechuan, and Shanghai," "Deem Sum," and "Mandarin." See San Francisco Convention and Visitor's Bureau, Pamphlet, *San Francisco Restaurant and Night Life Guide*, May 1984, OAK, VF, San Francisco County—1951—(II). The brochure for the annual convention of the Teachers of English to Speakers of Other Languages, meeting in San Francisco in 1990, also delineated the specific regions of China represented in restaurants. Brochure, *TESOL*, 1990, OAK, VF, San Francisco County—1951—(V); See also Ken Wong, "Chinatown Change," *San Francisco Examiner*, August 29, 1984.

70. Chen, *Chop Suey, USA*, 145–47.

71. William Peterson, "Success Story, Japanese-American Style," *New York Times*, January 9, 1966; "Asian Americans: A Model Minority," *Newsweek*, December 6, 1982, 39–44; David Brand, "The New Whiz Kids," *Time*, August 31, 1987.

72. In 2000, 47 percent of ethnic Chinese in the United States who were twenty-five years old or older held a four-year degree. The ratio was 67.11 percent for those who marked Taiwanese. For Asian Americans overall, 44 percent had a four-year degree. For the American population as a whole, the figure was 24.4 percent. *The Asian Databook* (Millerton, NY: Grey House Publishing, 2005), 965. See also Brand, "The New Whiz Kids," *Time*, August 31, 1987.

73. Cheng, "Out of Chinatown and into the Suburbs," 1074.

74. Chinese American Restaurant Association of Greater New York, *Directory, 1973*, in HML 93:15, Him Mark Lai Papers, Research Files, Restaurants, Organizations, Chinese American Restaurant Association of Greater New York, Inc., 1973. The directory had the following totals for each region: Queens and Long Island: 326, Manhattan: 321, Brooklyn: 202, New Jersey: 110, Bronx: 82, Westchester: 32, Staten Island: 15.

75. Patricia Unterman, "East Comes West," *San Francisco Chronicle*, October 30, 1991.

76. Quote from Ken Hom, "The Road to Canton," *New York Times*, June 5, 1988; Patricia Unterman "Bay's Best Cantonese Place Bigger, Better," *San Francisco Chronicle*, December 10, 1989. Another restaurant, Fook Yuen, had branches in Hong Kong, Singapore, and Australia, and Millbrae. See Michael Bauer, "Top 100 Bay Area Restaurants," *San Francisco Chronicle*, February 3, 2002.

77. On the presence of wealthy Chinese in the Bay Area suburbs, see Bernard Wong, *The Chinese in Silicon Valley: Globalization, Social Networks, and Ethnic Identity* (Lanham, MD: Rowan & Littlefield, 2006), 30–41. Shenglin Chang illustrates how Taiwanese Americans, many of them wealthy, cross back and forth between Taiwan and the United States, *The Global Silicon Valley Home: Lives and Landscapes within Taiwanese American Trans-Pacific Culture* (Stanford, CA: Stanford University Press, 2006), 107–14.

78. Menu, Hong Kong Fook Yuen Seafood Restaurant, Millbrae, CA, 1988, CCSF, Folder, Calif.—San Francisco, H–L.

79. John T. Edge, "Around a Midwest City, A World Comes to Eat," *New York Times*, February 23, 2011.

80. Calvin Trillin, *Feeding a Yen: Savoring Local Specialties from Kansas City to Cuzco* (New York: Random House, 2003). Trillin published many of these essays first in magazines, including the *New Yorker* and *Gourmet*.

81. R. W. Apple Jr., "An Asian Odyssey, Seconds from the Freeway," *New York Times*, April 17, 2002.

82. Nicole Mones, "Double Happiness," *New York Times*, August 5, 2007.

83. For population totals, see *The Asian Databook*, 1733–35. The changes in Monterey Park and the surrounding suburbs are documented in Timothy P. Fong, *The First Suburban Chinatown: The Remaking of Monterey Park, California* (Philadelphia: Temple University Press, 1994); Leland Saito, *Race and Politics: Asian Americans, Latinos, and Whites in a Los Angeles Suburb* (Urbana: University of Illinois Press, 1998).

84. "San Gabriel Square," *Goldsea* website, http://goldsea.com/parenting/malls/sgs .html (accessed February 19, 2008).

85. Merrill Shindler, "Affordable Feasts Save on Foreign Travel," *Los Angeles Daily News*, September 3, 1992.

86. Ibid.

87. Cecilia Chiang and others helped introduce kung pao chicken to Americans in the 1960s and 1970s. Janet Fletcher, "Cecilia Chiang's Epic Journey," *San Francisco Chronicle*, October 24, 2007.

88. "Best of Asian America: San Francisco Bay Area Dim Sum Restaurants," on *Goldsea* website at http://best.goldsea.com/100/dsnorcal.html (accessed February 19, 2008).

89. Michael Jones-Correa, "Reshaping the American Dream: Immigrants, Ethnic Minorities, and the Politics of the New Suburbs," in Kruse and Sugrue, eds., *New Suburban History*, 183–84.

90. Ray Kroc (with Robert Anderson), *Grinding It Out: The Making of McDonald's* (New York: St. Martin's, 1987); John F. Love, *McDonald's: Behind the Arches* (New York: Bantam, 1986); John A. Jakle and Keith A. Sculle, *Fast Food: Roadside Restaurants in the Automobile Age* (Baltimore: The Johns Hopkins University Press, 1999).

91. Lily Yau Lim-Chun, "Chinese Food, McDonald's Style Arrives in Hawaii," *China-town News* (Vancouver, BC), April 18, 1979, in HML, Carton 54:12, Research Files, Food and Cooking, 1947, 1970–1989.

92. Toni Lydecker, "Fast Food Goes Ethnic," *NRA News*, March 1985, 12.

93. Ibid.

94. The analyst is Michael Culp, quoted in Marc Schoifet, "Chinese Food Luring Chains," *NRA News*, June 17, 1985.

95. L.A. Chung, "Chinese Fast-Food Cafes Get Off to a Speedy Start," *San Francisco Chronicle*, September 9, 1985.

96. Ibid.

97. Chung, "Chinese Fast-Food Cafes," *San Francisco Chronicle*, September 9, 1985; Schoifet, "Chinese Food Luring Chains," *NRA News*, June 17, 1985.

98. The couple opened the Panda Inn in Pasadena, California, in 1973, eventually growing that chain to seven locations. Laura Kaufman, "Panda Express, On a Roll, Looks to Grow," *Los Angeles Times*, August 19, 1999.

99. Matt Krantz, "Panda Express Spreads Chinese Food Across USA," *USA Today*, September 10, 2006 (revised September 13, 2006); The chain listed 1,083 locations on March 1, 2008, at "Restaurant Locator," Panda Express website, http://www.pandaexpress.com/locations/locator .aspx?zip=Zip%20Code (accessed March 1, 2008)

100. Julie Tamaki, "Far East Restaurant Battle Heating up on West Coast," *Los Angeles Times*, September 6, 2004.

101. Panda Inn Mandarin Cuisine, "About Panda Inn," http://www.pandainn.com /default.asp?nav=about (accessed March 1, 2008). Panda Inn was the original restaurant opened by the Cherngs, and they maintained several locations with this name in Southern California. The Panda Inn restaurant was a full-serve establishment with a more extensive menu and higher prices than the Panda Express fast food spots.

102. David Shaw, "Matters of Taste," *Los Angeles Times*, April 27, 2005. Shaw was described as regarding dining as a form of "high art" and was known to fly across the world just to eat at a special restaurant, so his judgment may have been a bit harsh. See Jon Thurber, "David Shaw, 62," *Los Angeles Times*, August 2, 2005; Ken Reich, "A Memorial to David Shaw," August 5, 2005, on blog, *Take Back the Times*, http://takebackthetimes .blogspot.com/2005/08/memorial-to-david-shaw.html (accessed March 1, 2008).

103. Rose Dosti, "Orange Chicken, Sticky Rolls, Pickling Spice," *Los Angeles Times*, October 22, 1992.

104. Dosti, "Orange Chicken," *Los Angeles Times*, October 22, 1992. The Panda Express website says its recipe for orange chicken is secret, but does not call it orange-flavored chicken as noted in many newspaper articles. "Menu Items, Orange Chicken," Panda Express website, http://www.pandaexpress.com/menu/ofc.aspx (accessed March 1, 2008). On the prevalence of sweet tastes in American Chinese food, see Shun Lu and Gary Alan Fine, "The Presentation of Ethnic Authenticity: Chinese Food as a Social Accomplishment," *The Sociological Quarterly* 36, no. 3 (1995): 538–43.

105. "Totally Tubular Chinese Fast Food," *Asian Week*, June 11, 2004, http://news.asian week.com/news/view_article.html?article_id=ceb442358969cd59bfceb85b19badf84 (accessed January 22, 2008).

106. "Takeout at Home," *The Pioneer Woman*, Episode WU0802H, Food Network, http://www.foodnetwork.com/shows/the-pioneer-woman/800-series/takeout-at-home .html (accessed November 4, 2016).

107. In 2003, more than 10 percent of the Panda Express restaurants were housed in grocery stores. Karen Robinson-Jacobs, "Jack in the Box Heats Up Combo of Food, Groceries, Gasoline," *Los Angeles Times*, April 12, 2003.

108. Quotes from Jason Sheehan, "Second Helping: P.F. Chang's China Bistro," *Westword*, June 30, 2005. On Panda Express and P.F. Chang's, see James Flanigan, "Cooking up a Powerhouse of Chinese Fast Food," *Los Angeles Times*, October 8, 2001; Julie Tamaki, "Far East Restaurant Battle," *Los Angeles Times*, September 6, 2004; Karl Schoenberger, "Expatriate Entrepreneurs," *Los Angeles Times*, October 5, 1993.

109. "At Least 10,000 Asian Restaurants in State," *Asian Week*, August 12, 1982. That number did not include the many Asians serving other cuisines in their restaurants. An insurance broker, Ed Chin, decided to count the Asian restaurants so that he could sell health insurance and other services to Asian entrepreneurs, who he found were underserved.

110. Tamaki, "Far East Restaurant Battle."

111. "4th Annual Top 100 Chinese Restaurants in USA Awards Ceremony at Cultural Food New York," Press Release, *Chinese Restaurant News*, November 11, 2007, http://www.c -r-n.com/Jin_e/Content01Detail.aspx?id=301724023; Margot Adler, "Chinese Restaurant Workers in U.S. Face Hurdles," *Morning Edition*, NPR, May 8, 2007. This story says there were about forty thousand Chinese restaurants in the United States. This estimate differs significantly from the total found by a Taiwan government study in 1996, which estimated twenty thousand Chinese restaurants in the United States. It is unlikely that the number of restaurants doubled in the span of eleven years, so the real number may lie somewhere in between. For the twenty thousand estimate (which was really twenty-three thousand Oriental restaurants total, of which the study said 90 percent were Chinese), see Tang, "Chinese Restaurants Abroad."

112. Bruce Cost, "Grazing Meals," *New York Times*, September 7, 1986; Bruce Cost, "Advanced Course in Dining Chinese," *Los Angeles Times*, February 26, 1989; David Farkas, "Cost Structure," *Chain Leader*, July 2000.

113. Naomi Wise and Robert Lauriston, "In the Land of the Fun-Ethnics," *East Bay Express*, June 11, 1993; Ruth Reichl, "They're Leading Return of Bay Area Cuisine," *Los Angeles Times*, January 14, 1990; Stan Sesser, "Wonderful Monsoon Storms into SF," *San Francisco Chronicle*, December 15, 1989.

114. Wise and Lauriston, "In the Land of the Fun-Ethnics."

115. Jim Wood, "It's an Asian Potpourri," *San Francisco Examiner*, July 16, 1993; Jonathan Kauffman, "Asian Persuasion without Fusion Confusion," *East Bay Express*, May 21, 1999; Joan Zoloth, "Bruce Cost's Ginger Island Is Headed in the Right Direction," *Oakland Tribune*, June 25, 1993. Bruce Cost, *Bruce Cost's Asian Ingredients* (New York: William Morrow and Company, Inc., 1988); Bruce Cost, *Ginger: East to West*, revised and expanded edition, (Reading, MA: Aris Books, 1989)

116. "Emerging Markets," *Gourmet*, March 2002.

117. Bruce Cost, "History," at http://www.brucecostgingerale.com/history.html (accessed September 20, 2016).

8. TORTILLA POLITICS

1. Tortilla factory advertisements can be found in newspapers from around the Southwest dating to the early 1900s. Advertisement, "Tortilla Factory," *San Antonio Light*, December 27, 1915; Report of a fire in a tortilla factory in Miami, Arizona, "Another Blaze at a Tortilla Factory," *The Daily Silver Belt* (Miami, AZ), March 24, 1926; Advertisement, Gutierrez Tortilla Factory, *Yuma Daily Sun* (AZ), June 13, 1952. El Paso counted thirteen tortilla factories in 1954, in "Macaroni, Potato Chips, Tortillas, Salad Dressing Head Food Products," *El Paso Herald-Post*, April 24, 1954. Anita's Mexican Foods was in its fortieth year of business when it was featured in "Westside Merchants Offer Service, Savings for the Whole Family," *El Chicano* (San Bernardino, CA), March 13, 1975.

2. S. A. Eckert, "The Good That Can Come When You're 'Not Too Good to Do Anything,'" *Nation's Business*, October 1990, 14–15.

3. Galindo Family Papers, ca. 1867–1950, Benson Latin American Collection, General Libraries, University of Texas at Austin.

4. Laresh Jayasanker, "Tortilla Politics: Mexican Food, Globalization, and the Sunbelt," in Michelle Nickerson and Darren Dochuk, eds., *Sunbelt Rising: The Politics of Place, Space, and Region* (Philadelphia: University of Pennsylvania Press, 2011), 329.

5. "For the Cornivore," *Texas Monthly*, August 1974.

6. Susanna Person, "Tortilla Cos. Press On," *Austin Business Journal*, October 6–12, 1995, and Steve Greenhow, "Things Are Sent to Her," *Food and Service*, May–June 1990, in Austin History Center, Austin Public Library, AF Food F2500 (10), El Galindo, Inc.; Eckert, "The Good That Can Come'"; "After Surviving War, Man Turned Family Business into Tortilla Giant," oral-history interview of Tomas Galindo from September 2001 conducted by Antonio Gilb, US Latinos and Latinas and WWII Oral History Project, University of Texas at Austin, http://www.lib.utexas.edu/ww2latinos/template-stories-indiv.html?work_urn=urn% 3Autlol%3Awwlatin.135&work_title=Galindo%2C+Thomas, (accessed August 25, 2007); Pam Stephenson, "'Tortilla Lady' Learned Hard Work in Pflugerville," *Community Impact Newspaper* (Pflugerville, TX), September 9, 2006, http://impactnews.com/round-rock -pflugerville/history/279-tortilla-lady-learned-hard-work-in-pflugerville, accessed July 19, 2010; Richard Zelade, "Masa Marketing," *Texas Monthly*, May 1989, 132–41.

7. Patricia Sharpe, "Hot off the Presses," *Texas Monthly*, July 1981; Zelade, "Masa Marketing."

8. Jayasanker, "Tortilla Politics," 328, 329. Confirming Dark's estimate, I found that a ninety-tortilla package of Mission Foods Brand corn tortillas sold for $2.79 at an Austin, Texas, H-E-B in February 2004.

9. Steve Foster quoted in Person, "Tortilla Cos. Press On."

10. El Galindo was not a party in the lawsuit detailed below.

11. Jayasanker, "Tortilla Politics," 330. Data from the Census Bureau confirms Dark's suspicion. The number of tortilla producers increased from 1997 to 2002 (the only two years for which the bureau surveyed tortilla manufacturers), but the shipment value of the small firms (1 to 4 employees) paled in comparison to that of the large firms (250 to 999 employees). US Census Bureau, *Tortilla Manufacturing: 2002* (Washington, DC Government Printing Office, 2004), 4.

12. Patricia Sharpe, "Round and Round," *Texas Monthly*, April 2001, http://www.texas monthly.com (accessed February 5, 2004).

13. Jayasanker, "Tortilla Politics," 330.

14. Percentage of four largest manufacturers from Michael J. Harris et al., *The U.S. Food Marketing System, 2002* (Washington, DC: ERS-USDA, 2002), 65. Total value of shipments was $1.11 billion, from US Census Bureau, *Tortilla Manufacturing*, 1997 Economic Census, Manufacturing Industry Series (Washington, DC: Government Printing Office, 1999), 7.

15. After several telephone calls and visits to tortilla businesses and grocers in the Austin, Texas, area, I could not find El Galindo or its tortillas. W. Allen Dark's personal website stated that he was "winding up operations" for El Galindo in May 2009, http://www.linkedin.com /pub/w-allen-dark/13/834/873 (accessed January 14, 2010).

16. Mexican President Carlos Salinas de Gortari (1988–1994) earned a PhD in political economy and government at Harvard. President Ernesto Zedillo earned a PhD in economics from Yale. President Vicente Fox Quesada (2000–2006) was not a PRI member, but he was president of Coca-Cola Mexico and a board member on the United States–Mexico Chamber of Commerce. Also see Sarah Babb, *Managing Mexico: Economists from Nationalism to Neoliberalism* (Princeton, NJ: Princeton University Press, 2002).

17. Juan M. Rivera and Scott Whiteford, "Mexican Agriculture and NAFTA—Prospects for Change," in Juan M. Rivera, Scott Whiteford, and Manuel Chávez, eds., *NAFTA and the Campesinos: The Impact of NAFTA on Small-Scale Agricultural Producers in Mexico and the Prospects for Change* (Scranton, PA: University of Scranton Press, 2009), xv–xvi.

18. Strom C. Thacker, *Big Business, the State, and Free Trade: Constructing Coalitions in Mexico* (New York: Cambridge University Press, 2000), 1–11.

19. M. Angeles Villareal and Ian F. Ferguson, "The North American Free Trade Agreement (NAFTA)," *CRS Report*, April 16, 2015, at https://www.fas.org/sgp/crs/row/R42965.pdf (accessed September 9, 2015).

20. Rivera and Whiteford, "Mexican Agriculture," xii–xvi.

21. Douglas S. Massey, Jorge Durand, and Nolan J. Malone, *Beyond Smoke and Mirrors: Mexican Immigration in an Era of Economic Integration* (New York: Russell Sage, 2002), 78–82.

22. US Census Bureau, "Trade in Goods with Mexico" (years 1995–2014), at https:// www.census.gov/foreign-trade/balance/c2010.html#1994 (accessed September 4, 2015); Marla Dickerson and Jerry Hirsch, "Investment Money Pours in from Mexico," *Los Angeles Times*, May 5, 2007.

23. Grupo Bimbo, *Annual Report 2005*, 3. On the claim that it is the largest tortilla manufacturer in the world, see GRUMA, "This Is GRUMA," http://www.gruma.com/vIng /Acerca/acerca_esto.asp (accessed June 12, 2008); Walmart became the largest grocer in the United States in 2003, according to Tom Weir, "Walmart's the 1," *Progressive Grocer*, May 1, 2003, 35. Other estimates place it as the largest grocer by 2002. Walmart was the largest supermarket chain in Mexico by 2001. Rita Schwentesius and Manuel Ángel Gómez, "Supermarkets in Mexico: Impacts on Horticulture Systems," *Development Policy Review* 20, no. 4 (2002): 492; Archer Daniels Midland, *Annual Report 2008*. Walmart was the largest private employer in the world in 2018 and had the largest revenues of any company. Other companies had larger market capitalizations. "Forbes Global 2000," *Forbes*, https://www .forbes.com/global2000/list/#header:position (accessed October 4, 2018).

24. On the global expansion of Mexican food, see Jeffrey M. Pilcher, "Eating Mexican in a Global Age: The Politics and Production of Ethnic Food," in Warren Belasco and Roger

Horowitz, eds., *Food Chains: From Farmyard to Shopping Cart* (Philadelphia: University of Pennsylvania Press, 2009), 158–77.

25. Reinhold Wagnleitner and Elaine Tyler May, *"Here, There and Everywhere": The Foreign Politics of American Popular Culture* (Hanover, NH: University Press of New England, 2000); Benjamin Barber, *Jihad vs. McWorld* (New York: Ballantine, 1995); George Ritzer, *The McDonaldization Thesis: Explorations and Extensions* (Thousand Oaks, CA: Sage, 1998), esp. 84–87. For a counterargument see James L. Watson, ed., *Golden Arches East: McDonald's in East Asia* (Stanford, CA: Stanford University Press, 1997).

26. Globalization reconfigured the South too, Raymond A. Mohl, "Globalization, Latinization, and the Nuevo New South," *Journal of American Ethnic History* 22, no. 4 (2003): 31–66.

27. GRUMA, *Annual Report 2007*, 5–17; GRUMA, *Form 20-F for Fiscal Year Ended 1999*, 12–13; Rick Wartzman, "A Push to Probe Buying Habits in Latino Homes," *Wall Street Journal*, August 5, 1999.

28. GRUMA, *Annual Report 2007*, 3. That year, 33 percent of GRUMA's net sales were in Mexico.

29. Charles R. Handy and Suchada Langley, "Food Processing in Mexico Attracts U.S. Investments," *Food Review* 16, no. 1 (US Dept. of Agriculture) (January–April, 1993): 20–24.

30. David Bartsow, "Vast Mexico Bribery Case Hushed by Walmart after Top-Level Struggle," *New York Times*, April 12, 2012.

31. Weir, "Walmart's the 1," 35. Schwentesius and Gomez, "Supermarkets in Mexico," 492.

32. Allen R. Meyerson, "Lines Shift in Border War for Mexican Shopper," *New York Times*, April 25, 1994; Aïssatou Sidimé, "Mexican Nationals Call San Antonio Home," *San Antonio Express-News*, July 17, 2008.

33. Nelson Lichtenstein, "Walmart: A Template for Twenty-First-Century Capitalism," in Lichtenstein, ed., *Walmart: The Face of Twenty-First-Century Capitalism* (New York: The New Press, 2006), 4.

34. Bethany Moreton, *To Serve God and Walmart: The Making of Christian Free Enterprise* (Cambridge, MA: Harvard University Press, 2009), 253.

35. Kenneth J. Cooper, "House Approves U.S.-Mexico Canada Trade Pact on 234 to 200 Vote, Giving Clinton Big Victory," *Washington Post*, November 18, 1993; Moreton, *To Serve God and Walmart*, 248–63. Kenneth J. Cooper and Peter Behr, "Sun Belt vs. Rust Belt: Trade Pact Debate Causes Regional Conflict," *Washington Post*, November 6, 1993. The full vote on NAFTA was 61–38 in the Senate and 234–200 in the House. I calculated the Sunbelt percentage using Alabama, Arizona, California, Florida, Georgia, Louisiana, Mississippi, New Mexico, North Carolina, South Carolina, Texas, and Virginia. The Sunbelt vote was 16–8 in the Senate and 109–64 in the House. In the Senate, 9 Republicans and 7 Democrats voted for the bill, and in the House, 52 Republicans and 57 Democrats voted yes. In the House, the Sunbelt representatives that voted "no" were overwhelmingly in the Democratic Party. Notable congressional members voting "yes" included Newt Gingrich (R-GA), Nancy Pelosi (D-CA), Phil Gramm (R-TX) and J.J. Pickle (D-TX).

36. Statement of Senator John McCain, Senate Committee on Commerce, Science, and Transportation, *Hearings on Agricultural Trade with Mexico*, 103rd Cong., 1st sess., July 22, 1993, 68–74, 70.

37. Anthony Bianco and Wendy Zellner, "Is Walmart Too Big?" and "The Long Arm of Bentonville, Ark.," *Business Week*, October 6, 2003.

38. The discussion about Walmart, free trade, and antitrust is voluminous. See, for example, Barry C. Lynn, "Breaking the Chain: The Antitrust Case against Walmart," *Harper's*, July 2006; Steve Lohr, "Discount Nation: Is Walmart Good for America?" *New York Times*, December 7, 2003; Lichtenstein, *Walmart*.

39. Lichtenstein, *Walmart*, 13–15, gives an overall 25 percent lower wage than competitors. Bianco and Zellner, "Is Walmart Too Big?" and "The Long Arm of Bentonville, Ark.," estimate Walmart's labor costs as 20 percent lower than unionized grocers.

40. Lichtenstein, "Walmart," 15.

41. Elizabeth Tandy Shermer, "Counter-Organizing the Sunbelt: Right-to-Work Campaigns and Anti-Union Conservatism, 1943–1958," *Pacific Historical Review* 78, no. 1 (2009): 81–118.

42. Bartsow, "Vast Mexico Bribery Case . . .," *New York Times*, April 12, 2012.

43. "Hispanic Communities Fact Sheet," and "Texas Community Impact," www .walmartstores.com (accessed July 12, 2009).

44. On labor and Walmart, see Lichtenstein, "Walmart." Walmart's wages are high in Mexico relative to other retailers, in part because unions there have been successful in securing wage increases. See Chris Tilly, "Walmart and Its Workers: NOT the Same All over the World," *Connecticut Law Review* 39, no. 4 (May 2007): 1805–23. On farmworkers in the United States, see Daniel Rothenberg, *With These Hands: The Hidden World of Migrant Farmworkers Today* (Berkeley: University of California Press, 1998); Seth M. Holmes, *Fresh Fruit, Broken Bodies: Migrant Farmworkers in the United States* (Berkeley: University of California Press, 2013).

45. Chris Tilly and Marie Kennedy, "Supply, Demand, and Tortillas," *Dollars and Sense*, Spring 2007. Oxfam International, "Double-Edged Prices," Oxfam Briefing Paper, October 2008, http://www.oxfam.org.uk/resources/policy/conflict_disasters/downloads/bp121_food _price_crisis.pdf (accessed February 3, 2009), 19.

46. Rothenberg, *With These Hands*, 6–7.

47. Marilyn Halter, *Shopping for Identity: The Marketing of Ethnicity* (New York: Schocken Books, 2000); and Donna R. Gabaccia, *We Are What We Eat: Ethnic Food and the Making of Americans* (Cambridge, MA: Harvard University Press, 1999).

48. The discussion below owes a great debt to the work of Jeffrey M. Pilcher, especially *¡Que Vivan los Tamales! Food and the Making of Mexican Identity* (Albuquerque: University of New Mexico Press, 1998); and *Planet Taco: A Global History of Mexican Food* (New York: Oxford University Press, 2012).

49. The tortilla was eaten in what are now the southwestern states of the United States before European conquest and when Spain and Mexico controlled those lands, Pilcher, "Tex-Mex"; Sophie Coe, *America's First Cuisines* (Austin: University of Texas Press, 1994), 145–48.

50. Menu, Pepe's, Pier 39, San Francisco, 1980, CCSF, Folder: Calif.—San Francisco, Ethnic/Mexican.

51. Menu, Chi-Chi's, Timonium, Maryland, Copyright 1980, taken by customer on September 21, 1983, NYPLM, #1983-0007.

52. Elizabeth Paulucci, *Cookbook from a Melting Pot* (New York: Grosset & Dunlap, 1981), 221–24, quote on 221.

53. A newspaper story about Mexican restaurants in San Francisco from 1923 makes unfettered reference to tortillas, mole, and chilies without explaining what they are. Perhaps this was due to high Mexican immigration rates during the 1920s. See "Spanish-Mexican" by Robert H. Willson, from *San Francisco Examiner*, December 2, 1923, in Robert H. Willson et al., *Foreign Nationalities in San Francisco* (San Francisco, CA: n.p., 1951). Taco stands were common in Southern California during the 1950s. Andrew F. Smith, "Tacos, Enchiladas, and Refried Beans: The Invention of Mexican-American Cookery," paper presented at Oregon State University, 1999, http://food.oregonstate.edu/ref/culture/mexico_smith.html (accessed November 26, 2006). Both Anglos and Mexican Americans in Tucson had high consumption levels of "packaged, prepared tortillas" in the 1980s. Melanie Wallendorf and Michael D. Reilly, "Ethnic Migration, Assimilation, and Consumption," *Journal of Consumer Research* 10.3 (1983): 292–302.

54. Menu, La Festa, San Bruno, California, circa 1990s, CCSF, Folder, Ethnic-Mexican; Menu, Acapulco Restaurants, Inc., 1991 (the chain listed forty-eight California locations, mostly in the southern region); menu of Chipotle chain at http://www.chipotle.com/#flash/food_menu (accessed September 3, 2007).

55. GRUMA, *Annual Report 2010*.

56. The trade magazine *Progressive Grocer* shows the progression of tortillas from the "impulse-buy" category to a regular purchase for both Mexican and non-Mexican customers. See "QFI Helps Sales with an Ethnic Case," *Progressive Grocer*, January 1973, 94; Robert Dietrich, "As Easy as ABC: An Independent Brings Scanning to the Inner City," *Progressive Grocer*, September 1981, 123. In this article, Paul Kodimer, president of ABC Markets in South Central Los Angeles, said that tortilla sales had recently "gone wild" in his store. See also "Taco and Tortilla Chips Offered," *Progressive Grocer*, February 1972, 126, about how Wise Foods, a snack food manufacturer, first added tortilla chips to its product line. Tortilla chips were first listed as a separate food category in *Progressive Grocer* in its July 1978 issue. A typical story from a restaurant trade magazine in 1982 said, "Mexican cuisine has also been growing in popularity this year. A longtime favorite of the western states, its ethnic dishes are quickly becoming accepted nationwide." Elyse Cuttler, *NRA News*, December 1982.

57. Tom Caron was director of marketing for Happy Joe's Foods, a division of Tony's Pizza Service that manufactured frozen Mexican entrees. Quote in Mary Ann Linsen, "Three Hot Specialty Departments Where Grocery Is Growing," *Progressive Grocer*, October 1980, 129.

58. Del Monte was owned by RJR Nabisco. Bryan Salvage, "The 'New' Del Monte—Not Just a Canner Anymore," *Prepared Foods*, May 1985; and Advertisement, "A.1. Puts a Little Life into a Taco," (unknown pub.), February 8, 1986, in JWT-NEWBUS, Box 65, Folder Nabisco Del Monte File, 1987.

59. Marjorie Wold, "H-E-B's New Look: From Salsa to Sushi," *Progressive Grocer*, September 1991, 86–88. Quote from Paul Madure, vice president, store development, H-E-B. Tianguis chain also built these presses in the 1990s. Marian Burros, "Supermarkets Reach out to Hispanic Customers," *New York Times*, July 18, 1990.

60. Linsen, "Three Hot Specialty Departments," 129. Del Monte Foods introduced a line of frozen burritos in 1981, Advertisement, C20, *Progressive Grocer*, October 1981. See also Robert McCarthy, "Consumer Watch: Supermarkets Listen for That Resounding 'Ole,'" *Progressive Grocer*, August 1982, 32.

61. Jeffrey M. Pilcher catalogs the move from homebound, labor-intensive tortilla making to GRUMA's industrial dominance by the 1990s in "Industrial *Tortillas* and Folkloric Pepsi: The Nutritional Consequences of Hybrid Cuisines in Mexico," in Warren Belasco and Philip Scranton, eds., *Food Nations: Selling Taste in Consumer Societies* (New York: Routledge, 2002), 222–29; and *¡Que Vivan los Tamales!*, 99–111. See also "About GRUMA: Timeline," http://www.gruma.com/vIng/Acerca/acerca_historia.asp (accessed August 25, 2007).

62. Pilcher, *¡Que Vivan los Tamales!*, 105; "About GRUMA: Timeline."

63. Mission Foods Corporation, "About Us," http://www.missionmenus.com/pressroom (accessed April 11, 2009); Mission Foods Corporation, "Fun Factoids about Mission Foods," http://www.missionmenus.com/pressroom/MediaMaterials.aspx?t=470&id=6358 (accessed February 17, 2009). The twenty-nine billion figure is for 2007, and a quarter of all tortillas is for 2009.

64. GRUMA Annual Reports and 20-F statements, years 1999–2007.

65. Pilcher, *¡Que Vivan los Tamales!*, 101.

66. Ibid., 101–5. As with many inventions, there were fits and starts with these new technologies before they were widely adopted.

67. Pilcher, "Eating Mexican in a Global Age," in Belasco and Horowitz, eds., *Food Chains*, 160–61.

68. Patrice Duggan, "Tortilla Technology," *Forbes*, April 29, 1991.

69. GRUMA, *Annual Report 2006*, 11.

70. Tim Duffy, "Mexico Tortilla Deregulation Doesn't Boost Sales," *Wall Street Journal*, June 8, 1999.

71. Robert Donnelly, "Tortilla Riddle," *Business Mexico*, October 1, 1999.

72. GRUMA, *Annual Report 2001*, 1.

73. GRUMA, "Fourth Quarter 2008 Results," February 18, 2009, at http://www.gruma.com/Documentos/seccion_6/Categoria_448/4Q08-GRUMA.pdf (accessed February 22, 2009), 4.

74. Antonio Yunez-Naude, "The Dismantling of CONASUPO, a Mexican State Trader in Agriculture," *World Economy* 26, no. 1 (January 2003): 97–122.

75. Anthony DePalma, "How a Tortilla Empire Was Built on Favoritism," *New York Times*, February 15, 1996.

76. Enrique Ochoa, *Feeding Mexico: The Political Uses of Food since 1910* (Wilmington, DE: Scholarly Resources, 2000), 208–20.

77. Thacker, *Big Business, the State, and Free Trade*, 135–61.

78. Agrarian protesters have battled the Mexican government intermittently since the signing of NAFTA. The revision to the Mexican Constitution in December 1991 had also ended the requirement for state distribution of land. See Yunez-Naude, "Dismantling of CONASUPO." Kenneth Edward Mitchell, *State-Society Relations in Mexico* (Burlington, VT: Ashgate, 2001), 1–4, 37–40, 68–83. On the general progression of food policy and the

conflict that emerged from privatization, see Ochoa, *Feeding Mexico*, 208–20. On Cargill see John Ross, "Tortilla Wars," *The Progressive*, June 1, 1999.

79. Quote in Anthony DePalma, "Graft Inquiry in Mexico Ties Zedillo to Disputed Payment," *New York Times*, July 5, 1996. See also DePalma, "How a Tortilla Empire." Then CEO of GRUMA, Eduardo Livas Jr., disputed DePalma's allegations in a letter to the *New York Times* in "Mexico Tortilla Maker Won No Favors," February 21, 1996. See also Mitchell, *State-Society Relations in Mexico*, 48–83.

80. Ross, "Tortilla Wars."

81. Scott Kilman and Joel Millman, "ADM, Showing New Interest in Mexico, Agrees to Buy 22% Stake in Gruma SA," *Wall Street Journal*, August 23, 1996; Donnelly, "Tortilla Riddle."

82. José J. Yordán and Michael J. Mauboussin, *Grupo Industrial Maseca, S.A. de C.V. (GIMSA): 1993 Fourth Quarter and Full-Year Results* (New York: CS First Boston, 1994), 4; GRUMA, *Annual Report 2006*, 11.

83. Quoted in Joel Millman, "Mexican Tortilla Firms Stage U.S. Bake-Off," *Wall Street Journal*, May 10, 1996.

84. GRUMA, *Annual Report 1999*, 3.

85. Trey Garrison, "GRUMA Corp. Relocating to Metroplex," *Dallas Business Journal*, March 6, 1998.

86. "Owner Participation Agreement" between Rancho Cucamonga Redevelopment Agency and GRUMA Corporation Foods, Inc., January 18, 1996 (in possession of author), and e-mail correspondence with Tony Le-Ngoc, Redevelopment Analyst II, Rancho Cucamonga Redevelopment Agency, February 2, 2010. Though Governor Wilson sought to keep businesses in California, he likely was not personally involved in the Rancho Cucamonga plant deal. See also David Bacon, "Taking on the Tortilla King," September 22, 1996, at http://dbacon.igc.org/strikes/06tortil.htm (accessed January 12, 2010), but this gives the wrong figure of $400,000 for locating the plant in the city.

87. Joel Millman, "Foreign Firms also Outsource—to the U.S.," *Wall Street Journal*, February 23, 2004.

88. GRUMA built another tortilla facility in Panorama City, California, in 2008 that was about the same size as its Rancho Cucamonga plant. Dickerson and Hirsch, "Investment Money Pours in from Mexico"; GRUMA, *Form 20-F, Fiscal Year Ended 1999*, 14–15; Millman, "Mexican Tortilla Firms Stage U.S. Bake-Off"; Rick Wartzman, "Southern California Sees a Low-Tech Boom," *Wall Street Journal*, January 25, 1999.

89. GRUMA, *Annual Report 2004*, 22.

90. Trey Garrison, "GRUMA Corp. Relocating to Metroplex," *Dallas Business Journal*, March 6, 1998. In 1991, one estimate had GRUMA providing a third of Taco Bell's tortillas. See Duggan, "Tortilla Technology." See also "Mission Possible," *Snack Food and Wholesale Bakery*, July 1998.

91. "Mission Foods Parent in Move to Purchase Candy's," *Milling and Baking News*, April 19, 1994.

92. Matt Moffett, "U.S. Appetite for Mexican Food Grows, Cooking Up Hotter Sales for Exporters," *Wall Street Journal*, February 5, 1992; "Mexico: Maseca to Invest US$1bil in Asia over Five Years," *El Economista* (Mexico), March 8, 2006.

93. GRUMA opened a tortilla plant in Shanghai to fill Asian demand and reduce pressure on its Rancho Cucamonga, California, facility. "Wrapping the Globe in Tortillas," *Business Week*, February 26, 2007, 54; Mission Foods Press Release, "Mission Foods Opens Plant in China," November 2006, http://www.missionmenus.com/News.aspx (accessed April 2, 2009); Lu Haoting, "Mexican Mission," *China Business Weekly*, July 10, 2006.

94. Naresh Nakra, president and CEO of GRUMA USA, boasted that the Rancho Cucamonga facility would be the most technologically advanced in the world when the company was finishing it in 1996. Jay Sjerven, "Tortilla Industry: Capacity to Increase, But at a Slower Pace," *Milling and Baking News*, January 30, 1996.

95. Quote in Kilman and Millman, "ADM, Showing New Interest in Mexico." On the relationship between GRUMA and ADM, see GRUMA corporate website, "Investor Relations: Basic Questions," http://www.gruma.com/vIng/Relacion/relacion_preguntas.asp?idEmpresa=1 (accessed February 22, 2009); Archer Daniels Midland Company, *2008 Annual Report*, 5–6; "ADM Discloses Probe by Mexico on Pricing of Synthetic Lysine," *Wall Street Journal*, February 14, 1997; "ADM's Mexican Deal: Far from Corny," *Crossborder Monitor*, November 13, 1996; Kacey Culliney, "ADM Will 'Redeploy' $450m Gained from GRUMA Sale," *Bakery and Snacks.com*, December 18, 2012, http://www.bakeryandsnacks.com/Manufacturers/ADM-will-redeploy-450m-gained-from-Gruma-sale (accessed August 30, 2015).

96. Quote from GRUMA, *Form 20-F, Fiscal Year Ended 2003*, 21.

97. "3 Sentenced in Price-Fixing Plot," *Los Angeles Times*, July 10, 1999; Philip H. Howard, *Concentration and Power in the Food System* (New York: Bloomsbury, 2016), 72–78. Sachdev, "Andreas Released to Halfway House," *Chicago Tribune*, December 20, 2001; Kurt Eichenwald, "Archer Daniels Settles Suit Accusing It of Price Fixing," *New York Times*, June 18, 2004; Kilman and Burton, "Archer Daniels Inside Inquiry," *Wall Street Journal*, September 22, 1995; Kurt Eichenwald, "Archer Daniels Ousts Executive in Mexico," *New York Times*, October 7, 1995; "ADM Discloses Probe," *Wall Street Journal*, February 14, 1997.

98. Quote from "3 Sentenced in Price-Fixing Plot at Archer Daniels," *Los Angeles Times*, July 10, 1999. Howard, *Concentration and Power*, 72–78; Ameet Sachdev, "Andreas Released to Halfway House," *Chicago Tribune*, December 20, 2001.

99. Eichenwald, "Archer Daniels Settles Suit" *New York Times*, June 18, 2004. Another massive food processor, Cargill, also settled in the corn syrup case.

100. Scott Kilman and Thomas M. Burton, "Archer Daniels Inside Inquiry Triggers Departure or Suspension of Managers," *Wall Street Journal*, September 22, 1995; Eichenwald, "Archer Daniels Ousts," *New York Times*, October 7, 1995; "ADM Discloses Probe by Mexico of Pricing of Synthetic Lysine," *Wall Street Journal*, February 14, 1997. ADM also paid fines to the European Union for price fixing and was forced to pay fines for bribing Ukrainian officials. Gregory Meyer, "ADM to Pay $54m to Settle Bribery Charges," *Financial Times*, December 20, 2013, http://www.ft.com/cms/s/0/418a4d08-69ae-11e3-aba3-00144feabdco.html#ax zz4JXClzat4 (accessed September 6, 2016); "EU Court Cuts ADM Cartel Fine by 10.3 mln Euros," *Reuters*, July 9, 2009, http://www.reuters.com/article/archerdaniels-eu-court-idUSL 951583520090709 (accessed September 6, 2016).

101. Nixon said Andreas delivered the money in the fall of 1971. Nixon returned the cash to Andreas eventually, but also thought about having Andreas influence Democratic politics by blackmailing the Democratic National Committee chairman Larry O'Brien. Andreas

gave money to both Republican and Democratic candidates. Grand Jury Testimony of Richard M. Nixon, June 24, 1975, San Clemente, CA, at US Government Information, "Nixon Grand Jury Records," National Archives and Records Administration, https://www.gpo .gov/fdsys/pkg/GPO-NARA-WSPF-NIXON-GRAND-JURY-RECORDS/content-detail .html (accessed September 6, 2016), 124–26 152–59; Howard, *Concentration and Power*, 76–77; Scott Kilman, Bruce Ingersoll, and Jill Abramson, "Risk Averse," *Wall Street Journal*, October 27, 1995; "So You Want to Buy a President?" *Frontline*, http://www.pbs.org/wgbh /pages/frontline/president/players/andreas.html (accessed September 6, 2016); Keith Schneider, "Dwayne O. Andreas, Who Turned Archer Daniels Midland into Food Giant, Dies at 98," *New York Times*, November 16, 2016.

102. Schneider, "Dwayne O. Andreas," *New York Times*, November 16, 2016

103. Rivera and Whiteford, "Mexican Agriculture and NAFTA," Rivera et al., eds., *NAFTA and the Campesinos*, xix. American grain producers enjoyed greater subsidies and technological advantages, meaning corn yields measured 8.55 tons per hectare in the United States as compared to 2.50 tons per hectare in Mexico. See Manuel Ángel Gómez Cruz and Rita Schwentesius Rindermann, "NAFTA's Impact on Mexican Agriculture: An Overview," in *NAFTA and the Campesinos*, 4.

104. Cruz and Rindermann, "NAFTA's Impact on Mexican Agriculture," 14.

105. David Bacon, "Displaced People: NAFTA's Most Important Product," and Sergio Zermeño, "Desolation: Mexican Campesinos and Agriculture in the 21st Century," *NACLA Report on the Americas*, September–October 2008; Tim Duffy, "Mexico Deregulation Doesn't Boost Sales," *Wall Street Journal*, June 8, 1999; Anjali Browning, "Corn, Tomatoes and a Dead Dog: Mexican Agricultural Restructuring after NAFTA and Rural Responses to Declining Maize Production in Oaxaca, Mexico," *Mexican Studies/Estudios Mexicanos* 29, no. 1 (Winter 2013): 85–119.

106. Estimates vary concerning the decline in tortilla consumption, but reports consistently show a decline from 2000 to 2008. Price increases and alternative foods are typically cited as reasons. "Tortilla Consumption Continues to Decline in Mexico but Grows Steadily Overseas," *SourceMex Economic News and Analysis on Mexico*, June 23, 2004; "Agriculture Groups Offer Mixed Opinions on Pending Elimination of Corn Tariffs under NAFTA," *SourceMex Economic News and Analysis on Mexico*, December 12, 2007. For GRUMA's ascent, see Annual Reports, 1990–99.

107. *El Aquila Food Products v. Gruma Corp.*, 301 F. Supp. 2d 612 (S.D. Tex. 2003), 6. For background, see Marla Dickerson, "Small Tortilla Makers Lose Antitrust Suit Against Rival," *Los Angeles Times*, January 6, 2004.

108. *El Aquila Food Products v. Gruma Corp.*

109. Ibid., 12–13, 18.

110. *El Aquila Food Products. v. Gruma Corp*; see also Joel Millman, "Mexican Retailers Enter U.S. to Capture Latino Dollars," *Wall Street Journal*, February 1, 2001. The case was dismissed on appeal in 2005. See El Aguila Food Prods. Inc. v. Gruma Corp., 131 Fed. Appx. 450 (5th Cir. 2005).

111. Bill No. SB 582, April 11, 2005, CA Senate Committee on Business, Professions and Economic Development.

112. GRUMA, *Form 20-F for Fiscal Year Ended 1999*, 13.

113. "Mexican Firm Wins McDonald's Contract," *National Post* (Canada), August 4, 1999.

114. Joel Millman, "New Export Tiger Isn't Asian; It's Mexico," *Wall Street Journal*, May 9, 2000.

115. "Transaction Overview: A Transformative Opportunity," Grupo Bimbo press release (web cast), December 2008, http://www.grupobimbo.com/relacioninv/uploads/presentations /GB%20Webcast%20Final%20Web.pdf (accessed January 14, 2010).

116. "Grupo Bimbo Completes and Closes Weston Foods, Inc. Acquisition," Grupo Bimbo press release, January 22, 2009, http://www.bimbobakeriesusa.com/about_us/ media_center .php?id=1143 (accessed March 31, 2009); Bimbo Bakeries USA, "Our Brands," https://bimbo bakeriesusa.com/brands (accessed August 30, 2015).

117. Sonia Nazaro, "Teamsters Head Assails Tortilla Company at Rally," *Los Angeles Times*, August 19, 1996; Bacon, "Taking on the Tortilla King"; Christopher David Ruiz Cameron, "Labor Law and Latcrit Identity Politics: The Labyrinth of Solidarity: Why the Future of the American Labor Movement Depends on Latino Workers," *University of Miami Law Review* 53 (July 1999): 1090–91.

118. GRUMA, *Annual Report 2008*, 51.

CONCLUSION

1. Sidney W. Mintz and Christine M. Du Bois, "The Anthropology of Food and Eating," *Annual Review of Anthropology* 31 (2002): 99–119; Warren Belasco, *Food: The Key Concepts* (New York: Berg, 2008). At a protest at O'Hare airport against President Trump's Executive Order banning immigrants from seven nations, a Jewish and Muslim family met and exchanged their contact information. Later, they shared a Shabbat dinner as a way of bridging their cultural/religious divide, saying it was harder to "objectify" other people when you share experiences with them. Gregory Pratt, "Muslim, Jewish Families Share Dinner after Protest Encounter Captured in Viral Photo," *Chicago Tribune*, February 11, 2017.

2. Bud Kennedy, "Chip in to Keep Our Borders Safe," *Fort Worth Star-Telegram*, August 8, 2006.

3. Quotes from "About Minuteman Salsa," and "FAQs," www.minutemansalsa.com (accessed February 5, 2008); Vicki L. Ruiz, "Citizen Restaurant: American Imaginaries, American Communities," *American Quarterly* 60, no. 1 (March 2008): 1–21; Marisa Treviño, "Minuteman Salsa Leaves Chile Impression," *Latina Lista*, August 7, 2006, http://latinalista .blogspot.com; Betsy Guzmán, *The Hispanic Population: Census 2000 Brief* (Washington DC: US Census Bureau, May 2001).

4. Josh Harkinson, "White Nationalists See Trump as Their Troll in Chief. Is He with Them?," *Mother Jones*, January/February 2017, http://www.motherjones.com/politics/2016 /11/trump-white-nationalists-hate-racism-power (accessed February 2, 2017); "Alternative Right," Southern Poverty Law Center, https://www.splcenter.org/fighting-hate/extremist -files/ideology/alternative-right (accessed March 5, 2017); Graeme Wood, "His Kampf," *The Atlantic*, June 2017.

5. Josh Harkinson, "Meet the White Nationalist Trying to Ride the Trump Train to Lasting Power," *Mother Jones*, October 27, 2016, http://m.motherjones.com/politics/2016/10 /richard-spencer-trump-alt-right-white-nationalist (accessed February 2, 2017).

6. Ibid.; Alex Altman, "The Billionaire and the Bigots," *Time*, April 25, 2016. The Vietnamese restaurant, Nam Viet, is in Arlington, Virginia. See also Robert Ji-Song Ku, *Dubious Gastronomy: The Cultural Politics of Eating Asian in the USA* (Honolulu: University of Hawai'i Press, 2014); Mark Tanachai Padoongpatt, "Too Hot to Handle," *Radical History Review* 110 (Spring 2011): 83–108; Anita Mannur, "Asian American Food-Scapes," *Amerasia Journal* 32, no. 2 (2006): 1–5.

7. Frederick Douglass Opie, *Hog and Hominy: Soul Food from Africa to America* (New York: Columbia University Press, 2008), 36–38.

8. Lizzie Collingham, *Curry: A Tale of Cooks and Conquerors* (New York: Oxford University Press, 2006); Cecilia Leong-Salobir, "'Cookie' and 'Jungle Boy': A Historical Sketch of the Different Cooks for Different Folks in British Colonial Southeast Asia, ca. 1850–1960," *Global Food History* 1, no. 1 (2015): 59–80.

9. Kristin L. Hoganson, *Consumer's Imperium: The Global Production of American Domesticity, 1865–1920* (Chapel Hill: University of North Carolina Press, 2007).

10. Video at https://www.youtube.com/watch?v=ups4FeSuHvY (accessed February 3, 2017) and "Trump's Road to the White House," *Frontline*, January 24, 2017, http://www.pbs.org/wgbh/frontline/film/trumps-road-to-the-white-house/ (accessed February 2, 2017).

11. Views of "Edgar" and other students (no real names given) in US Commission on Civil Rights, *What Students Perceive* (Washington, DC: GPO, 1970), 2–23, 70–72.

12. Jessica M. Vasquez, *Mexican Americans across Generations* (New York: New York University Press, 2011), 64, 147. More generally, see Meredith E. Abarca and Consuelo Carr Salas, *Latin@s' Presence in the Food Industry: Changing How We Think about Food* (Fayetteville: University of Arkansas Press, 2016).

13. Tanya Broder, "Gastronaut: Passing Wind Gets Mexican Spaceman Banned from U.S. Shuttle Flights," *Weekly World News*, February 14, 1995, on GoogleBooks.

14. Statistics from Saru Jayaraman, *Behind the Kitchen Door* (Ithaca, NY: Cornell University Press, 2013), 2–3; Daniel Rothenberg, *With These Hands: The Hidden World of Migrant Farmworkers Today* (Berkeley: University of California Press, 1998); Seth M. Holmes, *Fresh Fruit, Broken Bodies: Migrant Farmworkers in the United States* (Berkeley: University of California Press, 2013).

15. Andrew P. Haley, "Restaurant Culture," in Michael D. Wise and Jennifer Jensen Wallach, eds., *The Routledge History of American Foodways* (New York: Routledge, 2016), 214.

16. Joe Fassler, "Restaurant Workers Aren't Allowed to Get Sick," *The New Food Economy*, http://newfoodeconomy.com/giving-kitchen-staplehouse/ (accessed February 3, 2016).

17. Akihiko Hirose and Kay Kei-Ho Pih, "'No Asians Working Here': Racialized Otherness and Authenticity in Gastronomical Orientalism," *Ethnic and Racial Studies* 34, no. 9 (September 2011): 1482–501; Ana Swanson, "Why So Many of America's Sushi Restaurants Are Owned by Chinese Immigrants," *Washington Post*, September 29, 2016.

18. Anthony Bourdain, *Kitchen Confidential: Adventures in the Culinary Underbelly* (New York: Bloomsbury, 2000).

19. "Authenticity," *Webster's Dictionary*, https://www.merriam-webster.com/dictionary/authenticity (accessed October 22, 2018).

20. Sarah Portnoy, "Authenticity (of cuisines)," in Ken Albala, ed., *Sage Encyclopedia of Food Issues* (Los Angeles: Sage Publishing Co., 2015). Also see Sarah Portnoy and Jeffrey

Pilcher, "Roy Choi, Ricardo Zárate, and Pacific Fusion Cuisine in Los Angeles," in Matthew Gutmann and Jeffrey Lesser, eds., *Global Latin America* (Oakland: University of California Press, 2015); Meredith Abarca, "Authentic or Not, It's Original," *Food and Foodways* 12, no. 1 (2004): 1–25.

21. One extended study of the search for authentic foods as a search for exotic adventures is Lisa M. Heldke, *Exotic Appetites: Ruminations of a Food Adventurer* (New York: Routledge, 2003). Other studies that examine authenticity and food include Sherrie Inness, *Pilaf, Pozole, and Pad Thai: American Women and Ethnic Food* (Amherst: University of Massachusetts Press, 2001); Tobias Döring, Markus Heide, and Susanne Mühleisen, eds., *Eating Culture: The Poetics and Politics of Food* (Heidelberg: Winter, 2003); and Lucy M. Long, ed., *Culinary Tourism* (Lexington: University Press of Kentucky, 2004).

22. Jeffrey M. Pilcher, "'Old Stock' Tamales and Migrant Tacos: Taste, Authenticity, and the Naturalization of Mexican Food," *Social Research* 81, no. 2 (Summer 2014): 449–50.

23. Ibid., 455–56. Sharon Zukin quoted in the article. Warren Belasco, *Appetite for Change: How the Counterculture Took on the Food Industry*, 2nd ed. (Ithaca, NY: Cornell University Press, 2007).

24. See menus from India House (no date, circa 1960s), San Francisco, CA, CCSF, Folder, Calif.—San Francisco, H-L; Menu, Senor Pico, (circa 1964), San Francisco, CA, Paul Padgette restaurant menu collection, 1945–1990, BANC; For a representation of Chinese restaurants in the 1960s, see Leonce Picot, ed., *Gourmet International's Recommended Restaurants of San Francisco* (Ft. Lauderdale, FL: Gourmet International, 1963). Also see Raymond Ewell, *Dining Out in San Francisco and the Bay Area*, 2nd ed. (Berkeley, CA: Epicurean Press, 1948). Also see photos of restaurants in the San Francisco and Los Angeles public library collections.

25. Heldke, *Exotic Appetites,* and author's observations in many cities/suburbs.

26. Chuck Williams and Howard Lester, *Volume II, Williams-Sonoma: Mastering the Homeware: 1994–2004,* an oral history conducted in 2004 by Victor W. Geraci (Regional Oral History Office, BANC, 2005) http://digitalassets.lib.berkeley.edu/roho/ucb/text/Chuck WilliamsBook.pdf (accessed February 1, 2008), 13–14.

27. Judith Jones told French cookbook author Simone Beck that "a good little store like Williams-Sonoma will always carry *Simca's Cuisine* but not so the big bookstore chains like B. Dalton and Walden's, which seem to be running the country these days." Judith Jones to Simone Beck, April 5, 1979, JJMC, Box 847.9. Also see Elisabeth Ortiz to Sally Berkeley (Judith Jones's assistant), August 14, 1978, JJMC, Box 854.2, where Ortiz advises that Williams-Sonoma carry tortilla presses and advertise cookbooks next to "relevant equipment."

28. Williams-Sonoma, Inc., "Corporate Timeline" and "Williams-Sonoma, Inc.— Company Overview," http://www.williams-sonomainc.com (accessed January 4, 2008).

29. Charles E. Williams, *Williams-Sonoma Cookware and the American Kitchen: The Merchandising Vision of Chuck Williams, 1956–1994,* an oral history conducted 1992–1994 by Lisa Jacobson and Ruth Teiser (Regional Oral History Office, BANC, 1995) http://digitalassets.lib.berkeley.edu/roho/ucb/text/williams_chuck_vol_1.pdf (accessed February 1, 2008), 89–91. Williams mentions selling woks as well as promoting Italian cuisine at his stores.

30. Ibid., 129.

31. Ibid., 180.

32. There are thousands of examples of these stories, but some of the more prominent in recent years are Richard Rodriguez, *The Hunger of Memory: The Education of Richard Rodriguez, an Autobiography* (New York: Bantam, 1982); Jhumpa Lahiri, *The Namesake* (Boston: Houghton Mifflin, 2003); V. S. Naipaul, *A House for Mr. Biswas* (London: A. Deutsch, 1961); Andre Dubus, III, *House of Sand and Fog* (New York: W.W. Norton, 1999); Amy Tan, *The Joy Luck Club* (New York: Putnam, 1989). The stories of Edward Said and Bharati Mukherjee are in André Aciman, ed., *Letters of Transit: Reflections on Exile, Identity, Language, and Loss* (New York: The New Press, 1999). The "Postcolonial Studies @ Emory" website created by the English Department at Emory University contains biographies of dozens of writers on these topics at http://www.english.emory.edu/Bahri/index.html (accessed February 12, 2008).

33. Juana de Hidalgo, quoted in Manuel Gamio, *The Mexican Immigrant: His Life Story* (Chicago: University of Chicago, 1931), 162–63. Hidalgo was a pseudonym for the real interviewee. Several other immigrants that Gamio interviewed in 1926 and 1927 spoke of the foods they liked, whether they were Mexican, American, or a hybrid, and their reasons for favoring one or another.

34. Krishnendu Ray, *The Migrant's Table: Meals and Memories in Bengali-American Households* (Philadelphia: Temple University Press, 2004), 72.

35. Peter Leung and Tony Waters, "Chinese Vegetable Farming," in *Origins and Destinations: 41 Essays on Chinese America* (Los Angeles: Chinese Historical Society of Southern California and UCLA Asian American Studies Center, 1994), 437–52; Valerie Imbruce, *From Farm to Canal Street: Chinatown's Alternative Food Network in the Global Marketplace* (Ithaca, NY: Cornell University Press, 2015).

36. Steven Stern, "Based on an Old Family Recipe," *New York Times*, June 7, 2011.

37. Kim Severson, "Eddie Hernandez Doesn't Care If His Food Isn't 'Authentic,'" *New York Times*, April 9, 2018.

38. "Badmaash" *The Migrant Kitchen*, KCET, https://www.kcet.org/shows/the-migrant-kitchen/episodes/badmaash (accessed October 26, 2018). Badmaash means mischievous or a wicked sense of humor.

39. Ibid.

40. Ibid.

41. Katie Rogers, "Oberlin Students Take Culture War to the Dining Hall," *New York Times*, December 21, 2015. Quote from Oberlin Review.

42. Quoted in ibid.

43. Michelle Gross, Oberlin Director of Dining Services, quoted in ibid.

44. Frederik deBoer identified as an academic in ibid.

45. Josée Johnston and Shyon Baumann, *Foodies: Democracy and Distinction in the Gourmet Foodscape* (New York: Routledge, 2010), 70–94.

46. Ibid., 72.

47. Ibid., 89.

48. Florence Nagy, a fifty-one-year-old administrative assistant from Pennsylvania, quoted in ibid., 90.

49. Steven Shaw, "Empire of Egg Rolls," *Saveur*, February 2018, 16.

50. Ibid. To explain the difference between egg rolls served in China and those served at Empire Szechuan, Shaw notes, "Soo Lon Moy, curator of the Chinese-American Museum

of Chicago, says they're derived from lighter, skinnier Cantonese spring rolls, which were supersized by restaurateurs for the American market in the 1930s."

51. Umberto Eco, *Travels in Hyperreality: Essays*, translated by William Weaver (San Diego: Harcourt Brace Jovanovich, 1986).

52. On New York, see Sharon Zukin, *The Cultures of Cities* (Malden, MA: Blackwell Publishers, 1995); On Las Vegas, see John M. Findlay, *Magic Lands: Western Cityscapes and American Culture after 1940* (Berkeley: University of California, 1992).

53. Charles McGrath, "What Happened in Vegas Stayed in Vegas His Novel," *New York Times*, January 27, 2008.

54. Jon Pareles, "A Fan Base without Borders," *New York Times*, March 18, 2012. He gave the speech at the SXSW festival.

55. Rachel Laudan, "Desperately Seeking Authentic," *Los Angeles Times*, December 19, 2001.

56. John Whiting, "Authentic? Or Just Expensive," in Richard Hosking, ed., *Authenticity in the Kitchen: Proceedings of the Oxford Symposium on Food and Cookery 2005* (Totnes, UK: Prospect Books, 2006).

BIBLIOGRAPHY

PRIMARY SOURCES

Archival Collections

Alice Statler Library, City College of San Francisco
Menu Collection

Arthur and Elizabeth Schlesinger Library on the History of Women in America, Radcliffe Institute for Advanced Study, Harvard University, Cambridge, MA.
Papers of Avis MacVicar De Voto, 1904–, Papers 1952–1968, A-167.
Papers of Grace Zia Chu, 1941–1986, MC 641, MP-42, Vt-91.
Papers of Julia Child, 1890–2004 (bulk), 1950–2001 (inclusive), MC 660.

Asian American Studies Archives, Ethnic Studies Library, University of California, Berkeley
Him Mark Lai Papers, 1778–2002 (bulk 1970–1995), AAS ARC 2000/80
Nancy Wey Papers, 1860–1994, AAS ARC 2000/50

Austin History Center, Austin Public Library
Folders, AF Food F2500
Folders, AF Groceries G4200
Folders, AF Restaurants R3800

The Bancroft Library, University of California, Berkeley
Richard Brautigan Papers, 1958–1984, BANC MSS 87/173c
Fang Family San Francisco Examiner Photograph Archive Negative Files, circa 1930–2000

Paul Padgette restaurant menu collection, 1945–1990
San Francisco Bay Area restaurant menu collection, ca. 1955–1960

Benson Latin American Collection, General Libraries, University of Texas at Austin
Galindo Family Papers, ca. 1867–1950

Berkeley Public Library, Main Branch, Berkeley History Room
Clippings Files, Festivals/Events
Clippings Files, Restaurants

California Historical Society, North Baker Research Library, San Francisco, CA
Menu Collections

Hagley Museum and Library, Wilmington, DE
Ernest Dichter Papers

Harry Ransom Humanities Research Center, University of Texas at Austin
Judith Jones Manuscript Collection, Alfred A. Knopf, Inc., Records, 1873–1996, Series V.
    Editor Files

John W. Hartman Center for Sales, Advertising & Marketing History, David M. Rubenstein
Rare Book & Manuscript Library, Duke University
J. Walter Thompson Company Archives
Nicole Di Bona Peterson Collection of Advertising Cookbooks

National Archives and Records Administration, Denver, Broomfield, CO
Record Group 188, Records of the Office of Price Administration Records of Regional Land
    District Field Offices, Region 7, Denver.

National Archives and Records Administration, Pacific Region, San Bruno, CA
Office of Price Administration, Region 8, San Francisco District Office Case Files, RG 188

New York Public Library, Rare Books Division, Humanities and Social Sciences Library,
Main Branch
Menu Collection

Oakland History Room, Oakland Public Library, Main Branch
Vertical Files, Bay Area cities and counties
Vertical Files, Restaurants
Vertical Files, Tour Guides
Clippings Files, Bay Area cities and counties
Clippings Files, Restaurants
Clippings Files, Grocery
Clippings Files, Safeway

San Francisco History Center, San Francisco Public Library, Main Branch (SFHC)
Vertical Files, Menus
Vertical Files, Tour Guides, various
Vertical Files, Tour Organizations, various
Vertical Files, Restaurants, various
Jack Shelton's Private Guide to Restaurants
Robert Finigan's Private Guide to Restaurants

San Francisco Maritime National Historical Park, San Francisco, CA
American President Lines Archives

San Jose Public Library, Martin Luther King, Jr., Branch
California Room, Clippings Files
San Jose Mercury News Clippings Files

Newspapers, Magazines, Radio Programs, and Television Programs

ABC News
Advertising Age
Agricultural Outlook
Alameda Times Star (Alameda, CA)
Albany Times-Union
Amber Waves
American Fruit Grower
The Argus (Fremont, CA)
Asia Society
Asian Week
The Atlantic
Austin American-Statesman
Austin Business Journal
Bay City News (San Francisco, CA)
Bay Weekly (Annapolis, MD)
BBC News
Berkeley Gazette
Berkshire Eagle
Boston Globe
Broadcast
Business Mexico
Business Week
Chain Leader
Chicago Tribune
China Business Weekly
Chinatown News (Vancouver, BC)
Chinese Restaurant News
Civic Center News (San Francisco, CA)

Community Impact Newspaper (Pflugerville, TX)
Corporate Report
CrossBorder Monitor
The Daily Meal
The Daily Review (Hayward, CA)
The Daily Silver Belt (Miami, AZ)
Dallas Business Journal
Denver Post
Dollars and Sense
East Bay Express (Emeryville, CA)
East West
The Economist
El Chicano (San Bernardino, CA)
El Economista (Mexico City)
El Paso Herald-Post
Expansion Management Magazine
Financial Times
Flavor and Fortune
Food and Service
Food & Wine
Food Field Reporter
Forbes
Fort Worth Star-Telegram
Frontline
The Globe and Mail (Toronto)
Goldsea
Gourmet
The Guardian (London)
Harper's
Holiday
Honolulu Magazine
The Independent (London)
Jack Shelton's Private Guide to Restaurants
The Jackson County Times Journal
KCET
Kirkus Reviews
KQED
Lebanon Daily News (Lebanon, PA)
The Lima News (OH)
Los Angeles Daily News
Los Angeles Times
Management's Food Processing and Marketing
McCall's
Meat Retailer

Menu Magazine
Mesa Tribune (AZ)
Milling and Baking News
Mother Jones
NACLA Report on the Americas
National Post (Toronto)
National Public Radio
Nation's Business
Nation's Restaurant News
The New Food Economy
The News Hour with Jim Lehrer
Newsweek
New York
The New York Review of Books
New York Times
The New Yorker
North Bay Bohemian (Santa Rosa, CA)
North Texas e-news
Northwest Arkansas Times
NRA News
NY Resident Magazine
The Oakland Tribune
Orange County Register
The Packer
PG&E Progress
Prepared Foods
Progressive Grocer
Public Broadcasting System
The Public Interest
Publisher's Weekly
Reason
Rediff India Abroad
Restaurants USA
Reuters
Robert Finigan's Private Guide to Restaurants
Safeway News
Sales Management
San Antonio Express-News
San Antonio Light
San Diego Union-Tribune
San Francisco Chronicle
San Francisco Examiner
San Francisco Focus
San Jose Mercury

San Jose Mercury News
San Jose News
Santa Fe New Mexican
Saveur
Seattle Times
Slate
Snack Food and Wholesale Bakery
SourceMex Economic News and Analysis on Mexico
Southern Poverty Law Center: Intelligence Report
South Florida Sun-Sentinel
Sponsor
The Stanford Daily
Sunset
Supermarket News
Tampa Tribune
Texas Monthly
Texas Observer
Time
Time Asia
Toronto Star
Transpacific (Venice, CA)
Tri-Valley Herald (Pleasanton, CA)
U.S. News and World Report
USA Today
The Valley Independent (Monessen, PA)
The Virginian Pilot (Norfolk, VA)
Wall Street Journal
Washington Post
Weekly World News
Westword
Where San Francisco
Yuma Daily Sun (AZ)

Government Documents

Agricultural Marketing Service, Fruit and Vegetable Division, Market News Branch., USDA. *Marketing Chile Fruits and Melons: 1981 Season.* Bronx, NY: USDA, 1981.

Agriculture Fact Book 2000. Washington, DC: USDA, 2000.

Agriculture Fact Book, 2001–2002. Washington, DC: USDA, 2003.

The American Presidency Project. http://www.presidency.ucsb.edu

Antitrust Division, United States Justice Department. "Public Workshops: Agriculture and Antitrust Enforcement Issues in our 21st Century Economy," https://www.justice.gov/atr/events/public-workshops-agriculture-and-antitrust-enforcement-issues-our-21st-century-economy-10#dates

Barnes, Jessica S., and Claudette E. Bennett. *The Asian Population: 2000, Census 2000 Brief.* Washington, DC: US Census Bureau, 2002.

Barriga, Claudio, in collaboration with Alejandro Leon, Manuel Saavedra, and Richard D. Abbott. *The Fruit and Vegetable Export Sector of Chile: A Case Study of Institutional Cooperation*. US Agency for International Development, 1990.

Bill No. SB 582, April 11, 2005, CA Senate Committee on Business, Professions and Economic Development.

Bolling, Christine, and Agapi Somwaru. "U.S. Food Companies Access Foreign Markets through Direct Investments." *Food Review* 24, no. 3 (2001): 23–28.

Bolling, Chris, Javier Calderon Elizalde, and Charles Handy. "U.S. Firms Invest in Mexico's Processed Food Industry." *Food Review* 22, no. 2 (1999): 26–29.

Bureau of Labor Statistics. "Women in the Labor Force: A Databook." Washington, DC: Bureau of Labor Statistics, 2006. http://www.bls.gov/cps/wlf-databook-2006.pdf (accessed December 5, 2007).

Calvin, Linda, and Roberta Cook. *U.S. Fresh Fruit and Vegetable Marketing: Emerging Trade Practices, Trends, and Issues*. Washington, DC: ERS-USDA, 2001. http://www.ers.usda.gov/publications/aer795/aer795.pdf (accessed June 28, 2007).

Centers for Disease Control. "NCHS Data Brief No. 219." November 2015. https://www.cdc.gov/obesity/data/adult.html (accessed April 26, 2019)

Day-Rubenstein, Kelly, and Paul Helsey. "Plant Genetic Resources: New Rules for International Exchange." *Amber Waves* (June 2003) http://www.ers.usda.gov/AmberWaves/June03/Features/PlantGeneticResources.htm (accessed March 1, 2008).

Economic Report of the President, 2002 Report Spreadsheet Tables. Washington, DC: US Government Printing Office. 2002. http://www.gpoaccess.gov/eop/tables02.html#erp8 (accessed June 28, 2007).

El Aguila Food Prods. Inc. v. Gruma Corp., 131 Fed. Appx. 450 (5th Cir. 2005).

El Aquila Food Products v. Gruma Corp., 301 F. Supp. 2d 612 (S.D. Tex. 2003).

Fishbein, Meyer H., and Elaine E. Bennett. *Preliminary Inventory Number 32: Records of the Accounting Department of the Office of Price Administration*. Washington, DC: National Archives, 1951.

Foreign Agricultural Service, Horticultural and Tropical Products Division, USDA. *United States Horticultural Import Situation, 2002*. http://www.fas.usda.gov/htp/News/News02/03-02/Freelance%20Graphics%20-%20IMSUMARY.pdf (accessed June 26, 2007).

Foreign Agricultural Trade Service, USDA. "World Horticultural Trade and U.S. Export Opportunities, March 1997." http://www.fas.usda.gov/htp2/circular/1997/97-03/mar97htp2.html (accessed July 19, 2007).

Fryar, Cheryl D., Margaret D. Carroll, and Cynthia L. Odgen. "Prevalence of Overweight, Obesity, and Extreme Obesity among Adults: United States, 1960–62 through 2011–2012." *Health E-Stat*, September 2014, https://www.cdc.gov/nchs/data/hestat/obesity_adult_11_12/obesity_adult_11_12.htm (accessed April 26, 2019).

Gallo, Anthony E. *Food Marketing Review, 1994–95, AER#743*. Washington, DC: ERS-USDA, 1995.

Gehlhar, Mark, and Anita Regmi. "Shopping the Global Market for High-Value Foods." *Agricultural Outlook* (December 2002): 38–42

Gibson, Campbell, and Kay Jung. *Historical Census Statistics on the Foreign-Born Population of the United States: 1850 to 2000*. Washington, DC: US Census Bureau, 2006. http://

www.census.gov/population/www/documentation/twps0081/twps0081.pdf (accessed March 18, 2007).

Handy, Charles R., and Suchada Langley. "Food Processing in Mexico Attracts U.S. Investments." *Food Review* 16, no. 1 (U.S. Dept. of Agriculture) (January–April, 1993): 20–24.

Harris, J. Michael, Phil R. Kaufman, Steve W. Martinez (coordinator), and Charlene Price. *The U.S. Food Marketing System, 2002.* Washington, DC: ERS-USDA, 2002.

Historical Tables: Budget of the United States Government, Fiscal Year 2004. Washington, DC: GPO, 2003. http://www.gpoaccess.gov/usbudget/fy04/pdf/hist.pdf (accessed December 14, 2007).

Hobbs, Frank, and Nicole Stoops. *Demographic Trends of the 20th Century.* Washington, DC: U.S. Census Bureau, 2002.

Hoeffel, Elizabeth M., Sonya Rastogi, Myoung Ouk Kim, and Hasan Shahid. US Census Bureau, *The Asian Population 2010.* March 2012. https://www.census.gov/prod/cen2010/briefs/c2010br-11.pdf (accessed October 23, 2016).

Huang, Sophia Wu. *Global Trade Patterns in Fruits and Vegetables.* Washington, DC: ERS-USDA, 2004. http://www.ers.usda.gov/publications/WRS0406/WRS0406.pdf (accessed June 28, 2007).

Hubbard, R. Glenn. "An Agenda for Global Growth." December 6, 2002. http://www.whitehouse.gov/cea/agenda_for_global_growth_dec6_2002.pdf (accessed September 6, 2007).

INS. *2000 Statistical Yearbook of the Immigration and Naturalization Service.* Washington, DC: INS, 2002.

———. *2001 Statistical Yearbook of the Immigration and Naturalization Service: Tables Only.* Washington, DC: INS, 2001. http://www.ins.gov/graphics/aboutins/statistics/immigs.htm (accessed February 27, 2002).

Jekanowski, Mark D. "Causes and Consequences of Fast Food Sales Growth." *Food Review* 22, no. 1 (1999): 11–16. http://www.ers.usda.gov/publications/foodreview/jan1999/frjan99b.pdf (accessed January 4, 2007).

Kaufman, Phil R., Charles R. Handy, Edward W. McLaughlin, Kristen Park, and Geoffrey M. Green. *Understanding the Dynamics of Produce Markets: Consumption and Consolidation Grow, AIB #758.* Washington, DC: ERS-USDA, 1999.

Legal Office, Food and Agriculture Organization, United Nations. "International Treaty on Plant Genetic Resources for Food and Agriculture." http://www.fao.org/legal/TREATIES/033s-e.htm (accessed March 1, 2008).

Lucier, Gary, Susan Pollack, Mir Ali, and Agnes Perez. *Fruit and Vegetable Backgrounder, VGS-313-01.* Washington, DC: ERS-USDA, 2006.

Martinez, Steve W. *The U.S. Food Marketing System: Recent Developments, 1997–2006, ERR #42.* Washington, DC: ERS-USDA, 2007.

Office of Price Administration (OPA). "Facts You Should Know." Statement No. 2, November 1943. http://arcweb.sos.state.or.us/exhibits/ww2/services/price.htm (accessed October 1, 2007).

Perez, Agnes. "Grape Expectations: Abundant Quantity, High Quality." *Agricultural Outlook* (December 2002).

Pollack, Susan L., and Linda Calvin. *U.S.-Mexico Fruit and Vegetable Trade, 1970–92, Agricultural Economic Report 704.* Washington, DC: ERS-USDA, 1995.

Putnam, Judith Jones, and Jane E. Allshouse. *Food Consumption, Prices, and Expenditures, 1970–97, Statistical Bulletin No. 965.* Washington, DC: ERS-USDA, 1999. http://www.ers.usda.gov/publications/sb965/sb965.pdf (accessed June 21, 2007).

Putnam, Judy, and Jane Allshouse. "Imports' Share of U.S. Diet Rises in Late 1990s." *Food Review* 24, no. 3 (2001): 15–22. http://www.ers.usda.gov/publications/FoodReview/septdec01/FRv24i3.pdf (accessed September 11, 2007).

Reeves, Terrance J., and Claudette E. Bennett. *We the People: Asians in the United States.* Washington, DC: Census Bureau, 2004.

Regmi, Anita, ed. *Changing Structure of Global Food Consumption and Trade/WRS-01-1.* Washington, DC: ERS-USDA, 2001.

"Report of the Joint Special Committee to Investigate Chinese Immigration." *S. Rept. 689,* 44 Cong., 2 sess. (1877).

Ruppel, Fred. "Globalization of the Processed Foods Market: Part One: U.S. Trade in Processed Foods." *Agricultural Outlook,* January–February 1997.

Senate Committee on Commerce, Science, and Transportation. *Hearings on Agricultural Trade with Mexico.* 103rd Cong., 1st sess., July 22, 1993.

Stewart, Hayden, Noel Blisard, Sanjib Bhuyan, and Rodolfo M. Nayga Jr. *The Demand for Food away from Home: Full Service or Fast Food? AER-829.* Washington, DC: ERS-USDA, 2004.

United Nations. "International Treaty on Plant Genetic Resources for Food and Agriculture." ftp://ftp.fao.org/ag/cgrfa/it/ITPGRe.pdf (accessed March 1, 2008).

United Nations Population Division. "World Population Prospects: The 2006 Revision." http://esa.un.org/unpp/ (accessed July 19, 2007).

US Census Bureau. "A Look at the 1940 Census," https://www.census.gov/newsroom/cspan/1940census/CSPAN_1940slides.pdf (accessed January 22, 2017).

———. "The Foreign-Born Population in the United States." https://www.census.gov/newsroom/pdf/cspan_fb_slides.pdf (accessed December 1, 2016).

———. *Historical Census Statistics on the Foreign-Born Population of the United States: 1850–1990,* Working Paper No. 29, February 1999. http://www.census.gov/topics/population/foreign-born.html (accessed July 24, 2007).

———. *Measuring 50 Years of Economic Change Using the March Current Population Survey, Current Population Reports, P60-203.* Washington, DC: GPO, 1998.

———. *1970 Census of Population.* Washington, DC: US Department of Commerce, 1973.

———. *1992 Census of Retail Trade.* http://www.census.gov/epcd/www/rc92html.html (Last modified, 02/27/97).

———. *Statistical Abstract of the United States.* Washington, DC: US Census Bureau, 1982–83, 1992, 2001, 2002, 2003.

———. *Tortilla Manufacturing.* 1997 Economic Census, Manufacturing Industry Series. Washington, DC: US Census Bureau, 1999.

———. *Tortilla Manufacturing: 2002.* Washington, DC: US Census Bureau, 2004.

———. "Trade in Goods with Mexico" (Years 1995–2014). https://www.census.gov/foreign-trade/balance/c2010.html#1994 (accessed September 4, 2015).

———. *Yearbook of the Department of Agriculture, 1900.* Washington, DC: USDA, 1901.

US Commission on Civil Rights. *What Students Perceive.* Washington, DC: GPO, 1970.

USDA-ERS. "Food Away from Home as a Share of Food Expenditures." http://www.ers .usda.gov/data-products/food-expenditures.aspx (accessed January 7, 2016).

US Department of Homeland Security. *Yearbook of Immigration Statistics (1996–2014).* https://www.dhs.gov/immigration-statistics.

US Department of Labor. *100 Years of Consumer Spending: Data for the Nation, New York City, and Boston, Report 991.* Washington, DC: U.S. Department of Labor, 2006.

US Government Information. "Nixon Grand Jury Records." National Archives and Records Administration, https://www.gpo.gov/fdsys/pkg/GPO-NARA-WSPF-NIXON-GRAND -JURY-RECORDS/content-detail.html (accessed September 6, 2016).

US Public Health Service. *The Surgeon General's Call to Action to Prevent and Decrease Overweight and Obesity, 2001.* Rockville, MD: GPO, 2001.

War and Price Rationing Board. "It's Amazing!" Washington, DC: OPA, 1945.

Welsh, Susan O., Carole Davis, and Anne Shaw. *USDA's Food Guide: Background and Development.* Hyattsville, MD: USDA, 1993.

Wilkins, Nadine. Agricultural Marketing Service News Release AMS No. 203-10, October 22, 2010. http://www.ams.usda.gov/AMSv1.0/ams.fetchTemplateData.do?template=Template U&navID=&page=Newsroom&resultType=Details&dDocName=STELPRDC5087188&d ID=139375&wf=false&description=USDA+Cites+O%3FLippi+%26+Co.+Inc.+for+PACA +Violations+&topNav=&leftNav=&rightNav1=&rightNav2= (accessed January 6, 2015).

Other Primary Sources

Acton, Eliza. *Modern Cookery, in All Its Branches: Reduced to a System of Easy Practice, for the Use of Private Families.* Philadelphia: Lea and Blanchard, 1858.

Archer Daniels Midland. *Annual Report 2008.*

Anheuser-Busch InBev. *2014 Annual Report.*

Award Winning Chinese Recipes. Englewood Cliffs, NJ: CPC International, 1983.

Beck, Simone. *Simca's Cuisine.* New York: Knopf, 1972.

The Berlitz Traveler's Guide to San Francisco and Northern California. 4th ed. New York: Berlitz, 1994.

Better Homes and Gardens New Cook Book. Meredith Publishing, 1953.

Boeing. "LanChile Adds Three Boeing 767-300 Freighters to Its Fleet," (press release). http:// www.boeing.com/news/releases/2000/news_release_001218a.html (accessed June 21, 2007).

Bourdain, Anthony. *Kitchen Confidential: Adventures in the Culinary Underbelly.* New York: Bloomsbury, 2000.

Caen, Maria Theresa. *San Francisco Epicure: A Menu Guide to the San Francisco Area's Finest Restaurants.* Seattle: Peanut Butter Publishing, 1986.

Chiang, Cecilia Sun Yun. *The Mandarin Way.* Revised and expanded edition, as told to Allan Carr. San Francisco: California Living Books, 1980.

Child, Julia. *The French Chef Cookbook.* New York: Knopf, 1968.

Child, Julia, Louisette Bertholle, and Simone Beck. *Mastering the Art of French Cooking, Volume I.* New York, Knopf, 1973.

Child, Julia, and Simone Beck. *Mastering the Art of French Cooking, Volume II.* New York: Knopf, 1970.

Chu, Grace Zia. *Madame Chu's Chinese Cooking School*. New York: Simon and Schuster, 1975.

———. *The Pleasures of Chinese Cooking*. New York: Simon and Schuster, 1962.

Chun King and Mazola Home Service Department. *Quick, Easy and Intriguing Ways with American Oriental Cookery to Add Zest to Your Menus*. Consolidated Book Publishers, 1962.

Cityguide 1989/90: Alameda and Contra Costa Counties. Danville, CA: Shandra Publications, 1989.

Claiborne, Craig, and Virginia Lee. *The Chinese Cookbook*. Philadelphia: J.B. Lippincott, 1972.

Cost, Bruce. *Bruce Cost's Asian Ingredients*. New York: William Morrow and Company. 1988.

———. *Ginger: East to West*. Reading, MA: Aris Books, 1989.

Dole Food Company, Inc. *2005 All about Dole (Annual Report)*. http://www.dole.com /CompanyInfo/Relations/AnnualReports.jsp (accessed August 8, 2007).

Ewell, Raymond. *Dining Out in San Francisco and the Bay Area*. 2nd ed. Berkeley, CA: Epicurean Press, 1948.

Food Marketing Industry Speaks, 2003. Washington, DC: Food Marketing Institute, 2003.

Food Marketing Industry Speaks, 2004. Washington, DC: Food Marketing Institute, 2004.

Garrido, David, and Robb Walsh. *Nuevo Tex-Mex: Festive New Recipes from Just North of the Border*. San Francisco: Chronicle Books, 1998.

Great American Menus. Chicago: National Restaurant Association, 1964.

Great Menus: 1983. Washington, DC: National Restaurant Association, 1983.

Great Menus: 1985. Washington, DC: National Restaurant Association, 1986.

Grigson, Jane. *The Art of Charcuterie*. New York: Knopf, 1968.

———. *Good Things*. New York: Knopf, 1971.

———. *The Mushroom Feast*. New York: Knopf, 1975.

Gruma Corporation. Annual Reports and Form 20-Fs, 1990–2015.

Grupo Bimbo. Annual Reports, 1990–2015.

Howarth, Karen. *Gourmet Tortillas: Exotic and Traditional Tortilla Dishes*. Santa Fe, NM: Clear Light Publishers, 2000.

International Fruit World, in cooperation with ProChile, eds. *Chile: An Exporting Country for Fruit and Vegetables*. Basel, Switzerland: International Fruit World, 1987.

Jaffrey, Madhur. *An Invitation to Indian Cooking*. New York: Knopf, 1973.

———. *Climbing the Mango Trees*. New York: Knopf, 2006.

———. *Madhur Jaffrey's World of the East Vegetarian Cooking*. New York: Knopf, 1981.

Jones, Judith. *The Tenth Muse: My Life in Food*. New York: Knopf, 2007.

Kennedy, Diana. *The Essential Cuisines of Mexico*. New York: Clarkson Potter, 2000.

La Choy Food Products. *The Arts and Secrets of Chinese Cookery*. Detroit: La Choy Food Products, 1931.

———. *The Arts and Secrets of Chinese Cookery*. Archbold, OH: Beatrice: 1949.

LAN Airlines, S.A. *Annual Report 2006*. http://plane.lan.com/files/about-us/lanchile /memoria2006.pdf (accessed June 21, 2007).

Leonard, Jonathan Norton. *Foods of the World: American Cooking: The Great West*. New York: Time-Life Books, 1971.

————. *Foods of the World: American Cooking: New England*. New York: Time-Life Books, 1970.

Los Angeles Public Library Online Menu Collection. https://www.lapl.org/collections -resources/visual-collections/menu-collection (accessed September 2, 2016).

Los Angeles Public Library Photo Collection. http://photos.lapl.org/carlweb/jsp/photo search_pageADV.jsp.

Manhattan Menus: The Great Restaurant Guide. New York, 1983.

McDonald's. "McDonald's Facts Summary." 2006. http://www.mcdonalds.com/corp/about /factsheets.html (accessed August 17, 2007).

————. *McDonald's Food: The Facts*. Oak Brook, IL: McDonald's Corporation, 1986.

Mortimer, Robert C., Charles C. Mortimer, and Eleanor Nelson. *The Menu Guide of Kansas City*. Pacific Palisades, CA: Corm Enterprises, 1976.

Mortimer, Robert C., and Charles C. Mortimer, eds. *The Menu Guide of Los Angeles*. Pacific Palisades, CA: Corm Enterprises, 1976.

Nathan, Joan. *The New American Cooking*. New York: Knopf, 2005.

Novas, Himilce, and Rosemary Silva. *Latin American Cooking across the U.S.A.* New York: Knopf, 1997.

Ortiz, Elisabeth. *The Book of Latin American Cooking*. New York: Knopf, 1979.

"Owner Participation Agreement" between Rancho Cucamonga Redevelopment Agency and GRUMA Corporation Foods, Inc. January 18, 1996 (in possession of author).

Pacific Bell Smart Yellow Pages. San Francisco: Pacific Bell, 2000.

Panda Inn Mandarin Cuisine. "About Panda Inn." http://www.pandainn.com/default. asp?nav=about (accessed March 1, 2008).

Paulucci, Elizabeth. *Cookbook from a Melting Pot*. New York: Grosset & Dunlap, 1981.

PepsiCo. *Performance with Purpose: PepsiCo Annual Report, 2006*. Purchase, NY: PepsiCo, 2007. https://www.pepsico.com/docs/album/annual-reports/2006-Annual-English.pdf. (accessed September 3, 2007).

P.F. Chang's China Bistro, Inc., "Corporate Overview." http://www.pfcb.com/Investor CorporateOverview.html (accessed August 30, 2016).

Phan, Charles. *Vietnamese Home Cooking*. Berkeley, CA: Ten Speed Press, 2012.

Picot, Leonce, ed. *Gourmet International's Recommended Restaurants of San Francisco*. Ft. Lauderdale, FL: Gourmet International, 1963.

Roden, Claudia. *A Book of Middle Eastern Food*. New York: Knopf, 1972.

Safeway, Inc. *Annual Reports*. Oakland and Pleasanton, CA: Safeway, Inc., 1960–2016.

Sinclair, Upton. *The Jungle*, ed. Christopher Phelps. Boston: Bedford/St. Martin's, 2005.

Sokolov, Raymond. *The Saucier's Apprentice: A Modern Guide to Classic French Sauces for the Home*. New York: Knopf, 1976.

Starbucks Corp. *10-K Filing with the United States Securities and Exchange Commission for 10/1/2000*. http://www.secinfo.com/dr643.524k.htm (accessed August 17, 2007).

Sung, Esther. "A Conversation with Charles Phan." Epicurious. http://www.epicurious.com /articlesguides/chefsexperts/interviews/charles-phan-interview-recipes (accessed June 6, 2013).

Thomas, Anna. *Vegetarian Epicure, Book Two*. New York: Knopf, 1978.

Van Aken, Norman. *Norman's New World Cuisine*. New York: Random House, 1997.

Wallach, Jennifer Jensen, and Lindsey R. Swindall. *American Appetites: A Documentary Reader*. Fayettville: University of Arkansas Press, 2014.

Willson, Robert H., George Hodel, and Emilia Hodel. *Foreign Nationalities in San Francisco*. San Francisco, CA: 1951.

Yellow Pages. San Francisco: Pacific Telephone, 1965–2005.

SECONDARY SOURCES

Abarca, Meredith E. "Authentic or Not, Its Original." *Food and Foodways* 12, no. 1 (2004): 1–25.

Abarca, Meredith E., and Consuelo Carr Salas. *Latin@s' Presence in the Food Industry: Changing How We Think about Food*. Fayetteville: University of Arkansas Press, 2016.

Abbott, Carl. *The Metropolitan Frontier: Cities in the Modern American West*. Tucson: University of Arizona, 1994.

Achaya, K. T. *A Historical Dictionary of Indian Food*. New Delhi: Oxford University Press, 1998.

Aciman, André, ed. *Letters of Transit: Reflections on Exile, Identity, Language, and Loss*. New York: The New Press, 1999.

Adas, Michael, ed. *Essays on Twentieth Century History*. Philadelphia: Temple University Press, 2010.

Albala, Ken, ed. *Routledge International Handbook of Food Studies*. New York: Routledge, 2012.

———. *Sage Encyclopedia of Food Issues*. Los Angeles: Sage Publishing Co., 2015.

Allison, Harry E., Charles J. Zwick, and Ayres Brinser. "Menu Data and Their Contribution to Food Consumption Studies." *Journal of Farm Economics* 40, no. 1 (1958): 1–20.

Almas, Reidår, and Geoffrey Lawrence, eds. *Globalization, Localization and Sustainable Livelihoods*. Burlington, VT: Ashgate, 2003.

Alvarez, Robert B. Jr. *Mangos, Chiles and Truckers: The Business of Transnationalism*. Minneapolis: University of Minnesota Press, 2005.

Anderson, E. N. *Everyone Eats: Understanding Food and Culture*. New York: New York University Press, 2005.

Appadurai, Arjun. "How to Make a National Cuisine: Cookbooks in Contemporary India." *Comparative Studies in Society and History* 30, no. 1 (1988): 3–24.

Archer, John, Paul J. P. Sandul, and Katherine Solomonson, eds. *Making Suburbia: New Histories of Everyday America*. Minneapolis: University of Minnesota Press, 2015.

Arndt, Alice, ed. *Culinary Biographies*. Houston, TX: Yes Press, 2006.

The Asian Databook. Millerton, NY: Grey House Publishing, 2005.

Atkins, Peter, and Ian Bowler. *Food in Society: Economy, Culture, Geography*. London: Arnold, 2001.

Ayto, John, ed. *An A–Z of Food and Drink, Oxford Reference Online*. New York: Oxford University Press, 2002. https://www.oxfordreference.com/view/10.1093/acref/97801928 03511.001.0001/acref-9780192803511.

Babb, Sarah. *Managing Mexico: Economists from Nationalism to Neoliberalism*. Princeton, NJ: Princeton University Press, 2002.

Bacon, David. "Taking on the Tortilla King." September 22, 1996, at http://dbacon.igc.org/strikes/o6tortil.htm (accessed January 12, 2010).

Barbas, Samantha. "'I'll Take Chop Suey': Restaurants as Agents of Culinary and Cultural Change." *Journal of Popular Culture* 36, no. 4 (2003): 669–79.

Barber, Benjamin R. *Jihad vs. McWorld: Terrorism's Challenge to Democracy.* New York: Ballantine Books, 2001.

Barkan, Elliot R., Hasia Diner, and Alan Kraut, eds., *From Arrival to Incorporation: Migrants to the U.S. in a Global Era.* New York: New York University Press, 2007.

Barrett, James R. *Work and Community in the Jungle: Chicago's Packinghouse Workers, 1894–1922.* Champaign: University of Illinois, 1987.

Basu, Shrabani. *Curry in the Crown: The Story of Britain's Favourite Dish.* Delhi: Harper Collins, 1999.

Bégin, Camille, and Jayeeta Sharma. "A Culinary Hub in the Global City: Diasporic Food-scapes across Scarborough, Canada." *Food, Culture and Society* 21, no. 1 (2018): 55–74.

Belasco, Warren. *Appetite for Change: How the Counterculture Took on the Food Industry.* 2nd ed. Ithaca, NY: Cornell University Press, 2007.

———. *Food: The Key Concepts.* New York: Berg, 2008.

Belasco, Warren, and Roger Horowitz, eds. *Food Chains: From Farmyard to Shopping Cart.* Philadelphia: University of Pennsylvania Press, 2009.

Belasco, Warren, and Philip Scranton, eds. *Food Nations: Selling Taste in Consumer Societies.* New York: Routledge, 2002.

Bellman, Jonathan. "Indian Resonances in the British Invasion, 1965–1968." *Journal of Musicology* 15, no. 1 (1997): 116–36.

Bender, David A. *A Dictionary of Food and Nutrition, Oxford Reference Online.* New York: Oxford University Press, 2005.

Berger, Peter L., and Samuel P. Huntington, eds. *Many Globalizations: Cultural Diversity in the Contemporary World.* New York: Oxford University Press, 2002.

Berghoff, Hartmut, Philip Scranton, and Uwe Spiekermann, eds. *The Rise of Marketing and Market Research.* New York: Palgrave Macmillan, 2012.

Beriss, David, and David Sutton, eds. *The Restaurants Book: Ethnographies of Where We Eat.* New York: Berg, 2007.

Bernstein, Charles. *Sambo's: Only a Fraction of the Action.* Burbank, CA: National Literary Guild, 1984.

Berube, Alan. "The State of Metropolitan America: Suburbs and the 2010 Census." Presentation and Remarks, July 14, 2011, Brookings Institution. https://www.brookings.edu/on-the-record/the-state-of-metropolitan-america-suburbs-and-the-2010-census/ (accessed September 17, 2016).

Bestor, Theodore C. "Supply-Side Sushi: Commodity, Market, and the Global City." *American Anthropologist* 103, no. 1 (March 2001): 76–95.

Bivens, Terry, Ken Goldman, and Charles Z. Yan. *Packaged Food, China: This Time It's for Real!* New York: Bear Stearns Equity Research, May 2007.

Block, Jason, Richard A. Scribner, and Karen B. DeSalvo. "Fast Food, Race/Ethnicity, and Income: A Geographic Analysis." *American Journal of Preventive Medicine* 27, no. 3 (2004): 211–17.

Bonnano, Alessandro, et al., eds. *From Columbus to ConAgra: The Globalization of Agriculture and Food*. Lawrence: University Press of Kansas, 1994.

Boskin, Joseph. *Sambo: The Rise and Demise of an American Jester*. New York: Oxford University Press, 1986.

Boyd, Harper W. Jr., and Sidney J. Levy. "New Dimension in Consumer Analysis." *Harvard Business Review* 41, no. 6 (1963): 129–40.

Bradley, Mark Philip. *Imagining Vietnam and America: The Making of Postcolonial Vietnam, 1919–1950*. Chapel Hill: University of North Carolina Press, 2000.

Brandt, Steven C. "Dissecting the Segmentation Syndrome." *Journal of Marketing* 30, no. 4 (1966): 22–27.

Brenner, Leslie. *American Appetite: The Coming of Age of a Cuisine*. New York: Bard, 1999.

Broda, Christian, and David Weinstein. *Globalization and the Gains from Variety, Working Paper 10314*. Cambridge, MA: National Bureau of Economic Research, 2004.

Brown, Linda Keller, and Kay Mussell, eds. *Ethnic and Regional Foodways in the United States: The Performance of Group Identity*. Knoxville: University of Tennessee Press, 1984.

Browning, Anjali. "Corn, Tomatoes and a Dead Dog: Mexican Agricultural Restructuring after NAFTA and Rural Responses to Declining Maize Production in Oaxaca, Mexico." *Mexican Studies/Estudios Mexicanos* 29, no. 1 (Winter 2013): 85–119.

California Table Grape Commission. "Commodity Fact Sheet: Table Grapes." http://www .cfaitc.org/Commodity/pdf/TableGrapes.pdf (accessed June 22, 2007).

Cameron, Christopher David Ruiz. "Labor Law and Latcrit Identity Politics: The Labyrinth of Solidarity: Why the Future of the American Labor Movement Depends on Latino Workers." *University of Miami Law Review* 53 (July 1999).

Cantú, Lionel. "The Peripheralization of Rural America: A Case Study of Latino Migrants in America's Heartland." *Sociological Perspectives* 38, no. 3 (1995): 399–414.

Casaburi, Gabriel. *Dynamic Agroindustrial Clusters: The Political Economy of Competitive Sectors in Argentina and Chile*. New York: St. Martin's Press, 1999.

Center on Hunger and Poverty and Food Research and Action Center. "The Paradox of Hunger and Obesity in America." http://www.agnt.org/humane/hungerandobesity.pdf (accessed April 29, 2019).

Chain Store Guide 2001 Directory of Supermarket, Grocery and Convenience Store Chains. Tampa, FL: Business Guides, Inc., 2001.

Chan, Bill, and Stephen Rich. *The Yet Wah Story*. Burlingame, CA: Advanced Pub., 1989.

Chan, Sucheng. *This Bittersweet Soil: The Chinese in California Agriculture, 1860–1910*. Berkeley: University of California Press, 1986.

Chan, Sucheng, and Madeline Y. Hsu, eds. *Chinese Americans and the Politics of Race and Culture*. Philadelphia: Temple University Press, 2008.

Chang, K.C. *Food in Chinese Culture: Anthropological and Historical Perspectives*. New Haven, CT: Yale University Press, 1977.

Chang, Shenglin. *The Global Silicon Valley Home: Lives and Landscapes within Taiwanese American Trans-Pacific Culture*. Stanford, CA: Stanford University Press, 2006.

Chen, Yong. *Chinese San Francisco, 1850–1943: A Trans-Pacific Community*. Stanford, CA: Stanford University Press, 2000.

———. *Chop Suey, USA: The Story of Chinese Food in America*. New York: Columbia University Press, 2014.

Cheng, Cindy I-Fen. "Out of Chinatown and into the Suburbs: Chinese Americans and the Politics of Cultural Citizenship in Early Cold War America." *American Quarterly* 58, no. 4 (2006): 1067–90.

Chinese America: History and Perspectives 1994. San Francisco: Chinese Historical Society, 1994.

Chinese America: History and Perspectives 1995. San Francisco: Chinese Historical Society of America, 1995.

Chow, Rey. "How (the) Inscrutable Chinese Led to Globalized Theory." *PMLA* 116, no. 1 (2001): 69–74.

"Chun King Chow Mein." Television Commercial, 1960, Historic Films Archive. http://www.historicfilms.com/search/?type=all&q=%22chun+king%22#p1t7096i204802109 (accessed September 24, 2014).

Cinotto, Simone. "'Now That's Italian!' Representations of Italian Cuisine in American Popular Magazines, 1950–2000." The Italian Academy for Advanced Studies in America (2004). http://www.italianacademy.columbia.edu/pdfs/cinotto.pdf (accessed March 19, 2007).

Civitello, Linda. *Cuisine and Culture: A History of Food and People*. Hoboken, NJ: John Wiley, 2011.

Clarke, Colin, Ceri Peach, and Steven Vertovec. *South Asians Overseas: Migration and Ethnicity*. New York: Cambridge University Press, 1990.

Coe, Andrew. *Chop Suey*. New York: Oxford University Press, 2009.

Coe, Sophie. *America's First Cuisines*. Austin: University of Texas Press, 1994.

Cohen, Lizabeth. *A Consumer's Republic: The Politics of Mass Consumption in Postwar America*. New York: Knopf, 2003.

———. *Making a New Deal: Industrial Workers in Chicago, 1919–1939*. New York: Cambridge University Press, 1990.

Collingham, Lizzie. *Curry: A Tale of Cooks and Conquerors*. New York: Oxford University Press, 2006.

Cook, Roberta. "Challenges and Opportunities in the U.S. Fresh Produce Industry." *Journal of Food Distribution Research* 21, no. 1 (1990): 67–74.

———. *The Evolving Global Marketplace for Fruits and Vegetables*. Davis, CA: Agricultural Issues Center, 2003. http://www.agmrc.org/NR/rdonlyres/DCE3CA96-A372-4522-BD18-1FFD84A0CFF1/0/globalmarketplace.pdf (accessed June 26, 2007).

Counihan, Carole M., ed. *Food in the USA: A Reader*. New York: Routledge, 2002.

Counihan, Carole, and Penny Van Esterik. *Food and Culture: A Reader*. New York: Routledge, 1997.

Coyle, L. Patrick Jr. *Cook's Books: An Affectionate Guide to the Literature of Food and Cooking*. New York: Facts on File Publications, 1985.

Crafts, Nicholas. "Globalisation and Economic Growth: A Historical Perspective." *The World Economy* 27, no. 1 (January 2004): 45–58.

Cronon, William. *Nature's Metropolis: Chicago and the Great West*. New York: Norton, 1991.

Cudahy, Brian J. *Box Boats: How Container Ships Changed the World*. New York: Fordham University Press, 2006.

Cullather, Nick. "The Foreign Policy of the Calorie." *American Historical Review* 112, no. 2 (2007): 337–63.

Cusack, Igor. "African Cuisines: Recipes for Nation Building?" *Journal of African Cultural Studies* 13, no. 2 (2000): 207–25.

Cwiertka, Katarzyna J. *Modern Japanese Cuisine: Food, Power and National Identity.* London: Reaktion, 2006.

Daniels, Roger. *Coming to America: A History of Immigration and Ethnicity in American Life.* New York: Harper Perennial, 1990.

Daniels, Roger, and Otis L. Graham. *Debating American Immigration, 1882–Present.* Lanham, MD: Rowman & Littlefield, 2001.

Davis, Netta. "To Serve the 'Other': Chinese American Immigrants in the Restaurant Business." *Journal for the Study of Food and Society* 6, no. 1 (2002): 70–81.

Denker, Joel. *The World on a Plate: A Tour through the History of America's Ethnic Cuisine.* Lincoln: University of Nebraska Press, 2003.

Deutsch, Tracy. *Building a Housewife's Paradise: Gender, Politics, and American Grocery Stores in the Twentieth Century.* Chapel Hill: University of North Carolina Press, 2010.

Didion, Joan. *Slouching Towards Bethlehem.* New York: Farrar Straus & Giroux, 1968.

Diner, Hasia R. *Hungering for America: Italian, Irish, and Jewish Foodways in the Age of Immigration.* Cambridge, MA: Harvard University Press, 2001.

Dinnerstein, Leonard, and David Reimers. *Ethnic Americans: A History of Immigration.* 4th ed. New York: Columbia University Press, 1999.

Doganis, Rigas. *Flying off Course: The Economics of International Airlines.* 3rd ed. New York: Routledge, 2002.

Döring, Tobias, Markus Heide, and Susanne Mühleisen, eds. *Eating Culture: The Poetics and Politics of Food.* Heidelberg: Winter, 2003.

Dubus III, Andre. *House of Sand and Fog.* New York: W.W. Norton, 1999.

Eckes, Alfred E. Jr., and Thomas W. Zeiler. *Globalization and the American Century.* New York: Cambridge University Press, 2003.

Eco, Umberto. *Travels in Hyperreality: Essays.* Translated by William Weaver. San Diego: Harcourt Brace Jovanovich, 1986.

Encyclopedia of American Industries, Online Edition. Farmington Hills, MI: Gale Group, 2006.

Ethnic Cuisines: A Profile. Washington, DC: National Restaurant Association, 1995.

Ethnic Cuisines II. Washington, DC: National Restaurant Association, 2000.

Faiguenbaum, Sergio, Julio A. Berdegué, and Thomas Reardon. "The Rapid Rise of Supermarkets in Chile: Effects on Dairy, Vegetable, and Beef Chains." *Development Policy Review* 20, no. 4 (2002): 459–71.

Feeney, Jonathan P., John Baumgartner, and John P. San Marco. "800 Lb. Gorilla Goes on a Diet." Equity Research Report. New York: Wachovia Capital Markets, LLC, 2007.

Fernández-Armesto, Felipe. "Global Histories of Food." *Journal of Global History* 3 (2008): 459–62.

Findlay, John M. *Magic Lands: Western Cityscapes and American Culture after 1940.* Berkeley: University of California Press, 1992.

Flandrin, Jean-Louis, and Massimo Montanari, eds. *Food: A Culinary History.* Translated by Albert Sonnenfeld. New York: Columbia University Press, 1999.

Floyd, Janet, and Laurel Forster, eds. *The Recipe Reader*. Burlington, VT: Ashgate, 2003.

Fong, Timothy P. *The First Suburban Chinatown: The Remaking of Monterey Park, California*. Philadelphia: Temple University Press, 1994.

"Food Industry Consolidation." *Produce Marketer's Association*. http://new.pma.com/cig /intl/usMarketAndTrends.cfm (accessed August 8, 2007).

Food Selection: From Genes to Culture. Paris: The Danones Institute, 2000. http://www .danoneinstitute.org/publications/book/pdf/food_selection_10_levenstein.pdf (accessed April 16, 2007).

Freedman, Paul, ed. *Food: The History of Taste*. Berkeley: University of California Press, 2007.

Freedman, Paul, Joyce E. Chaplin, and Ken Albala, eds. *Food in Time and Place: The American Historical Association Companion to Food History*. Berkeley: University of California Press, 2014.

Freidberg, Susanne. *Fresh: A Perishable History*. Cambridge, MA: Harvard University Press, 2009.

Frewer, L. J., E. Riskvik, and H. Schifferstein. *Food, People and Society: A European Perspective of Consumers' Food Choices*. Berlin: Springer, 2001.

Frey, William H. *Diversity Explosion: How New Racial Demographics Are Remaking America*. Washington, DC: Brookings Institution Press, 2015.

———. "Melting Pot Suburbs: A Census 2000 Study of Suburban Diversity." *The Brookings Institution: Census 2000 Series*. June 2001. http://www.frey-demographer.org/reports /billf.pdf (accessed February 8, 2008).

———. "Melting Pot Cities and Suburbs: Racial and Ethnic Change in Metro America in the 2000s." *Metropolitan Policy Program at Brookings*, Brookings Institution, May 2011. https://www.brookings.edu/wp-content/uploads/2016/06/0504_census_ethnicity_frey .pdf (accessed September 17, 2016).

Friddle, Charlotte G., Sandeep Mangaraj, and Jean Kinsey. "The Food Service Industry: Trends and Changing Structure in the New Millennium." Working Paper 01-02, The Retail Food Industry Center, University of Minnesota, March 2001. http://agecon.lib .umn.edu/cgi-bin/pdf_view.pl?paperid=3093&ftype=.pdf (accessed August 17, 2007).

Friedmann, Harriet, and Philip McMichael. "Agriculture and the State System: The Rise and Decline of National Agricultures, 1870 to the Present." *Sociologia Ruralis* 29, no. 2 (1989), 93–117.

———. "Feeding the Empire: Pathologies of Globalized Agriculture." In *Socialist Register 2005: The Empire Reloaded*, edited by Leo Panitch and Colin Leys, 124–43. London: Merlin, 2004.

Friedman, Thomas. *The World Is Flat: A Brief History of the Twenty-First Century*. New York: Picador, 2007.

Gabaccia, Donna R. "Is Everywhere Nowhere? Nomads, Nations, and the Immigrant Paradigm of United States History." *Journal of American History* 86, no. 3 (1999): 1115–34.

———. *We Are What We Eat: Ethnic Food and the Making of Americans*. Cambridge, MA: Harvard University Press, 1999.

Gamio, Manuel, *The Mexican Immigrant: His Life Story*. Chicago: University of Chicago, 1931.

Gereffi, Gary, and Miguel Korzeniewicz, eds. *Commodity Chains and Global Capitalism.* Westport, CT: Greenwood Press, 1994.

Gómez, Laura E. "The Birth of the 'Hispanic' Generation: Attitudes of Mexican-American Political Elites toward the Hispanic Label." *Latin American Perspectives* 19, no. 4 (1992): 45–58.

Goody, Jack. *Cooking Cuisine and Class: A Study in Comparative Sociology.* New York: Cambridge University Press, 1982.

Gujral, Monish. *Moti Mahal's Tandoori Trail.* New Delhi: Thomson Press, 2004.

Gutmann, Matthew, and Jeffrey Lesser, eds. *Global Latin America.* Oakland: University of California Press, 2015.

Guzmán, Betsy. *The Hispanic Population: Census 2000 Brief.* Washington, DC: US Census Bureau, May 2001.

Haber, Barbara. *From Hardtack to Home Fries: An Uncommon History of American Cooks and Meals.* New York: The Free Press, 2002.

Hackett, Alice Payne, and James Henry Burke. *80 Years of Best Sellers: 1895–1975.* New York: R.R. Bowker Company, 1977.

Halberstam, David. *The Fifties.* New York: Fawcett Columbine, 1993.

Haley, Andrew. *Turning the Tables: Restaurants and the Rise of the American Middle Class: 1880–1920.* Chapel Hill: University of North Carolina, 2011.

Halter, Marilyn. *Shopping for Identity: The Marketing of Ethnicity.* New York: Schocken Books, 2000.

Harpell, Ron. "Review of *Banana Wars: Power, Production and History in the Americas,* by Steve Striffler and Mark Moberg, eds." *Business History Review* 79, no. 3 (2005): 661–64.

Harrison, Paul, and Fred Pearce. *AAAS Atlas of Population and the Environment.* Berkeley: University of California Press, 2000.

Hastert, Theresa A., Susan H. Babey, Allison L. Diamant, and E. Richard Brown. "More California Teens Consume Fast Food and Soda Each Day Than Five Servings of Fruits and Vegetables." *UCLA Health Policy Research Brief,* September 2005. http://www.healthpolicy.ucla.edu/pubs/files/teen_fastfood_PB.pdf (accessed March 25, 2008).

Held, David, and Anthony McGrew, eds. *The Global Transformations Reader: An Introduction to the Globalization Debate.* 2nd ed. Malden, MA: Polity, 2003.

———. *Globalization Theory: Approaches and Controversies.* Malden, MA: Polity, 2007.

Heldke, Lisa M. *Exotic Appetites: Ruminations of a Food Adventurer.* New York: Routledge, 2003.

Helstosky, Carol, ed. *The Routledge History of Food.* New York: Routledge, 2015.

Hirose, Akihiko, and Kay Kei-Ho Pih. "'No Asians Working Here': Racialized Otherness and Authenticity in Gastronomical Orientalism." *Ethnic and Racial Studies* 34, no. 9 (September 2011): 1482–501

Hoganson, Kristin L. *Consumer's Imperium: The Global Production of American Domesticity, 1865–1920.* Chapel Hill: University of North Carolina Press, 2007.

———. "Cosmopolitan Domesticity: Importing the American Dream, 1865–1920." *The American Historical Review* 107, no. 1 (2002): 55–83.

Holmes, Seth M. *Fresh Fruit, Broken Bodies: Migrant Farmworkers in the United States.* Berkeley: University of California Press, 2013.

Holton, Robert. "Globalization's Cultural Consequences." *The Annals of the American Academy of Political and Social Science* 570 (2000): 140–52.

Hönnighausen, Lothar, Marc Frey, James Peacock, and Niklaus Steiner, eds. *Regionalism in the Age of Globalism, Volume 1: Concepts of Regionalism.* Madison: Center for the Study of Upper Midwestern Cultures, University of Wisconsin, 2005.

Hopkins, A. G. *American Empire: A Global History.* Princeton, NJ: Princeton University Press, 2018.

———. *Globalization in World History.* New York: Norton, 2002.

Horowitz, Daniel. *The Anxieties of Affluence: Critiques of American Consumer Culture, 1939–1979.* Amherst: University of Massachusetts Press, 2004.

HoSang, Daniel Martinez. *Racial Propositions: Ballot Initiatives and the Making of Postwar California.* Berkeley: University of California Press, 2010.

Hosking, Richard, ed. *Authenticity in the Kitchen: Proceedings of the Oxford Symposium on Food and Cookery 2005.* Totnes, UK: Prospect Books, 2006.

Howard, Philip H. *Concentration and Power in the Food System.* New York: Bloomsbury, 2016.

———. "Consolidation in the North American Organic Food Processing Sector, 1997 to 2007." *International Journal of Sociology of Agriculture and Food* 16, no. 1 (2009): 13–30.

———. "Organic Processing Industry Structure." Michigan State University. https://msu.edu/~howardp/organicindustry.html (accessed January 14, 2016).

Howsam, Leslie, ed. *Food, Cookery and Culture.* Windsor, ON: Humanities Research Group, University of Windsor, 1998.

Hsu, Madeline Y. *Dreaming of Gold, Dreaming of Home: Transnationalism and Migration between the United States and South China, 1882–1943.* Stanford, CA: Stanford University Press, 2000.

———. "From Chop Suey to Mandarin Cuisine: Fine Dining and the Refashioning of Chinese Ethnicity during the Cold War Era." http://www.instrcc.ubc.ca/History485_2008/Hsu.pdf (accessed February 18, 2008).

Hu-Dehart, Evelyn. "Globalization and Is Discontents: Exposing the Underside." *Frontiers: A Journal of Women Studies* 24, nos. 2–3 (2003): 244–60.

Hurley, Andrew. "From Hash House to Family Restaurant: The Transformation of the Diner and Post-World War II Consumer Culture." *Journal of American History* 83, no. 4 (1997): 1282–308.

Hydak, Michael G. "The Menu as Culture Capsule." *Modern Language Journal* 62, no. 3 (2002): 58–64.

Imbruce, Valerie. *From Farm to Canal Street: Chinatown's Alternative Food Network in the Global Marketplace.* Ithaca, NY: Cornell University Press, 2015.

Inglis, David, and Debra Gimlin. *The Globalization of Food.* New York: Berg, 2009.

Inness, Sherrie A. *Dinner Roles: American Women and Culinary Culture.* Iowa City: University of Iowa Press, 2001.

———, ed. *Kitchen Culture in America: Popular Representations of Food, Gender, and Race.* Philadelphia: University of Pennsylvania Press, 2001.

———. *Pilaf, Pozole, and Pad Thai: American Women and Ethnic Food.* Amherst: University of Massachusetts Press, 2001.

Isaacs, Harold R. *Images of Asia: American Views of China and India*. New York: Harper and Row, 1972.

Issenberg, Sasha. *The Sushi Economy: Globalization and the Making of a Modern Delicacy.* New York: Gotham, 2007.

Isserman, Maurice, and Michael Kazin. *America Divided: The Civil War of the 1960s*. 2nd ed. New York: Oxford University Press, 2004.

Jackson, Kenneth. *Crabgrass Frontier: The Suburbanization of the United States*. New York: Oxford University Press, 1985.

Jackson, W. L. *The San Francisco Wholesale Produce Market*. Berkeley, CA: 1926.

Jacobs, Meg. "'How about Some Meat?' The Office of Price Administration, Consumption Politics, and State Building from the Bottom Up, 1941–1946." *Journal of American History* 84, no. 3 (1997): 910–41.

Jacobson, Matthew Frye. *Roots Too: White Ethnic Revival in Post-Civil Rights America.* Cambridge, MA: Harvard University Press, 2006.

Jain, Usha R. *The Gujaratis of San Francisco*. New York: AMS Press, Inc., 1989.

Jakle, John A., and Keith A. Sculle. *Fast Food: Roadside Restaurants in the Automobile Age.* Baltimore: The Johns Hopkins University Press, 1999.

Jayaraman, Saru. *Behind the Kitchen Door*. Ithaca, NY: Cornell University Press, 2013.

Jayasanker, Laresh. "Tortilla Politics: Mexican Food, Globalization, and the Sunbelt." In *Sunbelt Rising: The Politics of Place, Space, and Region*, edited by Michelle Nickerson and Darren Dochuk, 316–34. Philadelphia: University of Pennsylvania Press, 2011.

The Jim Crow Museum of Racist Imagery. Ferris State University, Big Rapids, MI. http://www.ferris.edu/jimcrow/.

Johnston, Josée, and Shyon Baumann. "Democracy versus Distinction: A Study of Omnivorousness in Gourmet Food Writing." *American Journal of Sociology* 113, no. 1 (2007): 165–204.

———. *Foodies: Democracy and Distinction in the Gourmet Foodscape* (New York: Routledge, 2010).

Jurafsky, Dan. *The Language of Food: A Linguist Reads the Menu*. New York: Norton, 2014.

Kahn, Barbara E., and Leigh McAlister. *Grocery Revolution: The New Focus on the Consumer*. Reading, MA: Addison-Wesley, 1997.

Kandel, William, and Emilio A. Parrado. "Restructuring of the US Meat Processing Industry and New Hispanic Migrant Destinations." *Population and Development Review* 31, no. 3 (2005): 447–71.

Kennedy, David M. *Freedom from Fear: The American People in Depression and War, 1929–1945*. New York: Oxford University Press, 1999.

Kiefer, Nicholas. "Economics and the Origins of the Restaurant." *Cornell Hotel and Restaurant Administration Quarterly* 43, no. 2 (2002): 58–64.

King, Robert F., and Paul F. Phumpiu. "Reengineering the Food Supply Chain: The ECR Initiative in the Grocery Industry." Proceedings Issue, *American Journal of Agricultural Economics* 78, no. 5 (1996): 1181–86.

Kinsey, Jean. "A Faster, Leaner, Supply Chain: New Uses of Information Technology." Proceedings Issue, *American Journal of Agricultural Economics* 82, no. 5 (2000): 1123–29.

Kinsey, Jean D., Elaine M. Jacobson, Ajay S. Behl, and Jonathan M. Seltzer. *The 2003 Supermarket Panel: Annual Report*. St. Paul: The Food Industry Center, University of Minnesota, 2003. http://agecon.lib.umn.edu/cgi-bin/pdf_view.pl?paperid=13633&ftype=.pdf (accessed September 1, 2007).

Kiple, Kenneth F. *A Moveable Feast: Ten Millenia of Food Globalization*. New York: Cambridge University Press, 2007.

Kiple, Kenneth F., and Kriemhild Coneè Ornelas, eds. *The Cambridge World History of Food*. Vols. 1 and 2. New York: Cambridge University Press, 2000.

Kittler, Pamela Goyan, and Kathryn P. Sucher. *Food and Culture*. 3rd ed. Belmont, CA: Wadsworth/Thomson Learning, 2001.

Kroc, Ray (with Robert Anderson). *Grinding It Out: The Making of McDonald's*. New York: St. Martin's, 1987.

Krugman, Paul, Richard Cooper, and T. N. Srinivasan. "Growing World Trade: Causes and Consequences." 25th Anniversary Issue. *Brookings Papers on Economic Activity 1995*, no. 1 (1995): 327–77.

Kruse, Kevin M., and Thomas J. Sugrue, eds. *The New Suburban History*. Chicago: The University of Chicago Press, 2006.

Ku, Robert Ji-Song. *Dubious Gastronomy: The Cultural Politics of Eating Asian in the USA*. Honolulu: University of Hawai'i Press, 2014.

LaFeber, Walter. *The New Empire: An Interpretation of American Expansion, 1860–1898*. Ithaca, NY: Cornell University Press, 1963.

Lahiri, Jhumpa. *The Namesake*. Boston: Houghton Mifflin, 2003.

Lang, Robert E., and Patrick A. Simmons. "'Boomburbs': The Emergence of Large, Fast-Growing Suburban Cities in the United States." Fannie Mae Foundation Census Note 06 (June 2001). http://www.fanniemaefoundation.org/programs/census_notes_6.shtml (accessed September 3, 2006).

Larsen, Spencer A. *Air Cargo Potential in Fresh Fruits and Vegetables*. Detroit: Wayne University Press, 1944.

Laudan, Rachel. *Cuisine and Empire: Cooking in World History*. Berkeley: University of California Press, 2013.

LaVigne, David. "The 'Black Fellows' of the Mesabi Iron Range: European Immigrants and Racial Differentiation during the Early Twentieth Century." *Journal of American Ethnic History* 36, no. 2 (Winter 2017): 11–39.

Lechner, Frank, and John Boli. *The Globalization Reader*. 3rd ed. Malden, MA: Blackwell, 2008.

Lee, Khai Sheang, Guan Hua Lim, and Soo Jiuan Tan. "Limitations of Conventional Strategy Frameworks when Applied to SMEs: Lessons from a Case Study." Small Business Advancement Center, University of Central Arkansas. http://sbaer.uca.edu/research/icsb/1999/28.pdf (accessed October 2, 2014).

Leonard, Karen Isaksen. *The South Asian Americans*. Westport, CT: Greenwood Press, 1997.

Leong-Salobir, Cecilia. "'Cookie' and 'Jungle Boy': A Historical Sketch of the Different Cooks for Different Folks in British Colonial Southeast Asia, ca. 1850–1960." *Global Food History* 1, no. 1 (2015): 59–80.

Levenstein, Harvey. *Paradox of Plenty: A Social History of Eating in Modern America*. Berkeley: University of California Press, 2003.

Levinson, Marc. *The Box: How the Shipping Container Made the World Smaller and the World Economy Bigger*. Princeton, NJ: Princeton University Press, 2006.

Levitt, Theodore. "The Globalization of Markets." *Harvard Business Review* 61, no. 3 (1983): 92–102.

Lichtenstein, Nelson. *The Retail Revolution: How Walmart Created a Brave New World of Business*. New York: Metropolitan Books, 2009.

———, ed. *Walmart: The Face of Twenty-First-Century Capitalism*. New York: The New Press, 2006.

Light, Ivan. "From Vice District to Tourist Attraction: The Moral Career of American Chinatowns, 1880–1940." *Pacific Historical Review* 43, no. 3 (1974): 367–94.

Liu, Haiming. *From Canton Restaurant to Panda Express*. New Brunswick: Rutgers University Press, 2015.

Lo, Malinda. "'Authentic' Chinese Food: Chinese American Cookbooks and the Regulation of Ethnic Identity." Paper presented at the Association for Asian American Studies, March 2001. http://www.malindalo.com/chinesefood.htm (accessed March 23, 2007).

Lockwood, William G. "Ethnic Cuisines." In *Encyclopedia of Food and Culture*. Vol. 3. Edited by Solomon H. Katz, 442–46. New York: Scribner, 2003

Long, Lucy M., ed. *Culinary Tourism*. Lexington: University Press of Kentucky, 2004.

———, ed. *Ethnic American Food Today: A Cultural Encyclopedia*. Lanham, MD: Rowman & Littlefield, 2015.

Love, John F. *McDonald's: Behind the Arches*. New York: Bantam, 1986.

Lu, Shun, and Gary Alan Fine. "The Presentation of Ethnic Authenticity: Chinese Food as a Social Accomplishment." *The Sociological Quarterly* 36, no. 3 (1995): 535–53.

Lusk, Jayson L., Jutta Roosen, and Jason F. Shogren, eds. *The Oxford Handbook of the Economics of Food Consumption and Policy*. New York: Oxford University Press, 2011.

Lyon, David W. *Global California: The Connection to Asia*. San Francisco: Public Policy Institute of California, 2003.

Macbeth, Helen, and Jeremy MacClancy, eds. *Researching Food Habits: Methods and Problems*. New York: Berghahn Books, 2004.

MacCannell, Dean. "Staged Authenticity: Arrangements of Social Space in Tourist Settings." *American Journal of Sociology* 79, no. 3 (1973): 589–603.

MacMillan, Margaret. *Nixon and Mao: The Week That Changed the World*. New York: Random House, 2008.

Maddison, Angus. *Contours of the World Economy, 1–2030 AD*. New York: Oxford University Press, 2007.

———. *The World Economy: A Millennial Perspective*. Paris: Development Centre of the Organisation for Economic Co-operation and Development, 2001.

Mainer, Robert, and Charles C. Slater. "Markets in Motion." *Harvard Business Review* 42, no. 2 (1964): 75–82.

Mannur, Anita. "Asian American Food-Scapes." *Amerasia Journal* 32, no. 2 (2006): 1–5.

Marrewijk, Charles Van. *International Trade*. New York: Oxford University Press, 2017.

Martineau, Pierre. "Social Classes and Spending Behavior." *Journal of Marketing* 23, no. 2 (1958): 121–30.

Masson, Paul. "Globalization: Facts and Figures." IMF Policy Discussion Paper, No, 01/4. October 2001.

Massey, Douglas S., Jorge Durand, and Nolan J. Malone. *Beyond Smoke and Mirrors: Mexican Immigration in an Era of Economic Integration.* New York: Russell Sage, 2002.

Matthew, H. C. G, and Brian Harrison, eds. *Oxford Dictionary of National Biography.* Oxford: Oxford University Press, 2004.

McMichael, Philip. "Rethinking Globalization: The Agrarian Question Revisited." *Review of International Political Economy* 4, no. 4 (Winter 1997): 630–62.

Menu Analysis 1993. Washington, DC: National Restaurant Association, 1993.

Menu Analysis 1997. Washington, DC: National Restaurant Association, 1998.

Mercogliano, Salvatore R. "The Container Revolution." *Sea History* 114 (2006): 8–11. http://www.sname.org/newsletter/SeaHistoryContnrShps.pdf (accessed July 9, 2007).

Messinger, Paul R., and Chakravarthi Narasimhan. "A Model of Retail Formats Based on Consumers' Economizing of Shopping Time." *Marketing Science* 16, no. 1 (1997): 1–23.

Milani, Michael. *It Happens Every Morning: A Chronicle of the Bay Area Produce Industry.* San Mateo, CA: Papa's Publishing, 1996.

Mintz, Sidney. *Sweetness and Power: The Place of Sugar in Modern History.* New York: Penguin, 1985.

———. *Tasting Food, Tasting Freedom.* Boston: Beacon Press, 1996.

Mintz, Sidney W., and Christine M. Du Bois. "The Anthropology of Food and Eating." *Annual Review of Anthropology* 31 (2002): 99–119.

Mintz, Steven, and Susan Kellogg. *Domestic Revolutions: A Social History of American Family Life.* New York: The Free Press, 1988.

Mitchell, Kenneth Edward. *State-Society Relations in Mexico.* Burlington, VT: Ashgate, 2001.

Mohl, Raymond A. "Globalization, Latinization, and the Nuevo New South." *Journal of American Ethnic History* 22, no. 4 (2003): 31–66.

Moreton, Bethany. *To Serve God and Walmart: The Making of Christian Free Enterprise.* Cambridge, MA: Harvard University Press, 2009.

Muller, Peter O. "The Suburban Transformation of the Globalizing American City." *Annals of the American Academy of Political and Social Science* 551 (1997): 44–58.

Muscatine, Doris. *A Cook's Tour of San Francisco: The Best Restaurants and their Recipes.* New York: Charles Scribner and Sons, 1963.

Naipaul, V. S. *A House for Mr. Biswas.* London: A. Deutsch, 1961.

Newman, Jacqueline M. *Food Culture in China.* Westport, CT: Greenwood Press, 2004.

———. "La Choy: Going on Seventy-Five." *Flavor and Fortune* 11, no. 2 (Summer 2004): 5, 32–33.

Ngai, Mae M. *Impossible Subjects: Illegal Aliens and the Making of Modern America.* Updated ed. Princeton, NJ: Princeton University Press, 2014.

NPD Group. "U.S. Total Restaurant Count Increases by 4,442 Units over Last Year, Reports NPD." January 23, 2013. https://www.npd.com/wps/portal/npd/us/news/press-releases/us-total-restaurant-count-increases-by-4442-units-over-last-year-reports-npd/ (accessed January 11, 2016).

Nutrition Data: Know What You Eat. "Bananas, Raw Nutrition Facts and Calories." *Self.* http://www.nutritiondata.com/facts-C00001-01c20Tm.html (accessed August 8, 2007).

Nützenadel, Alexander, and Frank Trentmann, eds. *Food and Globalization: Consumption, Markets and Politics in the Modern World.* New York: Berg, 2008.

Oates, N. Stanley, ed. *Outlook for Air Cargo in Fresh Produce.* Detroit: Wayne University Press, 1944.

Ochoa, Enrique C. *Feeding Mexico: The Political Uses of Food since 1910.* Wilmington, DE: Scholarly Resources, 2000.

O'Connor, John M. "Food Product Proliferation: A Market Structure Analysis." *American Journal of Agricultural Economics* 63, no. 4 (1981): 607–17.

Oliver, Sandra. "Ruminations on the State of American Food History." *Gastronomica: The Journal of Food and Culture* 6, no. 4 (2006): 91–98.

Opie, Frederick Douglass. *Hog and Hominy: Soul Food from Africa to America.* New York: Columbia University Press, 2008.

Orfield, Gary, and Chungmei Lee. "*Brown* at 50: King's Dream or *Plessy*'s Nightmare?" Civil Rights Project, Harvard University, 2004. www.civilrightsproject.harvard.edu (accessed May 23, 2004).

Origins and Destinations: 41 Essays on Chinese America. Los Angeles: Chinese Historical Society of Southern California and UCLA Asian American Studies Center, 1994.

O'Rourke, Kevin H., and Jeffrey G. Williamson. "When Did Globalization Begin?" National Bureau of Economic Research Working Paper 7632, http://www.nber.org/papers/w7632 (accessed August 28, 2007).

Ortiz-Ospina, Esteban, and Max Roser. "International Trade." *OurWorldinData.org*, https://ourworldindata.org/international-trade (accessed March 1, 2018).

Osterhammel, Jürgen, and Niels P. Petersson. *Globalization: A Short History.* Translated by Dona Geyer. Princeton, NJ: Princeton University Press, 2005.

Oxfam International. "Behind the Brands." Oxfam Briefing Paper. February 2013, www.oxfam.org (accessed January 14, 2016).

———. "Double-Edged Prices." Oxfam Briefing Paper. October 2008. http://www.oxfam.org.uk/resources/policy/conflict_disasters/downloads/bp121_food_price_crisis.pdf (accessed February 3, 2009).

Oxford English Dictionary Online. 2nd ed. https://www.oed.com/.

Padoongpatt, Tanachai Mark. "Too Hot to Handle." *Radical History Review* 110 (Spring 2011): 83–108.

Papademetriou, Minas K., and Edward M. Herath, eds. *Deciduous Fruit Production in Asia and the Pacific.* Bangkok: FAO, 1999.

Paral, Rob. "No Way In: U.S. Immigration Policy Leaves Few Legal Options for Mexican Workers." *Immigration Policy in Focus* 4, no. 5 (2005). http://robparal.com/downloads/nowayin.htm (accessed February 8, 2008).

Park, Kyeyoung. "Use and Abuse of Race and Culture: Black-Korean Tension in America." *American Anthropologist* 98, New Series, no. 3 (1996): 492–99.

Paterson, Thomas G., ed. *American Imperialism and Anti-Imperialism.* New York: Thomas Y. Crowell, 1973.

Patterson, James T. *Restless Giant: The United States from Watergate to Bush v. Gore*. New York: Oxford University Press, 2005.

Pavesic, David V. *Restaurant Manager's Pocket Handbook*. New York: Lebhar-Friedman, 1999.

Peck, David R. "Beatles Orientalis: Influences from Asia in a Popular Song Tradition." *Asian Music* 16, no. 1 (1985): 83–149.

Peters, Erica J. *San Francisco: A Food Biography*. Lanham, MD: Rowman & Littlefield, 2013.

Pew Research Center. *The Rise of Asian Americans*. Washington, DC: Pew Research Center, 2013.

Pilcher, Jeffrey M. *Planet Taco: A Global History of Mexican Food*. New York: Oxford University Press, 2012.

———. "'Old Stock' Tamales and Migrant Tacos: Taste, Authenticity, and the Naturalization of Mexican Food." *Social Research* 81, no. 2 (Summer 2014): 449–50.

———, ed. *The Oxford Handbook of Food History*. New York: Oxford University Press, 2012.

———. *¡Que Vivan los Tamales! Food and the Making of Mexican Identity*. Albuquerque: University of New Mexico Press, 1998.

———. "Tex-Mex, Cal-Mex, New-Mex, or whose Mex? Notes on the Historical Geography of Southwestern Cuisine." *Journal of the Southwest* 43, no. 4 (2001): 659–80.

The Pioneer Woman. Food Network. www.foodnetwork.com.

Pirog, Rich. "Grape Expectations: A Food System Perspective on Redeveloping the Iowa Grape Industry." Ames, Iowa: Leopold Center for Sustainable Agriculture, 2002. http://www.leopold.iastate.edu/pubs/staff/grapes/Grape.pdf (accessed June 28, 2007).

Plunkett, Jack. *Plunkett's Food Industry Almanac*. Houston, TX: Plunkett Research, Ltd., 2003.

Pollan, Michael. *The Omnivore's Dilemma: A Natural History of Four Meals*. New York: Penguin Press, 2006.

Potrafke, Niklas. "The Evidence on Globalisation." *The World Economy* 38, no. 3 (March 2015): 509–52.

Prescott-Allen, Robert, and Christine Prescott-Allen. "How Many Plants Feed the World?" *Conservation Biology* 4, no. 4 (1990): 365–74.

Pretter, Yitzie. "Culture and Ethnicity in Consumer Decision Making." *TABS Journal*, Spring 2002: 167–74.

Produce Marketing Association. "U.S. Supply Chain Flow Chart." http://new.pma.com/cig/intl/usMarketAndTrends.cfm (accessed August 8, 2007).

Progressive Grocer. *Progressive Grocer's 1977 Marketing Guidebook*. New York: American Can Company, 1976.

———. *Progressive Grocer's 1992 Marketing Guidebook*. Stamford, CT: Progressive Grocer Trade Dimensions, 1991.

Purkayastha, Bandana. *Negotiating Ethnicity: Second-Generation South Asian Americans Traverse a Transnational World*. New Brunswick, NJ: Rutgers University Press, 2005.

Putnam, Robert. "*E Pluribus Unum*: Diversity and Community in the Twenty-First Century, The 2006 Johan Skytte Prize Lecture." *Scandinavian Political Studies* 30, no. 2 (2007): 137–74.

Radice, Judi. *Menu Design*. Locust Valley, New York: PBC International, 1985.

Ray, Krishnendu. *The Ethnic Restaurateur*. New York: Bloomsbury, 2016

———. *The Migrant's Table: Meals and Memories in Bengali-American Households*. Philadelphia: Temple University Press, 2004.

Ray, Krishnendu, and Tulasi Srinivas, eds. *Curried Cultures: Globalization, Food, and South Asia*. Berkeley: University of California Press, 2012.

Reardon, Joan. "Mastering the Art of French Cooking." *Gastronomica* 5, no. 3 (2005): 62–72.

Reardon, Thomas, and Julio A. Berdegué. "The Rapid Rise of Supermarkets in Latin America: Challenges and Opportunities for Development." *Development Policy Review* 20, no. 4 (2002): 371–88.

Reich, Ken. "A Memorial to David Shaw." *Take Back the Times*, August 5, 2005. http://takeback thetimes.blogspot.com/2005/08/memorial-to-david-shaw.html (accessed March 1, 2008).

Reicks, Marla. "Fast Food Consumption among Minority Adults and Adolescents." *Nutrinet*, January 2005. http://www.fsci.umn.edu/outreach/faculty_outreach/nutrinet/archives /january_2005/fast_food.html (accessed March 25, 2005).

Reimers, David M. *Still the Golden Door: The Third World Comes to America*. 2nd ed. New York: Columbia University Press, 1992.

———. *Unwelcome Strangers: American Identity and the Turn against Immigration*. New York: Columbia University Press, 1998.

"Reith Lectures 2000, Respect for the Earth." BBC. http://news.bbc.co.uk/hi/english/static /events/reith_2000/default.stm (accessed August 13, 2007).

Richards, John E. "Toward a Positive Theory of International Organizations: Regulating International Aviation Markets." *International Organization* 53, no. 1 (1999): 1–37.

Ritzer, George. *The McDonaldization Thesis: Explorations and Extensions*. Thousand Oaks, CA: Sage, 1998.

Rivera, Juan M., Scott Whiteford, and Manuel Chávez, eds. *NAFTA and the Campesinos: The Impact of NAFTA on Small-Scale Agricultural Producers in Mexico and the Prospects for Change*. Scranton, PA: University of Scranton Press, 2009.

Roberts, J. A. G. *China to Chinatown: Chinese Food in the West*. London: Reaktion Books, 2002.

Rodriguez, Richard. *The Hunger of Memory: The Education of Richard Rodriguez, an Autobiography*. New York: Bantam, 1982.

Rothenberg, Daniel. *With These Hands: The Hidden World of Migrant Farmworkers Today*. Berkeley: University of California Press, 1998.

Rotter, Andrew J. *Comrades at Odds: The United States and India, 1947–1964*. Ithaca, NY: Cornell University Press, 2000.

———. "In Retrospect: Harold R. Isaacs's *Scratches on our Minds*." *Reviews in American History* 24, no. 1 (1996): 177–88.

Rozin, Elizabeth. *The Flavor-Principle Cookbook*. New York: Hawthorn Books, 1973.

Rozin, Paul. "Food Is Fundamental, Fun, Frightening, and Far-Reaching." *Social Research* 66, no. 1 (1999): 9–30.

Ruiz, Vicki L. "Citizen Restaurant: American Imaginaries, American Communities." *American Quarterly* 60, no. 1 (March 2008): 1–21.

Russek, Audrey. "Appetites without Prejudice: U.S. Foreign Restaurants and the Globalization of American Food between Wars." *Food and Foodways: Explorations in the History and Culture of Human Nourishment* 19 (2011): 34–55.

Sahr, Robert C. "Consumer Price Index (CPI) Conversion Factors 1800 to Estimated 2015 to Convert to Dollars of 2001." http://oregonstate.edu/cla/polisci/faculty-research/sahr /cv2001.pdf (accessed March 26, 2008).

Saito, Leland. *Race and Politics: Asian Americans, Latinos, and Whites in a Los Angeles Suburb.* Urbana: University of Illinois Press, 1998.

Sanchez, George. *Becoming Mexican American: Ethnicity, Culture and Identity in Chicano Los Angeles, 1900–1945.* New York: Oxford University Press, 1993.

Saxenian, AnnaLee. *Local and Global Networks of Immigrant Professionals in Silicon Valley.* San Francisco: Public Policy Institute of California, 2002.

———. *Silicon Valley's New Immigrant Entrepreneurs.* San Francisco: Public Policy Institute of California, 1999.

Scheier, Lee M. "What Is the Hunger-Obesity Paradox?" *Journal of the Academy of Nutrition and Dietetics* 105, no. 6 (2005): 883–85.

Schlosser, Eric. *Fast Food Nation: The Dark Side of the All-American Meal.* New York: Perennial, 2002.

Schor, Juliet B., and Douglas B. Holt, eds. *The Consumer Society Reader.* New York: The New Press, 2000.

Schremp, Gerry. *Celebration of American Food: Four Centuries in the Melting Pot.* Golden, CO: Fulcrum Publishing, 1996.

Schulman, Bruce. *The Seventies: The Great Shift in American Culture, Society, and Politics.* Cambridge, MA: Da Capo Press, 2001.

Schwentesius, Rita, and Manuel Ángel Gómez. "Supermarkets in Mexico: Impacts on Horticulture Systems." *Development Policy Review* 20, no. 4 (2002): 487–502.

Scranton, Philip, ed. *Beauty and Business: Commerce, Gender, and Culture in Modern America.* New York: Routledge, 2001.

Sen, Colleen Taylor. *Food Culture in India.* Westport, CT: Greenwood Press, 2004.

Senauer, Benjamin, and Linda Goetz. "The Growing Middle Class in Developing Countries and the Market for High-Value Food Products." Paper prepared for the Workshop on Global Markets for High-Value Food. Washington, DC: ERS-USDA, 2003. http://www .farmfoundation.org/documents/Ben-Senauerpaper2--10--3-13-03_000.pdf (accessed February 13, 2008).

Senauer, Benjamin, and Luciano Venturini. "The Globalization of Food Systems: A Conceptual Framework and Empirical Patterns." St. Paul: The Food Industry Center, University of Minnesota, 2005. http://agecon.lib.umn.edu/cgi-bin/pdf_view.pl?paperid=15899 &ftype=.pdf (accessed August 16, 2007).

Shapiro, Laura. *Perfection Salad: Women and Cooking at the Turn of the Century.* New York: Farrar Strauss & Giroux, 1986.

———. *Something from the Oven: Reinventing Dinner in 1950s America.* New York: Penguin, 2004.

Shephard, Sue. *Pickled, Potted, and Canned: How the Art and Science of Food Preserving Changed the World.* New York: Simon & Schuster, 2000.

Shermer, Elizabeth Tandy. "Counter-Organizing the Sunbelt: Right-to-Work Campaigns and Anti-Union Conservatism, 1943–1958." *Pacific Historical Review* 78, no. 1 (2009): 81–118.

Shortridge, Barbara G., and James R. Shortridge. *The Taste of American Place: A Reader on Regional and Ethnic Foods*. New York: Rowman & Littlefield, 1998.

Silverstone, Roger, ed. *Visions of Suburbia*. New York: Routledge, 1997.

Smith, Andrew, ed. *The Oxford Encyclopedia of Food and Drink in America*. Vol. 1. New York: Oxford, 2004.

———. "Tacos, Enchiladas, and Refried Beans: The Invention of Mexican-American Cookery." Paper Presented at Oregon State University, 1999. http://food.oregonstate.edu/ref/culture/mexico_smith.html (accessed November 26, 2006).

Smith, Tom W. "Changing Racial Labels: From 'Colored' to 'Negro' to 'Black' to 'African American.'" *Public Opinion Quarterly* 56, no. 4 (1992): 496–514.

Smith, Wendell. "Product Differentiation and Market Segmentation as Alternative Marketing Strategies." *Journal of Marketing* 21, no. 1 (1956): 3–8.

Sokolov, Raymond. *Why We Eat What We Eat*. New York: Summit Books, 1991.

Soluri, John. *Banana Cultures: Agriculture, Consumption, and Environmental Change in Honduras and the United States*. Austin: University of Texas Press, 2005.

Som, Indigo. *Mostly Mississippi: Chinese Restaurants of the South*. San Francisco: Chinese Historical Society of America, 2005.

Spang, Rebecca. *The Invention of the Restaurant*. Cambridge, MA: Harvard University Press, 2000.

Spoehr, Luther W. "Sambo and the Heathen Chinee: Californians' Racial Stereotypes in the Late 1870s." *Pacific Historical Review* 42, no. 2 (1973): 185–204.

Stallberg-White, C., and P. Pliner. "The Effect of Flavor Principles on Willingness to Taste Novel Foods." *Appetite* 33 (1999): 209–21.

Staller, John E. *Maize Cobs and Cultures: History of Zea mays L.* New York: Springer, 2010.

Starczewska-Lambasa, Maria, ed. *Hofstra University Yearbook of Business*. Hempstead, NY: Hofstra University, 1982.

Strasser, Susan. *Never Done: A History of American Housework*. New York: Pantheon Books, 1982.

Strasser, Susan, Charles McGovern, and Matthias Judt. *Getting and Spending: European and American Consumer Societies in the Twentieth Century*. New York: Cambridge University Press, 1998.

Striffler, Steve, and Mark Moberg, eds. *Banana Wars: Power, Production, and History in the Americas*. Durham, NC: Duke University Press, 2003.

Tan, Amy. *The Joy Luck Club*. New York: Putnam, 1989.

Tang, Charles F., with Robert Goldberg. "Chinese Restaurants Abroad." *Flavor and Fortune* 3, no. 4 (1996).

Taylor, Timothy. "The Truth about Globalization." *Public Interest*, 147 (Spring 2002): 24–44.

Teaford, Jon C. *The Metropolitan Revolution: The Rise of Post-Urban America*. New York: Columbia University Press, 2006.

Tedlow, Richard S. *New and Improved: The Story of Mass Marketing in America*. Boston: Harvard Business School Press, 1996.

Teller, John W. "The Treatment of Foreign Terms in Chicago Restaurant Menus." *American Speech* 44, no. 2 (1969): 91–105.

Thacker, Strom C. *Big Business, the State, and Free Trade: Constructing Coalitions in Mexico.* New York: Cambridge University Press, 2000.

Tilly, Chris. "Walmart and Its Workers: NOT the Same All over the World." *Connecticut Law Review* 39, 4 (May 2007): 1805–23.

Tortilla Industry Association. *1991 Tortilla Industry National Research Survey.* Encino, CA: Tortilla Industry Association, 1992.

Trillin, Calvin. *Feeding a Yen: Savoring Local Specialties from Kansas City to Cuzco.* New York: Random House, 2003.

Turner, Bryan S., and Robert J. Holton, *The Routledge International Handbook of Globalization Studies,* 2nd ed. New York: Routledge, 2016.

Turner, Katharine Leonard. *How the Other Half Ate: A History of Working-Class Meals at the Turn of the Century.* Berkeley: University of California Press, 2014.

2005 Marketing Guidebook: The Blue Book of Supermarket Distribution. Wilton, CT: Trade Dimensions International, 2004.

U.S. Industry in 2000: Studies in Competitive Performance. Washington, DC: The National Academy Press, 1999.

Vasquez, Jessica M. *Mexican Americans across Generations.* New York: New York University Press, 2011.

Vial, Pablo M., Carlos H. Crisosto, and Gayle M. Crisosto. "Early Harvest Delays Berry Skin Browning of 'Princess' Table Grapes," *California Agriculture* 59, no. 2 (2005): 103–8. http://calag.ucop.edu/0502AMJ/pdfs/GrapeBrowning.pdf (accessed June 22, 2007).

Villareal, M. Angeles, and Ian F. Ferguson. "The North American Free Trade Agreement (NAFTA)," *CRS Report,* April 16, 2015. https://www.fas.org/sgp/crs/row/R42965.pdf (accessed September 9, 2015).

Voss, Kimberly Wilmot. *The Food Section: Newspaper Women and the Culinary Community.* Lanham, MD: Rowman & Littlefield, 2014.

Wagnleitner, Reinhold, and Elaine Tyler May, eds. *"Here, There and Everywhere": The Foreign Politics of American Popular Culture.* Hanover, NH: University Press of New England, 2000.

Wallendorf, Melanie, and Michael D. Reilly. "Ethnic Migration, Assimilation, and Consumption." *The Journal of Consumer Research* 10, no. 3 (1983): 292–302

Watson, James L., ed. *Golden Arches East: McDonald's in East Asia.* Stanford, CA: Stanford University Press, 1997.

Weaver, Thomas, James B. Greenberg, William L. Alexander, and Anne Browning-Aiken, eds. *Neoliberalism and Commodity Production in Mexico.* Boulder: University Press of Colorado, 2012.

Wilk, Richard, ed., *Fast Food/Slow Food: The Cultural Economy of the Global Food System.* Berkeley, CA: Altamira, 2006.

———. *Home Cooking in the Global Village: Caribbean Food from Buccaneers to Ecotourists.* New York: Berg, 2006.

Williams, William Appleman. *The Tragedy of American Diplomacy.* New York: W.W. Norton & Company, 1972.

Wise, Michael D., and Jennifer Jensen Wallach, eds. *The Routledge History of American Foodways.* New York: Routledge, 2016.

Wolfe, Tom. *From Bauhaus to Our House*. New York: Bantam Books, 1999.

Wong, Bernard. *Ethnicity and Entrepreneurship: The New Chinese Immigrants in the San Francisco Bay Area*. Boston: Allyn and Bacon, 1998.

———. *The Chinese in Silicon Valley: Globalization, Social Networks, and Ethnic Identity*. Lanham, MD: Rowan & Littlefield, 2006.

Wright, Wynne, and Elizabeth Ransom. "Stratification on the Menu: Using Restaurant Menus to Examine Social Class." *Teaching Sociology* 33, no. 3 (July 2005): 310–16.

Yankelovich, Daniel. "New Criteria for Market Segmentation." *Harvard Business Review* 42, no. 2 (1964): 83–90.

Yankelovich, Daniel, and David Meer. "Rediscovering Market Segmentation." *Harvard Business Review* 84, no. 2 (2006): 122–31.

Yee, Alfred. *Shopping at Giant Foods: Chinese American Supermarkets in Northern California*. Seattle: University of Washington Press, 2003.

Yordán, José J., and Michael J. Mauboussin. *Grupo Industrial Maseca, S.A. de C.V. (GIMSA): 1993 Fourth Quarter and Full-Year Results*. New York: CS First Boston, 1994.

Yunez-Naude, Antonio. "The Dismantling of CONASUPO, a Mexican State Trader in Agriculture." *World Economy* 26, no. 1 (January 2003): 97–122.

Zelinsky, Wilbur. "The Roving Palate: North America's Ethnic Restaurant Cuisines." *GeoForum* 16, no. 1 (1985): 51–77.

Zhao, Grace Q., Yifeng Zhang, Mark A. Hoon, Jayaram Chandrashekar, Isolde Erlenbach, Nicholas J. P. Ryba, and Charles S. Zuker. "The Receptors for Mammalian Sweet and Umami Taste." *Cell* 115, no. 3 (2003): 255–66.

Zukin, Sharon. *The Cultures of Cities*. Malden, MA: Blackwell Publishers, 1995.

Movies and Songs

Smith, Charles H., and Nancy Schimmel. "Little Boxes: Malvina Reynolds, Song Lyrics and Poems." http://www.wku.edu/~smithch/MALVINA/mr094.htm (accessed February 12, 2007).

Valley Girl. Directed by Martha Coolidge. 1983; MGM, 2003. DVD.

Wall Street. Directed by Oliver Stone. 1987; 20th Century Fox, 2010. DVD.

Weeds, Season 1. DVD. Santa Monica, CA: Lion's Gate Home Entertainment, 2006.

Unpublished Sources

Adema, Pauline. "Festive Foodscapes: Iconizing Food and the Shaping of Identity and Place." PhD diss., University of Texas at Austin, 2006.

Calleja Pinedo, Maria Margarita. "Distribution Channels in the U.S.A. for Mexican Fresh Fruits and Vegetables." PhD diss., University of Texas at Austin, 2001.

Casaburi, Gabriel. "Dynamic Production Systems in Newly Liberalizing Developing Countries: Agroindustrial Sectors in Argentina and Chile." PhD diss., Yale University, 1994.

Chiang, Cecilia. *Cecilia Chiang: An Oral History*. Oral History interview conducted in 2005–2006 by Victor Geraci. Berkeley, CA: Oral History Center, BANC, 2007.

Di Giorgio, Robert, and Joseph A. Di Giorgio. *The Di Giorgios: From Fruit Merchants to Corporate Innovators*. Oral history interview conducted in 1983 by Ruth Teiser. Berkeley, CA: Oral History Center, BANC, 1986.

Duvall, Rebecca Helen Carter. "Tracing the Trail of Table Grapes: The Globalization of the Sonoran Table Grape Industry." PhD diss., University of Arizona, 2002.

Feltault, Kelly. "Re: Eat Local and Seafood." Post to Association for the Study of Food and Society Digest (e-mail list service), September 3, 2007.

Gilb, Antonio. "After Surviving War, Man Turned Family Business into Tortilla Giant." Oral history interview from September 2001. U.S. Latinos and Latinas and WWII Oral History Project, University of Texas at Austin. http://www.lib.utexas.edu/exhibits/ww2latinos /narratives/05Galindo_Tom.html (accessed August 25, 2007).

Jayasanker, Laresh. "Difficulties Defining Equality: Mexican Americans in U.S. Education and Immigration Policy, 1964–1978." Master's thesis, University of Texas at Austin, 2004.

———. "Sameness in Diversity: Food Culture and Globalization in the San Francisco Bay Area and America, 1965–2005." PhD diss., University of Texas at Austin, 2008.

Lao, Chi Kien. "The Chinese Restaurant Industry in the United States: Its History, Development and Future." Master's thesis, Cornell University, 1975.

Lee, Christopher. "Bay Area Restaurateur." Oral history interview conducted by Kirstin Jackson in 2004. Berkeley, CA: Oral History Center, BANC, 2006.

Neidorf-Weinstein, Andrea. *Entrepreneurs of the West: James A. Collins.* An oral history conducted 1998–1999. Los Angeles: Oral History Program, University of California, Los Angeles, 2000.

Palmer, Hans Christian. "Italian Immigration and the Development of California Agriculture." PhD diss., University of California, Berkeley, 1965.

Ross, Drew Eliot. "Topography of Taste: Geography, Cultural Politics, and the Making of California Cuisine." PhD diss: University of Wisconsin-Madison, 1999.

Williams, Charles E. *Williams-Sonoma Cookware and the American Kitchen: The Merchandising Vision of Chuck Williams, 1956–1994.* An oral history conducted 1992–1994 by Lisa Jacobson and Ruth Teiser. Berkeley, CA: Oral History Center, BANC, 1995.

Williams, Chuck, and Howard Lester. *Volume II, Williams-Sonoma: Mastering the Homeware: 1994–2004.* An oral history conducted in 2004 by Victor W. Geraci. Berkeley, CA: Oral History Center, BANC, 2005.

INDEX

AB InBev, 45
advertising: Chun King marketing campaign, 48; cultural translators, food and, 11–13; ethnic food advertising, 61; to ethnic groups, 180n43; Kraft, Casino cheese campaign, 54; La Choy, 65; restaurant menus as, 73; segmented marketing, 13; tortillas, market expansion of, 126. *See also* media
agriculture: air freighting of produce, 28–29; biodiversity, fruits and vegetables, 30; decline of small farms, 131; farmworker wages, 131; meat, global consumption data, 44; NAFTA, effects of, 138; urbanization, effect on small farms, 10. *See also* fruit and vegetable trade
Ahold USA, 40
air freighted produce, 28–29
Albertsons, 33, 35, 40, 40*tab*, 139
Aldi, 46
Alfred A. Knopf, 79, 84, 86–88; cookbooks and culture translation, 93–96; Elisabeth Ortiz, Latin American cooking, 91–93; Jane Grigson, British cooking, 88–90; Julia Child, French cooking, 87–88; Madhur Jaffrey and, 90–91
Altria, 43
AmBev, 45
American audience: cookbooks, editorial decisions and, 80, 84, 85, 89–90; cultural translators, food and, 11–13; Indian restaurants, marketing of, 97, 105, 106–7; P.F. Chang's, marketing of, 112

American Meat Institute, 52
American President Lines, 20
An Invitation to Indian Cooking (Jaffrey, 1973), 79–82, 85, 87, 90–91, 94
Andreas, Dwayne, 137–38
Andronico's, 35
Anheuser-Busch InBev, 14, 45
antitrust violations, 137–38
A&P, 36, 54, 58–59
Apple, R. W. Jr., 119–20
Applegate Farms, 14
Archer Daniels Midland (ADM), 129–31, 137–38, 139
Arellano, Gustavo, 13
Argentina, 30, 44
Asia, container shipping routes, 20–21
Asian food: American-Oriental market, 65–67; ethnic food, holiday or every day, 62–65; sushi restaurants, growth in market, 69–70. *See also* Chinese food; Indian food
Asian grocery stores, growth of, 54–57
Asian population: history of immigration, 6–10, 7*tab*; independent, Hispanic, and Asian grocery stores, 54–57; suburban diversity, 11
Aunt Jemima, 77
Australia, 22, 29, 30, 44
authenticity trap, 15–16, 145–49

Badmaash, 148
bagged salad, 23–24

multinational corporations: history of globalization, 8–10; homogenization and consolidation, 14; trade policy, influence on, 9–10
Mumford, Lewis, 114

NAFTA (North American Free Trade Agreement),
26, 127–31, 135, 137, 138, 140
Najor, Victor, 55
Nankin Express, 121
National Chicken Council, 45
National Company of Popular Subsistence
(CONASUPO), 134–35
National Restaurant Association, 68, 69, 74
Nestlé, 14, 33, 43, 44
New, Ilhan, 65
New Zealand, 30
niche markets, 31
99 Ranch, 56, 57, 119, 120
Nixon, Richard, 118, 138
nutrition: food pyramid guide, 25, 164n36; fruits
and vegetables, 25, 28; McDonald's, nutrition
claims, 33

Oberlin College, 148
obesity: rise in, 3
Odwalla, 14
Office of Price Administration (OPA), 75
omnivore's dilemma, 4–5
Oroweat, 140
Ortega, 133
Ortiz, Elisabeth, 23, 87, 90, 91–93, 94, 95

Pakistan, 100, 102, 103, 104
Pakistani food, 100
Panda Express, 72, 113, 122, 123
Parkwood restaurant, 76
Pasta Manana, 23
Pathmark, 54
Patio, 133
Paulucci, Jeno, 47–51, 65, 66
PBS, cooking shows, 86, 116
Pei Wei Asian Diner, 122
Pepe's, 132
Pepsi, 54
Perdue, 45
P.F. Chang's, 112–13, 122, 124
Phan, Charles, 1–2, 4, 18
Pick Up Stix, 122
Pilcher, Jeffrey, 146
Pilgrim's Pride, 44
Pina, Roberto, 15–16
Piñata, 61–62

plant biodiversity, 30, 168n69
The Pleasure of Chinese Cooking (Chu, 1962), 110
Plumrose, 44
politics: ADM, political influence of, 137–38;
GRUMA and tortilla market, 125–27, 133–41,
139*tab*; NAFTA, effects of, 26, 127–31, 135, 137,
138, 140
Popeye's, 45
pork. *See* meat industry
poultry. *See* meat industry
poverty: fast food consumption and, 71; impact
of free trade, 10; obesity and, 3. *See also*
socioeconomic status
price fixing, 137–38
processed foods: calorie density of, 3; consumption
patterns, 43, 85; corn and soybean use in, 30,
32, 137; product development, 52; value-added
products, 42–43. *See also* food processors
Pro-Chile, 26–27
produce. *See* fruit and vegetable trade
Progressive Grocer, 51, 58, 61, 63
Prudhomme, Paul, 94
Publix, 40, 40*tab*
Puck, Wolfgang, 124
Punjab, 104

Quik Wok, 122

race: history of immigration, 6–10, 7*tab*; marketing strategies post-1960, 54, 180n45; racism
and food, 143–49; suburban diversity, 11,
114–15; white nationalists, 143–44
Ralphs, 55
Rampton, Suzanne, 60
Randall's, 40
Restaurant Brands International, 45
restaurants: age of the ethnic restaurant, 70–73;
authenticity trap, 15–16, 145–49; Cajun and
Creole, 94; chains (1950s and 1960s), 76–78;
Chinese food in America, 48, 111–24, 121*tab*;
cultural translators, food and, 11–13; fruit and
vegetable sourcing, 31; historical roots of,
72; immigrant labor in, 144–45; immigrant
ownership of, 101–3, 147–48; Indian food,
80, 97–109; meat and potatoes, mid-century
menus, 74–76; meat suppliers, 45; menu,
importance of, 73–74; Mexican food, growth
in market, 68–69; mixed menus at ethnic restaurants, 98; numbers of in U.S., 72; sales data
over time, 71; segmented marketing, 13; sushi,
growth in market, 69–70; World War II, price
controls and, 75–76. *See also* fast food

CALIFORNIA STUDIES IN FOOD AND CULTURE

Darra Goldstein, Editor

1. *Dangerous Tastes: The Story of Spices,* by Andrew Dalby
2. *Eating Right in the Renaissance,* by Ken Albala
3. *Food Politics: How the Food Industry Influences Nutrition and Health,* by Marion Nestle
4. *Camembert: A National Myth,* by Pierre Boisard
5. *Safe Food: The Politics of Food Safety,* by Marion Nestle
6. *Eating Apes,* by Dale Peterson
7. *Revolution at the Table: The Transformation of the American Diet,* by Harvey Levenstein
8. *Paradox of Plenty: A Social History of Eating in Modern America,* by Harvey Levenstein
9. *Encarnación's Kitchen: Mexican Recipes from Nineteenth-Century California: Selections from Encarnación Pinedo's* El cocinero español, by Encarnación Pinedo, edited and translated by Dan Strehl, with an essay by Victor Valle
10. *Zinfandel: A History of a Grape and Its Wine,* by Charles L. Sullivan, with a foreword by Paul Draper
11. *Tsukiji: The Fish Market at the Center of the World,* by Theodore C. Bestor
12. *Born Again Bodies: Flesh and Spirit in American Christianity,* by R. Marie Griffith
13. *Our Overweight Children: What Parents, Schools, and Communities Can Do to Control the Fatness Epidemic,* by Sharron Dalton
14. *The Art of Cooking: The First Modern Cookery Book,* by the Eminent Maestro Martino of Como, edited and with an introduction by Luigi Ballerini, translated and annotated by Jeremy Parzen, and with fifty modernized recipes by Stefania Barzini
15. *The Queen of Fats: Why Omega-3s Were Removed from the Western Diet and What We Can Do to Replace Them,* by Susan Allport
16. *Meals to Come: A History of the Future of Food,* by Warren Belasco
17. *The Spice Route: A History,* by John Keay
18. *Medieval Cuisine of the Islamic World: A Concise History with 174 Recipes,* by Lilia Zaouali, translated by M. B. DeBevoise, with a foreword by Charles Perry
19. *Arranging the Meal: A History of Table Service in France,* by Jean-Louis Flandrin, translated by Julie E. Johnson, with Sylvie and Antonio Roder; with a foreword to the English-language edition by Beatrice Fink
20. *The Taste of Place: A Cultural Journey into Terroir,* by Amy B. Trubek
21. *Food: The History of Taste,* edited by Paul Freedman
22. *M. F. K. Fisher among the Pots and Pans: Celebrating Her Kitchens,* by Joan Reardon, with a foreword by Amanda Hesser
23. *Cooking: The Quintessential Art,* by Hervé This and Pierre Gagnaire, translated by M. B. DeBevoise
24. *Perfection Salad: Women and Cooking at the Turn of the Century,* by Laura Shapiro
25. *Of Sugar and Snow: A History of Ice Cream Making,* by Jeri Quinzio
26. *Encyclopedia of Pasta,* by Oretta Zanini De Vita, translated by Maureen B. Fant, with a foreword by Carol Field

Founded in 1893,
UNIVERSITY OF CALIFORNIA PRESS
publishes bold, progressive books and journals
on topics in the arts, humanities, social sciences,
and natural sciences—with a focus on social
justice issues—that inspire thought and action
among readers worldwide.

The UC PRESS FOUNDATION
raises funds to uphold the press's vital role
as an independent, nonprofit publisher, and
receives philanthropic support from a wide
range of individuals and institutions—and from
committed readers like you. To learn more, visit
ucpress.edu/supportus.